The Polis
Bible Commentary

Volume 15
Jeremiah and Lamentations

URBAN LOFT PUBLISHERS

The Polis
Bible Commentary

Volume 15

Jeremiah and Lamentations

Biblical Exposition
Gary H. Hall

Urban Ministry Commentary
Mark S. Krause

Series Editor
Mark S. Krause

Senior Editor
Stephen E. Burris

URBAN LOFT PUBLISHERS

The Polis Bible Commentary: Jeremiah and Lamentations, Volume 15

Copyright © 2019 by Gary H. Hall

All rights reserved. Except for brief quotations in critical publications or reviews, no part of this book may be reproduced in any manner without prior written permission from the publisher.

Requests for information should be addressed to:

Urban Loft Publishers
6611 Aspen St.
La Vista, NE 68128

urbanloftpublishers.com

Stephen E. Burris, Senior Editor
Mark S. Krause, Series Editor

Scripture quotations are from New Revised Standard Version Bible, copyright © 1989 National Council of the Churches of Christ in the United States of America. Used by permission. All rights reserved worldwide.

ISBN: 978-1-949625-20-2

Cover picture: stairway of Mt. Sinai, Mark S. Krause

Table of Contents

Editor's Preface ii
Authors' Prefaces iii
Introduction to the Book of Jeremiah 1
    Historical Background 1
    Urban Setting 5
    Character of Jeremiah 9
    Outline of Jeremiah 9

Commentary on Jeremiah 11
    1. Prophecies of Doom (1-25) 11
        1.a. The call (1:1-19) 11
        1.b. Prophecies from the time of Josiah (2:1-6:30) 22
        1.c. Prophecies from the time of Jehoiakim (7:1-20:18) 57
        1.d. Prophecies Against King and Prophet (21:1-25:14) 164

    2. Introduction to Prophecies against the Nations (25:15-38) 196

    3. Destruction and Restoration (26-33) 200
        3.a. The temple sermon aftermath (26:1-24) 200
        3.b. Yoke Sermon, Hananiah's opposition, letters to exiles (27:1-29:32) 200
        3.c. The Book of Consolation (30:1-33:26) 219

    4. Jeremiah and the Last Days of Jerusalem (34-45) 252
        4.a. Jeremiah, Zedekiah, and Jehoiakim (34:1-39:18) 252
        4.b. The Fall of Jerusalem and Aftermath (39:1-45:5) 270

    5. Prophecies Against the Nations (46-51) 297
        5.a. Major Oracles against Nations (46:1-48:47) 299
        5.b. Lesser Oracles against Nations (49:1-39) 310
        5.c. Oracles against Babylon (50:1-51:64) 316

    6. Historical Epilogue (52) 325

Commentary on Lamentations 328
    Chapter 1 332
    Chapter 2 340
    Chapter 3 345
    Chapter 4 354
    Chapter 5 358

EDITOR'S PREFACE

This is the second volume to be released in an anticipated 30-volume set of commentaries for the entire Bible. Each volume will have Bible Exposition written by a capable Bible scholar and Urban Ministry Commentary sidebar insights written by an urban specialist. We have titled this series the ***Polis Bible Commentary***, using the Greek word πόλις (*polis*), the ancient designation for a city.

Ancient cities were centers for commerce, manufacturing, government, the arts, architecture, religious sites, and education. While the cities of Bible times had none of the technological features of modern cities, the difference between urban settings and rural settings was just as huge. Talent, ideas, and trends flowed to the urban centers from the rural world, with the urban influence coming back to rural residents with the city's stamp of influence.

This commentary series is written from the perspective that much of the Bible was written with cities in mind and intended for an urban audience. Urbanologists today have taught us that the cities of our world have great similarities and commonalities as opposed to their surrounding rural areas. Missions endeavors originating in the Western churches have long targeted rural populations in Africa and Asia. Now, the demographic trends that are building the urban populations have turned this focus to cities. It is the desire of the authors and editors of this series that the intentional inclusion of an urban perspective will better serve those who serve and live in these dynamic cities.

Gary H. Hall taught Old Testament for 40 years, including 26 years at Lincoln Christian Seminary. He retired in 2012. Dr. Hall held degrees from Milligan College (BA), Lincoln Christian Seminary (MDiv), Gordon-Conwell Theological Seminary (MTh in New Testament), and Union Presbyterian Seminary (PhD in Old Testament). Dr. Hall went to be with the Lord in June 2019.

Mark S. Krause teaches at Nebraska Christian College. His Ph.D. is from Trinity Evangelical Divinity School.

AUTHORS' PREFACES

My first serious engagement with Jeremiah began in 1976 when I started my research for my doctoral dissertation on Jeremiah 2 and 3. I continued my study of the book during my teaching career, offering exegetical courses at both the college and seminary level. However, I had never attempted a complete study of the book verse by verse until now. This commentary seems to be a fitting conclusion to decades of interaction with the book. I was reminded again of Jeremiah's grounding in the book of Deuteronomy.

Jeremiah is popularly known as the "Weeping Prophet" but to me he seems more like the "Suffering Servant." He shed tears over the fate of his people, but he shed as many tears over his own fate. His life was in danger several times and he survived only because of powerful friends. The response to his preaching was negative and he was unable to stem the nations headlong rush to catastrophe. He not only had a message of doom and devastation, he experienced the fulfilment of his words, living through the destruction of Jerusalem and the temple, and exile. One can only imagine his personal anguish which erupted into complaints to God.

Jeremiah's life is a reminder that when God calls someone, he calls them "to come and die" (Bonhoeffer). By most cultural standards, he was not successful. However, Jeremiah shows us that a long life of faithfulness is possible, even at extreme personal cost.

I am grateful to the editors of this series for inviting me to study Jeremiah again. I am especially thankful to Mark Krause for his hard work as editor of this commentary. To God be the glory.

Gary Hall

January 2017

It has been my privilege to work on this commentary, a tribute to my friend, Gary H. Hall. The book was delayed many times, and unfortunately, we were not able to get it published before Dr. Hall's death.

I have written the urban sidebars to correspond to the biblical exposition of Dr. Hall. Although I am not a trained urbanologist, I have lived in many different cities, including Seattle, Chicago, Los Angeles, and Omaha. I spent considerable time in several cities outside the United States including London, Kathmandu, Yangon, Manila, Bangkok, and Vancouver. In all places, I have been an observer and participant in the local church and various ministries. My love for the book of Jeremiah, often a neglected part of the Bible these days, gave me great motivation to add my insights based on the text and my forty years of urban living.

Mark S. Krause

October 2019

INTRODUCTION TO THE BOOK OF JEREMIAH

Historical Background

Jeremiah lived in a time of almost unparalleled political ferment in the ancient Near East (approximately 640 to after 587 BCE). It was also a time of unparalleled disaster for his home nation, Judah. The nation experienced independence and prosperity, vassalage, internal turmoil, partial destruction and captivity, and a final ravaging of Jerusalem and the temple, all within a few decades. Jeremiah's ministry and preaching were closely tied to these events. He warned, cajoled, condemned, pleaded with, and wept for his people and nation. He was opposed by people, kings, and family. He was ridiculed, shunned, threatened with death, and imprisoned.

Many of his sermons and the events in his life are dated and can be firmly placed into their historical setting. This gives a concreteness to Jeremiah's message and life that is missing from some other biblical prophets. Another important aspect of Jeremiah's ministry was his audience. He preached to his contemporaries in Judah before and after the catastrophes of 597 and 587 BCE. After the first deportation in 597 BCE, he also preached to the exiles in Babylon. Jeremiah had the distinction of seeing his grim portrayals of the future of God's people come to reality. The physical and emotional toll this took on the people is difficult to imagine. Their trust in God's providence was stretched to the limit and their faith in his power to save them from their enemies was shattered.

Consequently, it is important to understand a few of the historical events that marked this time period. In Jeremiah's lifetime the mighty Assyria, who had destroyed the northern kingdom of Israel in 722 BCE (2 Kgs 17) and ruled Mesopotamia, Palestine, and (sometimes) Egypt for over a century, collapsed at the end of the seventh century BCE. The neo-Babylonian empire rose to replace it and carried on almost constant battles with Egypt for control of the Fertile Crescent.

Josiah, the king of Judah during the first part of Jeremiah's ministry, came to the throne at age eight in 640 BCE following the assassination of his father Amon. Within eight years, by 631 BCE, he had begun a reform movement, and by his twelfth year he began to purge the country of pagan worship (2 Chron 34:3). This turn of events was quite remarkable, for Josiah's grandfather, Manasseh, was considered by the authors of Kings as the evilest king Judah ever had. Laid at Manasseh's feet was the blame for the eventual destruction of Judah and the ensuing exile (2 Kgs 21:11-15, *cf.* Jer 15:4). Josiah followed in the footsteps of his great-grandfather, the reforming king Hezekiah whom we know from his encounters with the prophet Isaiah (Isa 36ff.).

Ashurbanipal, the last great king of Assyria, died in 627 BCE, the year of Jeremiah's call (see below on chapter 1). Assyria began to weaken and was unable to maintain control over Palestine, thus paving the way for Josiah to carry out his reforms without interference.

In Josiah's eighteenth year, while the temple was being cleaned as a part of the reform, a scroll of the law was found (probably part or most of the book of Deuteronomy, though this is debated; 2 Kgs 22; 2 Chron 34:8-21).[1] This led to further reforms, including a magnificent celebration of the Passover (2 Kgs 23).

The year 612 is a pivotal date in the history of the ancient Near East. After struggling for years against the coalition of Medes and Babylonians, Nineveh, the capital of Assyria, fell. Assyrian survivors fled west to Haran, where the Egyptian Psammetichus joined the coalition. In 610 Haran fell and Assyria came to an end. Psammetichus died that same year and was succeeded by his son, Neco II. Determined to assert Egyptian influence in Palestine, Neco marched to Carchemish to try to help the remnant of the Assyrians against Babylon.

Josiah decided (foolishly) to intercede and met Neco at Megiddo (which Josiah now controlled), apparently to resist Neco's attempt to gain power. Josiah was killed, and his body was brought to Jerusalem (2 Kgs 23:28-30). His son, Jehoahaz II, took the throne, but he was removed within three months by Neco and taken captive to Egypt. (Neco, by the way, was too late to help the Assyrians.) Eliakim, Jehoahaz's brother, renamed Jehoiakim by Neco, was put on

---

[1] R.E. Clements, *Deuteronomy* (Sheffield: Sheffield Academic Press, 1989).

the throne as a vassal to the Egyptians. Egypt remained in control of Palestine and Syria for only five years as Babylon secured its eastern areas.

In 605 BCE Neco advanced to Carchemish in the north of Syria apparently to consolidate his power, but he was completely routed by the Babylonians under Nebuchadnezzar II.[2] In 604 BCE, Nebuchadnezzar marched into the Palestinian coastal plain and sacked Ashkelon. Jehoiakim wisely submitted to Babylon. Later (601 BCE) Babylon marched to Egypt but was firmly resisted. Jehoiakim apparently used this occasion to foolishly renege on his pledge to Babylon (2 Kgs 24:1).

In 598/97 BCE, Babylon returned to Palestine. Jehoiakim died just before the attack on Jerusalem and Jehoiachin, his son, became king. He was king only three months before Nebuchadnezzar captured Jerusalem, carried off much treasure and 10,000 captives, and put Mattaniah, Jehoiachin's uncle, on the throne, renaming him Zedekiah (2 Kgs 24:8-17). Jehoiachin was taken captive to Babylon, where he remained in custody for 37 years, until released and given a stipend by the king of Babylon (2 Kgs 25:27-30).

Zedekiah was a weak ruler, afraid of his advisors but secretly drawn to Jeremiah. His reign was a disaster, a time of continuous political intrigue with pro-Babylon, pro-Egyptian, and pro-independence parties jockeying for influence within Judah. An insurrection in Babylon in 595/594 BCE apparently led to a meeting of the foreign ministers of Edom, Moab, Ammon, Tyre, and Sidon in Jerusalem to plot revolt (Jer 27:1-3). It came to nothing, but Judah decided to follow a course of independence. Nebuchadnezzar returned in 588/87 BCE (2 Kgs 25), besieged Jerusalem for two years, and sacked it, carrying off numerous captives and more treasure, and destroying the city and temple. Jeremiah, who had been under guard (Jer 38) was freed by the Babylonians and treated with respect (Jer 39:11-14). The date 588/587 BCE usually marks the beginning of the exile,

---

[2] This name occurs in the OT as both "Nebuchadnezzar" and "Nebuchadrezzar" (only in Jeremiah and Ezekiel). In Jeremiah, it is "Nebuchadnezzar" eight times and "Nebuchadrezzar" twenty-nine times. This commentary will generally use the rendering of the NRSV in the verses under consideration, recognizing that the two names refer to the same person.

but captives had been taken to Babylon in 605 BCE and 597 BCE (including Daniel and Ezekiel). Gedaliah was made governor and the capital moved to Mizpah. However, some Judeans assassinated Gedaliah and then fled to Egypt, taking Jeremiah with them, against his advice and wishes (Jer 41-43). In 581 another deportation was taken to Babylon and Judah was subsumed under the province of Samaria. As far as we know Jeremiah died in Egypt.

In this context Jeremiah's message was one of almost constant doom and destruction. God's judgment was imminent because Judah had persisted in its disobedience of the covenant and in its dabbling in idolatry. Jeremiah's call (see chapter 1) was a call to persist in hammering his message home, and to resist the temptation to quit and give in to his enemies. His message was directed to both country and city, both Jerusalem and Babylon. These urban centers as heads of their countries symbolized the countries. In thought and deed the cities and nations were inseparable.

Jeremiah was given authority over both Jerusalem/Judah and Babylon/Babylonia because he was commissioned by the God who was sovereign over the whole world, *i.e.*, all nations and peoples. Therefore, his mission was not just to Judah but to the nations (Jer 1:5). Thus, the book of Jeremiah reflects this mission for it contains a block of oracles against the nations (chs. 46-51).

No one has reflected on this missional mandate in Jeremiah (and in the entire Old Testament) more than Christopher J. H. Wright.[3] Wright suggests the following points for reflection from the book of Jeremiah that were a part of Jeremiah's message and suggest ways for us to engage our world. According to Wright, Jeremiah's time featured international chaos with a breaking down of the old world order; religious confusion among God's people; rampant social evils; political abuse of power; abuse of religious power; the relevance of the message of God's sovereignty in history; the mission of

---

[3] C.J.H. Wright, *The Mission of God: Unlocking the Bible's Grand Narrative* (IVP, 2006), idem, *The Mission of God's People: A Biblical Theology of the Church's Mission* (Zondervan, 2010); idem, *Deuteronomy* (Hendrikson, 1996); idem, *The Message of Jeremiah* (IVP, 2015); idem, "Prophet to the Nations: Missional Reflections on the Book of Jeremiah," in Grand, Lo and Wenham (eds), *A God of Faithfulness* (T&T Clark, 2011), pp. 112-119.

God's people (even in exile); and grace in the end, hope for the future.4 These will provide a framework for reflections as we proceed through the commentary.

Another important theme arises from Jeremiah's conflict with false prophets throughout his lifetime as reflected in the book. The question was, who spoke for God? What was the nature of the word of God and who was the true deliverer of that word? Chapter 1 makes clear that Jeremiah was the spokesman for God. God's words were put into Jeremiah's mouth (1:9). The words of Jeremiah to Judah end with the challenge that now the people will know "whose word will stand – mine or theirs" (44:28). In between we see Jeremiah's words preached, opposed, written down and burned, rejected, and contradicted. We also see prophets who preach a different message, especially concerning the length of the exile (chs. 28-29) but also concerning the content of the message (23:16-17). But the word of God through Jeremiah, both in God's words and Jeremiah's words, will stand.5 That we have the book of Jeremiah in our Bibles is proof of that.

Urban Setting

Two cities dominate the book of Jeremiah: Jerusalem and Babylon.6 In the larger OT context these two cities are counterparts to each other. Jerusalem is God's elect city with the temple where he dwells. It is the Holy City. Babylon was the opposite, the city of Cain, in rebellion against God from the beginning (Gen 11), the city under judgment and curse.7

Jerusalem's origins are unclear. The Salem of Gen 14 may be the site and provides a link with the patriarch, Abraham. The site was called Jebus when Joshua led Israel into the Promised Land (Josh 18:28; Judg 19:10). It remained outside of Israelite control (Judg 1:21) until seven years into David's reign when his troops surprised the city

---

4 Wright, *Jeremiah*, pp. 38-39.

5 Andrew G. Shead, *A Mouth of Fire: The Word of God in the Words of Jeremiah* (IVP, 2012).

6 Jerusalem is referred to 89 times and Babylon 169 times.

7 NBD, "City, Theology of," 714.

defenders and took it for David (2 Sam 5:6-8; thus, the references to the city of David). Its location near the border between the tribes of Benjamin and Judah made it an ideal site for a capital city. When David brought the tabernacle to Jerusalem (2 Sam 6) its status as the capital and holy city was confirmed. Its status was further established when Solomon built a huge palace, other huge buildings (1 Kgs 7), and the temple on the high hill north of the city of David (1 Kgs 6). Thereafter, Jerusalem developed into an urban center as people and wealth converged. Different economic and cultural levels developed as the priesthood was established, the monarchy grew with the attendant growth of bureaucracy, tax revenue flowed into the temple and city, and a merchant class arose. Also during famine and war, people from the rural areas flowed into the capital and some stayed. The upper classes were characterized by several terms – elders, nobles, priests, officials, captains, and prophets (Isa 34:12; Jer 26:10, 17; 27:20).[8] 2 Kings 12 illustrates that a royal class of young men had been raised in privilege and wealth and were not about to give these things up.

The religious character of Jerusalem fluctuated over the years. Kings had great influence over the character of the country and city. Good kings obeyed the law and Israelite faith flourished. Evil kings apostatized to Canaanite and other religions. In time, this exacted a toll on the people. False prophets also played a role. By Jeremiah's time, the country had earned almost constant condemnation from the prophet. Just prior to his time the evil king Manasseh had led the country far astray and even is credited with killing many innocent people (2 Kgs 21). Punishment for his sins led to Judah's destruction (Jer 15:4). The situation was dire and even Josiah's reform (2 Kgs 22) did not turn things around. Faithful Torah followers were few and under great pressure to conform. The people, even under the shadow of the powerful Babylon, wanted to hear good news, not necessarily truth (Jer 23; 27). In Jeremiah's day Judah's religion had become legalistic and the temple almost a fetish (Jer 7). Ritual had replaced righteousness and foreign cults dominated (Jer 7:16-19).

---

[8] Frank Frick, *The City in Ancient Israel* (Scholars Press, 1977) chap. 3.

As we shall see, Jeremiah's ministry to this city was mostly negative, announcing judgment and destruction on it after a long history of covenant breaking through idolatry and foreign alliances. Theologically, the city stands for the nation of Judah, and both are condemned. However, judgment is not the end, and Jeremiah constructs a hopeful picture for the future with a coming new covenant and new relationship with God (Jer 30-31).

Babylon's origin goes back to the third millennium BCE, founded (according to tradition) by its high god, Marduk. In Genesis it is associated with Nimrod (Gen 10) and with the tower of Babel (Gen 11), an incident when the people attempted to build a tower to heaven and unify themselves. This was construed as disobedience to God, the people's language was confused, and they were scattered. Genesis makes an ironic word play, for the Hebrew for "confuse" *bll* (בלל), sounds like to Babel. The word Babylon comes from Semitic *bab-ilu* meaning "gate of the god."

Babylon is located 48 miles south of modern Baghdad on the Euphrates River (also called "the great river" in the OT, Deut 1:7; Jos 1:4). It gave its name to the territory and state of Babylonia which in its time of dominance stretched from the Persian Gulf to the northern regions of the Tigris River in modern day Iraq.[9] Babylonia had two periods of dominance, the Old Babylonian Kingdom under the Amorites (2000-1595 BCE), which included the famous king Hammurabi, and the Neo-Babylonian Kingdom (626-539 BCE). The latter era corresponds to the time of Jeremiah. Babylon was a highly literate society and left numerous clay tablets in cuneiform script detailing its myths, religious beliefs, administrative items, and history.

In Jeremiah's time, Babylon was a world class city, wealthy from conquest and trade. The city was known for its famous hanging gardens, highly decorated gates, palaces, and at least fifty-three temples. It also contained one of the most conspicuous monuments of ancient Mesopotamia, a ziggurat. This was a mud-brick, stepped pyramid with a temple to the gods on top. It was accessed by steps and a ramp. It reflected the highly religious nature of Babylon with

---

[9] In the OT the land is also called Shinar (Gen 10:10; 11:2; Isa 11:11; Jos 7:21) or "the land of the Chaldeans" in later texts (Jer 27:5; Ezek 12:17).

its long history of devotion to the many nature gods such Sin (moon-god), Shamash (sun-god), and Ishtar (mother goddess and goddess of love). In Babylon, Marduk was elevated to the king of the gods. Thus, the urban landscape of the city incorporated prominent religious elements.

Each god had its own cult, priests, festivals and rituals. The New Year Festival celebrated every spring was the most important festival. The statues of the gods were brought from other cities to Babylon and were joined by Marduk in procession to the *Akitu* house where rituals were performed, the king was humiliated, the creation myth was read, and a sacred marriage to insure fertility took place between the king and priestess. The religious professionals were therefore among the city's elite, even maintaining influence and power over the royalty. The Babylonian world-view included a three-storied universe, eternality of the gods, creation from conflict between the gods, and a universal flood.[10]

Popular religion was animistic which took the form of divination, magic, interpreting omens, rituals to ward off evil, and astrology. The premise was that the gods sent secret messages to the people and the priests had to devise ways to interpret them. The King of Babylon used magic to determine how to attack Jerusalem (Ezek 21:21, "He will cast lots with arrows, he will consult his idols, he will examine the liver."). By Jeremiah's time astrology was the major practice.[11] This religious world-view generated anxiety and uncertainty. Even some in Judah had adopted these practices and were strongly condemned by Jeremiah (Jer 14:14; 27:9; 29:8 [addressing the exiles in Babylon!]).

The exiles would have experienced culture shock upon entering this foreign world. They would have felt abandoned by God and desolate. Their first impulse would have been to isolate themselves and wish for an early return to Jerusalem (Jer 29). But Jerusalem's destruction made that impossible. However, Jeremiah's perspective is quite different, and he tells them to settle down, have families, and

---

[10] Parallels with Genesis are apparent. Some suggest parts of Genesis were intended to directly counter some of the Babylonian creation myth and flood story.

[11] Of the thousands of Babylonian texts discovered, divination texts are the most numerous. Amazingly, astrology still persists!

pray for the peace of the city (Jer 29). In other words, carry on an urban ministry in this alien context!

Character of Jeremiah

The book of Jeremiah is unique among the prophetic books in the quantity of biographical information we have about the prophet. This is the material in parts or all of chapters 19-21, 24, 26-28, and 34-45. Jeremiah is also unique in the amount of *auto*-biographical material it has, the so-called confessions in which Jeremiah offers intimate insight into his struggles with God. This is material in 1:4-19; 13:1-11; 16:1-8; 18:1-18; 19:1-3; and 20:7-18. Furthermore, Jeremiah is unique in the quantity of prose sermons it includes, the material in such chapters as 7, 11, 16, 18, and 23:23ff.

The book also includes the common range of prophetic speech forms that are found in other prophets, the prophetic oracles in poetic form. Chapters 1-26 have the largest amount of these poems. The common types include judgment speeches (5:1-6), covenant lawsuits (2:2-13), announcements of salvation (30:18-22; 31:1-6), disputations (3:1-5), symbolic acts (27), parables (18:1-11), and oracles against the nations (46-52). Chapters 30-33 contain a unified series of important promises of return and restoration and are called "The Book of Consolation" (sometimes extended to chs. 30-34).

Outline of Jeremiah

1. Prophecies of doom (1:1-25:14)

    a. The call (1)

    b. Prophecies from the time of Josiah (2-6)

    c. Prophecies from the time of Jehoiakim (7-20)

    d. Prophecies against king and prophet (21-25:14)

2. Introduction to prophecies against the nations (25:15-38)[12]

---

[12] The LXX version has a more logical order with the prophecies against the nations (MT chapters 46-51) following here after v. 38.

3. Destruction and restoration (26-33 [30-33 – book of consolation])

4. Jeremiah and the last days of Jerusalem (34-45)

5. Prophecies against the nations (46-51)

6. Historical appendix (52) (*cf.* 2 Kgs 25)

COMMENTARY ON JEREMIAH
1. Prophecies of Doom (1-25)

1.a. The call (1:1-19)

Structure of chapter 1

1. Introduction and setting: 1:1-3
2. Call and response: 1:4-10
3. First symbol – almond rod: 1:11-12
4. Second symbol – boiling caldron: 1:13-16
5. Charge to and encouragement for Jeremiah: 1:17-19

Jeremiah 1 fits the genre of the call narrative that appears in Exodus 3-4, Isaiah 6, and Ezekiel 1-3.[13] These include an initial call, a response (usually some objection), a Divine response and assurance, and a commission or description of the task. Jeremiah's call also includes two visions and a strong assurance of salvation (vv. 8, 17-19) with the characteristic "do not be afraid."[14] In the light of Jeremiah's ministry experience, the assurance was needed.

1:1-3

The verses in this section set the stage for everything that follows, identifying for us Jeremiah's family and the historical context (see Introduction). Jeremiah's career, beginning in 627 BCE, would continue until the fall of Jerusalem in 587 BCE and even beyond (Jer 40-44). Jeremiah was from a priestly family that could trace its heritage back to Abiathar, David's high priest, who incurred the wrath of Solomon and was banished to the little village of Anathoth

---

[13] See also Isa 1:1, Amos 1:1, Mic 1:1.

[14] This is rather common in the OT, beginning in Gen 15. God is continually reassuring his people that he is in control, especially in situations when the person has every right to be afraid. The consistent Hebrew phrase is *'al tīrāh* (אַל־תִּירָא).

(I Kgs 2:26-27).[15] There could very well have been some long-held resentment in his family against the Zadok line that had ruled in Jerusalem since the time of Solomon (1 Kgs 2:35).

"The words of Jeremiah" (vs.1) and the "word of the Lord" (vs. 2) are juxtaposed here. These phrases occur throughout the book and there seems to be little distinction between them. God's word comes through Jeremiah's words. Jeremiah's words comprise the book of Jeremiah, but their authority is grounded in the fact that ultimately, they are God's words. The book of Jeremiah also ends with an inclusion, a reference to "the words of Jeremiah" (51:64).[16] So we are intended to conclude that the whole book, whether it is a sermon, poetry, biography, or history is God's word.[17]

The mention of the three kings (Josiah, Jehoiakim, Zedekiah) not only sets the historical context but hints at what becomes apparent throughout the book – Jeremiah interacts often with the political authorities, bringing the word of the Lord into the political arena. Much was expected from the kings as leaders of God's people (Deut 17:14ff.), but many failed. So, for the most part Jeremiah's words were not good, encouraging words. Josiah was a good king (Jer 22:15-16; 2 Kgs 22:2; 23:25) but Jehoiakim and Zedekiah "did evil in the eyes of the Lord" (2 Kgs 23:37; 24:19). Therefore, Jeremiah's words of God's judgment coming through Babylon did not resonate well with these kings and their advisors, and he was jailed more than once (Jer 37, 38). The prophet Isaiah had had many wonderful things to say about God's blessings on Zion and Jerusalem and its prosperous future (Isa 1:26-27; 2:1-5; 4:2-6; 31:5; 37:35),

---

[15] Jeremiah's father was not the high priest Hilkiah of Josiah's reign (2 Kgs 22:4).

[16] Jer 52 is an historical appendix almost identical to 2 Kgs 24:18-20 and 25:1-21.

[17] The noun form of Hebrew דבר (*dbr*, "word") occurs more often in Jeremiah than any other book in the OT. Further, such phrases in vv. 1 and 2 and the phrase "oracle of the Lord" occurs more often in Jeremiah than in any prophet (Wright, *Jeremiah*, 32-33).

but that was a word for an earlier day. Circumstances were different in Jeremiah's time and the message from God was also different in tone and content.

Verse 3 foreshadows the end of the story of Jeremiah and joins with 52:27b-34. So, the reader knows from the beginning that Judah is doomed but is still fascinated with how all this will work out. From these words we also know that no matter what the kings may think about their importance and control of the history of the nation, it is a delusion. They may think their decisions make a difference in the political process and affairs of the nation but not so. God is sovereign and works out his will, which in this case means imminent exile.[18]

The exiles, who preserved Jeremiah's sermons, were living with the consequences of the exile in Babylon. They now knew Jeremiah's words were vindicated, although many had doubted before the fact. This is part of the reason for so much passion in the book of Jeremiah (the "weeping prophet"). God and Jeremiah weep for the obstinate and rebellious people because after centuries of warning, the end has come and there is no escape. Yet, even then there is hope, as we shall see.

1:4-10

This section and the rest of the chapter switches to the first person – God addresses Jeremiah directly and he responds. Verse 5 describes God's personal selection of Jeremiah as a prophet with the use of three loaded words: "knew," "consecrated," and "appointed."

The verse has three parallel lines describing the "before" of Jeremiah.

---

[18] Walter Brueggemann, *To Pluck Up, to Tear Down (Jeremiah 1-25)*, (Eerdmans, 1988), 21-22. This seems a particularly relevant observation for people who live in a constitutional democracy and go through the throes of a regular election cycle in which candidates promise their programs will solve all problems and save the future of the nation.

> Before I formed you in the womb I knew you,
> and before you were born I consecrated you;
> I appointed you a prophet to the nations.

The verb "form" of the first line (יצר, *yṣr*) recalls Genesis 2:7 and 19 where God formed the man and the animals from the ground. The verb is not a synonym of Hebrew create (ברא, *brʾ*) but is closely related. It signifies an object of God's care. The servant of Isaiah 44 and 49 is also formed in the womb (44:2; 49:1, 5, 8). In Isaiah the verbal "form" is almost always used of Israel and indicates her election and purpose. That is certainly the focus here for Jeremiah as well.[19]

The verb "know" (ידע, *ydʿ*), which has a wide range of meaning, here is used in the sense of election to the office of prophet. It is intended to give encouragement and denote a special relationship as when God spoke to Moses (Exod 33:17) and to Israel (Amos 3:2). Jeremiah's ministry is laid out for him before his birth, and he will only be able to find his purpose and fulfillment in life if he obeys God's summons.

Jeremiah is also "consecrated" or set apart to the task. The verb (קדש, *qds*, to make holy) is often used of material items used in worship of God – the temple, utensils, ark of the covenant, but also of the nation and gifts given to God (Exod 19:6; 33; 28:38; 29:33; 40:9-10; I Kgs 8:4). Jeremiah is the only prophet consecrated. His is a holy task.

"Appointed" translates the very common verb "to give" (נתן, *ntn*) which here takes on a special meaning from the context and syntax. God appoints Moses as "God to Pharaoh" (Exod 7:1), Ezekiel as a "watchman" (Ezek 3:17), and the servant as a "light to the nations" (Isa 49:6). This emphasizes the special circumstances and special task. The extraordinary time and circumstances require an extraordi-

---

[19] Jer 18 illustrates the total control of God over Israel with the analogy of the potter forming the clay pot.

nary servant of God. All three verbs (know, consecrate, appoint) imply Jeremiah belongs to God and is the man for the job.[20]

The scope of the task is breathtaking – it is "the nations."[21] This recalls the call of Abraham (Gen 12:1-3) which was ultimately for the nations also. This also recalls Isaiah's word to the servant in Isaiah 49:6:

> It is too light a thing that you should be my servant to raise up the tribes of Jacob and to restore the survivors of Israel; I will give you as a light to the nations, that my salvation may reach to the end of the earth.

The Creator of the universe chose Israel for his people to carry out his purpose. His purpose was that the whole world would know that he was God. Ultimately his desire was to do more than just call rebellious Israel back to himself. He also desired that all nations would hear his word, so we find several prophetic sermons addressed to the nations (Amos 2-3; Isa 13-23; Ezek 25-32; and Jer 46-51).

Jeremiah's response (v. 6) is negative. He does not see himself fit for the task because he is just a lad, a young man. The translations use "Ah" for the first word, which is too weak. It is a cry of alarm such as "Oh no" or "Alas." In a culture that honored age and paralleled it with wisdom his objection makes sense. It looks like God has determined Jeremiah's path, but he is not confident he can do it. He is in good company, for Moses did not wish to follow God's initiative (Exod 3-4) and Isaiah thought he was unworthy (Isa 6). Jeremiah's freedom to object foreshadows the many dialogues he has with God throughout his life. It also suggests that despite the determinate language of his call there is still room for his dissent.

However, God brushes his concerns aside (v.7). When God calls, ability, age, sinfulness, nor anything else is relevant. God is the actor and Jeremiah's role is obedient servant.

---

[20] Wright, *Jeremiah*, 50

[21] See Wright, *The Mission of God*.

Jeremiah is not to say that he is a child, but he is to say what God tells him to say. The import of the negative command is "Never say ..." and parallels the negative command in verse 8, "Never be afraid."[22] If God stands with his person or people then how can they fear anybody or any circumstances? God will not just "rescue" Jeremiah, he will "snatch him away" from his enemies. This verb is often used of God delivering his people from hostile hands such as delivering Israel from Egypt (1 Sam 10:18) or David from danger (2 Sam 22:1). The psalmists often plead for God to deliver them from enemies and violent people, and then affirm his deliverance (see e.g. Ps 18:1, 17; 25:20; 34:19; 71:2, 11; 72:12). But despite the assurances we must admit that the fear is real and cannot be denied. "Fear is one of the most potent obstacles to obedience."[23] The only antidote to fear is obedience.

The promise that God will "be with him" is a typical promise that follows God's command to not fear (*e.g.*, Gen 15:1; 26:24; Isa 41:10). This reassurance is repeated in verse 19.

The second half of God's response shows why Jeremiah's objection is useless (v. 9). It is God's word that Jeremiah will be speaking, not his own. The source is God, so Jeremiah's ability or lack thereof is irrelevant. The introduction to Jeremiah's response in verse 6 ("Ah, alas") is repeated by God in verse 9 (translated "Now"), but here highlights a strong affirmation (NET Bible, "Most assuredly"). The response also recalls Deut 18:18 where God assures Moses he will raise up a prophet like him into whose mouth God will

---

[22] This is a common command in the OT beginning in Gen 15:1 and occurring dozens of times. It is addressed to people who in the circumstances have every reason to be afraid. It is usually followed by the promise from God, "for I am with you" (as here). For a few examples see Gen 26:24; Deut 1:21; Josh 8:1; Isa 43:1; 44:2; Jer 30:10; Ezek 2:6; Dan 10:19.

[23] Wright, *Jeremiah*, 52.

put his words.[24] Of course Christians interpret Deuteronomy 18 messianically, but within the context of the Old Testament, Jeremiah is one of those prophets.[25] Thus, to hear Jeremiah is to hear God. This was often denied by Jeremiah's audience during his lifetime, but the exiles who preserved his sermons understood that indeed his words were God's words.[26]

The charge of verse 5 is now explained (v. 10). Jeremiah is a prophet to "nations and kingdoms" (see chs. 25, 46-51) for a purpose. This purpose is expressed with six verbs in three pairs, four with negative outcomes and two with positive outcomes. These verbs (or various combinations of them) appear throughout the rest of the book (Jer 31:28 [6 of them]; 18:7-10 [5]; 12:14-17; 24:6; 42:10; 45:4 [4]; 31:38, 40 [3]). The first four (pluck/pull down, destroy/overthrow) are word pairs used often in other prophets as well. They denote the devastating judgment of God against his disobedient people, but here these are actions against other nations also. The powerful spoken word of God can change history and the fortunes of all nations. Prophets like Isaiah, Amos, and Ezekiel also spoke words against the nations. These verbs give the scope of Jeremiah's prophetic authority.[27]

The last word pair (build/plant) contrasts with the first word pair for these verbs speak of restoration and blessing (see also Isa 65:21; Amos 9:14-15; Ezek 36:36). Unfortunately, this blessing does not come until after the first pair are accomplished, a fact that many of Jeremiah's opponents found unbelievable (see Jer 28-29). Remarkably, this

---

[24] A human example is provided in Exod 4:15-16 when God tells Moses that he will tell his brother Aaron what to say and that Moses will be "as God to him."

[25] Christians will recall that when Jesus asked his disciples who people said that he was one of the suggestions was Jeremiah (Matt 16:14).

[26] The New Testament authors had the same conviction that they were speaking God's word – 1 Cor 2:13; 2 Pet 1:21.

[27] Wright, *Jeremiah*, 55.

unbelief continued even after the destruction of Jerusalem and the exile (Jer 44).

Verse 10 sets the agenda for the rest of the book by defining the intent and content. The long history of Israel's disobedience to God has finally exhausted his patience and there is no more time for repentance. The end of Israel is assured. That is not the total end, as God's grace will ultimately shine through, but the status of the nation is grim.

> **Jeremiah 1:10**
>
> *See, today I appoint you over nations and over kingdoms,*
> *to pluck up and to pull down,*
> *to destroy and to overthrow,*
> *to build and to plant.*
>
> Civilizations and empires are defined by great cities. In Jeremiah's day, the city of Babylon expanded its influence to crush the remnants of the Assyrian empire and its great city, Nineveh. The dominance of Babylon continued to the defeat the Egyptians at the battle of Carchemish in 605 BCE. Judah's King Josiah played a role in this epic history, attempting to delay Pharaoh Neco's march to the north with his Egyptian armies to meet the Babylonians. Josiah lost his life fighting the Egyptians in the Battle of Megiddo, 609 BCE (2 Chr 35:20-27). Josiah and his sons figure prominently in the writings of Jeremiah. The reign of these men set the parameters for the book (see Jer 1:2-3).
>
> In Jeremiah's day, Josiah's Jerusalem was a small city and a minor player on the world stage. Transnational empires were based in large cities where weaponry was produced, armies were raised, and ambitious men organized conquests. Resources, talent, and innovation flowed into the great cities from their provinces and streamed out of the cities in dominating government and culture.

> We live in the age of great cities. The United Nations counted thirty-three "urban agglomerations" in 2018, megacities with 10 million or more residents.[28] While these cities are not the seat of empires as they were in Jeremiah's day, they wield enormous influence among the people of their countries, regions, and continents. The two megacities of the United States exercise outsized influence considering their relatively small percentage of the American population. New York City is a world power in the economic arena. Los Angeles's entertainment industry has world-wide cultural impact.
>
> In this urban milieu, both ancient and modern, the Lord is involved. In his initial charge, he appoints Jeremiah to pluck and to plant when it comes to kings and kingdoms. These are city-based rulers and empires. Jeremiah's messages, given to him by God, speak deeply into the future of cities. His words are intended for urban ears. He will prophesy the building and the destruction of city-based empires, those who may seek to lord it over the less powerful in rural contexts. A primary message of Jeremiah is that God is Lord over all the kings, all the kingdoms, and all the cities.
>
> Mark S. Krause

In verse 5 God had "appointed" Jeremiah as a prophet and in verse 10 he also does this, but there is an important difference indicated by a different word in the Hebrew. *Pqd* (פקד) here carries the idea of commissioned or assigned and suggests his authority more strongly. But it is derived authority and it will be God who carries out the word that Jeremiah will speak.

The theology of the word of God is on display in this text. That word comes through the prophet and exercises control over all nations. Tied to this sovereign power of God is

---

[28] United Nations, Department of Economic and Social Affairs, Population Division (2019). World Urbanization Prospects: The 2018 Revision (ST/ESA/SER.A/420). New York: United Nations, 81.

the theology of God's call, for he exercises his divine will through the instrumentality of frail humans. Jeremiah may think he is too young, but with God as the initiator that is no problem, for it is God's work being done. The mystery is that God's word works through people, thus the need for both a commission and assurance. It is both an honor to be chosen by God and an impossible task to do. This tension follows Jeremiah through his whole life.

1:11-16

The next section in this chapter, verses 11-16, gives Jeremiah two visions of affirmation that show that God will be faithful to his word. The first vision of the almond tree (vv. 11-12) provides a strong memory key for Jeremiah because it is based on a word play. The Hebrew word for almond tree (שָׁקֵד, šāqēd) sounds like the word for watch (v. 12, שֹׁקֵד, šōqēd). Thus, Jeremiah could easily remember the word of encouragement but also would be reminded of this word every time he saw an almond tree. At the end of the book of Jeremiah, God is still watching over his word (44:27) for the survivors who have gone to Egypt are still resisting it and earn a death threat. Scripture affirms throughout that the word of the Lord stands firm (Isa 40:8; 55:10-11; Ps 119:89; 1 Pet 1: 24-25).

The second vision (verses 13-16), in showing Jeremiah a boiling pot tipped to the south, affirms that the devastation and destruction promised earlier will come from the north. This was a geographical truth for Israel. Other than Egypt which lay to the south, any threat that came to the nation came from the north (Syria [Arameans in 1 and 2 Kgs], Assyria, or Babylon). Only occasionally did the small nations to the east of the Jordan threaten Israel. Because of the great Arabian desert to the east the only route the Mesopotamian countries could follow was to travel northwest up the Euphrates river valley and come down through Syria. In Jeremiah's day this was firm assurance that Babylon, the dominant nation at that time, was coming. These Babylonians would do what a conquering nation usually does, set up their temporary thrones near the city gates and watch the army besiege and destroy the city of Jerusalem (v. 15).

All of Israel's sin is described in one word (v. 16), they have "forsaken" God. The word (עזב, 'zb) in this kind of context is a covenant term and refers to a breaking of the covenant (used with this nuance about 100 times in the OT[29]). It is a common word in Jeremiah (*e.g.*, 2:13, 17, 19; 5:7; 9:13) and provides a clear description of what it means to sin against God. Jeremiah 9:13 says the people have forsaken the law and 22:9 says they have abandoned the covenant. Chapter 16:11 is comprehensive, *"then you shall say to them: It is because your ancestors have forsaken me, says the LORD, and have gone after other gods and have served and worshiped them, and have forsaken me and have not kept my law…"*

The forsaking is public and pervasive, described as idolatry or worshipping what their hands have made (v. 16). This is a violation of the first commandment and tells us that God's judgment is based in morality and theology, not politics or economics.[30] The irony and reproof are thick. The God of Israel was the creator of the universe and of humans. He was the creator of his people. Yet they turned aside from honoring this great God to worship puny, lifeless, powerless things they had made with their hands (see on chapter 10). They were created in the image of God but created something in their image to worship (*cf.*, Rom 1:23). Isaiah 44:12-20 is the delightful spoof of this action. It well describes moderns who abandon God and create their own gods involving wealth, power, and sex. These are not the ancient physical idols but are idols just the same.[31]

1:17-19

Jeremiah's call narrative ends with a warning and words of assurance which remind the reader of God's warning to

---

[29] Robert L. Alden, "עזב", NIDOTTE, 3:365.

[30] Brueggemann, *To Pluck Up*, 27.

[31] See an older work but still relevant: Herbert Schlossberg, *Idols of Destruction: The Conflict of Christian Faith and American Culture*. Wheaton, IL: Crossway, 1990. He names as the major categories: history, humanity, mammon, nature, power, and religion.

Joshua (Josh 1:6-9). The warning of stiff opposition justifies Jeremiah's earlier objection. How could a young lad expect to stand firm against such odds let alone a mature prophet? Who would voluntarily take on such a formidable task? The warning defines Jeremiah's future and is borne out by future events recorded in the book. God warns him (v. 18b) that he will be opposed by kings (see ch. 36), its officials (ch. 26), priests, and the people of the land (11:18-21, which includes his own family). God could also have added, prophets (chs. 28-29). Jeremiah's life was in danger more than once and it took powerful friends to rescue him. These events led to some of Jeremiah's most poignant complaints to God as we shall see. The warning in verse 17 also carries a threat! God is gracious and supportive but also a stern commissioner who expects obedience.

As Abraham discovered, the one who calls and commissions also provides (Gen 22). Therefore, God would enable Jeremiah to stand against the opposition just as the strongest city, or pillar, or wall can stand against opposing forces (v. 18a). The call is rounded off by a deliberate repetition of the assurance of verse 8b.

1.b. Prophecies from the time of Josiah (2:1-6:30)

The first sermons in the book are undated. A general date is given in 3:6 as during the reign of Josiah. This suggests that the early chapters are perhaps from that same general time. The sermons were thus delivered during the time of Josiah's reform (2 Kgs 22-23) which for the prophet and the faithful was a hopeful time. The law book (some form of Deuteronomy?) found in the temple, became the basis for extensive excising of the pagan elements in Judah. The hopeful note in 3:6ff. perhaps reflects this time.[32] However, Josiah's untimely death and the subsequent reign of evil Jehoiakim dashed these hopes (see Jer 26 and 36; 2 Kgs 23:37).

---

[32] Some suggest all of Jeremiah's early sermons are in chs. 1-20.

1.b.i. Marriage and divorce (2:1-3:5)

Jeremiah's first sermon in the book introduces us to many features that mark his preaching style. This includes a remarkable talent for memorable figures of speech, incisive questions for his audience, and interaction with his audience that reflects the constant push back he received.[33] A major figure of speech in this section which first appears in Hosea 1-2 is the marriage metaphor. The prophet conceived of God as the husband and Israel as the wife involved in a covenant relationship that mirrored human marriage. With this metaphor he was able to formulate strong images displaying the depth of Israel's sin against God. Hosea suggested that Israel was an unfaithful wife and had committed prostitution with Canaanite fertility gods. Jeremiah builds on this image and adds his own insights. Ezekiel carried the image into even more harsh terms.[34]

2:1-3

A brief command to speak is followed by the first assertion of the sermon. God remembers Israel's early history as a time of love and devotion, a honeymoon period when she was a new bride and followed her husband. This reflects the exodus from Egypt and the early wanderings in the wilderness. This is a somewhat idealized version since the accounts in Exodus and Numbers suggests a complaining, restive people.

Two key words are "devotion" (חסד, *ḥesed*) and "love" (אהבה, *'ahabah*). *Ḥesed* is the premier covenantal word and portrays the deepest of loyalty and faithful loving kindness. It originates with God but was expected from his people also. God's *ḥesed* meant that he freely gives his people exactly

---

[33] Wright counts 16 questions and 19 different images in the section (*Jeremiah*, 59-60)

[34] I explored this imagery in my Ph.D. dissertation at Union Theological Seminary (now Presbyterian Theological Seminary) in 1980. Gary H. Hall, *The Marriage Imagery in Jeremiah 1-2: A Study of Antecedents and Innovations in a Prophetic Metaphor* (unpublished). See Ezekiel 16 and 23.

what they need so that they can live as his people. On the other hand, Israel owed everything to God, so they were expected to show loyalty and faithfulness to him. The marriage metaphor was a perfect symbol for expressing this relationship.

'Ahabah was not an obvious choice of words to express the relationship because it suggested a more sensual side, but it fit the metaphor. This is the only place in the Old Testament that states that Israel loved God. Elsewhere, as in Deuteronomy, Israel is commanded to love God. This love also was a part of commitment and loyalty.

Verse 2 provides the thematic framework for 2:1-3:5, what Holliday calls the "harlotry cycle."[35] So we will expect the language to refer to the metaphor as the chapter progresses.

Verse 3 shifts to considering the status of Israel before God, rather than her relationship to him. She is "holy" to the Lord which means she is set apart from the other nations for an express purpose and shares his holiness. Those who oppress her are guilty before God of violating his holy nation. She is also God's "first fruits", a concept grounded in the law of the harvest (Lev 23:9-14) which also reflects on her status, so although Israel may be guilty of forsaking God (vv. 4-13), those nations that might take advantage of her also incur guilt, because she still is God's nation.[36]

2:4-13

This section is marked by a specific prophetic genre and a specific rhetorical structure. The genre is a covenant lawsuit in which God brings a legal charge against his people that is grounded in their covenant unfaithfulness. The key word is *rîb* (ריב), "contend, accuse, bring a charge against"

---

[35] William Holliday, *The Architecture of Jeremiah 1-20* (Lewisburg: Bucknell University Press, 1976).

[36] Some have speculated that there may be a missional aspect here as well, since Israel as first fruits could imply that she is the first of the nations and that eventually all nations will come to God.

in verse 9. God puts her on trial and is the prosecuting attorney, judge, and jury (*cf.* Mic 6:1-2; Hos 4:1). The rhetorical structure is a chiasm, an X form, in which the section begins and ends with the same thoughts, with the focal point in the middle, in this case verse 9. On each side of verse 9 in verses 5 and 13 the main charge is made: Israel has turned away from God. This charge is elaborated on in verses 6-8 and 11.

Israel's status is that they are following idols (v.5) and have forsaken God (v.13). This contrasts with their early devotion of following only God and represents a complete about face in loyalty and service (there is great emotion in the plaintive "What fault did your fathers find in me..." of v. 5). What is even worse is that the gods they now follow are not even gods, they are nothings (הֶבֶל, *hebel*). This is the word often translated as "vanity" in Ecclesiastes. The idols have no substance. They are but a brief puff of wind. Jeremiah states a "law" of life, a person (or nation) becomes that to which they devote their energies. In this case since they had devoted themselves to "nothings" that is what they became. It still is true and can be seen all around us. Empty human values replace divine ones and people lead desperate lives, always seeking the next thrill or high, or giving into despair. Only if God is the object of our desires will we, or the church, become everything that God wants for us. Anything less side tracks us into pursuits that take over our lives and can destroy us.

The parallel verse 13 asks the question, how could Israel give up, forsake, the source of life for nothing, for death, for a cracked cistern. The forsaking of God is one of Jeremiah's major terms for Israel's apostasy (see 2:17, 19; 5:7, 19; 16:11; 17:13; 22:9). This is the exact opposite of election and the loyal following after of her honeymoon period of verse 2. How could this have happened? The people ceased pursuing God (vv. 6-7). They forgot their history, all the great things God had done for them by electing them as his people. They forgot his rescuing them from slavery in Egypt, taking them safely through the wilderness, and bringing them into the Promised Land. Furthermore, Israel's leadership totally failed (v. 8). The priest, rulers ("shepherds" in the Hebrew text), and prophets were all to blame. Ignorance, rebellion, and false prophecy led Israel into their current state. At every level there was complicity in turning away from God. The proper pursuit and knowledge of God had been replaced by adopting the pagan nations' pursuits, a lethal substitution. When the unreal is substituted for the real, only disaster can follow. The substitutes for the worship of the one true God are ultimately demeaning to the worshipper and offer nothing for them.

Forsaking God had left an emptiness in their lives, so Israel did what even the pagan nations did not do, they substituted other gods for their God (v. 11), replaced the reality of God's presence for "nothings." This was even appalling to nature! Why would they want to replace God for idols? Was he too demanding? Did he stand in the way of human goals? Was his glory a terrible thing?

God the prosecutor made his case and proved it beyond doubt. The defendant had no excuse nor a response. Israel was guilty as charged. Much of the rest of the book of Jeremiah is only a variation on this theme.

The church too has a great history of Christians' faithful service down through the centuries. The influence on western culture is enormous and encompasses all aspects of our current lives from modern science and medicine to art and music to abolition of slavery to education to respect for women to the rule of law to hospitals to morality to the sanctity of life, and on and on.[37] Under the pressure of the now the church could easily forget this legacy and the evidence of God at work in the world, and be tempted to turn inward and focus on the all-important "me".

Christians should remember that God has remained faithful to all his promises and they are "yes" in Christ (2 Cor 1:20). Further Jesus Christ is the faithful one who was obedient to the father even to death on the cross. He is also the living water and he who drinks will never thirst (John 4). Therefore, the good news can be preached with confidence

---

[37] Alvin Schmidt, *How Christianity Changed the World* (Grand Rapids: Zondervan, 2001, 2004).

to the whole world. But woe to the church, like the Ephesian church, who loses its first love (Rev 2:4).

2:14-19

The focus shifts for a moment from idolatry to Israel's foreign alliances and trust in other countries. But this is equal to idolatry because it involves placing trust in something other than God and thus "forsaking" him (vv. 17 and 19).

This section has two parts, each introduced by a rhetorical question (vv. 14 and 17). The first raises the issue of her slavery. Israel spent several hundred years as a slave in Egypt but that was not their origin, and God rescued them. But now they have reversed their history and become slaves again. How? They have formed alliances with foreign countries, especially Assyria or Egypt. These two countries are referenced twice, in a chiastic style. Assyria (the lion) appears in verses 15 and 18b, and Egypt appears in verses 16 and 18a. Near the end of the northern kingdom's history, King Ahaz had appealed to Assyria for help against his enemies, but it only led to disaster (2 Kgs 16). Hezekiah apparently hoped for help from Egypt during his "Assyrian crisis" in 701 BCE, but they fled home (2 Kgs 18:21). These alliances were harmful to Israel.[38] Foreign alliances also subjected Israel to pagan religious influence. Jeremiah returns to this theme in verse 35.

The second rhetorical question in verse 17 suggests they have brought all this trouble on themselves. Israel had abandoned the living water (v. 13) so now she was seeking to slack her thirst elsewhere (v. 18) which could not succeed.

Jeremiah calls Israel's turning to foreign nations "backsliding" in verse 19. This word (מְשׁוּבָה, *m^ešûbāh*) becomes a favorite word of his in chapter 3 to characterize the religious apostasy of the Northern Kingdom. There the word is translated as "faithless" in the NIV (see 3:6, 8, 11, 12, 22). For Jeremiah, foreign alliances fit the same category as

---

[38] Ezekiel especially pursues these connections in his extended harlotry metaphor in ch. 23.

idolatry and can be characterized as spiritual adultery/harlotry as well. In fact, one cause of turning to idolatry was probably assimilation of foreign religions because of foreign alliances.

The result is "evil and bitter" for Israel. They committed two "evils' against God (v. 13) and this has come back on them.[39] In other places "evil" is translated "disaster" which fits many contexts. The evil that comes back on Israel here is the disaster that Babylon is about to bring on her by destroying Jerusalem and the temple (see chs. 39-44 and the use of "evil" there). Jeremiah uses evil often in chapters 2 and 3 (2:3, 13, 19, 27, 33; 3:2, 5, 7) for it is an appropriate word for both their sin against God and their punishment.[40] Its two-sided meaning fits well, for evil can refer to both moral wickedness and amoral calamity. The people are immoral and will thus suffer calamity (see Jer 4:6; 5:12-13; 6:1; 23:10, 12). But the calamity is not an impersonal event. God is its author, for Israel is God's people and they have deeply offended him.[41]

The psalmist declared, *"Some trust in chariots and some in horses, but we trust in the Lord our God"* (Ps 20:7). God's people are continuously faced with the challenge of trust. All kinds of powers vie for influence and ultimate meaning in peoples' lives: wealth, power, politics, military might, fame, but none bring the kind of security that people want. They usually bring calamity. Christians are not immune from these temptations as the culture brings great pressure on them to pursue "worldly" goals. It is truly difficult to trust solely in God. Israel failed, and her leadership often practiced the *realpolitik* of the world rather than remaining faithful to the covenant. Jeremiah will return to this theme again and again.

---

[39] Translations vary for v. 13 from "sins" to "wrongs" to "evil." Evil is the correct translation.

[40] Jeremiah uses the word evil an astounding 116 times!

[41] For the same concept in other prophets see Hos 8:4-7; 7:1-2; 12:3, 15; Amos 3:6; Mic 2:1-2.

2:20-25

This section is a continuation of the charges of the lawsuit laid out for us in verses 4-13. Jeremiah returns to the sexual metaphor for these charges. He also directly quotes the people three times (vv. 20, 23, 25) to illustrate their confusion and to support his accusations. In other words, he is not making this stuff up. How can the people say they will not serve God (v. 20), or it is no use because they love foreign gods (v. 25), and yet claim that they are not defiled (v. 23)?

Jeremiah uses some of his most picturesque descriptions here and allows us to get a glimpse into some of the popular religion in his day. The details and graphic descriptions are supported by heavy sarcasm.

The section begins with a simple, precise accusation – Israel had refused to serve the Lord and she has prostrated herself in Canaanite worship, acting like a prostitute (v. 20). She was elected as a choice vine but has turned rotten (v. 21) so that nothing can purify her (v. 22). Yet she protests her innocence (v. 23a). However, her innocence cannot be sustained, for she is as uncontrollable as a young camel, as a female ass in heat (vv. 23b-24). Despite this, the Lord desires that she restrain herself (v. 25a). but she finally admits the hopelessness of the situation – she is determined to continue in her love and pursuit of foreign idols (v. 25b).

The first figure in verse 20 recalls a rebellious, uncontrollable ox. The yoke is used to hitch cattle to the wagon (1 Sam 6:7). The word then became a figure for servitude (1 Kgs 12; Deut 28:48). The servitude here is service to the Lord which is positive. However, her refusal to serve is negative and open rebellion (Jer 5:5). Jeremiah coined a phrase to express this rebellion, "break yoke and burst bonds."[42]

---

[42] Parts of this phrase occur elsewhere but Jeremiah is the only one to put together "break yoke" and "burst bonds" (see Nahum 1:13; Ps 2:3; 107:14; Lev 26:13; Ezek 34:27).

But Jeremiah hastens to point out that they have indeed served, only it is Baal not the Lord. The description of where they served pictures idolatry at the Canaanite cultic centers. The "high hill" and the "green tree" throughout the Old Testament are the places of illicit worship. The whole phrase or some variant of it occurs sixteen times in the Old Testament.[43] This phrase is a succinct description of Israel's popular religion. The practices are those of the Canaanite fertility cult. The sanctuaries of the cult were on the hills and mountains, usually adorned with a stone pillar or wooden pole (if no tree was nearby). Jeremiah called this established practice "harlotry/prostitution" following Hosea's daring formulation. Israel's worship of other gods is a prostitution of her faith. This code word has two referents – the religious apostasy and the actual sexual prostitution that took place at the cultic centers. Verses 25 and 33 make clear this is not just a casual liaison, but Israel actively seeking out the object of worship (love).

The accusation continues in verse 21 under the figure of the vine. In the Hebrew text the "I" is in an emphatic position contrasting what God had done with what Israel had become. Jeremiah intends to emphasize the quality of Israel's beginning. A select, healthy vineyard was a source of great pleasure in Palestine. Such was Israel/Judah, but she has become a rotten vine, alien to the Lord. Her sin is so great that cleansing is impossible (v. 22).

Yet Israel responds by protesting her innocence (v. 23. "I am not defiled..."). She is unclean without a doubt, both religiously and sexually. Jeremiah develops some vivid figures to accuse her of her sin. Her "way in the valley" is probably a reference to offering child sacrifice in the valley of Ben-Hinnon near Jerusalem (see Jer 7:31; 19:5; 2 Kgs 23:10). The people made many paths as they pursued Baal worship throughout the country. Their behavior is unrestrained, like animals. A young camel lacks control of its limbs and if on the loose no one dares get near it. The wild

---

[43] See 1 Kgs 14:23; 2 Kgs 17:10; Deut 12:2, 12, etc. See William L. Holladay, "On Every High Hill and Under Every Green Tree," VT 11 (1961):170-76.

female ass is the one who initiates action when she is in heat. She searches for the scent of the male and then races wildly after him. Their behavior is both uncontrolled and lustful. Jeremiah reduces Israel's idol worship to the level of animal behavior.

The people themselves seem to recognize they are caught up in this passionate pursuit and cannot turn back (v. 25, another quote of the people). Their love for the strange gods contrasts to their earlier love for the Lord in verse 2, and the original devotion is now directed to others. Israel's earlier history stands in judgment on her present history. Her early faithfulness and trust, her reliance on the Lord to bring her into the good land has been abandoned. Her turning to other gods has not brought her blessing, but servitude and privation. The blessings she could be experiencing are not now open to her because her history in the land has been one of abandonment of the Lord of the covenant for other gods. These are false gods who have no history of relationship with the people. In light of God's elective love, Israel's apostasy is breathtaking.

2:26-28

Israel's quest for blessing and profit from pursuing the Canaanite false gods results in their shame. In ancient cultures shame and honor were deep seated values. To bring shame on someone or experience shame was the worst of social stigmas. Consequently, Israel's attempts to find benefit and guidance from the false gods did not result in what they hoped for, fertility and success, but in deep shame. Part of that shame was discovering that the false gods were helpless to provide any kind of assistance. They were not worthy of the loyalty that the people gave them (see Hos 10:3-6). This same thought is repeated in verse 36 but there it is the foreign alliances that have failed and brought shame. The irony was that when Israel got in deep trouble then she appealed to the Lord (v. 27) but it is too late. How could she claim a relationship with the idols and still appeal to God to come to her aid? The fault also lay at the feet of the leadership which failed at every level (v. 26).

Jeremiah 2:16

Moreover, the people of Memphis and Tahpanhes have broken the crown of your head.

Jeremiah mentions two Egyptian cities, Memphis and Tahpanhes, as historic oppressors of the people of Israel. For centuries, Memphis was the capital and chief trading center of Egypt. Tahpanhes was a garrison city near the Palestinian frontier to the east of the Nile delta. In this oracle, the cities serve as warnings against hostile foreign powers. Yet later in the book, both serve as cities of refuge for the Judeans fleeing the Babylonian pillage of Judea and Jerusalem (Jer 43:7, 44:1).

Vancouver, British Columbia, has long had a large population of ethnic Chinese citizens. With the rise in economic power in China and particularly in Hong Kong, Chinese investment cash flowed to Vancouver in the late twentieth century to purchase properties and businesses, leading to dramatic rises in home prices.[44] The transfer of Hong Kong back to the mainland Chinese government in 1997 led to more than the influx of Chinese money to Vancouver. Because of Hongkongers' status as residents of the British Commonwealth, some relocated to the Canadian cities as well-healed "refugees." Not all were wealthy, however, and the flood of Chinese people coming to Vancouver has changed the city permanently with "Chinese" now being the largest percentage for any ethnic group in the city. The vestiges of the British Empire, which dominated China in the nineteenth century, now provides refuge in a Canadian city.

People whose lives and livelihoods are endangered seek to immigrate. They become refugees who face hostility to relocate. Cities absorb immigrants at a high rate, making

---

[44] See "The City that Had Too Much Money," Bloomberg Businessweek, October 20, 2018, accessed at https://www.bloomberg.com/news/features/2018-10-20/vancouver-is-drowning-in-chinese-money.

> them diverse in language, culture, and religion. In the period 2002-2018, my state (Nebraska) received nearly 12,000 refugees.[45] Over 80% of these people located in the state's two larger cities, Omaha and Lincoln even though these comprise a little more than a third of Nebraska's population. Just as the people of Judah had to flee from Jerusalem to Memphis and Tahpanhes, so families from across the world seek refuge in Vancouver, Miami, Houston, Minneapolis, Toronto, Lincoln, and Omaha today. Will we "break the crown" of their heads, or will we welcome and support them in their time of disorientation and need?
>
> *Mark S. Krause*

There is more irony in verse 27. In the Baal cult it was the tree that represented the goddess Ashtorah and the stone represented the god Baal. Jeremiah reveres these concepts as a deliberate spoof of Israel's foolishness.

2:29-37

This long section transitions to chapter 3, looking back to verses 14-19, and ahead to chapter 3 by introducing the use of the key word "return" (שוב, *shub*) which appears throughout chapter 3. The accusations of the covenant lawsuit are affirmed and the possibility of Israel's ability to return to the Lord from her apostasy (literally "turning away") is raised. The rhetoric is a disputation style. Jeremiah continues to quote the audience (vv. 31, 35) and disputes their perspective by listing facts about their conduct.

The people have been complaining against the Lord, but that is incomprehensible for they are the ones who turned against him (v. 29). Their rebellion is demonstrated in several ways: they rejected the discipline of the prophets and in fact murdered them (v. 30, 34); they rejected God's lordship ("we will roam", v. 31); they forgot the Lord (v. 32); and they sought other gods (v. 33). In spite all of this they claim innocence and take comfort in the Lord's mercy (v. 35a). But they will be punished (v. 35b). Despite what they

---

[45] See "Refugee Resettlement" provided by the Omaha World-Herald, https://dataomaha.com/refugees.

say, their fickleness is apparent as they continually change gods and alliances (v. 36) so there can only be one result – judgment that will bring shame and grief (vv. 36b-37).

Verse 29 is shocking. Jeremiah has listed copious evidence that Israel is guilty of covenant breaking and that the lawsuit of verses 14-19 is appropriate. But Israel thinks she can charge the Lord with covenant breaking. Impossible! They are the rebellious party! They have rejected their prophets and forgotten God (vv. 30-32)! This was the original charge raised in 2:2. To forget is not just a loss of memory but an active turning against God. A bride would never forget her special day and her ornaments, but Israel, as a bride (v. 2), has done just that. Moreover, she has sought other "lovers" (v. 33), that is other gods, instead of being faithful and loyal to her spouse. Hosea used this term in his extended reflection on Israel's infatuation with Canaanite gods which he called adultery and prostitution (Hos 2:5, 6, 12, 13). This is a harsh and poignant metaphor for the people's broken relationship with God.

That this rebellion was intentional is fortified using the word "seek" in verse 33 (NIV, "pursuing"). This is a conscious act of the will with a specific goal in mind and often involves a great deal of effort, shrewdness and imagination.[46] This seeking involves worship but extends to non-cultic life as well (Hos 5:6; Ps 27:8; 105:4). In Jeremiah's day Israel was expending her energy on seeking other gods, and doing so well they could teach sinners new tricks.

Verse 34 is perhaps a reference to the Manasseh era when great evil was done by this evil king (2 Kgs 21:16). There could be no more serious charge of complete social disintegration. The referent here to innocent blood is founded on the law in Exodus 22:2 which addresses the issue of how to treat someone breaking into one's home. Only if it is at night is death warranted. But even in this simple case Israel in Jeremiah's time has violated the law. This is a clear example of the principle that Jeremiah emphasized earlier

---

[46] Siegfried Wagner, "*biqqēsh; baqqāshāh*", *TDOT*, 2:230.

– the object of the people's worship determined what they became, and in this case, they lost their respect for innocent life.[47]

After the long indictment of chapter 2, Jeremiah finally adds words of judgment, something we might have expected sooner. Her seeking help from other countries would fail and she would suffer exile. Jeremiah will return to this theme in detail later.

3:1-5

This passage completes the marriage metaphor begun in chapter 2:2 by contemplating the results of Israel's numerous violations of the marriage covenant. The imagery implied strongly in chapter 2 is now explicit. God is the husband and Israel is the wife. This analogy continues throughout chapter 3 (vv. 1, 2, 3, 6, 8, 9, 14, 20). Chapter 2 detailed the unfaithfulness of the wife and her subsequent estrangement. This section contemplates the possibility of reconciliation between the parties. Though Israel seems to think it possible, Jeremiah refers to the law to show that it is impossible. The law on divorce and remarriage is in Deuteronomy 24:1-4. Although this is often referred to as the law on divorce, it is the law about the consequences of divorce and the impossibility of remarriage if the divorced wife has married someone else, been divorced, then wants to return to her first husband. The law is marked by several conditional clauses and divorce is assumed at the beginning. A reconciliation after the second divorce would defile the land (Deut 24:5).[48]

Israel seemed to assume "cheap grace." She was guilty of all the sins Jeremiah outlined but was sure God would allow her to come back. Jeremiah disabuses them of that naive assumption. Israel had not just gone after one other

---

[47] A clear example that what one choses to worship has serious consequences for all of life. There is evidence that Canaanite worship at times involved child sacrifice.

[48] See Gary H. Hall, *Deuteronomy* (Joplin: College Press, 2000), 357-360.

lover, she had pursued many. Thus, her break with the Lord was complete. The breach of faithfulness and loyalty was beyond the point of healing.[49]

Israel's thinking suggests a common human perception – my wrongdoings are not too bad and God, who is characterized by love and mercy, will always be willing to take me back. A writer years ago pointed out why we think this way: we do not take our sins seriously enough, nor do we take the holiness of God seriously enough.[50]

Jeremiah introduces a key word here that appears 16 times in verb and noun forms in chapter 3, the root word *šûb* (שׁוב), which can mean turn back, turn away, return, or other similar nuances (vv. 1 [2], 7 [2], 10, 12, 14, 19, 22; the noun *mᵉšûbāh* (משׁובה), vv. 6, 8, 11, 12, 22; the adjective *šōbab* (שׁובב), vv.14, 22). The noun and adjective are usually translated as backsliding or faithless. Apostate would be a good rendering. All three forms occur in verse 22.[51]

Jeremiah supports his stance on reconciliation by reminding Israel once again of their despicable behavior (v. 2) with harsh language reminiscent of 2:23-24. She was not an innocent victim but actively sought the false idols. The harlot sitting at the roadside reminds us of Tamar in Genesis 38:14ff. and the seductive woman of Proverbs 7:12.

The result (v. 3) was the exact opposite of why Israel sought the Canaanite gods in the first place. Baal was the god of the storm and thunder and Ashtorah was a fertility goddess. Israel thought they were insuring both rain and fertility by worshipping these gods. But Jeremiah insists that the Lord was the source of both, and he withheld the rain they needed to make it clear just who was the God of the land, nature, and the world.

---

[49] However, Jeremiah does hold out the hope of reconciliation as we shall see in 3:12-14, 22-25. But it comes only after repentance.

[50] Richard Lovelace, *Dynamics of Spiritual Life: An Evangelical Theology of Renewal* (Downers Grove: IVP, 1979).

[51] The root occurs 115 times in the whole book. More discussion follows on verses 6ff. below.

The calamity of no rain apparently brought Israel to their senses and they appealed to God for help (v. 4-5a). But here they refer to God as their father (in contrast to Jeremiah's persistent use of the marriage metaphor). This is a title they also used for the idols (2:27) so their total confusion about their religious commitments is plain. The appeal here seems superficial and insincere, and Jeremiah calls them on it in verse 5. They may appeal to God for mercy, but their actions give lie to their words. They expect that God will not be angry forever, but Jeremiah suggests otherwise.[52]

Is it possible that God's people can become so immersed in a rebellious, faithless life that no reconciliation is possible? Jeremiah seems to be saying yes. Is repentance and return possible for those who have turned away? And will God return to his rebellious people? The answer awaits us in the next section. But what this Old Testament text needs is a mediator who can bring the two estranged parties together, not through cheap grace, but through sacrificial atonement for sin. Thanks be to God for his gift of Jesus Christ.

1.b.ii. Return faithless Israel (3:6-4:4)

3:6-11

Jeremiah now explores the crucial issue raised in 3:1-5, can reconciliation occur between the wayward wife and the husband? While the law said no, perhaps there is grace in the end.[53]

Stylistically the section is characterized by the interchange between prose and poetry (prose in vv. 6-11, 14-18, and poetry in vv. 12-13 and 19-4:4). It is not clear why this is so, but the book of Jeremiah is noted for its extensive prose sections.

The passage consists of five sections: vv. 5-11 which contrasts the northern and southern kingdoms of Israel and

---

[52] Therefore, the statement in 3:12 comes as a surprise.

[53] This phrase comes from J. G. McConville, *Grace in the End: A Study of Deuteronomic Theology* (Grand Rapids: Zondervan, 1993).

Judah; vv. 12-14 which offer mercy; vv. 15-18 which suggest a new day and a new perspective is possible; vv. 19-25 which contain another accusation but also the hope of repentance; and 4:1-4 which adds a warning to an offer of repentance. The theme is that reconciliation is possible but only if the people sincerely return to the Lord (repent).

In verse 6, Jeremiah switches to prose and introduces the northern kingdom, Israel, as a separate nation. He had addressed Judah as Israel in chapter two, four times (vv. 3, 4, 14, 26). There he probably had in mind more of a theological entity than a political one. But here the political distinction is crucial to his argument.

The theme of the section develops logically. The northern kingdom had committed the same kind of idolatry that Judah had, and God expected them to return to him, but it did not happen (vv. 6-7). Therefore, he divorced her (v. 8a). This refers to Israel's defeat by the Assyrians and their subsequent exile (2 Kgs 17; the year was 722 BCE). Judah at the time would have entertained some thoughts of spiritual superiority for they not only survived, but were still independent and thriving over 100 years later. But they were no better than Israel. God desired that they learn a lesson and repent. But they did not (vv. 8b-10). In fact, God deemed Israel as more righteous than Judah because she did not have an object lesson like Judah did (v. 11).

The details of Israel's idolatry are familiar because it was the same kind as Judah, apostasy to the Canaanite cultic practices. Judah is addressed by a new adjective here, "treacherous/faithless/unfaithful" (בגד, *bgd*). She had not only turned against God, she had broken her commitment to the covenant (the adjective of *bgd* in vv. 7 and 10, the noun in vv. 8 and 11, and the verb twice in v. 20).[54] This was a singular act of treachery for a lesson not learned.[55]

This section draws together Jeremiah's vocabulary for Judah's rebellion against the Lord. All the sexual and marriage imagery that he can muster comes into focus in the graphic descriptions of her guilt (harlotry, adultery, divorce, faithlessness, apostasy). It is almost as if the Hebrew language is inadequate to express the gravity of Israel and Judah turning away from their covenant God for other gods!

There are historical implications from this apostasy. Israel's history came to an end because of her idolatry/harlotry. Judah's can too as 3:1 hints. In fact, Judah is living on borrowed time. 2 Kings 24-25 detail the tragic end. The exilic readers of this sermon would know how short the time was. They would know that the reforms of Josiah were short-lived. They would also recognize in despair that they should have listened to Jeremiah.

3:12-14

These verses stand in sharp contrast to the proceeding sections but are connected to them using the root *šûb* (שׁוּב). They are specifically connected to verses 1-5. There a return to God is out of the question according to the law, here it is made possible. There God's anger is assumed as ongoing, here is a promise it will end. We must understand that God's anger is not a part of his character but a description of his response to sin and human evil. This response can change, especially if repentance occurs. However, his love and grace are fundamental to his nature and will never

---

[54] See Seth Erlandsson, "*baghadh,*" *TDOT*, 1:470; Robin Wakely, "בגד," *NIDOTTE*, 1:587.

[55] Elsewhere the word is used in parallel with rebellion, sin, wickedness. See Hos 5:3-7 where harlotry and treachery are also put together. Isaiah 24:16 uses forms of the word in a highly alliterative phrase.

change. Jeremiah has more to say about God's anger in chapter 25.

These verses also anticipate verses 19ff. with the repetition of the key phrase in verses 12, 14, and 22, "Return apostate Israel." This is a word play difficult to reflect in English – *šûbāh mᵉšûbāh yiśrā'ēl*. John Bright suggests, "Come back, back-slidden Israel."[56]

Some may be surprised that Jeremiah can introduce God's covenant faithfulness here. Too often Christians have a negative view of the Old Testament God and seem to think that grace came only with Jesus Christ (John 1:17).[57] The word in verse 12 is *ḥasīd* (חסיד), an adjectival form which can refer to covenant faithfulness or covenant love. But in this context, it certainly equals the idea of mercy or grace.[58] The only reason that reconciliation is possible is because the Lord is loyal to his covenant and to his character, even if Israel is not. Therefore, he will show faithfulness to the covenant by offering his elect people forgiveness of their rebellion against him and the covenant. This reminds us of Hosea 11:1-11 which is the most profound statement of God's compassion and forgiveness in the Old Testament.

For forgiveness to happen Israel must meet one condition, "acknowledge" her guilt. That is, she must confess her sin and repent – of her rebellion, her Canaanite worship practices, and her disobedience (v. 13). This is addressed to a people who constantly said they were not guilty (2:23, 35), a big lie! They must come to their senses, as the prodigal son had to. In one sense Israel had not misread God's grace back in verses 1-5, he would accept them back. But they had misunderstood what it would take from them. It would

---

[56] Bright, *Jeremiah* (Garden City: Doubleday, 1965), 22.

[57] Several years ago, a colleague reported to me he had encountered this argument in an email discussion with a Christian college professor.

[58] The Hebrew verb for mercy is *ḥnn* (חנן), which occurs 78 times in the OT; the noun occurs 69 times and the adjective 13 times. See Lam 4:16

take a contrite confession, a confession[59] which is provided for them in verses 22-25 (see also Hosea 14:2-3). God's declaration as a faithful husband (v. 14) strikes a subtle blow at Judah's apostasy. The verb often translated "husband" is *b'l* (בעל) which means "be lord/master." The corresponding noun, *ba'al*, was the name of the Canaanite male fertility god (2:23). Therefore, God is again decisively declaring that he is the true lord and master of Judah, not some nothing god (the "I" is in the emphatic position in the Hebrew).[60]

Yet, even then only partial restoration of the people to the land would result (v. 14). God's grace cannot overturn the consequences of Judah's rebellion and she must suffer those consequences. But her relationship with God can be restored. "To take/choose" is election language. Judah can once again experience the loving relationship with the Lord that they had at first, but only by God's grace.

Coming to "Zion" introduces an eschatological element that Jeremiah will return to in chapters 30-31. Scattered Israel will once again experience the proof of God's steadfast love through restoration to God's place (31:6, 12; 50:4-5).

3:15-18

Now Jeremiah promises a new life without the Ark of the Covenant. This will be inspired by new leadership (v. 15), the kind God intended from the beginning ("after his own heart" or will/desire) who are able to inspire the people to deeper knowledge and understanding (*cf.* Prov 1:3; 21:11). A new type of leader is required because the current leadership had completely failed (2:8, 26).

---

[59] "Vv. 12 and 13 together show us the tension within the heart of God that human sin produces. There is the powerful yearning of the merciful husband (12), alongside the profound recognition of the sheer evil of evil and the assault that it makes upon his will and integrity (13)." Wright, *Jeremiah*, 82-83.

[60] See Hos 2:16-17 for another significant play on words on this topic.

The center focus of the religious life since the exodus had been the Ark of the Covenant in the tabernacle, and later the temple, where God maintained his presence (Exod 25:22; 30:31; 34:29; 1 Kgs 8-10). Early in Israel's history in the land, the Ark moved from place to place (1 Sam 1-7) but David finally established it in Jerusalem. The Ark also held a copy of the law (Deut 31:9). Israel's worship without it would be unthinkable. Yet that future day is near when the Ark will be gone.[61]

Jeremiah then envisions a time (v. 17) when Jerusalem, not the Ark, will be God's throne and thus the center of worship.[62] Furthermore, not just Israel will worship him there but all nations. This is one of those projections of the universality of God's honor that are seeded in the Old Testament (*cf.* Isa 2:2ff.; 56:6-8; 60:11-14; Mic 4:1ff.) but await their realization in the New Testament. This filling out takes place in two phases – in Jesus Christ whose kingdom is not of this world, and at the end of time in the new heaven (new Jerusalem) where there is no temple because God is there (Rev 21-22).

The transition will not be easy for it will require a complete change of heart from Israel's current stubbornness to a new heart (v. 17b, implied). The stubborn heart is a favorite Jeremiah phrase to describe Israel's rebelliousness. The heart is the seat of the guiding will and moral intention. Israel's heart was evil and hard.[63] Genesis 6:5 describes the ultimate evil heart: *"every inclination of the thoughts of his*

---

[61] The Ark disappeared in 587-86 BC with the destruction of Jerusalem and the temple. Its fate is unknown but perhaps it was taken to Babylon as spoils of war (2 Kgs 25; Jer 39).

[62] Compare Ezekiel's vision in which he sees the Glory of God depart from the temple before its destruction (Ezek 10-11) and its return to the new temple (Ezek 43).

[63] The phrase "stubborn heart" occurs 10 times in the OT, 8 times in Jeremiah – here plus 7:14; 9:14; 11:8; 13:10; 16:12; 18:12; 23:17. Five times it is also "evil".

heart was only evil all the time." This could be a good description of Israel's idolatrous heart.[64] Jeremiah tells us later that a circumcised heart (4:4) and even a new kind of heart is required (31:33).[65] That means a complete conversion and transformation of character. Christians know this can come only through the preaching of the Gospel.[66]

The consequences of this conversion will be restored unity and restoration to the land (v. 18).

3:19-20

Now we hear God's plaintive plea. His heart's desire was to always give his best, but his hopes have been dashed by the reality of Israel's heart. This plea is a summary of chapters 2 and 3. This is one of the most beautiful statements of God's plan for Israel in the Old Testament. He wanted his people, his "son", to enjoy the wonderful "promised land." Deuteronomy 8:7-9 describes this land:

> [A] good land, a land of brooks, springs, and fountains flowing forth in valleys and hills, a land with wheat and barley, vines and fig trees, pomegranates, olive oil and honey; a land where you will eat food without scarcity, in which you will not lack anything; a land whose stones are iron, and out of whose hills you can dig copper." (NIV).

The desired outcome is also stated there, although in the context of a warning against self-sufficiency (vv. 12-13):

> [W]hen you eat and are satisfied, when you build fine houses and settle down, and when your herds and your flocks multiply, and your silver and gold multiply, and all that you have multiplies...

---

[64] Unfortunately, many cultures during the centuries have sunk to this level of depravity, perhaps our own is well on the way

[65] Ezek 11:19; 36:26 looks for a new heart.

[66] John Ortberg, "Who is This Man," claims that Jesus first introduced the idea of conversion into the world. Video presentation, session 4, Zondervan, 2012.

This was God's deepest desire. It was to be the most beautiful gift among all the nations. He gave his people the opportunity to live in peace and to prosper. It was a most glorious land.[67] But they threw it away.[68]

God wished to treat her like the first-born son and give her the rightful inheritance. Jeremiah adds now the father-son imagery to the husband-wife metaphor. Israel had called the idols "father" (2:27) and had also insincerely referred to God as "father" (3:4). But from the first God had considered her to be his son (Exod 4:22; Hos 11:1). This was still the relationship he sought. But (v. 20 – a very strong "but") as the wife she had continued in her treacherous unfaithfulness (3:7, 8, 14). God's joyful desire to gift his people was extinguished by her desire to continue to follow the idols.

3:21-25

However, God's grace means that this was not the end. There is one more chance for reconciliation to occur. If they confess their sins. In this section God even provides the words for their confession. There are four parts: a cry of dereliction (recognition of sin) – 21; a call to return – 22a; a statement of intention – 22b; the confession of sin – 23-25.

Verse 21 mirrors verse 2 but here the people weep as they realize their pursuit of the idols was a waste. They have come to their senses and now see that the abandoning of God was destructive. They lament at the high places now rather than worship.[69] This paves the way for the confession in verses 23-25. Verse 22a reiterates the call to return

---

[67]The Hebrew text has a word repetition that functions as an emphatic phrase.

[68] The Promised Land is referred to elsewhere as the "beautiful land" – Deut 11:16; Dan 11:16, 41; Ezek 20:6, 15.

[69] This is how most translations interpret the verse. The NET Bible offers an alternative. It suggests the "because" in line 3 (כִּי, $kī$) is not causal, but contrastive and should be translated "surely/indeed". This

from verse 14 with a promise of healing. This language suggests they have a sickness of the soul. This healing is elsewhere in Jeremiah part of the future restoration of Israel (30:17; 33:6).[70]

So, Israel is portrayed as finally coming to her senses, or at least if they do, Jeremiah provides a confession for them (vv. 22b-25). There cannot be reconciliation without a recognition of sin, confession of the sin, and repentance. It begins with confronting the truth of who God is. He is not the nothings of the idols (2:5, 11, 23) but the Lord of Israel. The confession in verse 25 has two parallel assertions, each beginning with "indeed/surely" (the same word as in v. 20). Bright calls this a "liturgy of penitence."[71] They must confess two contrasting truths: idol worship is a lie, and salvation lies only in the Lord. This is the proper response to the call for confession in verse 13. Indeed, any idol worship, ancient or modern, is a lie and only useless "commotion/agitation" (NRSV, "delusion"; NAS, "deception"). The practical lie for Israel was that they sought fertility and rain from the idols on the hills, when only God gave those gifts.[72] The idolatry also consumed much of their possessions in sacrifice, including their children, and returned nothing. Idolatry was, and is, costly. It deceives the worshipper for it can never meet his expectations. The idols are powerless, products of human imagination and creation. It is also costly for it cannot return any benefits equal to its demands. In fact, there is no beneficial return. Modern idols fit this description as well. They consume and ultimately destroy their adherents. Israel's living God stands in sharp contrast to ancient and modern idols.

---

would not be a cry of dereliction then but descriptive of the pagan practice.

[70] In 51:8-9, there is no healing for Babylon!

[71] Bright, *Jeremiah*, 35.

[72] Ps 121:1-2 – salvation came not from the hills but from the Lord, the maker of heaven and earth.

Israel's shame was complete (v. 25). Only the truly penitent could admit such a humble spirit, but just such a humble spirit is the basis for forgiveness. God will not despise a "broken and contrite heart" (Ps 51:17). This is the only way that opens the future.

The tragedy is that Israel apparently never appropriated this confession (nor the parallel one in Hos 14:1-3).[73] She persisted in her disobedient ways until the very end. However, some may have returned to the Lord during Josiah's reign (2 Kgs 22). Josiah himself is described as the best king Judah ever had. He was a Deuteronomy kind of king (2 Kgs 22:2; 23:3). However, whatever reform happened did not last. Within two decades of Josiah's death Jerusalem was decimated.

This Old Testament theology of confession and repentance is central to the New Testament gospel of the kingdom, whose focal point is Jesus Christ, the only true Son of God (Mark 6:12; Luke 13:3, 5; Acts 2:38; 3:17, 26; 2 Pet 3:9; Rev 2:5, 6, 22, etc.). The projected outcome is also the same, salvation through our Lord, or destruction and death.

4:1-4

These verses conclude the section begun in 3:1 with a final call to repent and return to the Lord, plus a final warning. The word šûb (שׁוּב) connects 3:1 and 4:1 and the latter verse answers the question in the former. Šūb's double use in 4:1 may mean something like, "if you would turn around/turn back, then turn back to me." It would be useless to turn elsewhere. This is another and final offer of reconciliation.

Verse 1 has two parallel conditional clauses followed by an unmarked conditional clause in verse 2a, which lead to the concluding "then" clause of 2b. If all conditions are met, Israel's reconciliation could have profound results for the nations. Condition 2 (v. 1a) is not new. The idols must go. Condition 3 (v. 2a) connects repentance with acts of social endeavor, which, following Deuteronomic ethics, involves practicing care for the widow and orphan (justice), caring

---

[73] A confession also followed by words of healing in verse 4ff.

for truth (and not lies), and establishing an intimate relationship with God. They must value not only cleaning up their worship but cleaning up their lives. They must do the will of God.

They must also take an oath of covenant loyalty (v. 2a) – "As the Lord lives." This acknowledges that in contrast to the lifeless idols, the God of Israel is the one, true living God.[74] Using God's name in vain was forbidden in the Decalogue (Exod 20:7) so this oath apparently did not fit into vain use. It was an affirmation of who God was and could be used to bind a person to his word or conviction.[75] In the context of Jeremiah 2-3 this assertion was crucial to re-establish the peoples' obedience to God.

The ancient cultures were serious about their oaths and took the gods seriously. Therefore, oath taking was extremely important, and care was taken to get it right. One did not want to offend the gods. Our culture is saturated with oaths and swearing. Sadly, it does not reflect serious commitment but a causal vulgarizing and profaning of life.

If the conditions of verses 1-2a are met, then the nations will be blessed (v. 2b) and glorify God. This is an overt missionary statement and deliberately recalls the promise in Abram in Genesis 12:1-3. The goal of calling Abram from his homeland was so that the nations would be blessed through him. That promise has not been canceled by Israel's disobedience but still is God's desire.[76] The promise to Abram is foundational to the mission of the church as

---

[74] A converted Buddhist from Thailand and graduate of Lincoln Christian Seminary always refers to the Biblical God as "the living God." This distinction is particularly acute in southeast Asia which is full of statues of the Buddha.

[75] The phrase occurs 42 times in the Old Testament, mostly in 1 and 2 Samuel in the narrative about David and in 1 Kings 19 to 2 Kings 5 in the Elijah and Elisha stories. Jeremiah and Hosea are the only prophets to use it (here and Hos 4:15). Twenty-two times God swears by himself, "as I live." Sixteen of these are in Ezekiel. See Jeremiah 22:24 and 46:18.

[76] See the repetition of the promise in Genesis 12:2, 3; 18:18; 22:18; 26:4; and 28:14 using the same verb as here.

well and provides an important part of Paul's argument that God always intended to bring the Gentiles into the kingdom (Gal 3:8).

However, God's blessing requires a total change of heart, a new way of life (vv. 3-4). Jeremiah recognizes here that the physical circumcision of an eight-day old baby boy carried a much more important spiritual symbolism. If repentance was to happen the people needed a total transformation of their will and intention. They needed a drastic heart operation (literally "cutting off the foreskin"). Deuteronomy 6:5 demanded that Israel love God with their whole heart, but Moses also realized that this was not a natural response. He too asserted that Israel needed a circumcised heart. Obedience and faithfulness required a profound change in the will (Deut 10:16). In fact, Moses realized that only God could circumcise the heart (Deut 30:6)! Jeremiah later compared unrepentant Israel to the surrounding nations who were physically circumcised but whose heart was not devoted to God (9:25-26).[77] Ezekiel advances this theology further and suggests that in the future Israel will need a new heart (Ezek 11:19; 36:26).[78]

The section that began with encouragement to repent and even offered the words of confession ends with a dire warning (v. 4). If they do not repent, God's wrath will burn like a hot fire on them. This anger is not a part of God's character but a response to the persistent rebellion of the people. By Jeremiah's time God's patience had expired and Israel was doomed to destruction.[79] God's grace and patience does

---

[77] Other nations practiced circumcision but not as a covenant sign with God. The Philistines were noted for being uncircumcised (Judg 14:3; 1 Sam 14:6; 17:26). See Leslie Allen, "Circumcision," NIDOTTE, 4:474-476; Hall, *Deuteronomy*, 199-200. Jeremiah also refers to uncircumcised ears (6:10). See Paul's reflections on circumcision in Rom 2:25-29; Galatians 5:1-12.

[78] See also Jer 31:31-34 and comments there.

[79] 40% of the uses of the word for wrath occur in Jeremiah and Ezekiel – 17 times in Jeremiah, 33 times in Ezekiel. This reflects the historical circumstances that in their day the time of wrath had come. See Gale B. Struthers, חמה, NIDOTTE, 2:170-171.

have a limit. Even the New Testament affirms this (2 Pet 3:9-10).

1.b. iii. Disaster from the North – 4:5-6:30

The preceding section concluded with a dire warning – if Israel did not repent God's wrath would break out on her like a burning fire. Apparently, Israel did not repent, for this section announces that that wrath is coming in the form of an invading army from the north to devastate the land. This is a horrible "disaster" (4:6, "evil", רָעָה, *ra'ah*). Literally Jeremiah says that they have done all the evil they can (4:5) so God is bringing evil on them. The punishment fits the sin, evil for evil.[80] The rebellion against God which Israel seemingly undertook lightly, has consequences beyond what they could have imagined.

This disaster takes the form of an invading army from the north and is vividly portrayed in two parallel passages, 4:5-8 and 6:1-12. This army, unidentified here, is God's instrument to carry out his judgment. But it is certainly a foreign army, that is, a pagan nation. Jeremiah's response is deep anguish as we shall see. However, there is a deep theological issue at work here, which Jeremiah's contemporary prophet Habakkuk raised: how can a Holy God use a pagan nation for his purposes (Hab 1:12-17)? The assumption is that God would not have anything to do with pagans. His eyes were "too pure to look on evil" (Hab 1:13). But God surprised Habakkuk with his answer. Since he is sovereign over the whole world all nations are under his ultimate authority. Therefore, he will do what he needs to do to work out his purposes.

The judgment amounts to Holy War in which God is fighting against his people. Always before he had fought for his people, especially in the exodus and conquest, but Israel's disobedience over the centuries had turned her into God's enemies. How tragic that events had come to this!

---

[80] See the use of "evil" in 4:14, 18, 22.

This long section has a certain symmetry to it, with repetitions and a circular kind of reasoning common to the Old Testament. Martens has proposed two parallel sections, each introduced by the imperative verb "announce" in 4:5 and 5:20.[81] The text also has some rhetorical markers (some form of "this is what the Lord says") in 5:14; 6:6, 16, 21, 22. Because of the repetitions and parallel material this commentary will not follow a verse by verse or section by section exposition but will adopt a topical approach.[82] We will organize our exegesis under five themes.

Theme 1: An invading army brings disaster – 4:5-8, 11-18, 29-31; 6:1-12, 22-26

The description of the invading army is vivid and detailed as if the prophet is an eyewitness. A trumpet blast was the warning sign of danger and warned the people in the villages and towns to hurry to fortified cities for safety (*cf.* Amos 3:6). In Judah the principle cities were Jerusalem and Lachish in the southwest, though there were several other fortified cities.[83] Jeremiah's language of the invasion is not hyperbole. Enemy armies in the ancient world were savage and showed no mercy, even to children and the elderly. They slaughtered at will, took slaves, destroyed everything in sight, cut down trees, burned what they could, and took the leadership into exile (if they did not kill them). The northern kingdom had experienced the Assyrian conquest in 722 BCE and Judah had barely survived the Assyrians in 701 BCE.[84] This was long before Jeremiah's time but stories and traditions of the disasters as

---

[81] Elmer Martens, *Jeremiah,* (Scottsburg, PA: Herald Press, 1986) 60.

[82] Suggested by Wright, *Jeremiah,* 92, though I do not follow his arrangement.

[83] The Assyrian king Sennacherib who invaded Judah in 701 BC during Hezekiah's reign reported there were 46 strong cities that he devastated, plus numerous other villages.

[84] Sennacherib celebrated his 701 BC conquest of Lachish with carved reliefs on a room in his palace. It depicts Judeans impaled on stakes, being skinned alive, and being led away to exile. These reliefs can be seen today in the British Museum in London.

well as written records were probably known to his audience.

That this army would come from the north was anticipated in 1:13-14 with the boiling pot vision. Palestine was only accessible by land from the north or south, especially for the empires of the Mesopotamian valley. Geographically, Mesopotamia was to the east, but the great Arabian desert blocked any direct access. Therefore, armies from there had to go northwest up the Euphrates and then come south through Syria.

Everyone flees (4:29) but that is certainly futile. Where was there to go except into the wilderness? Some apparently decided to try a ruse and compromise with the invaders (4:30) but this was also futile. They had already consorted with foreign gods. Trying to seduce an army was senseless, but it reflected a mindset already adept at self-deception.

The details of the invasion in 6:1-12 picture the army getting closer and closer to Jerusalem, step by step. The impending doom cannot be stopped. The attack is described again in 6:22-26 with more details of an army equipped for battle – with bows, spears, horses, troops formed into battle lines. The only response can be deep mourning with sackcloth and ashes (see also 4:8). "Terror is on every side (6:25)." This is rare phrase appropriated by Jeremiah to describe their plight.[85] Later Jeremiah used this phrase for his priestly foe, Pashur (20:3), but his enemies also used it against him (20:10).

The vocabulary in 6:1-12 for the devastation brought by the invaders is extensive, at least eight different verbs, but they are basically synonyms to describe the destruction of the people and land. Jeremiah uses these verbs more than any other prophet. God's judgment is sure, and the time is near. This devastation of Israel is only a part of the larger picture of God's judgment on his creation and human history. It is a part of the metanarrative of the Bible. It began

---

[85] In Hebrew the phrase is alliterative, *māgōr missābîb*. See 46:5 also.

in Genesis 6 and continues to the end in Revelation. It represents God's judgment at work until ultimately all opposition to his will is destroyed. This is a function of his justice, for only through the destruction of evil can he restore the creation to its original design.

Theme 2: Continued accusations – 4:22; 5:1-13, 20-31; 6:13-15

Even as God's judgments are detailed Jeremiah continues to describe more accusations against the people to emphasize their guilt. They are foolish and senseless and know only how to do evil (4:22). Jeremiah conducts a thorough search in Jerusalem but cannot find one honest person (5:1-2), even among the leaders who had already been condemned for malfeasance (v. 5). The drive to idolatry is compared to lusty stallions who blindly follow their instincts (v. 8). Their idolatry is ascribed to a false view of God. They saw him in the same category as the lifeless idols and concluded he "would do nothing" (v.12). This was a part of the great collection of lies they believed. Apparently, the memory of God's mighty acts in the past had faded and the present was void of any divine presence. Like most secular people (even today) they evaluated everything by personal experience and could not point to anything that indicated God was present. There was certainly some wishful thinking here as well for they were convinced that "no harm would come to them." How could they so misread their relationship with God? Their fear of the Lord was gone (5:24) so we should not be surprised. Part of the cause was their wealth.[86] It had saturated their hearts (vv. 27-28) and made them impervious to their sinful conduct. It especially deadened them to social injustice with its oppression of the economically deprived (vv. 27-28). Even their prophets had given in to the malaise and told lies and falsehoods (vv. 19, 31). They preached peace and safety when the discerning heart would have seen what was coming (6:13-15).

---

[86] There are many echoes in this section from Deut 32:15ff.

This thought should haunt every preacher. Is my message a word from God for this time and for my audience, or have I succumbed to the ethos of the culture? Am I, in God's eyes, just a windbag?

Jeremiah asks a final, penetrating question for the people that echoes through the centuries. "... my people love it this way. But what will you do in the end?" (5:31b)

> **Jeremiah 5:26**
>
> *For scoundrels are found among my people;*
>   *they take over the goods of others.*
>
> There are many ways the poor of cities are exploited and kept from thriving. One of the most widespread and insidious ways is the "payday loan" industry. In this system (sometimes labeled "predatory lending"), poor people borrow against future paychecks while paying high fees and incurring exorbitant interest rates.[87]
>
> In 2014 the National Association of Evangelicals (NAE) passed a resolution against predatory loans, stating, "Scripture upholds principles of just and honest commerce, while prohibiting usury, exploitation and oppression of those in need." The resolution calls for churches to help families in crisis so they may avoid taking out a devastating payday loan.[88] In every city in America, poor neighborhoods have seen a proliferation of "quick loan stores," siphoning off the money of the poor to wealthy backers outside the community. Churches have members trapped in this vicious economic cycle. The NAE resolution and many other Christian voices call for economic justice in this area, to circumvent the "scoundrels [who] take over the goods of others."
>
> Mark S. Krause

---

[87] U.S. News has reported that some predatory loans have an effective annual interest rate of over 400%. See "What Is a Predatory Loan?" https://loans.usnews.com/what-is-a-predatory-loan.

[88] https://www.nae.net/predatory-lending.

Theme 3: Anguish – 4:10, 19-21 (4:31); 6:9-11

Jeremiah is called the weeping prophet and we see why in this passage. He is committed to God as a faithful prophet, but his message takes a toll on him emotionally (4:10). He is not sure his message is an honest one. God seems to have sent other prophets who preached peace, but Jeremiah is preaching judgment and destruction. It is not clear what he is referring to. Perhaps he is referring to the other prophets of his day who were claiming to speak on God's behalf and were preaching peace and safety (see 6:18; 8:11; 14:12; 23:17; Ezek 13:10).[89] In his heighten state of emotion Jeremiah seems to give them more legitimacy than they deserved.

Jeremiah expressed his deep distress even more strongly in 4:19-21 when he hears the battle sounds. Fear grips the pit of his stomach and his heart pounds.[90] He is totally devastated by the destroying army's advance into Jerusalem. He is not a disinterested bystander but suffers with his people. We will see in chapters 37-40 that he physically suffered from his people, for he was imprisoned twice during Jerusalem's final days. In fact, the Babylonians treated him better than his people did. Yet, here he weeps over his city. The Christian will recall Jesus who, too, wept over Jerusalem (Matt 23:37-39).

In another passage not quite so emotional, Jeremiah decides that it is no use to go on (6:9-11b). No one will listen so why bother? It is certainly easy to give up if there is no response.[91] Yet he could not stop preaching, for he could not hold in God's words. He does not control them, and they burst out (4:19). Later, in ch. 20:9, Jeremiah declares that God's word is like a fire in his bones and he cannot

---

[89] See comments on chapters 27-29 where Jeremiah personally encounters some of these prophets.

[90] Literally he cries out "My bowels, my bowels." The heart was the seat of the will and lower abdomen the seat of emotions.

[91] No preacher wants to preach to a totally unresponsive audience. It is interesting that the prophet Isaiah was warned of failure from the beginning (Isa 6:9-11).

hold it in. Every preacher worth his calling should have the same burning desire to preach.

We also hear another cry of anguish in the text, that of Israel. She is portrayed as a woman giving birth to her first child (4:31; 6:24). The pain and anguish of a woman giving birth was familiar to everyone in the ancient world (and many present cultures) since children were born at home. Not only was there great anguish but often the mother died. Israel was in her death throes, but she denied it to the end. Only Jeremiah seemed to have the godly insight that the signs of the times meant the end.

Theme 4: Consequences – 4:23-28; 5:14-18; 6:16-21, 27-30

The outcome of an invading army was certain, yet Jeremiah devoted some space to detailing the results. He sees the great destruction as a reversal of creation (4:23-28). He saw four things: an empty earth, an empty and dark sky, empty cities, and an empty land. The language is a deliberate reference to Genesis 1 and 2. Indeed, 4:23 is the only place in the Old Testament that the phrase "formless and empty" occurs beyond Genesis 1:2. The darkness of verse 25 also reverses the first act of creation, the giving of light. The land, empty of humans and animals, reverses Genesis 1:21-31. This is an amazing passage! God's judgment on his people had cosmic implications. It was not just a minor event limited to a small geographical space. When God is at work any act can be earth shaking.

Another consequence was the destruction of the country side detailed with the use of the word "devour" (5:17). The harvests, the children, the flocks and herds, and the fruit crops all were eaten up by the enemy. Again, in the ancient world, or during any war, this would be unremarkable, but the unrelenting descriptions of destruction should have impressed on Israel the great damage she had done to herself. Even if some should survive the onslaught, which we know some did, there would be little left for them.

The result is also made explicit in 6:27-30. God had tested Israel and she had failed every time. She had rejected her Lord, so he rejected her. Like ore tested by fire, Israel had been tested and became like rejected dross. Israel's heart was just as hard as the hard metals like iron and bronze. She was so full of impurities that she could not withstand God's purifying fire and was discarded. God's judgment fire (4:4) would carry out its task.

Theme 5: Hope – 4:27; 5:10b, 18-19

Amid the sustained grim pictures of destruction in this section are a few faint glimmers of hope. The first, brief hint is 4:27: the land will be ruined but not destroyed completely (see also 5:10). Jeremiah does not explain further here what that might look like. What is left? A few people, or crops, or livestock, or houses? We will have to wait to see. In 5:18 we learn that a few people will survive but they will be in exile. Would some also survive in the land?[92] Therefore, in the middle of God's consuming judgment fire, grace breaks through, but it is still after the judgment and the survivors are just that, survivors. They still must go through the judgment.[93] Many of the Judeans would have been faithful and "innocent" of the gross sins of the majority. Many would have responded positively to Josiah's reform, but they were still part of the nation and suffered with it. They were the audience for God's word to Habakkuk, "the righteous shall live by his faith" (Hab 2:4).

---

[92] We have to wait for chs. 30-32 to discover Jeremiah's hopeful vision for the future.

[93] We are reminded of Isa 7-10. Isaiah pictures the end of the northern kingdom at the hand of the Assyrians but a major theme is the survival of a remnant.

1.c. Prophecies from the time of Jehoiakim (7:1-20:18)

1.c.i. The temple sermon and its aftermath – 7:1-8:3; 26:1-24[94]

We now enter a new section of Jeremiah that includes his sermons after the death of Josiah. The historical background is crucial for understanding the sermon in chapter 7. The date is 609/608 (see chapter 26:1).[95] Josiah was killed by the Egyptians during his ill-fated march north to Megiddo to stop them from going up to Syria (2 Kgs. 23:29). In an instant, Judah's world collapsed. Josiah's reforms, Judah's independence and prosperity vanished, and she became a vassal of Egypt. Josiah's son, Jehoahaz, was made king but in three months the Egyptians had taken him to Egypt and put their puppet, Eliakim (renamed Jehoiakim) a brother of Jehoahaz, in his place. The two world powers, Egypt and Babylon, were battling for control of Palestine and Judah was in the middle. Within ten years Babylon would be on Jerusalem's doorstep and initiate the first deportation (2 Kgs 24:10-14).

Responding to this crisis, people were flocking to the temple to seek safety and comfort. Jeremiah addressed them there but not with what they wanted to hear. They wanted words of hope and assurance. He gave them words of condemnation and disaster.

The sermon as we have it has four sections: the sermon proper in 7:1-15 and three elaborations in verses 7:16-20, 7:21-26 and 7:27-8:3. The sermon style is stylistic prose with repetitions, alliterations, key words, and lyrical phrases. The book of Jeremiah is noted for its several styles of writing including the vivid poetry we have seen in the

---

[94] We are commenting on chs. 7 and 26 together. Ch. 26 is most likely about the same event and concentrates on the reaction of the people to the sermon. Jeremiah is almost lynched.

[95] Early in Jehoiakim's reign probably means his accession year.

previous chapters, the sermonic prose here, and long biographical sections. In addition, there are intense autobiographical pieces.[96]

The background for the sermon is the covenant law as presented in the book of Deuteronomy. This is demonstrated by the reference to the ten commandments, the language style, and the repeated reference to "place" in 7:3, 6, 7, 12, 14, 20, 31; 8:3.[97] The sermon also answers the question of 5:19, "Why has the Lord our God done all this to us?"

7:1-15

This part of the sermon has three parts after the introduction in verses 1-2, that is, verses 3-7, 8-11, and 12-15. Verses 3 and 4 set the stage with a command and a warning. Verses 5-7 explain the command and verses 8-11 explain the warning.[98] Verses 12-15 provide historical evidence that God means what he says.

Verses 1-2 stress that the sermon is God's word through Jeremiah. Jeremiah is preaching on God's authority. Israel is to hear the word.[99] The location is central to the impact of the sermon; it is at the temple gates. People are pouring into the sanctuary for assurance that God will protect them in this time of crisis.[100] They are anxious for a word from God's prophets, but Jeremiah does not have a message

---

[96] This reason for this variety has been debated for some time. Many use the differences to offer a dating scheme for the book with varying amounts seen as having their origin in the exile. There now seems to be more interest in the text as a whole rather than in theoretical dates. See Hall, "Jeremiah," in Mark Mangano, *et al.*, *Old Testament Introduction* (Joplin, MO: College Press, 2005), 468-74.

[97] Deuteronomy refers to the "place" where God will put his name nine times, referring to the location of the tabernacle and later the temple. There were several places where this could happen. The referent for "place" in Jer 7 is either the temple, the land, or Jerusalem.

[98] Wright, *Jeremiah*, 108.

[99] But verses 21-28 refer to "not listening" five times!

[100] Remember after September 11, 2001 the churches were packed, but only for a while!

they want to hear.[101] God assures them he will let them live in the place (v. 3), but they must first repent. Literally they are to "do good" ("amend" in many translations). A change was needed. Jeremiah could have used the word for repent he used in chapters 3 and 4, "turn around" (3:14; 4:1) but the idea here is the same. The command came with a promise: he would let them live in the Jerusalem (or the land, "this place").[102] A threat is implied. If they do not change their ways, they will not be allowed to live in the place.

Verse 4 gives the warning. They are trusting in the wrong thing. They trust a lie.[103] What is the lie? The belief that simply because the temple is in their midst they are safe from all danger. It appears they had developed a mantra, repeating over and over, "the temple of the Lord". They could well ask, just how is that a lie? After all they had history, tradition, and God's word on their side. The temple was the locus of God's presence (1 Kgs 8). Furthermore, he had in the past delivered Jerusalem from the Assyrians and promised through the prophet Isaiah that all who trusted in Jerusalem and the temple would be safe (Isa 36; 37:33-35). They also had many Psalms that glorified the temple and Zion (46, 48, 72, 132:6-10). Jeremiah returns to what the big lie is in verses 9-11.

Verses 5-8 reveal exactly what God means by changing their ways. They are to follow the heart of God and do justice. What is justice? Jeremiah refers to Deuteronomy's concerns: taking care of the poor of the land, specifically the orphans, aliens and widows. These were always the

---

[101] Imagine a modern preacher setting up the pulpit in the doorway of the church and telling the people that it will do them no good to go inside.

[102] Two ancient versions have "I will dwell with you"; a somewhat different nuance but still reassuring. See Wright, *Jeremiah,* 108, for a discussion of the different texts.

[103] Hebrew *seqer* (שקר) is a common word in Jeremiah.

first to suffer privation.[104] The condemnation of shedding innocent blood is perhaps a reference to the reign of Manasseh when the streets ran with the blood of the innocent, that is, those slaughtered for no reason (2 Kgs 21:16; 24:4). Sacrificing children would be another example (7:31; Ps 106:38). Justice in the Old Testament meant treating everyone with dignity and respect and dealing fairly across all social and political structures, not just in a legal setting as is the case in modern times. God loved justice (Ps 37:28) and the kings (Jer 21:12) and all society was to imitate him.[105]

The presentation is in the form of three conditional clauses ("if" in vv. 5 and 6). The assumption seems to be that they do not and will not meet the conditions, but if they do, then God will be faithful to his promises to the forefathers and let them continue to live in the land (v. 7). The burden is on them. God is faithful, will they be? No, they would rather listen to a lie, than repent (v. 8).

Jeremiah 7:6-7

[I]f you do not oppress the alien, the orphan, and the widow ... then I will dwell with you in this place ...

Homelessness is omnipresent in most North American cities. There are many causes such as lack of affordable housing, mental illness, addictions, or loss of jobs. The 1990s saw an increase in homeless families, having exhausted all their personal resources and left with no options for housing.

Omaha, Nebraska, has a remarkable institution, the Open Door Mission (ODM),[106] that attracts urban mission people

---

[104] This priority was codified in the law numerous times: Exod 22:20-21; 23:7-9; Lev 19:33-35; Deut 14:29; 16:11; 24:14-22; 26:11-13. See Hall, *Deuteronomy*, 201-202.

[105] The Hebrew word for justice occurs 32 times in Jeremiah. James's view in the New Testament of pure religion is grounded in the Old Testament truth stated in this text (Jas 1:27; see also his exposition in chapter 2).

[106] See https://www.opendoormission.org.

from all over the U.S. to study its successful practices. ODM is unapologetically Christian, and this repels some donors and community leaders. But ODM acts in a non-discriminatory and non-sectarian way such that it receives financial support from some of the largest corporations in the metro region.

ODM's operations support families, especially single-mother units. This includes the new Lydia House, a facility with safe shelter for up to 72 single women and 46 families without male adults (men are housed in another facility). In addition, ODM provides low-cost transitional housing (apartments) for stabilizing families nearly ready to return to the community. While ODM provides Bible-based worship times and training programs, much of what it does is simply designed to meet the needs of the urban poor and homeless. Over 1.3 million meals are served each year at no cost. I have helped with these meals as a volunteer and I marvel at the quality of the food (much of it donated) and the respect with which clients are served. In addition, ODM maintains a thrift "store" where approved families may shop once a month for clothing, personal items, and household goods, but do not pay. My wife and I have given many bags of clothing and other items to support this effort.

Jeremiah agrees with other prophets that justice in a community is measured by its care for "aliens, orphans, and widows" (see Zechariah 7:10). The sprawling scope of homelessness and family dislocation may seem so overwhelming that we are paralyzed into inaction. Organizations like the Open Door Mission may have flaws but supporting them as a person is able shows mercy to widows (single women/mothers), orphans (children), and aliens (refugees).

Mark S. Krause

Verses 9-11 demonstrate why their trust in the temple is a lie. They have broken the basic law of God, the Ten Commandments. Four commandments dealing with interpersonal relationships are listed (numbers 6, 7, 8, 9), and one about true worship (both numbers 1 and 2). The cultural ethos that allowed injustice had no concern for obedience either. It had objectified the temple and used its presence as a shield against fidelity toward God. Actions and words did not match. To believe under these circumstances that they "were safe" was a delusion. How could the people think they could come to the temple and worship, and God not care? God and Jeremiah were incredulous. Religious ritual by itself counts for little. The Holy God may be in his Holy temple, but an unholy people can turn the temple into an unholy place. Jeremiah compares it to a "den of thieves" (v. 11).[107]

The audience would have been horrified to hear that God might desert the temple, so Jeremiah provides a little history lesson (vv. 12-15). Shiloh was a small village about eighteen miles north of Jerusalem where the tabernacle was first set up after the conquest of the land (Josh 18:8; Judg 18:31; 21:16). By Samuel's time a sanctuary had been constructed there (1 Sam 1:3; 3:3). But the Ark of the Covenant housed there had become like a talisman, and Eli's sons took it from the tabernacle into battle to ensure victory. They were defeated, and the Philistines captured the Ark (1 Sam 4). Part of Shiloh was destroyed at that time (and in Jeremiah's day) was in ruins. The lesson was clear. God did not protect Shiloh just because the Ark and tabernacle were there, so why would he protect Jerusalem just because the temple was there? Obedience was more important than sacrifice (7:21-23; 1 Sam 15:22; Hos 6:6; Amos 5:21-25; Mic 6:6-8). Furthermore, God would treat them like the northern kingdom and drive them out of the land (v. 15).

This sermon resonates through the centuries with the truth that ritual worship of God by itself is worthless. The Bible is consistent throughout the Old and New Testament. Visible institutions of worship are not mechanical means of grace. Security comes from doing God's will. Persistent disobedience can exhaust God's patience. The Christian is reminded of several New Testament teachings. Jesus said both that the place of worship was not important (John 4) and that he was the temple (John 2:19). Paul expanded this

---

[107] Jesus accused the Jews of his day of doing the same thing – Matt 21:13.

to include the church and individual Christians as the temple (1 Cor 3:16ff.). Jesus condemned the Pharisees for meticulous attention to ritual details while ignoring justice (Matt 23). Paul called on Christians to be living sacrifices (Rom 12:1-2). Jesus's challenge to his disciples was the same as Jeremiah's challenge to Israel – love and obey God (John 14-15). Therefore, it is somewhat disconcerting that Christians call their places of worship "sanctuaries"! Who then may approach God? Psalm 15 and 24 still ring true.

7:16-20

This first elaboration of the temple speech is a classical judgment speech with the accusation in verses 17-19, followed by the hinge preposition "therefore" and announcement of judgment in verse 20. A personal word to Jeremiah introduces the speech, "Do not pray for this people..." (v. 16). This is the first of three specific commands to Jeremiah forbidding intercessory prayer (see 11:14; 14:11; see also 15:1). Intercessory prayer was a part of a prophet's calling, with Moses and Samuel as good examples (Exod 32-34; 1 Sam 7). How are we to understand such a shocking divine command to Jeremiah? Apparently, Israel's long history of disobedience had reached its climax. There were no more chances. God's judgment was now inevitable and the time for intercession was past.

Amos 7:1-9 is a parallel passage. Twice God relents after Amos's protest, but not the third time. The situation is hopeless.[108] Prayer is useless because God will not listen. In this he mimics the people who are charged with not listening four times in the following passage (vv. 24, 26, 27, 28). If they don't listen, he won't either. He will be like the false idols who cannot hear or act. Israel will be completely forsaken. What will they do then (5:31)?

---

[108] Jeremiah does intercede later: 21:2; 37:3, but the answer is similar. After the exile he prays at the survivors' request, 42:1ff. In 29:7, 9, Jeremiah commands the people in exile to pray . . for their captors the Babylonians!

The accusation in verses 17-18 is a new form of idolatry, in addition to the Canaanite forms already condemned. The "Queen of Heaven" cult came from Mesopotamia. The offering of cakes to the goddess was very common in Babylon, often used in the cult for the worship of Ishtar, the goddess of war and fertility. She could be the referent here, or perhaps it was the Canaanite Anat or Ashtorah.[109] Israel had adopted the worship of the goddess of the very nation God was using for judgment on them for their idolatry![110] It was not just the religious leaders who were involved in idolatry now, but whole families. God interprets this idolatry as a deliberate effort to insult him,[111] but rather than insulting him they have brought harm and shame on themselves (v.19).

False worship harms the worshipper. Sin has consequences that come back on the sinner. In this case the harm is God's anger and wrath that comes as a burning fire to devour all the fruits of their labor, which is why they were worshipping the fertility goddess.[112] They poured out their drink offerings, God will pour out his anger. They lit fires to burn the cakes, God's fire will burn everything they have.[113]

7:21-29

Jeremiah began the sermon by attacking the temple. Now he attacks what was done there, the sacrifices.

The basic laws for the sacrifice are given in Leviticus 1-7. The first was the burnt offering (chapter 1) or whole burnt offering. This offering was unique in that the whole thing

---

[109] John Walton, et al, *The IVP Background Commentary: The Old Testament* (Downers Grove: IVP, 2000), 649.

[110] A reference to the worship of the Queen of Heaven reappears in 44:15-19. See comments there.

[111] NIV, "provoke to anger"; NET Bible, "just to trouble me"; the Jewish translation "vex". Jeremiah uses this verb eleven times, all in the context of idolatry.

[112] See also Jer 4:4; 11:16; 13:14; 15:6, 14; 17:4, 27.

[113] Wright, *Jeremiah,* 115.

was burnt on the altar. The other sacrifices allowed the worshipper to share in the meat or grain of the offering. Now it makes no difference whether they violate the sacrificial law or not. They might as well eat even the meat of the burnt offering since the offering is useless. In fact, Jeremiah casts aspersions on the whole sacrificial system, suggesting it was not what God desired (v. 22). This statement seems to contradict the teaching of the Pentateuch, but we need to read the text carefully. Jeremiah is referring to the period of the whole exodus experience detailed in Exodus 1-19, before the law was given at Sinai (Exodus 20ff.). Jeremiah alludes to Exodus 19:5-6. God did tell Israel that obedience would make them his people before he revealed the law. This was a solemn promise.[114]

Despite the promise, Israel had a hearing problem – she would not listen (vv. 23, 24, 26, 27, 28; cf. v. 13). This was more than being deaf. The Hebrew verb "hear" in covenantal contexts like this has the nuance of "obey".[115] This usage is found throughout Deuteronomy.[116] It wasn't faulty hearing, it was stubborn and evil hearts (v. 24) or stiff-necks (v. 26). They had turned their backs on God (v. 24c)[117] and had no interest in loyalty to God or the covenant. Wright raises the question – if they would not listen why did God send Jeremiah to preach to them?[118]

Isaiah had a similar commission, and the purpose of his preaching was to harden the hearts of the people so that they would not repent (Isa 6:9-10)! Wright offers three

---

[114] There is another possible way of reading the text. To make a point the Old Testament sometimes would contrast two opposing ideas, not meaning that it was one or the other. It was both. But one thought or action was the most important. NIV tries to indicate this tension by adding "just" before "give."

[115] NIV translates "hear" as "obey" in vv. 23 and 28

[116] The phrase often is "listen to the voice of the Lord your God" (13 times). Compare here "listen to my voice" in vv. 23 and 28 (see footnote above).

[117] This is one way of interpreting "going backward and not forward".

[118] Wright, *Jeremiah*, 117-118.

possible reasons here: the preaching of Jeremiah was to further harden their hearts as judgment time approached and to make it clear they were not innocent (like Isaiah); it made it clear that God gave plenty of warning; and it challenged the exiles who were reading this sermon with the question, "will you listen now?" All these objectives could be true, to show how greatly God desired to give Israel every chance to repent and turn back to him (1 Tim 2:1-4).

At the end of this section (v. 28) Israel is characterized as disobedient, impervious to divine discipline and correction, and no longer able to recognize or speak the truth. This is the consequence of believing lies (vv. 4, 8). Those who promote falsehoods eventually become unable to distinguish between truth and deceit.[119]

The only possible response to this horrific situation is lament (v. 29; *cf.* 4:8).

7:30-8:3

The final elaboration of the temple sermon is a death notice. Jeremiah introduces another form of idolatry, the worst of all – child sacrifice. The consequence is a culture of death that reaps its own reward – death and exposure for everyone.

Idols had been erected in the temple itself (v. 30) during the time of Manasseh (2 Kgs 21:3, 5, 7; 23:4) and removed by Josiah (2 Kgs 23:4), but they were erected again after Josiah's death (Jer 19:5; 32:34; Ezek 8:3, 5, 10-12). Even more shocking, Israel had adopted a pagan practice of child sacrifice (v. 31), a practice far removed from the heart of God. Manasseh had sacrificed his own son (2 Kgs 21:6). Topheth was apparently the name of the altar where the sacrifices took place. This name rhymes with the Hebrew word for "shame" (בשת, *bosheth*) which was damnation by

---

[119] Modern political campaigns are a good example. We know that ads are propaganda and mostly false. Yet we seem to accept this as natural, and then expect the politicians we vote for to suddenly become paragons of honesty and keep their promises.

innuendo. Ben Hinnom was in a valley southwest of Jerusalem and it eventually became a garbage dump and a metaphor for Hell.[120] Jeremiah says it will be renamed the valley of Slaughter (v. 32) because of the enormous pile of bodies left there during the conquest of Jerusalem.

One can hardly imagine a more horrible practice than child sacrifice. It apparently was rare in ancient Mesopotamia but was practiced in North Africa through Phoenician influence.[121] How could it have slipped in Israelite worship, especially since it was absolutely forbidden in the law (Lev 18:21; Deut 12:31; 18:10)?

The consequences of this gross crime were a judgment that fit the sin. Ben Hinnom would become a burial place but would not be able to hold all the bodies put there. They would be left on top of the ground to be exposed to the elements, beast, vultures, and the heavenly bodies that the people worshiped (vv. 32-33). The Babylonian destruction of Jerusalem would bring this vivid scene to life. (2 Chr 36:17). Another consequence was the end of normal life (v. 34). Only the poor were left behind after Jerusalem's destruction and many of them fled to Egypt (Jer 39:10; 43:4-7).

However, something more tragic awaits (8:1-3). The already dead and respectfully buried will be dug up and their bones exposed to the elements, a horrifying and shameful end. At that time bodies were buried with honor, and bones in tombs were considered sacred. Disturbing tombs was an especially strong form of sacrilege.[122] Again the punishment fits the crime. The people had worshipped the sun, moon, and stars as gods, but these natural objects will mutely look on, helpless to came to their aid.

---

[120] The Greek translation was *ge hennom* which became in Latin and English Gehenna (Matt 5:22; 10:28; 18:9; 23:15; Jas 3:6)

[121] Patricia Smith, "Infant Sacrifice? The Tale Teeth Tell," *BAR*, July/Aug 2014.

[122] Even in modern Israel, bones unearthed by archaeologists or by building construction must be properly disposed of by Orthodox rabbis.

Moses had appealed to the people to choose life (Deut 30:19-20) but they had chosen death. The end truly had come.

One wonders what Jeremiah would say to our modern culture of death, especially the treatment of children. Killing of the unborn, child sexual abuse and sex slavery, child labor, disintegrating families are all signs of a brokenness in our world that will surely stand under God's judgment. Christian and non-Christian can agree that these are evils that must be fought.

26:1-24

This chapter covers the same event as Chapter 7 and we will offer exegesis of it here rather than in its sequence in the book. The book context of chapter 26 is chapters 26-29, which are narratives (probably from Baruch) that detail some of Jeremiah's experiences with other prophets.[123] We have the sermon in chapter 26, Jeremiah's message that contradicts the other prophets in chapter 27, his conflict with Hananiah in chapter 28, and his letter to the exiles that condemns other prophets in chapter 29.[124]

We are familiar with the prophets in Israel and Judah whose messages were recorded for us and preserved in the canon. However, there were always many other prophets at work in the two nations. These are often referred to in 1 and 2 Kings. For example, Elijah's great contest with the prophets of Baal is well known (1 Kgs 18). A lesser known example is Micaiah's conflict in 1 Kings 22. In Jeremiah's day they were still active. Their message conflicted with Jeremiah's. They preached peace, not destruction (23:17). Of course, the people preferred that message to Jeremiah's. In chapter 26 the prophets are only one of the groups that opposed Jeremiah (see v. 7).

---

[123] We would call them false prophets, but the Hebrew Bible does not. However, they are called false prophets in the LXX, Greek translation.

[124] We could add ch. 23 also, which extensively condemns the other prophets.

The plot line of the narrative in chapter 27 is masterful. The narrator sets the stage with a summary of Jeremiah's temple sermon (vv. 2-6), which arouses strong opposition from several groups who threaten Jeremiah's life (vv. 7-9). Two important groups, some court officials and the elders of the land, come to his defense and apparently his life is safe and the tension eases (vv. 10-19). But a cautionary story is told of a later prophet Uriah who was executed by the king (vv. 20-23), so perhaps Jeremiah is not safe either. Only at the very end of the narrative is the tension finally resolved when a certain Ahikam rescues Jeremiah from the mob. The narrative provides a fascinating study of the competing social and political forces at work in Jerusalem in her last days. We will see more of these forces at work later in the book of Jeremiah.

The chapter begins with a precise date for the sermon, which we can place as 609 BCE.[125] This was a critical year for Israel. Chapter 7 left us wondering how the audience may have reacted to Jeremiah's strong words.[126] Apparently what disturbed the audience the most was Jeremiah's contention that God could and would make Jerusalem like Shiloh. They took the "temple/Zion" theology of Isaiah and the Psalms seriously and considered it a permanent promise from God.[127] The response was universal and overwhelming. "The priests, the prophets[128] and all the people" gathered around Jeremiah in a mob to seize him and demand his execution. The cause for the death declaration may have been perceived blasphemy against the temple, but it is more likely the perception that he was a false prophet (Deut 18:20). How could he be speaking for God when he seemingly contradicted most of the other prophets, including Isaiah?

---

[125] See the discussion on 7:1 above.

[126] I think that is probably our reaction to many of Jeremiah's early sermons.

[127] See the texts listed above in the exegesis of chapter 7.

[128] Note this group.

The uproar was loud enough to reach the palace complex just to the south of the temple so some of the royal officials came up to the temple to intervene (vv. 10-11).[129] They gathered at the New Gate, whose location is unknown, but it was probably in the temple wall, not the wall of the city. They arrayed themselves as an official court to hear the case, since gates were the locus of judicial proceedings (Deut 21:19; 22:15; Ruth 4:1: Amos 5:12). Jeremiah was allowed his defense and he insists that he was sent by God (vv. 12-15).[130] He throws himself on the mercy of the court but with a threat. The officials (now joined by the fickle "people"!) declare him innocent (v. 16).

> **Jeremiah 26:11**
>
> *Then the priests and the prophets said to the officials and to all the people, "This man deserves the sentence of death because he has prophesied against this city, as you have heard with your own ears."*
>
> Jeremiah 26 records a dramatic encounter between the prophet and the court officials of Jerusalem. Jeremiah's message is that because of their failure to heed his warnings and change their behavior, God would make their city a place of desolation.
>
> This is not well received by the king's priests and prophets. Rather than listen to or dialog with Jeremiah, they condemn him and demand his death. His great crime? Jeremiah has "prophesied against this city."
>
> Church leaders are sometimes called to speak up against injustice and oppression in their communities. In 2014, in a non-affluent suburban city of St. Louis, Missouri named Ferguson, tensions rose, and the threat of violence persisted after the death of a young black man, killed by a Ferguson policeman. This fueled the already established

---

[129] These may be some of the same officials mentioned in chapter 36.

[130] This episode illustrates why God needed to make him an iron pillar and bronze wall to stand against the whole land (1:18).

"Black Lives Matter" (BLM) movement that demands justice in the cases of the deaths of black men and women at the hands of police officers.

Through friends living in the area, I experienced different versions of the tensions of Ferguson in those days. One friend, a white man who lived in Ferguson, was afraid to drive to work through that area. His view was that the protests were expressions of lawlessness and had no legitimacy. Soon after, he moved out of state. Another man (whom I did not know personally) is a black pastor and led the mobilization of the African American church community to rally against what was seen as systemic racism in the city government. Sometimes a righteous voice needs to be raised in the community against its own government.[131] Ferguson's history of racism included many years as a "sundown town" where black people were not allowed after sunset.[132]

In a class I was teaching at the time, a black woman student gave a report on the BLM movement. She, herself, having been raised in a peaceful suburb of Omaha, did not really understand the basis or urgency of the BLM until she began to research some of the complaints. She, like others, questioned why we need an organization to say Black Lives Matter. Her eyes were opened when she discovered mean spirited parodies of this like the "White Lives Matter" counter-organization. The bottom line of her research: why do we need a Black Lives Matter? Answer: because some people in our cities, in our world, even in our churches,

---

[131] For more on the impact the Black Lives Matter movement has had on the church, see interviews compiled by Antonia Blumberg and Carol Kuruvilla, "How the Black Lives Matter Movement Changed the Church," *Huffington Post*, August 8, 2015, accessed at https://www.huffpost.com/entry/how-the-blacklivesmatter-movement-changed-the-church_n_55c4f54ce4b0923c12b2c8c0

[132] Richard Rothstein, "The Making of Ferguson: Public Policies at the Root of Its Troubles," published October 15, 2014, accessed at https://www.epi.org/publication/making-ferguson.

> don't think that they do, and the church cannot tolerate that.
>
> The next event is one of the most unusual in the Old Testament prophets. Some leaders from the villages step forward in defense of Jeremiah, and quote verbatim the prophet Micah (vv. 17-19) from the time of Hezekiah, 100 years earlier. This is the only such quote in the Old Testament prophets.[133] The elders' intent is to defend Jeremiah from the accusation of false prophecy. They point out that Micah had made similar comments about Jerusalem (Mic 3:12) and the great king Hezekiah, rather than seeking the prophet's death, sought the favor of God, who in turn relented and spared Jerusalem.[134] The elders foresaw disaster if their contemporaries did not do the same.
>
> *Mark S. Krause*

Is Jeremiah safe? Maybe no, and Baruch offers a cautionary story (vv. 20-23). It seems there was another prophet, Uriah,[135] who also prophesied similar messages. This displeased the king Jehoiakim and he sought Uriah's death, but the prophet fled to Egypt for safety. However, Jehoiakim was a vassal of Egypt and was able to send some men to bring Uriah back. It is possible Jehoiakim personally executed Uriah.[136]

Only when an official named Ahikam intervenes is Jeremiah's survival assured (26:34). Jeremiah was fortunate to have the support of the Shaphan family, an important political power in the last decades of Jerusalem. Shaphan was an official of Josiah, something like the state secretary

---

[133] The elders must have had a written copy of Micah's sermons that had been preserved and passed down. The prophet's words carried authority. This text has implications for the development of the Old Testament canon. In the seventh century, and probably earlier, there were written texts preserved and cherished as God's word.

[134] See Isa 37-38 and the parallel in 2 Kgs 19.

[135] Otherwise unknown.

[136] Elnathan, Jehoiakim's envoy, is also mentioned in 36:11-19, 25 as a supporter of Jeremiah. He may have been Jehoiachin's father-in-law (2 Kgs 24:6, 8).

(scribe), to whom Hilkiah the priest reported the discovery of the law scroll in the temple (2 Kgs 22:3). He also read the scroll to Josiah. Ahikam had two brothers, Elasah who took Jeremiah's letter to the exiles (Jer 29:3) and Gemariah who advised Jehoiakim not to burn Jeremiah's scroll (Jer 36:11). A grandson of Shaphan, Gedaliah, was appointed governor of Judah after the destruction in 587 BCE and aided Jeremiah (Jer 39).

Jeremiah was caught between the competing political forces in Jerusalem and this would not be the last time his life was in danger. What is clear here is that the religious establishment opposed him and the people (but they vacillated). The Christian is reminded of Jesus who encountered the religious establishment also, to his detriment; and the crowds who were for and then against him.

1.c.ii. A stubborn people and their tragic fate: 8:4 – 10:25

The text returns to the poetic style of chapters 2 to 6. Prose picks up again in chapter 11 which justifies us taking 8:4 to 10:25 as a unit. The themes are like chapters 2 through 6 with descriptions of Israel's sins, coming judgments, and laments. But they seem more intense in places. These sermons are undated but probably fit the same general context of chapter 7, or maybe a little later. Josiah's reforms had failed and his successor, Jehoiakim, returned to doing evil (2 Kgs 23:36-37).

The structure of these chapters is not clear, except chapter 10 seems to be a discrete section, denouncing idolatry. For convenience the exegesis will divide this unit in three sections: 8:4-9:2; 9:3-26; and 10:1-25.

8:4-13

The section is a typical judgment speech, with a list of sins (vv. 4-9), the hinge "therefore" (v.10a), and the announcement of judgment (vv. 10-13). The judgment section includes a list of sins also.

The first accusation is familiar from chapters 3 and 4. The people refuse to repent. The verb *šûb* ("turn," "return, שוב)

predominates (six times in vv. 4-6).[137] Jeremiah sets the stage with examples from normal life. If someone falls into the dirt or mud they of course get up. Or if they wander off the road they will return to it. But Jerusalem in her present condition is not normal. Common sense has fled. Her sin has impaired her judgment and she prefers her wayward path. She is fine with being lost, so she refuses to turn back (v.5). She charges on like a battle horse who is well trained to go headlong into the fight.[138] She apparently has no idea she has done wrong ("What have I done?", v. 6). This claim to innocence is a pattern already established in chapter 2. If one cannot think clearly, then one does not have a moral compass for what is right.

In sharp contrast to Israel, even the animal kingdom exhibits common sense. The stork by instinct migrates according to a pattern and other birds know what to do at the right time (v. 7).[139] Jeremiah follows the tradition of comparing Israel to animals. Isaiah pointed out that the ox and donkey knew better than Israel (Isa 1:3). The key word is "know". Animals understood their place. Israel was expected to have an intimate relationship with God but rejected him.[140] They even had the law to make them wise in the ways of the Lord and to lead them to the right understanding of God. But they refused to take advantage of it.[141]

It was delusional to claim to have the law because it was easy to demonstrate their disobedience. For Israel, having the law was no better than having the temple or the sacrifices (ch. 7). The scribes had the responsibility of copying the law and teaching it to the people (see Ezra in Neh. 8) but they were like the priests and the prophets and led the

---

[137] Compare the discussion at 3:12.

[138] In 5:8 she was compared to a lusty stallion.

[139] The Hebrew for stork (חסידה, ḥasîdāh) sounds like the word for covenant love (חסד, ḥesed).

[140] Jesus compared the Jews unfavorably to baby chickens who knew enough to gather under the protection of their mother's wings (Luke 13:34).

[141] This was foreseen in the Song of Moses in Deut 32:28-29.

people astray (v. 8). They had a lying pen (see the extended discussion on deceit in 9:3-6 below) so they could not be expected to tell the truth. They were part of the big lie.

The law was given as a conduit to understanding and doing the will of God, but it had become a barrier. One wonders how can the word of God become a barrier to understanding and obeying the words of God? This is a continuous danger for God's people. Fidelity to God's word is crucial to doctrine and practice, but if the words becomes the main goal, then attention to the compassionate side of his will can suffer. This is a temptation that afflicts many in the church. We may be right in our convictions but wrong in the way we treat those who need to see the love of God in action. How will the church fare if its leaders are also self-deluded?

Verse 9 prompts the question, can there be no wisdom apart from the word of God? Jeremiah seems to think so, at least for the people of God. A survey of secular cultures would seem to confirm his observation. What passes for wisdom seems so often to turn into power plays or self-centeredness. Even in the church, attempts to enforce rigid right thinking can turn into control issues.

The failure to heed truth does have consequences, which Jeremiah announces in verses 10a and 13. The deceitful leaders will lose family, property and crops. Their richly blessed land will be taken away. The blessings of Deuteronomy 8 will be reversed. Their greed will turn back on them. They have a false message of "peace" which at that time was only empty words. They are shameless but will be humbled. They are incorrigible in their sin.[142]

8:14-9:2

One must pay careful attention to the speaker in this section. The people, God, and Jeremiah all speak. The people

---

[142] Verses 10-12 repeat 6:12-15 almost exactly. This is one example of several places in Jeremiah where earlier words are taken up in a new context.

are despondent and full of fear, God is steadfast in judgment, and Jeremiah is in tears.[143]

It appears that the people finally awoke to the grave danger they faced. Verses 14-16 read like a response to an invading army (described already in 4:5-9 and 6:1-8). Perhaps these verses reflect the events of 598 BCE (2 Kgs 24:10-17) after the death of Jehoiakim when the Babylonians invaded Judah the first time. The people realize there is no hope. Even fleeing the fortified cities, the last bastion of protection, will not save them (v. 14a). They finally believe Jeremiah and know their suffering is from God. They have sinned and that is final (v. 14).[144] They had often listened to messages of peace from the prophets but now know they were lies (v. 15). Jeremiah had predicted "terror on every side" (6:25) but only now do they understand (*cf.* 14:19). Their plaintive cry is full of pathos. They had hope, wished for peace, sought good, and desired healing. All these were gifts from God, but now was not the time for those gifts. The Hebrew text stresses their despair by its cryptic phrasing. There are no nouns and only eight words: "hope for peace, but no good; for a time of healing, but look, terror!"[145]

The army is already upon them, in Dan in the north, and coming fast. The cavalry of trained battle horses charges ahead, running over defenders and refugees alike who get in the way.[146] The enemy will indeed devour the land as Jeremiah predicted in 5:17.

---

[143] Some contend that God and Jeremiah speak as one. If so God is in tears also.

[144] Are they blaming God for their suffering? Wright thinks so (*Jeremiah*, p. 126).

[145] God is not just late, he is not coming at all (Wright, *Jeremiah*, 126).

[146] It is difficult for moderns to understand the horror expressed here. Before mechanized warfare, battle horses were the tank regiments, from ancient times even up to the end of the nineteenth century. They could easily destroy troop formations and trample foot soldiers. See the vivid descriptions in Bernard Cromwell, *Waterloo: The History of Four*

God is unmoved by the people's despair (v. 17). He responds with a cryptic metaphor. Judgment is coming like poisonous snakes and will mortally wound the people. His determination is stated with the Hebrew emphatic construction: "Indeed, I..." Poisonous snakes were and are common in Palestine, probably some sort of viper (same word in Isa 11:3; 59:5; Prov 23:32). Even ancient magic could not stop them. The vividness of the reality of snake bites in the ancient world makes this metaphorical use here powerful. Who could escape from the Lord? No one.[147]

Jeremiah's response, as before, is lament (vv. 18-19a; *cf.* 4:10, 19-28). He is fainthearted from anguish and in deep sorrow. The people are still fatally misguided. Is God no longer among his people, they ask? Despite Jeremiah's sermons they still cling to hope that God's presence will stave off destruction. The rhetorical style seems to expect the answer, yes, and if God is present in Zion then how can Jerusalem fall? Jeremiah had clearly said that God had abandoned his people, but they could not accept it.

God responds to his people with his own question: why has Israel provoked him with idolatry (literally, "with their foreign nothings", v. 19b). There is no comparison between the creator of the universe and the nothings so why should he not punish them?

Provoking God to anger is a charge that has a long background in Israelite history. The king frequently provoked God's anger by leading the people into idolatry (1 Kgs 14:9, 15; 15:30; 16:2, 13, 26, 33). Jeroboam, who led the northern kingdom in its rebellion against Rehoboam, was the prototype for this behavior, and all the northern kings followed in his steps. Jeremiah had already made this charge

---

Days, Three Armies, and Three Battles (New York: HarperCollins, 2011).

[147] See Amos 5:19.

in the temple sermon (7:18-19) and he makes it twelve more times (*cf.* 32:29-32).[148]

The people respond in despair (v. 20):

> The harvest is past, the summer is ended,
>   and we are not saved.

Time has run out and salvation has not come. Perhaps, the expression here is a proverbial expression that time marches on.[149] One hundred years earlier the people had a more optimistic attitude – God would come like the spring rain (Hos 6:3) but even back then that hope was dashed.

Jeremiah again responds with lament (vv. 21-9:2). He identifies with his people. He mourns with them and experiences their horror. He is a reminder that preaching against sin should bring no joy, only Godly sorrow that it is necessary. What they need is healing but there is none. Even though medication is available, and practitioners are ready, the peoples' wounds are incurable. He is thinking of spiritual wounds here and the medicine of obedience to the law, loyalty to God, and doing justice.[150] He as a prophet can administer this medicine, but the people have refused.[151]

Jeremiah's emotions are intense and profoundly mixed. On the one hand he doesn't have enough tears as he weeps

---

[148] Ps 78:58-59 explains God's motive for responding as he does, because of his jealousy for the purity of his people.

[149] NET Bible comment.

[150] A cure was offered in 3:22.

[151] Balm came from the sap of the storax or mastic tree. Currently there are no such trees in Gilead but there may have been in ancient times. Gilead may have been a trade center in the Old Testament era. The Ishmaelite traders of Gen 37:25 carried balm. The ointment would provide soothing to the wound and a pleasant aroma to cover the smell of decaying flesh. Israel's wound was also incurable according to Jer 10:19; 14:19; 15:18; 30:12-15. There was no healing balm for Egypt (46:11) or Babylon (51:8-9) either.

(9:1).[152] On the other he wishes he did not have to deal with the people at all because they are so sinful (9:2).

If God is speaking here, then we have a reflection of his suffering for or because of his people. Many Christians have trouble with the concept of a suffering God. Perhaps we have been too influenced by some fancy Greek concepts about the nature of God, rather than closely reading the Biblical text. If God is the rejected husband as Jeremiah contends then we would expect his love for his bride to involve grief at her leaving. Certainly, for the Christian we understand that in the incarnation Jesus, as God, suffered greatly. This should encourage us, for we know that when we suffer God understands. We certainly hope that he is not impassable in these situations.[153]

9:3-11

This section continues with a second round of accusations, lament and judgment and the interchange of speakers. The accusations are new in a sense, though they are the logical outcome of idolatry. The people are full of deceit and lies. In 3:23, they acknowledged that they believed in a lie that the idols could save them (at least if they adopted the offered confession). Jeremiah had already characterized them and their leaders as liars (5:2, 31; 8:8) and that they trusted in lying words (7:8). But here he clarifies that lying is at the very heart of their society. The people are well armed, with a tongue like a bow, to lie (v. 3; in v. 8 the tongue is an arrow). Truth had died. The accepted way to advancement was deceit. At the foundation of this sickness of the soul was a refusal to know God and his instruction (*cf.* v. 6).

The social structure was completely broken. A person could not even trust a friend or neighbor (vv. 4-5). The Hebrew is harsh, "Guard yourself from your neighbor." The "you" is

---

[152] The Hebrew and English text differ here in versification. English 9:1 is Hebrew 8:23.

[153] A modern classic study is: T. E. Fretheim, *The Suffering of God: An Old Testament Perspective* (Philadelphia Fortress, 1984).

not Jeremiah but anyone or everyone.[154] In an ironic twist, the Hebrew word for "neighbor/friend" sounds like the Hebrew for "evil." The picture is of a society with no moral restraints. Such a social situation cannot endure long. Imagine living in a culture where you could not trust even your closest friend or family member. You had always to be vigilant in your relationships. Unfortunately, that is how many people must live, even today. There is no "normal" life possible. There are many modern examples. Perhaps the most endemic lie is that of the modern secular culture that believes it can operate successfully, without regard for possible divine purpose or intervention.[155]

Another ironic word play is the word "deceive." It is the same verb root from which the name Jacob comes and is repeated twice – literally everyone is a "deceiving Jacob" (Gen 27:36) or a "deceiving deceiver" (v. 4). The insinuation is there is a tradition of deception in their heritage which they continue.

The tragedy is that rather than teaching each other the law of God as instructed in Deuteronomy (4:5, 14; 5:31; 11:13; *cf.* also Ps 25:4, 5; 119) they have taught themselves how to lie. When they worship a lie, how can they expect to be honest? Their character is the exact opposite of God's.[156] This kind of life is extremely taxing (v. 5c). A person of deceit expends energy trying to remember the last lie or falsehood and still tell a good tale. A liar also tends to gossip, and gossips love to run to and fro delivering the latest tidbit. The addiction to self-pleasure is exhausting and in the end, empty. On the other hand, honesty and virtue invigorate a person and gives them a sense of freedom.

---

[154] Though Jeremiah's own physical brothers betrayed him in 12:6.

[155] Wright, *Jeremiah*, 129.

[156] Christians will remember Jesus's claim to be the truth (John 14:6) and John's claim that truth came through Jesus Christ (John 1:17). Numerous times Jesus began his teachings with the statement, "I tell you the truth...."

The word of the Lord comes again in an announcement of judgment of divine consequences ("Therefore" in v. 7). The announcement is marked by three questions: What else can I do? (v. 7), Should I not punish them for this?, and Should I not avenge myself? (v. 8). There is a plaintive quality to these questions for God would really like to do otherwise.[157] But this is the only just thing he can do. The impurities of deceit must be purged out. The avenging here is not revenge, but calling Israel to account for their actions.[158] It is God's prerogative to hold his people accountable and try to restore order and obedience. God had promised Israel he was slow to anger, yet he would not leave the guilty unpunished (Exod 34:6-7).

God's compassion is emphasized by the lament of verse 10. Here he laments for the barrenness of the land he gave to Israel. The conquering army had devastated it so thoroughly that even animal life is gone, and the holy city is a heap (v. 11). This is another undoing of creation like that depicted in 4:23-28.

9:12-16

These verses are a brief prose interlude to explain in a different way why Israel is undergoing judgment. It offers a brief respite from the divine lament and tears of the previous section and the wailing of verses 17-22. It combines two major Old Testament themes, wisdom and the law. Verse 12 asks three more questions to focus the reader again on why God destroyed the land. These have the combined effect of asking, is anyone wise enough to understand what is going on (*cf.* Eccl 8:1)? The expected answer seems to be, no, but those well-grounded in the law should be wise. The law also explained why the land was ruined.

---

[157] Wright – we see the broken heart of God here (*Jeremiah,* 129).

[158] The verb is used 43 times in Jeremiah, but has a range of meaning beyond call to account on occasion. In Jer 1:10, its nuance is "to appoint." Both OT and NT remind us that vengeance belongs to God (Deut 32:35; Rom 12:19),

Verses 13-14 echo Deuteronomy in several ways. The main accusation is they have forsaken the law. This is equal to forsaking God, for the law is his expressed will for his people.[159] Deuteronomy often counseled obeying the law (literally "listening to the voice of God/my voice") and walking in it. Jeremiah uses these two phrases here to condemn their lack of obedience. Perhaps Jeremiah was thinking of Deuteronomy 10 which is a rich reflection on all the different ways Israel could follow the will of God – fearing God, loving God, walking in his ways, serving him, and obeying the commands (Deut 10:12-13).[160] It was their "stubborn heart" that led them to disobey, a favorite accusation for Jeremiah (*cf.* 3:17; 7:24; 11:8; 13:10; 16:12; 18:12; 23:17). This stubbornness led the fathers to teach their children the way of the Baals rather than the way of the Lord.

This was also a direct violation of a main Deuteronomic directive. Fathers were to "teach" their children the law and to love God, all the time and by several different methods.[161] This seemed like a simple plan. The law was the revealed will of God so that his people would know how to live and please him. It was a gift not a burden. But somehow Israel lost her way and forgot or ignored it. She was seduced by pagan idolatry and perverted obedience into legalism (chap. 7).

Deuteronomy also contained extended curses on the people if they disobeyed, so God's judgments should have not been a surprise. In fact, God was pessimistic about Israel's ability to obey and predicted what Jeremiah describes in verse 15-16 (and in nearby contexts; see Deut 29:15-22; 28:49-52).

Deuteronomy's demands on Israel were simple – love God and obey him. Jesus's demands on the Christian are the

---

[159] See the earlier charges of forsaking God in 1:6; 2:13, 19; 5:7, 19 and also later in 16:11; 17:11.

[160] See Hall, *Deuteronomy*, 197-198. Deut 10 also calls the people to circumcise the heart which Jeremiah echoed in 4:4.

[161] Deut 11:18-20 repeats Deut 6:7-8 but replaces "recount" in 6:7 with "teach."

same – love him (and thus God) and obey him (John 14:15, 23-24; 15:9-10; *cf.* 1 John 2:3-5). What detours us from this simple path – cultural seduction, stubborn evil hearts, idols of our making, legalism, ignorance?

9:17-22

Jeremiah takes us back to lament. Now the people are called to join Jeremiah and God in weeping (see 9:1-2). God's word is coming through Jeremiah, but Jeremiah seems to be the one speaking (see the "us" of v. 18). The best of the lamenting (NIV, "wailing") women are called for (v. 16).

In ancient cultures and in Israel women skilled in mourning could be hired to provide adequate crowds for proper wailing at funerals. This is attested in both Egyptian reliefs and Mesopotamian texts.[162] The ritual included wailing, tearing clothes, throwing dust, putting on sackcloth, and fasting.[163] That the women were to teach their daughters (v. 20) suggests the mourning would extend beyond the present generation. The formal laments in verses 19, 21 and 22 suggest the great devastation wrought by the Babylonian army as it swept through Judah and destroyed Jerusalem. The houses are gone (v. 19), death like a thief in the night has come in through the windows and slaughtered children and young men alike (v. 21), and the dead bodies cover the ground like dung (v. 22; *cf.* 8:2).

The Hebrew lament style (קִינָה, *qînāh*, vv. 10, 20) sharpens the horror and emotion of the moment. There is a staccato like three-two emphasis that adds punch to the words. This can even be seen in the English translations of the three verses. Verse 19a declares, "How ruined we are! How great is our shame!" (NIV; each phrase is two words in Hebrew, nominal clauses with unexpressed verbs). Verse 22a declares, "The dead bodies of men will lie, like refuse on the

---

[162] Walton, et al, *Old Testament Background Commentary*, 650.

[163] See David's instruction for mourning for Abner in 2 Sam 3:31-35. These customs are still followed in some Middle Eastern countries.

open field" (NIV). The book of 2 Chronicles says Jeremiah wrote laments for Josiah (35:25) which were perhaps similar to this passage.[164]

Jeremiah wants the people's weeping (v. 18) to equal his own (v. 1). Under the circumstances that would seem likely. As Wright points out, it is always the women who are left after war to weep.[165] The men and boys are dead.[166]

9:23-24

These two verses do not fit the pattern of accusation, judgment, and lament that we have been seeing. They offer a respite from the negativity and provide guidance for the people.[167] Though somewhat of an aside, they do offer a counter balance to other comments in chapters 8 and 9. Two triads form a contrast between the two verses with verse 23 listing three things important to humankind and verse 24 listing three things important to God. The human propensity is to boast of one's achievements, whether it be wisdom (intelligence) or power or wealth.[168] Many see these accomplishments coming from personal talent or work, and as measures of one's value and a source of security. In the context of chapters 8-9 they have already shown their inadequacy in the present crisis. Wisdom did not work (8:8-9), strength was useless (8:14-17), and wealth failed (8:10).

If God's people want to boast, then it should be in their relationship with God – that they know him. That is, that

---

[164] The book of Lamentations is dominated by the *qînāh* pattern. See the commentary there.

[165] *Jeremiah*, p. 131.

[166] When I taught in England in 1986, I preached in churches and visited the families. One family pointed out that a whole generation of men was missing from Britain because of WWI.

[167] The editorial activity and objectives in the book is sometimes unclear, though chapter 36 gives some clues.

[168] These are very much a part of non-religious or anti-religions value systems even today. It is a tragedy that they sometimes seem to have invaded the church.

they have an obedient, personal relationship with him. We have already learned that Israel did not know God (8:7) and failed to acknowledge him (9:3, 6), but these missing qualities should be at the heart of being his people. God's triad in v. 24 comes from his character: loving faithfulness (חֶסֶד, ḥesed), justice (מִשְׁפָּט, mišpāt), and righteousness (צְדָקָה, ṣᵉdāqāh). These are the "holy trinity" of God's virtues, first expressed in Exodus 34:6-7. They are expressed in his long relationship with Israel with the loving faithfulness and righteousness predominating. However, as we have seen, now is the time for justice, which means judgment on Israel's rebellion against God. But this is also an expression of his love and mercy for he will manifest himself in the exile and lead Israel back to the land in restoration (salvation). This is a divine pattern that should earn praise from the nations also (see Ps 47). God's sovereign reign over the whole earth benefits everyone. This vindicates God and his character. The final expression of this duality and God's ultimate vindication is in the cross.[169]

> ### Jeremiah 9:24b
>
> *I act with steadfast love, justice, and righteousness in the earth, for in these things I delight, says the Lord.*
>
> Jeremiah lifts up a great triad of virtues found in the Lord: "steadfast love" (mercy, חסד), "justice" (judgment, מׁשפט), and "righteousness" (צדקה). God wants a society permeated by long-lasting love, a deserved reputation for justice in its legal system, and right living rather than lawlessness.
>
> Sadly, many urban areas seem harsh and unfair. The remarkable success stories we sometimes hear of new arrivals making it big do not mention the cycle of violence and poverty that bedevils people in poor neighborhoods. Some of this is systemic. A distrust of law enforcement has a basis in remembered brutality or official indifference to injustice. Residents of upscale suburbia may believe that blighted communities are only getting what they deserve.

---

[169] Wright, *Jeremiah*, p. 133.

> I was sad some years ago to attend a suburban church and see a man wearing a T-shirt for a local police force that had the motto, "Keeping crime north of Harrison for fifty years". Harrison Street is the southern border of much of Omaha, and the implication was that the job of this officer was to push criminals out of his community into the city that deserved them. This was disappointing to me, because criminality exists in the suburbs, too! It reminds me of the premise of the old movie, "Escape from New York," projecting a dystopian future where the island of Manhattan had become so crime infested that it had been turned into a maximum-security prison.
>
> This stereotype of cities ignores the many kind and righteous people who live there. Rather than flee to fortress suburbia, churches and individual Christians should bring God's mercy, justice, and righteousness to inner urban neighborhoods. Jeremiah promises this will "delight" the Lord.
>
> *Mark S. Krause*

9:25-26

These verses continue the interlude of verses 22-24 by looking briefly at the future, speaking of the nations.[170] "The days are coming" is an introduction for future events that occurs almost exclusively in Jeremiah in the Old Testament[171] though the Old Testament has plenty to say about the future.[172] God will punish[173] the nations around Judah who are called the circumcised, from Egypt to the desert

---

[170] Some suggest 4:1-4 and 9:24-25 which both speak of circumcision form a frame around 4:5-9:23.

[171] Out of the twenty times this expression appears in the Old Testament, fourteen are in Jeremiah, 70%

[172] Other introductory phrases are "in that day" (109 times in the prophets, ten in Jeremiah) and "the day of the Lord" (fifteen times, none in Jeremiah). Both the near and distant future is addressed depending on context.

[173] Same verb as 9:8 and also in 5:9, 29; 6:6, 15.

tribes. Astonishingly, Judah is in the middle of the list and treated like one of them. These nations did practice circumcision but not as a covenant sign as Israel did. Circumcision had become only a ritual divorced from the heart, so in reality the fleshly circumcision was useless.[174]

Jeremiah was relentless in his condemnation of Israel's ritual symbols. The ark (3:16), the temple (7:4), the sacrifices (7:21), pride in the law (8:8), and now circumcision were of no value in God's eyes. A rebellious heart cancelled out any good they might have had. This is the final insult in the long litany of faults that God found in Israel in this large section.

10:1-16

Jeremiah 10:1-16 presents one of the strongest attacks on idolatry in the Old Testament, equal to Isaiah 44:12-20 in sarcasm and devastating critique.[175] The immediately following section, 10:17-22, reprises the destruction coming from the north. The next section, 10:23-25, gives Jeremiah's prayer for justice.

The attack on idolatry is grounded in the Song of Moses in Deuteronomy 32.[176] The poetry here is notable for the sharp contrast made between the idols and God as it toggles back and forth between the two. God is superior in every way.[177] The worthless idols are described in verses 2-5, 8-9, 11, and 14-15, while the greatness of the creator God is expressed in verses 6-7, 10, 12-13, and 16.

Verse 2 begins with an introductory warning not to mimic the nations. The Babylonians and Assyrians deified the

---

[174] See comments at 4:4.

[175] See also Isa 40:18-20 and 41:5-7.

[176] Wright, *Jeremiah*, lists five major parallel themes between Deut 32 and Jer 8:4-10:25 (p. 135, note 30).

[177] A student once remarked, the idols are awful, but God is awe full.

sun, moon, stars, and other natural elements and worshipped them. They developed rituals and magic to placate them and gain their favor, but these methods were based on uncertainty. The people lived in fear, assuming that fate controlled the universe. They believed the gods gave them signs and developed written records of omens and their interpretation. By 1000 BCE these records covered 70 tablets and were consulted for centuries.[178] Israel's temptation to worship the heavenly bodies is illustrated by Jeremiah 8:2 and 2 Kings 21:3, 5. Josiah tried to stop the practice in his reforms (2 Kgs 23:4).

Worship of nature is a part of many religions, ancient and modern. Fear of nature and fate is endemic in animistic cultures which results in hopelessness. Fatalism even sneaks into modern culture. How often does one hear "it was meant to be," sometimes even from Christians? What do references to "Mother Nature" mean? How many really believe the banal pontifications in the newspaper astrology section?

Verses 3-5 give a scathing critique of the man-made idols. First of all, they are worthless. This is the *hebel* (הבל) of 2:5; the nothingness or vanity of Ecclesiastes (*cf.* v. 15 and 51:18). How worthless? They are just a tree that was shaped by an artisan and covered with thin sheets of gold and silver. Isaiah 44 points out that the carpenter uses half the tree to warm himself and half for an idol to bow to. Nothing could be more absurd. The idol is so powerless that it has to have nailed on supports. However, these carved and decorated idols were given great honor in the ancient world with their own temples and feast days. The idols that the exiles would have seen in Babylon would have been impressive in size and adornment. This reality check would have been important for them.

Jeremiah's parody creates one of the most sarcastic word pictures ever made: idols are nothing more than scarecrows in a vegetable garden, a common sight in Israel (v.

---

[178] Walton, et al, *Old Testament Background Commentary*, p. 651.

5). And like scarecrows they are dumb and helpless.[179] Furthermore, they cannot do a thing, whether good or evil; literally "it is not in them to do good" (NRSV). Good and evil cover the whole spectrum of action. So why would one fear them? The Psalmists loved to point out the dumbness of the idols:

> They have mouths, but do not speak;
> > eyes, but do not see.
> They have ears, but do not hear;
> > noses, but do not smell.
> They have hands, but do not feel;
> > feet, do not walk;
> > they make no sound in their throats.[180]

Logic tells us this is true, but Isaiah points out that reason is not an idolaters' forte: *"no one stops to think; no one has the knowledge or understanding..."* (Isa 44:19).

In sharp contrast there is no one like Israel's God (vv. 6-7). This phrase frames the two verses to emphasize God's uniqueness. His power is incomparable, so he is the one to be feared not the idols![181] God is the great King of the universe and his power and authority is absolute.

God and the idols are different is essence also (vv. 8-9 and 10). The idols are lifeless, just blocks of wood dressed up. "Blockheads try to learn from blocks of wood."[182] Covered in the best of silver and gold makes no difference.[183]

---

[179] One recalls the helplessness of the Baal who could not come to the aid of the prophets opposed to Elijah, even though they cried out long and hard and mutilated themselves (1 Kgs 18).

[180] Ps 115:5-7; see also Ps 135:16-17; Isa 44:18.

[181] See Jer 5:22; 32:29.

[182] From the NEB as quoted in Martens, *Jeremiah*, p. 85.

[183] A missionary friend in Myanmar remarked on the highly decorated Buddhas everywhere which the people worshipped.

Tarshish is commonly thought to be in Spain and Uphaz is unknown unless it is a misprint for Ophir which was famous for its gold (I Kgs 5:22; Job 28:16). The word for "wise men" in verse 7 and "skilled worker" here are the same, providing an ironic pun in the Hebrew. Is the skilled worker really skilled then? In contrast God is the living God, the one and only true and eternal God (see on 9:3ff.). God is the God of truth (Isa 65:16), an important assertion in the ancient world and today when truth seems to be only a social construction.[184] It is this living God of truth who administers justice on the earth (his anger and wrath are his just response to sin and evil; see Jer 25:15-31).[185]

Verses 11-13 offer another contrast, this time on creativeness. The idols cannot create a thing, but God created the universe. The powerless gods will perish, which indeed they have. We know of the ancient gods only through old texts and archaeological discoveries.[186] No one worships them anymore, whether it be Assyrian, Babylonian, Greek or Roman.

Verse 11 has puzzled scholars because it is in Aramaic, not Hebrew, even though it seems to be the center point of verses 1-16.[187] However, Aramaic was the universal language of the Middle East for centuries commencing around Jeremiah's time so perhaps its appearance here is not that unusual.[188]

---

[184] Which ironically one could say the same of the ancients' approach to reality.

[185] Jeremiah 10:4-11 is very different in the Hebrew text and in the Greek Septuagint with the latter much shorter. Hebrew texts of Jeremiah discovered at Qumran support both versions! The scholarly discussion is long and technical. The NET Bible probably is the most accessible and easiest to understand. See the note on verse 10.

[186] Wright, *Jeremiah,* p. 137, "history is the graveyard of the gods."

[187] William Holladay, *Jeremiah,* I:324-25, 334-35.

[188] Kidner, *Jeremiah,* p. 57.

There is only one Creator, the God of Israel (verses 12-13 are repeated in 51:15-16 in the context of judgment on Babylon). The language here is reminiscent of the creation hymn in Psalm 104. Verse 12 has three parallel clauses, expressing three aspects of his creative genius. God did it through power, wisdom, and understanding. These stand in sharp contrast to the powerless, senseless gods and those who worship them.

God's skill and wisdom in creation is perhaps understood today more clearly than ever before. The overwhelming scientific evidence for design in the universe and the immense complexity of DNA are only two modern examples.[189] There are also three verbs for making the universe: make (used often in Gen 1), establish, and stretch out (*cf.* Jer 33:2). "Make" is often parallel with create. "Establish" suggests a solid and eternal foundation. It is used often of the earth (Ps 24:2; 93:1; 96:10) or of David's kingdom (2 Sam 5:12; 7:12) or justice and equity (Ps 99:4) or God's throne in heaven (Ps 103:19). "Stretch out" is often combined with "like a tent" as in Psalm 104:2 and reminded the Israelite of the common practice of erecting a tent, or a house. This language made the universe seem more personal and feel like home.[190]

Jeremiah gives us a sampling of what God's sovereign control of the universe looks like (v. 13). Nothing is outside of his control and what moderns would call "natural" events

---

[189] Numerous resources are available. Perhaps a good place to start is Francis Collins, *The Language of God* (Free Press, 2006), and Guillermo Gonzalez and Jay W. Richards, *The Privileged Planet: How Our Place in the Cosmos is Designed for Discovery*. (Regnery Publishing, 2004). Others will have their favorite books. It is fascinating that Richard Dawkins in his *The Blind Watchmaker* (Norton and Co., 1987) devotes a long chapter to making a case for design in the universe, and then asserts that it is all an illusion!

[190] I have explored this concept at length in an unpublished paper and suggested it was a way to make the Israelite feel more at home in the world. In fact, there are distinct parallels between Genesis 1 and 2 and the construction of the tabernacle and temple. See Isa 40.22; 44.24; 45.12; 51.13; Jer 10.12; 51.15; Zech 12.1; Job 9.8; Isa 48.13.

ultimately find their origin in God. The world is alive with testimony to God's power and activity. We know what Jeremiah (and the rest of the Bible) would say to Carl Sagan's pompous announcement that "the Cosmos is all that is or was or ever will be." This is a naturalist creed that cannot be supported by science. However, modern Christians are probably more naturalists and less jeremianic than we would like to admit.

Jeremiah's analysis put alongside the Genesis 1 affirmation about humans made in God's image suggests interesting parallels between God and humans. Humans are created in God's image and reflect him in several ways. One important way is in their "creativity." Humans have been very successful in the arts, music, literature, science, philosophy, and other areas. Each of these is open ended and continues to inspire further creativity. But as Jeremiah shows, humans have also used their creativity to manufacture objects that are a dead end. In this case, humans make idols who are nothings and cannot create nor inspire creativity. This is a gross misuse of the gifting God has given us. There are modern dead-end idols as well that are lifeless and deadly. No wonder God condemns these efforts which cost so much in time, work, and wealth.

Verses 14-15 repeat points made earlier about the worthlessness of idols. For the first time Jeremiah uses the word for idol, *pesel* (פסל). This noun comes from a verb "to chisel out." *Pesel* is the word used in the Decalogue of Exodus 20:7 and Deuteronomy 5:8. Deuteronomy 4:15-20, 25 warns against making an image for God of any shape that resembles any created animal, human, or object.[191] Idolatry is both foolish, and rebellion against God's law. The idolaters will suffer shame and ultimately will perish. Their inheritance is death.

However, the godly will inherit God (v. 16). God is the "portion of Jacob." This phrase is grounded in Israel's in-

---

[191] It was impossible to make an image of God because he was invisible. See Hall, *Deuteronomy*, pp. 98-100.

heritance of the Promised Land. Every tribe received a portion of property except the Levites. They depended on God for their portion and lived on the tithes and offerings of the other tribes. To be God's portion, then, is to have him provide for all ones needs. Deuteronomy 32:9 is the obvious source of this verse (*cf.* Ps 15:2, 5-6; 119:57).

Jeremiah and other prophets are quite clear that false gods are not real. Paul condemns foolish pagans who exchanged God's glory for images of humans and animals (Rom 1:18-25). He also associates idols with demons (1 Cor 10:14, 20). For those who believe in idols, however, they are very real and exert great power and influence. These may be religious icons or secular idols that vie for control over people's lives.

Even in modern times idolatry is a challenge to the church. Its task is to show the emptiness behind these false "gods" and point their devotees to the one and only living, creator God, and to his Son, Jesus Christ, who is the way, the truth, and the life. But when Paul calls greed, idolatry (Col 3:5), he shows how varied it is and how it can creep into the Christian life. Christians need to be especially alert in a culture where image is everything.

10:17-22

In shocking contrast to verse 16 which honors Israel as God's inheritance is the description here of that same people going into exile. The verbs in verses 17-19 are feminine singular and thus picture Jerusalem addressed as a single woman. She is doomed. Ezekiel was told to mimic going into exile by packing up his things in a bundle and digging through the wall (Ezek 12:1-7). Exiles carrying their belongings in bags on their backs was common and are shown in Assyrian reliefs. Jerusalem's wound is great and incurable.[192] The comparison would be especially effective in the ancient world which had few resources to treat injuries and illnesses. She was not only wounded, she was leaderless and scattered (v. 21). Therefore, the enemy from the

---

[192] Jeremiah often compares Israel's suffering to wounds – 8:22-23; 14:19; 15:18; 30:12-15.

north would devastate the land (v. 22; *cf.* 4:5-8, 13-17; 6:1-8).

10:23-25

After contemplating the words just spoken, Jeremiah breaks out into another lament, seeking justice for Israel and punishment on her enemies. Jeremiah understands human limits, recognizes that punishment must come, but pleads for mercy. He knows that God is using the nations for his instrument, but they should still be held accountable. Isaiah 10, addressed to the Assyrians that God used against the northern kingdom, also asserts that God will hold them accountable. Deuteronomy 32:27-42 describes the same divine action.

This divine purpose can be used against Israel as well. If the nations who reject God are held accountable, how much more his people who have rejected him.

1.c.iii. The broken covenant – 11:1-17

For the first time, Jeremiah directly introduces the covenant. Since all his sermons up to this point have assumed the covenant arrangement between God and Israel, this section would have fit well at the beginning of the book, but that is not how the editor has given this book to us. Two features stand out here, the demand for obedience and the covenant curses. These make sense when we understand the ancient near Eastern background to the Mosaic covenant.[193]

International relationships in the Mesopotamian world from the eighteenth to the seventh centuries BCE were governed by various treaties, each had its own form and content. The so-called "suzerain-vassal treaty" is important for understanding the Mosaic covenant, especially as presented in Deuteronomy. Such treaties governed the relationship between a powerful nation, like the Hittites or Assyrians, and conquered countries. The treaties required

---

[193] Walton, et al, *Background Commentary: Old Testament*, p. 172.

loyalty and obedience from the vassal, and their conduct was carefully prescribed. If the vassal broke the treaty they would suffer multiple curses explained in the treaty. The older Hittite treaties began with an historical prologue which detailed the history of the relationship between the Hittite king and the vassal nation.

This is the form that dominates the book of Deuteronomy.[194] God is the great King and Israel is his vassal. His history with her is well attested in the Pentateuch (summarized in Deut 1-4), his demands are made clear (Exod 20-24; Deut 5-26), and blessings or curses that will follow obedience or disobedience are detailed (Lev 26; Deut 28). Jeremiah's sermon presupposes these formulations.

The sermon is in prose like the temple sermon in chapter 7, and has several parallels with it, especially with 7:16, 22-26. The sermon also exhibits the repetitious and verbose style of many of the prose sections in Jeremiah. Rhetorical phrases divide it into three sections: vv. 1-5, 6-8, and 9-17. Perhaps Josiah's reforms and the reading of the book of the Law were fresh in everyone's minds (2 Kgs 22-23; 2 Chr 34), because Jeremiah refers to "this covenant" or "the covenant" (vss. 2, 3, 6, 8, 10).[195] However, the reforms were short-lived and Josiah's successor, Jehoiakim, returned to the sins of the fathers.

11:1-5

Jeremiah, at God's direction, sets the sermon and admonitions firmly in the context of giving of the covenant as a part of the exodus. He specifically addresses the people of Judah and Jerusalem in verses 2, 6 and 9, but broadens the audience to the houses of Judah and Israel in verses 10 and 17. His text could be Exodus 19ff. and Joshua. He briefly

---

[194] Hall, *Deuteronomy*, pp. 24-25 and sources cited there. There were other types of treaties such as parity treaties and land grants which appear in the Old Testament but do not fit the form of the Mosaic covenant.

[195] The next heavy concentration of references to the covenant is in chs. 31-34 (fourteen times).

mentions God saving Israel from Egypt to set the background, but his focus is on the covenant curses.

Israel was in the fruitful land because of God's grace in keeping his promise to the forefathers (v. 5).[196] The "oath" was sworn in Exodus 3:8 and repeated several times (see Deut 6:3; 11:9; 26:9). God had kept his part of the covenant, but Israel had not kept hers. Her responsibility was to obey ("listen" or "listen to the voice of" in Hebrew equals obey) but she had not (vv. 2, 3, 4, 6, 7, 8, 10, 11, 14).[197] Her rebellion against the great King could not be tolerated, so the curses of the covenant (Deut 27:9-26; 28:15-68) would come.[198]

The reward of obedience was a special place in the world – "you will be my people and I will be your God" (v. 4). This was first promised in Exodus 6:7 as a result of God redeeming Israel from Egypt, and repeated as a covenant blessing in Leviticus 26:12:

> And I will walk among you, and will be your God, and you shall be my people.

Jeremiah repeats this affirmation more than any other book in the Old Testament, especially in chapters 30-32. It speaks to the uniqueness of Israel's relationship with God. Of all the nations, only she was chosen to be God's people, so her rebellion was even more serious. How could she treat this gift so lightly?

This passage also speaks to the paradox of God's gracious gift of redemption to Israel and his demands on her. The gift was free but keeping it required obedience. The gift was free, but the recipients were not then free to do as they pleased. Their goal was to please God and he gave them the law to provide guidance for how to please him. The analogy

---

[196] "[A] land flowing with milk and honey" seems quaint to the modern audience but it reflected by analogy the bounty of a fertile land.

[197] This is often demanded in Deuteronomy.

[198] These long curse sections mirrored the eighteenth century Hittite treaties.

with the ancient treaties shows us how to understand this. God the great King was faithful to his part of the covenant. Israel's faithlessness required that God carry out of the curses.

Paul, in the New Testament, takes the same approach. He enumerates God's great free gift of salvation and then details how that works out in daily living, which requires obedience.[199]

11:6-8

This is a repeat of the above section with more emphasis on God's history with Israel. Her rebellion is highlighted here by emphasis on how often God warned them about sin. NRSV's "persistently" translates a Hebrew word which literally means "rising early" which we have seen already in 7:13, 25, plus the word for "repeating." God was persistent from the judges onward through the prophets, warning the people for centuries to be faithful, but it did not work.

> ### Jeremiah 11:6
>
> *And the Lord said to me: Proclaim all these words in the cities of Judah, and in the streets of Jerusalem: Hear the words of this covenant and do them.*
>
> Where should we proclaim the Word of the Lord? Jeremiah's history reveals his general reluctance to do as God directed him, but also his great faithfulness to obey these directives. Here was perhaps his hardest task: speaking for God in the "streets of Jerusalem." His message was simple, "You know the expectations of covenant with God; now meet them!"
>
> Street witnessing is to an uninterested, skeptical, and hurried crowd. I once accompanied a group of frightened yet eager college students to a park in downtown Seattle to hand out clothing and snacks, and to 'speak a good word for Jesus" (as I told them). The young people, mostly from rural Nebraska and Iowa, were surprised at their reception.

---

[199] This is a clear theme in Romans, but found throughout Paul's letters.

> Some of the street people in the park were willing to listen to these Christian students tell of their love for Jesus and their passion for ministry.
>
> Like my students, Jeremiah grew up in a rural setting, a priestly family living in tiny Anathoth in the territory of the tribe of Benjamin. His call to the city would likely have been both terrifying and exciting. His message, though, was hard, calling the city to obedience. Did he anticipate results like the famous Jonah a few generations earlier, sent to the huge and hostile Assyrian city of Nineveh to issue a call for repentance? The Lord needs faithful people, sometimes from rural backgrounds, to bear faithful witness in the streets of our cities today.
>
> Mark S. Krause

11:9-17

This rebellion was so intentional that Jeremiah calls it a plot. He implies that the people have deliberately come together to plan how to break the covenant. Jeremiah called for the people to return to God (chs. 3-4) but what they return to is the sin of the fathers (v. 10). They also turned to their many gods who were powerless to help. Jeremiah implies there was an idol in every village, which suggests everyone was involved. Perhaps even worse was the large number of idols in Jerusalem where the temple was.[200] "Therefore" (v. 11) God's only recourse is to bring disaster. Wright points out there are four reasons they cannot escape the disaster: God won't listen (vv. 11b, 14b), the other gods won't help (vv. 12-13), Jeremiah won't pray for them (v. 14), and their sacrifices won't work (v. 15).[201]

We have often seen the strong feelings God has for his people in Jeremiah, such as calling Israel his wife, and we see

---

[200] These could be references to the "high places" that Josiah destroyed. Jerusalem was also full of idols. See 2 Kgs 23.

[201] Wright, *Jeremiah*, pp. 144-45.

it again here.[202] She is God's "beloved" (v. 15) as a wife should be, but this affection has been wasted.[203] She is also called God's beloved in Isaiah 5:1. There she is compared to a lovingly planted vineyard whose owner lavished great care on it, but which in the end produced only bad grapes. Jeremiah compares her to a wonderful, lush olive tree with beautiful fruit. But her destiny was a fiery destruction because of her idolatry. They burned incense to the idols and in turn would be burned up (v. 17).

This grim section would seem to spell the end to the covenant. Israel had completely failed to keep it. Jeremiah returns to the topic in chapters 31-34 and holds out hope for the future, but, as we shall see, it will take a new covenant for that hope to be realized.

1.c.iv. Jeremiah's compliant and God's response – 11:18-12:17

This text is the first of several accounts of persecution of Jeremiah. In the call of Jeremiah in chapter 1, God warned the prophet of coming difficulties and encouraged him to stand strong (1:17-19). Now we see why. We will encounter further persecutions in 18:18-23; 20:1-18; 28; 37, and 38. We have seen a few brief laments from Jeremiah before (4:10, 19-21; 6:9-11), but these persecutions are personal and extended. This is also the first of some eight complaints in chapters 11-20 (11:18-20; 12:1-4; 15:10, 15-18; 17:14-18; 18:18-23; 20:7-13, 14-18). Traditionally they have been called "Confessions" but they are similar in content and form to laments in the Psalms and therefore fit better as a complaint or lament genre.

Jeremiah registers two complaints with God, 11:18-23 and 12:1-13. They are presented in parallel with similar structures. Chapter 11:18-20 is a complaint, with a two-fold answer in 21-23. The second complaint is chapter 12:1-4 with

---

[202] Vv. 15-16 resort to poetry again, perhaps to better express the emotion.

[203] God loved Solomon and gave him a second name, "beloved of the Lord" (2 Sam 12:24-27 – Jedidiah).

a two-fold answer in 5-13. The two complaints are marked by vivid images and metaphors and repetition of key words.

11:18-23

In the first complaint, Jeremiah presents himself as totally innocent of any inkling of trouble until God revealed it to him (v. 18).[204] He offers a vivid image of innocence – he was like a docile lamb led to the slaughter (v. 19). The Psalmists and Isaiah like this image too. Psalm 44:11 and 22 picture the persecuted Psalmists also as innocent like a lamb.[205] Isaiah's "suffering servant" is like a lamb led to the slaughter (Isa 53:7).[206]

The Hebrew word for lamb in these texts is used mostly for sacrificial lambs, largely in the book of Numbers.[207] The Christian will make the connection to Jesus in the New Testament who is "the lamb of God who takes away the sin of the world" (John 1:29) and who is the lamb who was slain in Revelation (5:6, 12; 6:1; 7:17; 8:1).

The plotters' plan was to destroy any reminder of Jeremiah's existence (v. 19b). If he had no children ("fruit") he would not have any descendants to carry on his name, and thus there would no memory of him. In the ancient world, this was a personal disaster. There is irony here in this part

---

[204] The NRSV follows the literal Hebrew, "the Lord make it known to me and I knew it (*i.e.*, understood it)".

[205] Paul quotes Ps 44:22 in Rom 8:36 as encouragement to Christians.

[206] Isaiah also says he was silent like a sheep before the shearers. I vividly remember as an early teen watching shearers shear my grandfather's sheep. The sheep would struggle until flipped on their back, then lie quietly as the wool was shaved off. Lambs could be docile and easily led but I had a pet lamb when I was 12 and he was pretty feisty as he grew older.

[207] This seems like a deliberate choice since there were other words for lamb or sheep in Hebrew.

of the plot for we learn later that God had forbidden Jeremiah to marry, so he would not have any descendants anyway (16:2).

Jeremiah was confident of his innocence. He was also confident in God as the just judge (v. 20). He knew with Abraham that "Shall not the Judge of the whole earth do what is just?" (Gen 18:25). Therefore, he appealed directly to God to come to his aid. He was unable to take his own retribution, but he was confident that God could and would. In 5:9 (see also 5:29 and 9:8), God had pronounced retribution on the nation,[208] so Jeremiah can identify with the divine desire in his own personal life. Many translations use the word "vengeance" in verse 20.[209] The NRSV "retribution" conveys the meaning more accurately here.[210] In 51:6 the noun is parallel with "pay back/repay."

What Jeremiah wants is justice for himself, and since he is innocent that must mean some penalty for the plotters who wish him dead. In this case also the idea of vindication is included. If God will punish the plotters, then Jeremiah's innocence is proven.[211] That is why Jeremiah is confident that he can present his "cause" to God. "Cause" is the translation of the Hebrew *rîb* (ריב) which is often used in legal settings and in covenant lawsuits, as in 2:9. Jeremiah was sure he had a just legal claim. (Jeremiah will use this word again in 12:1, but in a different sense.)

Only after Jeremiah's appeal does God reveal who the plotters are (v. 21). They are Jeremiah's own hometown people. Worse than that, they include his family (12:6). Why would they want to kill him? Should they not be proud of their famous son? Also on what grounds did they decide that he

---

[208] This is a persistent theme in Jeremiah which correlates with the historical fact that God's patience is at an end and he is bringing his righteous judgment to bear on Israel and the nations (noun and verb 18 times in the book).

[209] He repeats the request in 20:10 in another persecution account.

[210] Often vengeance is associated with revenge which is not the idea here.

[211] Jeremiah makes a similar appeal in 15:15.

deserved death? We do not know but perhaps can surmise a few factors.

There was a strong priestly influence in Anathoth since they were descendants of the abolished priest Abiathar (Jer 1:1; 1 Kgs 2:26). Anathoth was also a city given to the Levites (Josh 21:18), so the people could have taken offense at Jeremiah's critique of the temple and its sacrifices, the law, circumcision, covenant, and priestly leadership. Thereby, Jeremiah attacked their very identity as servants of God. In this context they must have identified him with the kind of prophet described in Deuteronomy 13 who was condemned to die because he channeled divination or enticed Israel to worship other gods.[212] Or they may have interpreted such a relentless attack on the hallowed foundations of Israel's faith as blasphemy.[213] Or they might have seen him as a supporter of Josiah's reforms which included the destruction of altars and high places in the towns and villages, thus putting many priests out of work. Whatever the reason, they felt justified in calling Jeremiah to account. Jeremiah's life truly was in danger, for another prophet, Uriah, was put to death for speaking against Jerusalem and the land (Jer 26:20-23).

God's response, introduced by a double "therefore" in verses 21 and 22, proves that Jeremiah was in the right, not his accusers. The righteous judge pronounces sentence on the plotters. They will suffer the destruction brought by military invasion – death by sword and famine. Twenty-two times Jeremiah refers to death by the sword, a common expression for death in war in the Old Testament.

---

[212] But the exact opposite was true. Jeremiah consistently condemned going after other gods or idols! False prophecy was among the 18 or so cases of capital crimes listed in the Pentateuch. See David Fiensy, "A Christian Perspective on Capital Punishment," in Larry Chouinard, David Fiensy, and George Pickens (eds), *Christian Ethics: The Issues of Life and Death* (Parma Press: 2003), pp. 233-260, especially pages 238-39. However, these kinds of prophets were not called false prophets in the Hebrew Bible, even though they certainly fit the description.

[213] Wright, *Jeremiah*, p. 147.

Famine suggests military siege (see 2 Kgs 25:1-4; Jer 52:6). The result was catastrophic, no one left at all.

This dire result apparently was not completely carried out, for we know that after the fall of Jerusalem there was a remnant left that fled to Egypt (*cf.* 23:3; 31:7; chs. 40-44) and Ezra 2:33 lists 128 men from Anathoth who returned from exile.

Christians will recognize several parallels between Jeremiah and Jesus. Both were rejected by their home town folk. Both were rejected by family. Both were described as a lamb for slaughter. Both were condemned to die. But there are two important differences. Jeremiah asked for retribution on his persecutors, Jesus prayed for their forgiveness. God rescued Jeremiah from his enemies, but he did not intervene when Jesus was crucified. Interestingly, some in Jesus's day thought he might be Jeremiah (Matt 16:14).

Since God answered Jeremiah's complaint and pronounced judgment on his foes, the case appears settled, but Jeremiah wants a further word with the judge.

12:1-6

Jeremiah's second complaint is in the style of a legal charge against God. He can address God in this way because he knows God is righteous and does what is just. In the light of his persecution his question concerns equity in the universe. If God is righteous, good and sovereign, which he is, then why do the wicked prosper? Surely a just God would not allow that to happen. A Psalm of Asaph asks the same question and lays out even more details of the perceived good life of the wicked (Ps 73:3-12).

The "treacherous" in verse 1 (or "faithless" in the NIV) have been described before. They are the nation as a whole who played the prostitute (3:8, 11, 20), those who think God will do nothing (5:11-12), and the people who Jeremiah wanted to escape from (9:1). They also turn out to be his family (12:6). So, the question for Jeremiah is existential. Why should such people seem to enjoy success? Those who love the Lord should be the ones to prosper (Ps 122:6).

Jeremiah's charge is grounded in Deuteronomy 28 which clearly promises blessings on the obedient and curses (stated as graphic punishments) on the disobedient (or wicked). His position is both theologically and Biblically sound. He could have as well stated the opposite side of the problem, which we often hear, that is, why do the righteous suffer persecution.[214] Is the divine Judge really just?

Jeremiah sees Psalm 1:3 turned on its head. Rather than the lover of the law being firmly planted in the land, it is the wicked that he sees blessed by God. The moral order of the universe is at stake. Is God who he says he is and is he in control of the world or not? Does he not recognize the duplicity of these people who talk piously but care little for him (v. 2b)? The people apparently had not changed much from Isaiah's day a century earlier when he described them as drawing near with mouth and lips but with hearts far from God (Isa 29:13).

On the other hand, Jeremiah is confident he is on God's side and that God knows it (v. 3a; *cf.* 1:5). God sees into his heart and knows that his thoughts, motives, and will are just. Therefore, Jeremiah's desire that the wicked get the punishment they deserve is in line with God's. After all, God had already revealed his will by announcing judgment on the people on several occasions. Jeremiah felt like he was a sheep led to slaughter so he desires the wicked be led to slaughter (v. 3b). Jeremiah could have written Psalm 109 which has an extended description of how the author wants the wicked punished (vv. 6-19 with v. 20). Vengeance may be the Lord's (Deut 32:35) but as with the psalmist, Jeremiah had some suggestions.

In verse 4 we find another reason for Jeremiah's complaint. They wicked want his life, but also their conduct had dire results for the land. The land was a good land given to Israel by God (Deut 8), but disobedience and sin caused it to suffer. The land even "mourns", an idea that

---

[214] Or, why do bad things happen to good people, as a popular book put it years ago – Harold Kushner, *Why Do Bad Things Happen to Good People* (New York: Anchor Books, 1981). Other authors have used similar titles recently, Melvin Tinker in 2006 and David Arnold in 2008.

Hosea probably originated (Hos 4:1-3, as part of a lawsuit God brings against Israel). This destructive effect Jeremiah had already noted in 4:23-25 and 9:10-12 and he will return to the drought theme in chapter 14. We are reminded of the vivid historical account of a three-year drought caused by royal sin in 2 Kings 17-18 involving the prophet Elijah.

Jeremiah was also concerned about the attitude of the people. They did not think God saw what they did. They were the same ones who thought God did nothing (5:12). This is practical atheism. The belief in many gods did not make them more religious, but totally insensitive to the one true God. Yet he was the one who had acted on their behalf in history, rescued them from slavery and given them the good land. How, then, could they think he did nothing or was blind to their actions? This is also a characteristic of the wicked described in the Psalms (Ps 10:11; 73:11; 94:7).

The question Jeremiah raised echoes through time and is still a pressing concern today. Every generation experiences injustice, and every culture seems to produce wealth and poverty, power and oppression, wicked and good without rhyme or reason. What seems to be endemic evil does call into question God's sovereignty and goodness and has provided fodder for the so-called "New Atheists" who use evil as good reason for not believing in God.[215] The whole Bible is based on the premise that God is righteous,[216] but the issue of evil calls into question his faithfulness and reliability to look after his people. Therefore, with Jeremiah we await God's response.

To our surprise, the response does not answer the question. Rather, God interrogates Jeremiah with two challenges (v. 5). The gist is "if you think life is hard now what are you going to do when things really get tough?" There is

---

[215] Two examples are: Richard Dawkins, *The God Illusion* (New York: Haughton Mifflin, 2006) and Christopher Hitchens, *God is Not Great: How Religion Poisons Everything* (New York: Twelve Hattachette Group, 2007).

[216] Brueggemann, *To Pluck Up, To Tear Down*, p. 112.

a huge difference between racing with humans and with horses, or walking in smooth country and forging one's way through the thickets along the Jordan River.

How should we understand this response? In chapter one God was quick to encourage Jeremiah by the admonition not to fear for he would deliver him (1:8, 19). But here the word from God is disheartening. Jeremiah's life is in danger and he cannot even trust his family (v. 6) but things will get worse?[217] God deflects Jeremiah's legitimate question and moves in another direction. Why does he not answer? Isn't this issue one of the most profound challenges facing God's people?

Jeremiah is in the company of Job and Habakkuk who both asked similar questions of God and received no direct answer. God's response to Job's question about his suffering was a long litany of the mysteries of creation and a challenge to Job for an explanation (Job 38-41). God's response to Habakkuk's complaint about the divine use of an evil nation was to remind the prophet that the "righteous shall live by their faith" (Hab 2:4). Asaph found his answer in worship, not in a divine explanation (Ps 73:17, 27-28). In the New Testament, Paul's response to those who would question God's mercy is "Who are you, O man, to talk back to God?" (Rom 9:20).

It seems, then, that when it comes to profound questions of theodicy (God's control over the universe), God doesn't seem to be interested in them. What he most desires for his people is faithful trust. There may be legitimate answers[218] but God thinks there are more important issues, such as his people's obedient relationship to him. Isaiah commented that God's ways are not ours nor his thoughts ours (Isa 55:8-9). Although the question is urgent, uncertainty remains, for Jeremiah (and the others) get no relief. What God wants his people to understand is that fidelity has its

---

[217] And they do as we shall see in chapters 36-38.

[218] Jews and Christians over the centuries have provided several solutions.

own reward.[219] Indeed, the righteous must live by faith (Gal 3:11). The best response may be Isaiah 40:27-28 – those who wait on the Lord will mount up like eagles, "they shall run and not be weary, they shall walk and not be faint."[220]

12:7-13[221]

God has a second response to Jeremiah, but it comes in the form of a complaint of his own.[222] He shares Jeremiah's pain at the conduct of the people. He is done with them; his patience is at an end. Perhaps in some way this is God's response to Jeremiah's question in verse 1 – the evil may prosper now but their end is coming.

God's words are harsh toward Israel. Verse 7 begins with a triple statement: *I have forsaken.... I have abandoned.... I have given into*. He is treating the nation the same way they treated him (Jer 2:13, 19). We have read many announcements of judgment up to this point, but this declaration seems more final than the others. God really is at the end of his rope with his people, but it is deeply painful because these are "*my house, ... my heritage ... my beloved.*"[223]

There is a long history of mercy and love behind these words. "Heritage" signifies a hereditary possession gained

---

[219] Brueggemann, *To Pluck Up, To Tear Down*, p. 115.

[220] Note that Jeremiah and the Psalmists are frank with God and are not afraid to complain to him. They have an intimate relationship with God and are seeking understanding. That can come only through open and honest dialogue, not through pious phrases and the quelling of serious questions. God can handle anything we ask.

[221] This section is marked by verbs in the perfect tense, which in Hebrew indicates past action. But the context suggests that the action is in the future. Scholars refer to this phenomenon as the "prophetic perfect." Since God is announcing the action it is put in the past because it is assured to occur and considered already done. The NIV, alone among modern translations, translates the verbs in the future tense,

[222] Brueggemann: we see the pathos of God here (*To Pluck Up*, p. 115).

[223] And "*my vineyard*" in verse 10. See Isa 5:1-7.

through great effort. God brought Israel out of Egypt with great signs and wonders to be his beloved people.[224] This included the plagues, the crossing of the Red Sea, the provision in the wilderness, and finally the conquest of the Promised Land. Israel was therefore God's "treasured possession" (*segullāh*, סְגֻלָּה, Deut 7:6; 9:29; 14:2; 26:18; 32:9). This is a singular word expressing how precious Israel was to God.[225] How could he abandon them? Hosea 11 poses the same possibility. Israel the beloved son had rebelled against God and deserved exile but in the end God could not give him up (v. 8). But that was 140 years earlier. Now God's patience has come to an end and he can give them up, but we must still hear the deep hurt behind these words.

Israel had become like a lion roaring at God (v. 8) and his love had turned to hate. This is not an emotional human level hate, but the measured response of a holy God to his unholy people, an aversion toward them. They had become his enemy, so he eventually becomes theirs. This put them in the same category of other things God hated such as sin, rebellion, and false worship (*cf.* Deut 12:37; Ps 5:5; Isa 61:8; Amos 5:2). Therefore, nature and the nations turn against the beloved people and share in her destruction (vv. 9-10). The result is "desolation" (four times in verses 10b-11). The picture is of the Promised Land completely emptied of all life (a scene already portrayed in 4:23-26). Jeremiah later describes the scene as *"without inhabitants, human or animal"* (30:10).[226] Despite all this no one cares (v. 11b) – except God.

---

[224] Deut 4:20; 1 Kgs 8:5.

[225] Walter Zorn, "*Segullah*: A Word of Worth,' in Jason T. LeCureux, J. Blair Wilgus, and James Riley Estep, Jr., *Deuteronomy, The Prophets and the Life of the Church* (Preston, Australia: Mosaic Press, 2013), pp. 36-54.

[226] "Desolation" is a favorite word of the prophets to describe the results of God's judgment, used around 60 times.

This desolation is brought by invading armies and perhaps has the events described in 2 Kings 24:1-4 in mind. The invaders are not doing this on their own, their swords are actually "*the sword of the Lord*" that devours the land and people. That is, God uses the other nations as his instruments to punish his people. Isaiah already saw how this worked out as he spoke of Assyria as "*the rod of my [God's] anger*" to punish the northern kingdom in 722 BCE (Isa 10:5).[227] No one will escape the sword (v. 12c). Genesis 3:18 has come full circle (v. 13a) and Israel's pursing worthless idols has come to fruition, that is to nothing (see 2:8, 11; 7:8).

12:14-17[228]

The section ends with an echo of chapter 1:10. God is going to start plucking and destroying ("plucking" in verses 14 [twice] 15, 17 [twice][229] and "destroying" in verse 17).[230] Verse 14 also echoes verses 7 and 8 by referring to God's "heritage."

Jeremiah declares a word of hope for both Israel and then the nations, one of many Old Testament texts to reflect the promise to Abraham in Genesis 12:1-3. First, he will save Israel from the nations he had appointed to destroy her by

---

[227] It was this idea that caused Habakkuk so much anguish in Hab 1:5-14.

[228] Some scholars find the positive tone of these verses incompatible with verses 7-13 and suggest that some later editor has inserted them. But if modern scholars can see this disjunction, why would not some ancient editor? He was certainly just as intelligent. These hopeful words are similar to others that Jeremiah inserted into negative sermons (cf. 3:15-18; 5:18-19) and, therefore, most likely came from him.

[229] The verb occurs twice but the second is in an infinitive form which syntactically signals emphasis, so most translations rightly translate "completely uproot."

[230] The Hebrew word for "pluck" (or "uproot", NIV) is *ntš* (נתש). The NIV is consistent in translating "uproot" in each instance and helps the English reader see the emphasis. The NRSV is less consistent by translating the verb as "pluck" in vv. 14 and 15, but "uproot" in v. 17. In 1:10 it uses "pluck." Repetitions like this are often significant and English translations should aid the reader in seeing them.

plucking her out of their clutches (vv. 14-15). He will indeed have compassion, a gift that seemed impossible in verses 7-13 but which we saw dominates Hosea 11. We are to understand that rescue will follow the events foretold in the previous verses. Second, to those nations who dare bother his heritage he will pluck up from their land just as they plucked Israel from hers (v. 14). If these nations learn the way of Israel and confess the name of God then they will live in the midst of Israel (v. 16), but if they do not, then destruction is their lot (v. 17).

Both Israel and the nations are under the sovereign will of God, but both also control their destinies. God is just and will bring justice on both for rebellion against him, but he is also merciful, and his judgments are not the end for his people. They and the nations can turn to God and be forgiven and restored. The exiles who were hearing Jeremiah's words may have had deep doubts about that for they were in the throes of despair (Ps 137), but there is hope, and Jeremiah will fully explore what this hope looks like in later sermons (chapters 30-34).

1.c.v. *Two Symbols and Two Warnings – 13:1-27*

In chapter 13 we find the first of many symbolic acts in the ministry of Jeremiah. Other prophets engaged in symbolic acts but none like Jeremiah.[231] These acts and their interpretations present a message in a powerful and memorable way. People remember better what they see then what they hear, but these presentations combine both.

The chapter contains two symbols (vv. 1-11, 12-14), and two separate warning to the people (15-17, 18-27). The references to garments in the first and last sections holds it together

13:1-11

This first event in verses 1-11 is somewhat unusual since it seems to be only for Jeremiah and he is not instructed to

---

[231] In Jeremiah see chapters 16, 18, 19, 25, 27-28, 32, 35, 43, and 51. See also Hos 1, Isa 8, Ezek 4.

present it to the people. There was a public aspect to it, too, as we shall see. If the first audience for the act were the exiles it would have certainly had a strong impact on them. The event has a six-part structure arranged in an a, b, c, c, b, a, chiastic pattern. There are three commands which are interpreted in reverse order, that is verses 1-2 are interpreted in verse 11, verses 3-5 in 10, and verses 6-7 in 9.[232] The key to the meaning of the symbolic act is verse 11.

Jeremiah is commanded to buy a new linen loincloth (אזור, *'zwr*) wear it for a while, then go to the Euphrates (see below), hide it in some rocks for a time, go back and get it, and observe that it had rotted and was good for nothing. This seems rather straightforward but there are some interpretative issues. First, there is disagreement on what the loincloth was exactly. The NIV has "belt" and other translations have "girdle" or "waistband." The NRSV "loincloth" seems the most accurate. Verse 11 indicates it was something worn close to the body that clung tightly. A loincloth that went from the waist to the knees fits best this description. Was it an inner or outer garment? Loincloth suggests an inner, basic garment (NET "linen shorts"). But the fact that it may have been observable suggests something worn over a robe. Elijah had a leather one (2 Kgs 1:8) that was visible. The Hebrew word is used only 14 times in the Old Testament and 8 of the occurrences are here.[233] That it was linen suggests a priestly garment (Exod 28) and a holy character. A linen garment gave the priest a special glory (compare v. 11). This fits with Jeremiah's priestly heritage from Anathoth.

Verse 4 instructs Jeremiah to go to the "Euphrates." This was a major river of Mesopotamia some 500 hundred miles from Judah. This seems like an extreme distance and would have taken months. Jeremiah had to go twice. Therefore, some have suggested that the Hebrew word here actually refers to a place near Anathoth named Parah listed in Joshua 18:23 (so NIV). In support of the latter is the fact

---

[232] Brueggemann, *To Pluck Up*, p. 122.

[233] Isa 11:5 uses it in a metaphorical sense.

that although Hebrew *pᵉrath* (פְּרָת) always refers to the Euphrates elsewhere, the word always occurs with the words "river of" or in a context that makes it clear that the Euphrates river is meant (see *e.g.* Gen 2:16; 15:18; Deut 1:7; Jer 46:2). Parah seems more likely. However, the exilic readers would have immediately made the connection with the river in Babylon where they were. They were the ruined loincloth.

The interpretation (vv. 8-11) condemns Judah and Jerusalem for their pride. The pride specifically is their worship of other gods which became the mainstay of their lives. They were stubborn in defiance of God and insistent that their way was the right one. This arrogance marked a self-serving, self-centered way of life that was doomed to fail. In the end it was, like the loincloth, "good for nothing."

Verse 11 is the crux of the passage. God chose Israel as his people and intended that they cling to him like a loincloth so that they would bring him "a name, a praise, and a glory." The clinging (דבק, *dbq*) was like that of the first man who was to leave his family and cling to his wife (Gen 2:4), or that of each tribe clinging to their allotted land (Num 36:7).

Deuteronomy 26:18-19 is the foundation for God's purpose for Israel,

> Today the LORD has obtained your agreement: to be his treasured people, as he promised you, and to keep his commandments; for him to set you high above all nations that he has made, in praise and in fame and in honor; and for you to be a people holy to the LORD your God, as he promised."[234]

This was a great honor with a great purpose, to bring glory to God among the nations and to be a light to the nations (Isa 42:6; 49:6), so their turning against God not only ruined their glory, it cancelled out their mission mandate,

---

[234] See also Deut 7:6.

their very reason for existence.[235] They sought glory for themselves rather than God and turned inward rather than outward. Like the loincloth they were good for nothing.[236]

The New Testament has a great deal to say about the glory of God which was revealed through Jesus Christ (John 1; Phil 2) and who brought glory to God. Christians, as was ancient Israel, are to bring glory to God also (1 Cor 6:19-20). This glory is for both Jew and Gentile who are saved by God's glorious grace (Eph 2) and results in God's glory (v. 21). Peter encourages his readers that their present suffering will ultimately result in *"praise and glory and honor when Jesus Christ is revealed"* (1 Pet 1:7). Ultimately all glory will go to God as all the saved from every nation will surround the throne of God and give him praise and honor and glory (Rev 4:9-11; 5:12-13).

13:12-14

Jeremiah uses another symbolic message which is not acted out, but presented through the use of a common object, a wine jar. This message was to be delivered directly to the people and took the form of a dialog. Jeremiah begins with a common observation that every wine jar should be filled with wine. This was so obvious that the people reply with a strong hint of disdain – of course, we know that! Beyond this reply there were probably some common assumptions the people had about wine. It was one of the great blessings of the Promised Land (Deut 7:13; 8:8; Num 13:23) and the people might have thought of the overflowing cup of Psalm 23:5. They might also associate a full wine cup with the presence of God himself (Ps 16:5) or the cup of salvation (Ps 116:13). They had no reason to anticipate the coming negative message.

---

[235] Wright, *Jeremiah*, p. 159.

[236] Phillip Ryken explores this theme in his sermon on this text with the key Latin phrase that means "the corruption of the best is the worst corruption." See Phillip Ryken, *Jeremiah and Lamentations: From Sorrow to Hope* (Wheaton: Crossway, 2001), pp. 233-235.

On the other hand, the downside of too much wine of course was drunkenness with all its attendant complications. It is this downside that becomes the object lesson for Israel. God will not bless them with the full cup of wine but will make them drunk, so drunk that they will destroy each other. This will involve every level of society, from the kings down through all the leadership to even all the inhabitants of Jerusalem, including the children. Drunkenness causes such personal and social stress and dislocation that it becomes an apt metaphor for God's wrath against his sinful people. Jeremiah will explore this further in chapter 25 and apply it to the nations.[237]

The terrible conclusion to the message is that God will have no compassion on his people as he destroys them in his wrath. God is pictured as the direct agent here, but we know from history that the direct agent for this destruction was the Babylonians. They showed no pity or compassion (Jer 21:7). The theological principle established in the discussion on chapter 12 is that God's uses nations to carry out his judgments. It was this aspect of God's activity that upset Habakkuk so much (Hab 1). He could not understand how God could use an evil nation like the Babylonians to bring judgment of his people.[238] Nor could King Jehoiakim, who burned Jeremiah's scroll of sermons when he heard the message (Jer 36:29). Yet this is how God has determined to work in the world.

13:15-17

These verses stand in tension with what precedes and what follows. They suggest a possibility of repentance when the surrounding statements are quite clear that the end has come. Commentators differ on their intention. They do seem to offer a last chance but the conclusion in verse 17 looks negative. Perhaps the intent is to allow some who are penitent to enter exile remaining firm and knowing they

---

[237] See also Isa 51:17-23; Ps 60:1-3; Hab 2:15-16.

[238] It is ironic that Habakkuk wanted God to judge the sinful people, but he could not accept the method.

still have a relationship with God.[239] Perhaps there is hope that repentance could take place.[240] Perhaps this is an offer for them to face up to their sin, acknowledge their guilt, accept their fate, and thus bring glory to God.[241]

These verses apply common jeremianic themes. He has challenged them numerous times to listen (obey) and described their disobedience (7:13 23, 24, 28; 4:13; 11;4; 16:2). This challenge frames the text (vv. 15 and 17). He addressed their pride in the preceding section (and elsewhere) and here in verse 15 and 17. He is still concerned about bringing glory to God (v. 16), but the warning is new – deep darkness is coming if they do not listen to his message. Darkness is an apt metaphor for judgment. It reminded them of creation when darkness prevailed before God acted (Gen 1:2, 4, 5, 18). It reminded Israel also of the plague that God brought on Egypt (Exod 10:15). It was also associated with God's theophany at Sinai (Deut 4:11; 5:22). More ominously, darkness was a part of the covenant curses (Deut 28:29). It was associated with the dreaded day of the Lord in Joel (2:2, 3). Metaphorically it was also connected to disaster, punishment, imprisonment, death, the grave (*sheol*). The three different Hebrew words used in verse 16 for darkness paint a dreadful picture of what is coming. There is no protection now from the "deep darkness" of Ps 23:4.[242]

God's judgment was just but it was not done with any joy. In fact, it was accompanied by copious weeping (verse

---

[239] Fretheim, *Jeremiah*, p. 209.

[240] Brueggemann, *To Pluck Up*, p. 125.

[241] Wright, *Jeremiah,* p. 162. He cites Joshua's challenge to Achan in Josh 7:19-20 which uses the same language of bringing glory to God. Achan does confess his guilt and takes his punishment.

[242] It is difficult to tell in the NRSV that "deep darkness" here and the "darkest" valley of Ps 23:4 is the same word. The traditional translation "valley of the shadow of death" conveys well the horror of the prospect of God withdrawing his protection. See Ps 107:10.

17).²⁴³ Though Jeremiah speaks and weeps, it is God also speaking and weeping. We have already seen Jeremiah weeping in 9:1, which also may reflect God weeping. In fact, Jeremiah weeps often for his destroyed people (14:17; Lam 2:11; 3:48), but he is not the only one who weeps – Isaiah did (Isa 22:4) as did the psalmist (Ps 119;136). How could there be anything but sorrow over the stubborn disobedience of the people that earned such judgment? The concept of a vengeful God who enjoys inflicting punishment on innocent people is the figment of a lively (and perverse) imagination.²⁴⁴ Jeremiah is considered a weeping prophet because he served a weeping God. Jesus weeping over Jerusalem (Luke 19:41) reflected his weeping father.

13:18-27

This last section of the chapter concludes with a familiar litany of the sins of the people that have earned the judgment of God, but it does address briefly a new group in the nation, the royal family (vv.18-19). The leadership has been condemned several times (2:8, 26; 6:13; 8:8-12), but this the first time the king and queen mother have received a word of the Lord. The book of Kings lists almost all of the queen mothers in Judah, and some have suggested this was an official position in the kingdom.²⁴⁵ If so, the queen mother would have wielded strong influence (see 1 Kgs 23:31, 36; 24:8). One queen mother, Athaliah, seized the throne for six years (2 Kgs 11). The message is that a complete humbling of the royal family is coming, which in fact did happen with Jehoiachin who was taken to Babylon and imprisoned (2 Kgs 24:8-12). The message is clear, even the political class could not save the nation. The threat of exile has been in the background since 1:3 but now it is made explicit and it involves "all of Judah" who will be "wholly

---

²⁴³ Three occurrences of the root weep (2 verbs and a noun) and the word tears.

²⁴⁴ Richard Dawkins, *The God Delusion* (New York: Houghton Mifflin, 2006).

²⁴⁵ Walton, *Bible Background*, pp. 357, 653.

taken." Indeed, the beautiful, lofty crown will come crashing down.[246]

The addressee of verses 20-27 is unclear. The pronouns are second feminine in the Hebrew and verse 27 addresses Jerusalem. Perhaps the city and queen mother are both in view, the latter representing the former. The passage continues the familiar charges against the nation we have already seen: their iniquity (v. 22), their evil deeds (v. 23), their forgetting the Lord and trusting in lies (v. 25), and their abominations, adulteries, and prostitutions (v. 27).

Now, a new image is introduced to describe the judgment, the "lifting of the skirts" to reveal their shame (vv. 22, 26). The experiential background is probably two-fold. An adulterous wife was shamed by her husband by exposure (Hos 2:3, 10; Ezek 16:39) and ancient conquering armies routinely pillaged and raped. Since Israel was the adulterous wife, God was justified in exposing her shame to the nations by sending her into exile.[247] Further, since God used as his agent the conquering Babylonians, the people would suffer the ravages of war.[248]

Perhaps the most amazing thing is that the people could not understand why this was happening (v. 22). How could they be so obtuse? God's response generated a famous proverb in verse 23, one that still resonates into modern times: can a person change the color of their skin or can a leopard change its spots? The implied answer is: of course not. Many things in nature are beyond human control. When applied to Israel this is devastating. They were so deep in sin there was no chance they could change. The time of repentance was past, and the future was sealed.

---

[246] Wright, *Jeremiah*, p. 163.

[247] The Hebrew verb for "lift up, expose" and "go into exile" are the same.

[248] The same image is used of Assyria in Nah 3:5. Nakedness and humiliation are reflected in a different way in ancient international relations, such as when Hanun mistreated King David's envoys in 2 Sam 10, or in the Assyrian treatment of the Egyptians in Isa 20:4.

They were like the wicked of Psalm 2, fit only to be scattered like chaff before the wind (v. 24). Early in their history their lot and portion had been the gift of the land and the security that brought (Num 26:53; 33:54; Josh 15:1) but now their lot and portion was a much different gift from God, shame (v. 26).

The only possible response was "Woe" (v. 27; cf. 4:13; 6:4; 10:19; 45:3; 48:46), a profound expression of despair in the face of coming judgment. In light of this, can Israel be made clean? That question hovers over the whole book until chapters 32-33.

1.c.vi. Drought, famine and sword – 14:1-15:9

This section is dominated by catastrophe, fervent appeals, and denunciations. It is styled on the lament pattern seen in many Psalms (e.g. Ps 74, 79, 80) which usually contain a complaint, an appeal to God's mercy, an implied response, and a concluding thanksgiving. Psalm 74 offers several parallels to Jeremiah's lament here. Individual laments like Psalm 13 and 22 offer more hope at the end than a communal lament like Psalm 74. The communal lament often has a note of accusation to God as if somehow, he was to blame for the trouble. This section favors a communal lament as we shall see.

The structure of the section is in the form of repeated themes in two cycles:

- A - Lament and appeal – 14:1-9
- B - God's response – 14:10-11
- C - Denunciation of lying prophets – 14:12-16
- A' - Second lament and appeal – 14:17-22
- B' - God's response – 15:1-4
- B"- Further affirmation of Israel's destruction – 15:5-9

This structure suggests that the focus is on the lying prophets who had led the people astray and were responsible for the coming judgment. Although up to this point Jeremiah has emphasized the role of the people's apostasy in their downfall, he has also indicted failed prophetic leadership (2:8; 4:9; 5:13, 31; 6:13; 8:10). Now he makes it more explicit.

Verses 12-16 contain two key words that dominate – sword and famine (vv. 12, 13, 15, 16, 18; 15:2). Both 14:12 and 15:2 add a related word – pestilence. These are some of Jeremiah's favorite words to describe God's judgments on Israel. Sword and famine occur 29 times together and they are joined by pestilence ten times in Jeremiah.

These are interconnected terms. Famine is devastating in marginally arid countries where in even good times rainfall is limited. If the rain fails, then all life is under threat and death is imminent. War (the sword) also causes famine as invading armies pillage and burn everything they can. Famine would also increase death from diseases which were common in the ancient world. Jeremiah paints a grim picture and the question would immediately arise, who could survive? The many word pictures and metaphors in the section re-enforce the message – the destruction of God's people is certain.

14:1-9

The first lament is in verses 1-9 and is marked by the verb "to mourn" (אבל, *'bl*) which often occurs with references to "weeping" (בכה, *bkh*; see 13:17 above).[249] Judah is the one mourning here but more often in Jeremiah it is the land that is mourning, for it suffers the consequences of the judgment that God brings on Judah and Israel (Jer 4:28; 12:4, 11; 23:10).

The lament has two parts: a description of the drought which causes the lament (vv. 1-6) and an appeal to God for help. The cause of the lament is "droughts" (plural in Hebrew) so Jeremiah could be referring to several, whose cumulative effects are vividly described. The most remembered drought in Israel was during the time of Elijah in 1 Kings 17-18. Drought was a covenant curse in Deuteronomy 28:22-24, described in stark, realistic terms – "bronze sky" and "iron ground." The three verbs of verse 2 picture the consequences: mourning, gloom, and crying/wailing.

---

[249] Gen 37:34-35 and 50:3, 10-11 are good examples.

Bitter wailing was a part of ancient mourning customs (and still is a part of many cultural mourning rites).

The drought is described in detail in verses 3-6. Two things are emphasized – its effects on all levels of human life and its effects on animal life. Thus, it strikes the nobles (v. 3) and farmer (v. 4), and deer (v. 5) and asses (v. 6). There are no privileged classes when God's judgment comes. Verses 3-6 are also marked by the refrain, no: no water (v. 3), no rain (v. 4), no grass (v. 5), and no herbage (v. 6). Jeremiah balances two levels of human society with two levels of the animal kingdom. Water is essential for one and herbage for the other. Therefore, all of life is affected by the drought. Jeremiah also hints that creation has been reversed. The word for "herbage" is the same one used in Genesis 1:11-12, 29-30, and 3:18. There is also a reversal of the provisions made by creation as listed in Psalm 104:23-30. Drought is anti-creation and no respecter of persons. All anyone can do is mourn and cover their heads, rich and poor alike (vv. 3 and 4).

The lament is followed by a confession of sin and an appeal for help (vv. 7-9). It is unclear who is speaking here. Is it Jeremiah or the people? Opinions vary. Several think it is the people as in a normal communal lament.[250] On the other hand can we imagine the people who are entrenched in their idolatry saying these words? Elsewhere they claimed not to have sinned (2:35). The same issue arises with verses 19-22 in the second appeal. Perhaps Jeremiah is constructing a confession for the people to use should they decide to return to God, as he did in chapter 3:22b-25.

The confession admits they are deep in guilt which bears witness against them.[251] They have abandoned their original beliefs ("apostasies") and they have "sinned" against God (see Ps. 51). Jeremiah has already described these apostasies in some detail (2:19; 3:6, 8, 11, 12, 22 – see comments there). Their evil is comprehensive and could only

---

[250] Wright, *Jeremiah*, p. 169; Brueggemann, *To Pluck Up*, p. 129.

[251] There is a Hebrew word play for the word for iniquity and testify have the same consonants.

have been more so if they had added "rebellion", the other major word for sin in the Old Testament. "Against you" is the key admission. Ultimately all sin is against God even if it only seems to be "personal" or "victimless" (a modern invention). Joseph recognized that even sexual sins like adultery were a sin against God (Gen 39:11). This sensitivity is crucial to understanding our status before God but is rare in modern culture. The addiction to sin distorts this theology of sin.

The appeal to God to "act" is ironic. Had he not always been acting on Israel's behalf, all the way from creation through the exodus and conquest to ordaining Israel's leaders like kings and prophets? They seem to have had a limited view of God's sovereignty over the world.[252] They also appeal to God's honor. He should forgive them for his "name's sake." This was an appeal to show his honor among the nations (Ezek 20:9). Never mind that they had brought shame on God by turning to idolatry!

The appeal goes deeper. They had abandoned God for idols, but now he is the "hope of Israel" (v. 8; *cf.* 17:13; 50:7). God is their hope because it is through him that Israel can expect deliverance (*cf.* Jer 2:11; 31:19; Hos 2:15; Zech 9:12). This is not mere wishful thinking but is grounded in confidence in God's trustworthiness and grace.[253]

Four "why" questions dominate verses 8-9. Only two whys are stated but the other two are implied (see the four lines in 8b-9a).

> [W]hy should you be like a stranger in the land,
> [why] like a traveler turning aside for the night?

---

[252] There is a modern parallel in the statement that it was "a God thing" when something fortuitous happens. Isn't everything in the Christian's life or the church's life a "God thing"?

[253] He had shown that over and over through his faithfulness to the covenant. For the Christian our hope is in the same faithfulness demonstrated through Jesus's incarnation, crucifixion, and resurrection.

> Why should you be like someone confused,
> [why] like a mighty warrior who cannot give help?

The questions seem to suggest subtly that God was somehow to blame for their plight because he seems to have been disinterested in them. He was like a "stranger." Jeremiah uses the Hebrew technical word *gēr* (גר), which normally refers to a non-Israelite living in Israel as a temporary resident or newcomer, or foreigner who decided to reside among the Israelites. They were among the protected class along with widows and orphans (Jer 7:6) and were expected to keep the Israelite law (see Deut 10:18-19; 24:19-21; Lev 16:29; 17:8-16). It is ironic that Israel populated the high hills and high places with idols (ch. 2) then laments that God is absent!

They also see him as confused, a hero who cannot help, but the reader knows who was confused. What they failed to realize is that God is always present, but he does not force himself on anyone.

14:10-12

God's two-fold response is harsh. First, he will not heed their plea (v. 10) because of their unrestrained behavior (which in 2:24-25 was likened to wild donkeys). He will punish their iniquities and sins, not forgive them. He will remember them, not forget them. This is in contrast to Israel who had not remembered but had forgotten him (2:32; 3:21; 13:25; 18:15, etc.).

Secondly, he tells Jeremiah not to pray for them (for the third time, see 7:16 and 11:14). Prayer and worship are conversations with God, an important part of Israel's relationship with God, but now God withdraws from communication.[254] If God will not listen then Israel has no hope.

Further, Israel is no longer "my people" but "this people". This was not how it was supposed to happen. God was supposed to respond with grace and salvation as expressed in Psalm 85: 2-3, 8-13, but this time requires a different response. God will not be manipulated. Worship and prayer

---

[254] Brueggemann, *To Pluck Up*, p. 130.

are not magic. A just God holds his people accountable for their sin (see on Jer 7 above). All Israel can look forward to is sword, famine, and pestilence (v. 12), that is, defeat and destruction by the Babylonians (see 15:2).

14:13-16

Maybe the people are not totally to blame. Jeremiah identifies other prophets who have been giving the people a different message and leading them astray. These other prophets played a significant role in Jeremiah's life and he attacks them again in chapter 23:9-40. Hananiah was named as one who took a lead role in opposing him in chapter 28. Who the others were, we do not know, but we do know from Deuteronomy and the historical books that there were many prophets in Israel over the years, sometimes hundreds.[255]

Jeremiah is distressed by this contradiction to his message.[256] Will these other voices drown out his words and will the people follow them? Their message was certainly more acceptable to the people and met their felt needs. It offered them a way out of the impending doom that Jeremiah saw. They also had Isaiah's so-called "Zion theology" on their side.[257] Who does not want to hear positive preaching and words of peace? Who does not want to hear a good word from the audience?[258] The contradiction was direct: sword and famine will not come (v. 13).[259]

God's response told Jeremiah to look at the source of their message and their authority (v. 14). The message came from lies, divination, and their deceitful minds, so their

---

[255] Deut 13; 18; 1 Kgs 18; 22; 2 Kgs 4. These were not true prophets, but they often led king and people astray.

[256] The Hebrew translated "Ah" is used in other contexts as a cry of alarm (see Judges 11:35; 2 Kgs 3:10; 6:5, 15).

[257] Often Isaiah asserted the safety and secureness of Jerusalem/Zion. See for example Isa 14:32; 26:1; 28:16; 31:5.

[258] Did Jesus have these false prophets in mind in Luke 6:26?

[259] Notice how these two words dominate these verses.

words could not be true.[260] Also God did not send them, command them, or speak to them as he had Jeremiah. Thus, they had no standing as speakers of truth, but their words did have a certain perverse truth. What they had said would not happen to the people would actually happen to them (v. 15)!

The "therefore" introduces the judgment statement after an accusation. This punishment was an exact fit for the sin. That seems just, but there is a tragedy here also, for the people who listened to them will suffer the same fate (v. 16). We know they were not innocent, but it still seems harsh. Yet again this is just, for it is the people's "wickedness" that brought this on them. The word for wickedness (or evil) is a double duty word that both can refer to the act of doing evil and the result of such an act which is disaster or evil (see Jer 1:14, 16; 2:13, 19, etc.).

God's people always wrestle with what is a true word from God. Not only did Jeremiah have to deal with false preachers, but the early church did also (Mark 13:22; I Tim 6:5; 2 Pet 2:1; I John 4:1; Rev 16:13). Jesus warned about false prophets (Matt 7:15-23) and Paul about false apostles (2 Cor 11:26). Jeremiah helps us understand that good tests of truth are both source and content.

14:17-22

These verses begin the second cycle of lament and appeal (parallel to 14:1-9), but this lament is from God himself (vv. 17-18). We have already seen Jeremiah's tears (8:18 – 9:3; 13:17) and the people's tears. Now we see God's tears (although Jeremiah's tears may have been God's also.

The truth about the nature of God is made clear here – he is just and will bring judgment, but not without great feelings. As any loving father, it costs him pain and sorrow

---

[260] Deut 13 instructs the people to examine the content of a messenger who claims to be from God.

also.[261] The "let" is a permissive idea but it states, when used of God, a fact — his eyes do run down with tears.

The judgment is more tragic because it is the "virgin daughter" (also 18:13; 31:4, 21) who is suffering the "crushing blow" and "wound." In Israelite culture the virgin daughter held a special place of honor and was strongly protected by family and the law (Deut 22:13-29) against male predators and other dangers. Her virginity until marriage was highly valued.[262] Yet it was God the father who had abandoned her and allowed her to experience the Babylonian invasion which brought the sword and famine (v. 18). Death was in the land and in the city. Again, the blame is laid at the feet of the prophets and priests (2:6; 5:13; 6:13; 8:16).

The lament is followed by another appeal and confession of guilt (*cf.* vv. 7-9). This confession also suggests that God is partly to blame for the disaster (*cf.* v. 9). Now the people say he has rejected them. They ignore the fact that they already have rejected the law (6:19) and his word (8:3). They seem to think that the present is divorced from the past and that God's patience should be his controlling attribute (Exod 34:6-7a). As before they acknowledge their wickedness, iniquity and sin (v. 7) and they appeal to God's honor, reputation and the covenant (v. 21; *cf.* 8-9). They want God to keep his side of the covenant though they could break it with impunity (ch. 11). They seem to finally realize that the idols are useless, and their hope is in God (v. 22), so they wait for another word from the Lord. Will he relent this time?

15:1-4

The answer comes swiftly, and it is the same as before (14:10-11). God will not relent. Even if the two greatest in-

---

[261] This is certainly not the impassive God of the philosopher or systematic theologian.

[262] See Hall, *Deuteronomy*, 335.

tercessors in Israel's history, Moses and Samuel, stood before him in prayer for his people, he would not relent (v. 1). He had responded to Moses' and Samuel's prayers before,[263] but that was a different time and circumstance. They could not assume that God's past actions guaranteed his future actions. Their covenantal relationship with God was not static and involved interaction and response: obedience and blessing or disobedience and curse. Jeremiah had enumerated their disobedience in great detail. They might want to stand before him in worship (7:10) but the divine verdict was "Send them out of my sight."

Israel's broken-hearted response "Where shall we go?" (v. 2) receives a harsh answer – to whatever judgment will fit. Some would suffer disease, others death by sword, others famine, others captivity. In other words, Israel would not escape the Babylonian invasion and all the people would greatly suffer.[264] "Captivity" introduces a new dimension to the original three but Jeremiah's readers in Babylon would understand very well what that meant.

The covenant curse is made explicit in verse 3. The animal kingdom which before was pictured as suffering the judgment with the people and land (7:20; 12:4) will be an instrument of God's punishment. War produces many dead, and they normally would not be buried. Thus, all the scavengers would swarm around the bodies – dogs to drag them away and birds and beasts to feast on the flesh (Deut 28:26; Lev 26:22). This is a common threat throughout Jeremiah (7:33; 12:9; 16:4; 19:7; 34:30) and contributes to

---

[263] See Exod 32:11-14, 30-34; Num 14:13-19; Deut 9:6-29; 1 Sam 7:5-9; 8:1-22; 12:17-23; Ps 99:6.

[264] The NRSV's fourfold "destined" in verse 2 is somewhat misleading. The word is not in the Hebrew text. In fact, the Hebrew lacks any verb and has just four staccato phrases, "those for the pestilence for the pestilence, those for the sword for the sword, those for the famine for the famine, those for the captivity for the captivity." The repetition also involves assonance and would have assaulted the ear with the drumbeat of a death sentence.

the shame and distress that surrounded unburied bodies in ancient Israel.

Up until now in Jeremiah, the people had been held accountable for their own sin, but now the prophet invokes the theology of the author of 2 Kings. The cycle of sin and disobedience that condemned Israel to God's judgment could be traced all the way back to King Manasseh. In Kings, not even the reforms of the great king Josiah, who was a king after God's own heart, could reverse the path to judgment initiated by the evilness of Manasseh (2 Kgs 23:25-27; 24:3-4).[265] The great evils of Manasseh detailed in 2 Kings 21:1-16 set the wheels of God's justice into motion and in Jeremiah's time these wheels had finished their fine grinding and the end had come. Manasseh died in 642 BCE, about the time Jeremiah was born. Within half a century after Manasseh's death the tragic trajectory he set in motion came to fruition. The people, however, were not innocent for they allowed themselves to be led astray (2 Kgs 21:9).[266]

> **Jeremiah 15:4**
>
> *I will make them a horror to all the kingdoms of the earth because of what King Manasseh son of Hezekiah of Judah did in Jerusalem.*
>
> Jeremiah bears witness to the sinful excesses of King Josiah's grandfather, Manasseh. Manasseh's 55-year reign was the longest of any king in the line of David. He promoted idolatry, sacrificed his son to a false god, and "filled Jerusalem" with innocent blood from one end to another (2 Kings 21:16). It is the verdict of Jeremiah that despite the reforms of Josiah, Manasseh's sins were so great that

---

[265] Josiah is described in 2 Kgs 23:25 as the perfect Deuteronomy man who loved God with his whole heart, soul and might (Deut 6:5).

[266] 2 Chr 33:10-19 reports that Manasseh was taken captive by the Assyrians, repented and prayed to God, was returned and initiated a reformation. It did not make any difference because his successors continued in his evil ways. Assyrian records do show that Manasseh was a prisoner for a time but do not mention his release, although it was their practice to often release captive kings (Walton, *Bible Background*, 456).

God's judgment of Jerusalem was inevitable. The corruption of a long-serving politician dug a hole so deep that a well-intentioned reformer could not climb out of it in a single generation.

Cities suffer when their leaders are corrupt. Needed funds are misappropriated. Justice in the courts is perverted. The wealthy are accommodated while the poor are exploited.

Although construction in now proceeding, for many years a mass transit subway line to the westside of Los Angeles was blocked by politicians, particularly one powerful County Supervisor. While various excuses were given, when I lived in L.A., I was told by more than one person that the real reason was to prevent the poor residents of other parts of L.A. from having easy access to upscale westside communities like Beverly Hills, Bel Air, and Santa Monica. The unstated rationale was that if poor people were allowed easily to travel to the enclaves of the rich, they would bring crime and gangs. Ironically, in this traffic clogged city, the lack of a subway train required the low-income domestic servants of these wealthy households to commute to work from east or south L.A. via much slower bus routes, often changing busses multiple times.

Sadly, this economic and racist obstruction was unopposed by any of the wealthy churches of the area. Such a simple thing as mobility within the urban area was rationed and reserved. The rich avoided the traffic woes by using limo drivers and, in some cases, helicopters to fly over congestion nightmares they helped perpetuate.

As with Jeremiah's condemnation of Manasseh, corruption and greediness of civic leaders may cause injustice that endures for generations. City believers should hold politicians to high standards of ethical behavior, making decisions in the best interests for all citizens.

Mark S. Krause

15:5-9

This section ends with a re-affirmation of God's intention to destroy Israel. Despite the two confessions of sin in 14:7-

9 and 19-22 God refused to relent in 14:11-12 and 15:1-4. Jeremiah introduces new images here to further establish God's determination. He first suggests that nobody cares about what happens to Israel (v. 5). No one will pity them or mourn their passing. Second, he confirms that God is fed up with them (v. 6). Israel was called to walk in the way of the Lord (Deuteronomy), but they had gone backward (*cf.* 7:24). Just as God was sorry he made humankind (Gen 6:6), he was tired of feeling sorry for Israel (NRSV "weary of relenting"). He was throwing them to the wind like chaff (v. 7a). The sword, famine, and pestilence would destroy them, cause great mourning, and create more widows than could be counted (vv. 7-8).[267] War always takes the young men and husbands first and a whole generation can be swept away almost overnight. Even the honor of having a full family will be destroyed (v. 9).[268]

The three-fold affirmation in this section that God will not relent and will indeed destroy his people is disturbing. Had he not promised to be compassionate and slow to anger (Exod 34:6)? But even Isaiah a century earlier testified to the fact that God was weary of his people (Isa 1:14; 7:13; 43:24). After the exile Malachi witnessed to the fact that Israel still wearied God (Mal 2:17).

How did God become weary? By continually bearing with their sins and extending opportunities to repent (Isa 43:24).[269] After time that burden became intolerable, and justice had to be done.

In the New Testament we discover that God in the person of Jesus Christ bears the sin on himself and suffers even to death on the cross. The Gospel answers the concerns left

---

[267] An allusion to the promise to Abraham that God would make his descendants more numerous than the sand of the sea (Gen 22:17).

[268] Having seven sons was a matter of pride and honor – Ruth 4:15; 1 Sam 2:5.

[269] Terrance Fretheim explores this theme in his *The Suffering of God: An Old Testament Perspective* (Philadelphia: Fortress, 1984).

hanging by the Old Testament. There is grace without limit.[270]

1.c.vii. Jeremiah's Third Complaint – 15:10-21

Jeremiah once again raises a lament to God in the form of a complaint about his treatment at the hands of his people (see 11:18-23 and 12:1-6). This complaint raises crucial issues about God's call to ministry, reception of the message, and the validity of the call. While the issues are clear, part of the text is marked by a degree of uncertainty of meaning.

There are two complaints and two divine responses: the complaints are in verses 10 and 15-18; the responses in verses 11-14 and 19-21. However, verses 11-14 are difficult to translate and understand. If they are a response they do not address directly Jeremiah's complaint, but they seem to address Jerusalem.[271] We will explore the complaints first and then the responses.

First of all, Jeremiah wishes he had not been born (v. 10). Perhaps the message on the shamed mothers of the previous sermon (v. 9) led him to reflect on his own mother and his circumstances.[272] It is clear he was in the depths of despair. His life had not turned out as he had planned or hoped, and he was deeply disillusioned. All his preaching had done was cause strife and contention. Was this a strife for his audience as he continued to pronounce judgment and destruction, or a strife that he experienced from his constant negative preaching? Though both are true, probably the latter is in view. He was continually rejected and

---

[270] Wright, *Jeremiah*, 175.

[271] Commentators and translations differ. Brueggemann thinks that through verse 12 are a part of the complaint (*To Pluck Up*, p. 137). Lalleman and Fretheim think they are a response (Lalleman, *Jeremiah*, p. 154; Fretheim, *Jeremiah*, p. 126). Wright thinks the verses are an intrusion and does not deal with them (Wright, *Jeremiah*, p. 176).

[272] In another complaint in 20:14 he curses the day he was born; see Job 3:1-12.

persecuted (v. 15) as later chapters in the book demonstrate (see chs. 26, 36, 37, 38, and 40-44).[273] He had done nothing to earn this treatment (perhaps the enigmatic "I have not lent, nor have I borrowed" is sort of a proverbial expression of ways to create social friction[274]).

Second, he had suffered insult on God's behalf (v. 15) and was experiencing God's absence. He wanted God to take vengeance on his persecutors (see 5:9, 29) just as God himself was taking vengeance. He also desired God's patience with him.

This was not the way he began his ministry. Then he was full of joy and delight (v. 16). He made God's word an integral part of his life,[275] cultivated an intimate relationship with God, and anticipated a long and fruitful ministry in the name of the Lord. In fact, God's word was burning within him and he could not hold it in (20:9). Further, he was literally a Psalm 1:1 person (v. 17), not associating with the evil and wicked, but bearing up faithfully under the weight of God's message. Yet, he endured isolation and rejection. His private joy was extinguished by his public experience.

Finally, he could not understand why he suffered (v. 18). This is the focus of his complaint. He thinks God has failed him. Wounds were the result of God's judgment (10:19; 30:12, 14) so he interprets his suffering in the same way. Faithfulness should bring healing, not more pain; comfort not more darkness. Further, he felt God had deceived him. He had earlier proclaimed God as a life-giving cistern of water (2:13), but now God seemed more comparable to a dry wadi in a desert, a mirage that appears real but fades

---

[273] Unfortunately, his most difficult days of ministry were still ahead!

[274] Fretheim, *Jeremiah*, p. 235. See Ps 15:5.

[275] An experience that Ezekiel shared (Ezek. 3:1-3).

into nothing as one approaches.[276] So God who called him and promised to be with him, was absent and unreliable.

These complaints seem to be Jeremiah's "dark night of the soul." Many Godly people admit to experiencing times of spiritual drought and a loss of the sense of God's calling and presence, not once but many times. The Christian world was shocked in 2007 to learn that the saintly (and now sainted) Mother Teresa had experienced long periods of darkness and the loss of the sense of divine presence.[277] Even her closest colleagues were stunned. Yet she remained faithful to her calling and ministry. Many wonder how she could keep up her ministry under such spiritual struggles. If this was in fact Jeremiah's situation he did not keep silent, as Mother Teresa, but made his sense of abandonment abundantly clear. Jeremiah shows that a calling from God is a not a guarantee of a life of joyful service. In many cases it seems to be the opposite – lack of "success",[278] suffering insults, feeling the full weight of God bearing down. Consequently, Jeremiah gave in to bitter resentment and self-pity.[279]

God's first response was a re-affirmation of the word of destruction against Israel and Jerusalem that Jeremiah had often announced (vv. 11-14).[280] This word of destruction

---

[276] Compare Job 6:15-20 who speaks of his friends in the same way.

[277] Mother Teresa and Brian Kolodiejchuk, *Come Be My Light: The Private Writings of the Saint of Calcutta* (New York: Doubleday, 2007).

[278] Mother Teresa: "God did not call me to be successful but to be faithful." It is easier to preach positive messages to gain popularity than to challenge people to change or to repent. The false prophets took the path of preaching peace. Ultimately God's servants must decide what success looks like and from whose perspective. Even resistance, rejection and failure may be success (Fretheim, *Jeremiah*, p. 244).

[279] Wright, *Jeremiah,* pp. 178, 181.

[280] Some take Jeremiah as the addressee but verses 13-14 are against that interpretation, plus "enemies" in Jeremiah always refer to the enemies of the people, not Jeremiah. The verb forms are in the second masculine singular, but these forms have been used already with

confirms Jeremiah's message and paradoxically is "good" for Jerusalem (see 25:5-6). Destruction and exile will in the long run work to the good of the people which is beyond their sight at the time. Even if the nation is like iron, the iron of the conqueror will be stronger (v. 12). Exile is assured and thus Jeremiah is vindicated (vv. 13-14; *cf.* 17:3-4).

The second divine response is two-fold and addresses Jeremiah directly (vv. 19-21). This response is dominated by the Hebrew root *šûb* (שוב) which we have seen several times already (four times in v. 19; see 3:1-4:4 and comments there). First, God does not answer Jeremiah's complaint directly but presents him with a challenge – to return to his calling (v. 19). Israel was called to repent with this same language (ch. 3) but that does not seem to be the intent here. Jeremiah had not sinned by calling God to account and did not need to repent. What he needed was to abandon his worthless words of complaint and return to speaking God's words that had originally give him such joy (v. 16). He had seemed to be turning toward the people by listening to them more than to God. If he indeed returned to his calling, the people would turn to him. He needed a reorientation of his focus.[281] If he did this, he could become like a Moses and serve again as God's mouth (*cf.* Exod 4:15-16; 7:1-2). The challenge lifts Jeremiah's eyes up above his circumstances to once again consider what service to God's will means.[282]

The second part of God's response repeats his original commission and his promise to make Jeremiah strong and to be with him (v. 20; *cf.* 1:18-19). Jeremiah can stand against the opposition. The job is not finished, and the mission goes on.[283] God did comfort Jeremiah in one way. He

---

references to Israel and Jerusalem in 2:28-29; 4:1-2; 5:17-18 and elsewhere (*cf.* the NET Bible on these verses).

[281] Brueggemann, *To Pluck Up*, p. 142.

[282] This is similar to how God dealt with Elijah in 1 Kgs. 19.

[283] Wright, *Jeremiah*, p. 178.

recognized that Jeremiah was dealing with real opposition and wicked, abusive people and he promised to deliver him (v. 21). This rang true in many of Jeremiah's later experiences.[284]

Jeremiah's suffering seems to have caught him by surprise even though at his call God had warned him that he would need to stand firm against opposition (ch. 1). The Christian, however, should not be surprised by suffering for the faith. Jesus our Lord suffered and died and warned his followers that they would also (John 16:33; Matt 10:34-39; 16:24). The apostles and early Christians suffered for preaching the gospel (Acts). Paul, Peter, and John addressed the suffering of early Christians (2 Cor 1:6; 1 Thess 2:14; 1 Pet 1:6-7; 4:12-16; Rev 2:10). The default circumstance for many Christians in our world is suffering but they hold on to the promise of eternal life (1 Pet 1:6-9).

1.c.viii. *Normal life cancelled and more accusations – 16:1-17:18*

These two chapters continues the announcements of judgment on Israel, but with some unique features. They also contain a surprising word of hope for the future. Jeremiah's life is once again disrupted, and he ends in chapter 17 with a prayer for vindication. The writing style returns to prose and exhibits several repetitions like we have found earlier.

The first section, 16:1-13, has two parts – an announcement of judgment in verses 1-9 and a response from the people in verses 10-13.

16:1-9

God commands Jeremiah not to marry (v. 1). Normally Israelite men married early, perhaps in their late teens, so this command would have come early in his life. This added to his rejection and isolation for it would have aroused opposition for his opting out of normal community life. Jeremiah was not the only prophet whose ministry

---

[284] See ch. 26; 36; 37:11-16; 38:1-13.

calling affected his married life. Hosea was called to suffer the abuse of an unfaithful wife to mirror God's suffering at Israel's unfaithfulness (Hos. 1-2). Ezekiel experienced the death of his wife and was forbidden to mourn to mirror the pain God's people would experience at God's judgment (Ezek 24:15-24). Here Jeremiah's pain of isolation would mirror God's pain at the rejection by his people.[285] A faithful prophet did not often experience peace, acclaim, or popularity.

Despite the impact of God's command, its importance for this text is as a departure point for the main message. This is demonstrated by the structure and content of verses 2-9 with their parallel content. Verse 3-4 parallel verses 6-8, so verse 5 forms the center focus. Verse 9 adds another negative assessment of community life. Jeremiah would not experience the blessing of children, a major expectation in ancient Israel, but he would be spared the agony of those parents who did have children. Children would experience the worst outcome of a conquering army – death by disease, famine, and sword,[286] and subsequent exposure of their dead bodies to the elements (vv. 3-4).[287] Circumstances would not permit any mourning for these unfortunate victims. Verse 6-8 expand this theme by detailing the precise mourning rites that would not be observed. Some of them seem to reflect pagan rites that were forbidden in Israel, especially the gashing (Lev 19:28)! Verse 9 adds another important social and cultural practice that would not occur – the joy of a wedding and its attendant feasting and community celebration.[288] The coming disaster would destroy all normal social life, from marriage to death, which means the end of the community.

---

[285] Wright, *Jeremiah*, p. 186.

[286] See comments on 14:12 above.

[287] See on 7:33 above.

[288] The restoration of the joy of weddings is a part of the restoration detailed in Jer 33:10-11.

The parallel structure draws our attention to verse 5. The horrors of the judgment come on Israel because God has withdrawn from his covenant. The three most important gifts of his grace that formed the basis of the covenant are gone – his peace (שׁלוֹם, šᵊlôm), his steadfast love (חסד, ḥesed, covenant faithfulness), and his mercy (רחמים, raḥamîm, compassion).[289] So the covenant collapses and Israel is doomed. If life with God ends, then so does Israel's community life, for it was grounded in the covenant.[290]

We see again how strongly Jeremiah's life embed the word of God. He not only spoke the word, he lived it out in what he was and what he did.[291]

16:10-13

The people respond to this emotional message the same way they had before in chapter 14:7-9 and 19-22 – why? What was their sin and iniquity (v. 10; *cf.* 14:7)?[292] God's response is similar to his previous responses (14:10-12 and 15:1-9). The time for hope is past and destruction is inevitable. The answer is brief, but the rhetorical balance emphasizes two things. Verse 11 provides the reason for the coming judgment – Israel's ancestors had forsaken God (*cf.* 1:16; 2:13, 17, 19; 5:7 etc.) and his law and had committed idolatry (*cf.* 7:9; 11:10; 13:10). Therefore, God will forsake them (v. 13 – "hurl" them out of the land; 22:26, 28[293]) where they will continue serving other gods. The punishment takes the form of the accusation. God tells them – since you are determined to worship other gods I will put you in a situation where you will experience what

---

[289] See Exod. 24:6-7 for these terms in God's self-revelation of his character.

[290] Brueggemann, *To Pluck Up*, p. 146.

[291] Fretheim, *Jeremiah*, p. 248.

[292] The spiritual blindness of the question is astonishing (Wright, *Jeremiah*, p. 187).

[293] The covenant curses of Deut 28:63-67 list plucking them from the land, scattering them among the nations, serving other gods, and experiencing trembling hearts, failing eyes, languishing spirits, and days and nights of dread.

an idolatrous life apart from me really is like. The punishment fits the sin.

Verses 11 and 13 enclose verse 12 which explains the reason for Israel's persistence in idolatry. Their "stubborn evil will" led them to abandon God (*cf.* Jer 3:17; 7:24; 9:14; 11:8; 13:10). This reflects an attitude of destructive self-centeredness that prevented them from exercising a humble obedience, the proper response to God's gracious gift of the covenant (expressed throughout Deuteronomy). A synonymous phrase was "stiff-necked" (Deut 9:6, 13; Jer 7:26; 17:23; 19:15).

Earlier in chapter 16 Jeremiah had emphasized death as the consequence of apostasy. Here it is exile. The two results are not in conflict but complimentary as the history in 2 Kings 24-25 shows. Many died during the Babylonian invasion, many were taken into exile, and some were left in the land (Jer 40-42). In every case the covenant life with God was shattered.

Self-centered stubbornness is just not an ancient malady but a modern one. How many church conflicts can be ascribed to stubborn hearts and stiff necks (but are always presented in terms of defending orthodoxy)? How many of the conflicts in our current culture are grounded in self-absorption? Autonomy and self-sufficiency are the hall marks of our age and are the path to destruction, just as they were for Israel.

16:14-18

This section begins with an astounding disconnect from the context – a message of hope in the form of a promise of restoration to the land (vv. 14-15). This message seems so ill-suited to Jeremiah that critical scholars all agree some later editor has put these verses here.[294] But if Jeremiah could not have said this, why would some later editor think these words would fit here? Verse 14 begins with "Therefore" which usually connects two statements together, most

---

[294] Brueggemann, *To Pluck Up*, p. 147.

commonly announcing a judgment following an accusation. Here the word clearly connects restoration with the judgment of the preceding verses, so we understand that judgment is not the end of Israel, but it must come before God can announce hope. These are two sides of God's dealing with his people. Judgment is earned because Israel broke the covenant, but God's grace continues, and the covenant continues.

The restoration is stated in almost exaggerated terms. The return from exile will supersede the exodus (v. 15). The exodus was the central salvation event for Israel and defined her beginning as God's covenant people. Israel was expected to celebrate it every year with the Passover (Deut 16:1-7) and the people confessed their faith in God who brought them out of Egypt every time they brought their first fruits to the priests (Deut 26:5-8). The exodus was God's great act in their history, often referred to as the operation of his "mighty hand and outstretched arm" (Exod 7:4-5; 9:15; 15:1-18; Deut 5:15; 6:21-23). It was their redemption from slavery and emergence as God's holy people (Exod 19).

Now, Jeremiah says that great event and confession will fade away because of an even greater act of God's power – the bringing of the exiles back from all the foreign lands to which they were taken! It is difficult for us to imagine the power of these words. They would seem to negate everything Israel had believed up to this point. Their history would begin anew with a new great act of salvation, a new exodus.[295] The one enduring promise is that the land is still theirs for God had promised it to their ancestors. Jeremiah will repeat this theme and repeat the promise in 23:5-8.

Nevertheless, the exile "first" still has to happen (v. 18). The NRSV and other translations omit the "first" but it is in

---

[295] The promise of a new exodus is not unique to Jeremiah. Isaiah included the concept often in his vision for Israel's future in chapters 40-55. See Isa 40:3-4; 41:17-20; 43:14-21; 51:9-11. See also Ezek 20:34-38.

the Hebrew and is an important connecting word. The return will occur, but first the judgment must take place. Jeremiah uses some different imagery here, that of hunting and fishing (v. 16), but the message is the same.[296] Everyone will experience the exile. No one will escape it.[297] There is nowhere to hide, for God is the all-seeing God. Nothing is hidden from him. His eyes range throughout all the earth keeping watch (2 Chr 16:9; *cf.* Ps 33:13-14; Prov 15:3; Zech 4:10). It is foolish to think that anything could be hidden from God, but how many, not just ancient Israel, have deceived themselves into thinking it is possible. Israel will receive full compensation for her sin. The idiom "doubly repay" does not mean twice as much but full payment for a debt due.[298]

16:19-21

Chapter 16 ends with a statement of trust in God that mirrors several Psalms of trust (v. 18; *cf.* Ps 18:1-2; 22:19; 27). Often in the Psalms a statement of trust is followed by a complaint, but Jeremiah asserts that the nations will come to put their trust in the Lord as well. They will recognize the contrast between the God of Israel who is indeed a refuge and stronghold, and the gods they have invented who are worthless (v. 19-20). Jeremiah made this point already in 2:11 with the same words. The idols are worthless and of no profit. The irony is that it seems the nations will come to recognize this, but will Israel?

There is more. This recognition by the nations will open them up to instruction and God will take the opportunity to teach the truth, who the true God really is (v. 21).

---

[296] See Amos 4:2; 9:3; Hab 1:14-17 for similar imagery.

[297] In Isa 2 the crevices and crags are where the people go to escape the coming judgment of God. But as Jeremiah shows, here is no escape.

[298] See Deut 15:18 for same phrase which the NRSV translates as "services worth the wages..." (Hebrew: "twice as much").

> Therefore, I am surely going to teach them, this time I am going to teach them my power and my might, and they shall know that my name is the LORD.

This is perhaps the most important missional statement of the book. Beyond the judgments lies not only the restoration of Israel, but the nations entering into the blessing of God. We are all included in these nations.[299]

17:1-18

If we ignore the chapter divisions, which were not in the ancient Hebrew text, and compare 16:21 with 17:1-4 the contrast is "striking and tragic."[300] In 16:21 the nations are coming to the Lord so that they may <u>know</u> him. In 17:1-4 God's chosen people are so hard-hearted that they will be driven into a land they do not <u>know</u>. Jeremiah explains how that is possible.

This section is another series of judgment scenes followed by another of Jeremiah's pleas for vindication. The connecting word is "heart" (vv. 1, 5, 9, 10) with a back and forth between negative and positive statements. The structure is: the hard heart (vv. 1-4), the cursed heart (vv. 5-6), the blessed heart (vv. 7-8), the devious heart (vv. 9-11), and Jeremiah's heart (implied, vv. 12-18).

17:1-4

Jeremiah implies that the peoples' hearts were so hard that it took an iron pen with a hard point to write on them (v. 1).[301] He speaks of the tablets of their hearts as a deliberate allusion to the law that was written on tablets of stone by the finger of God (Exod 31:18). These laws were to be on their hearts (Deut 6:6), but in Jeremiah's day it was their sins that was inscribed on their hearts.

---

[299] Wright, *Jeremiah*, p. 191.

[300] Wright, *Jeremiah*, p. 196.

[301] NRSV has "diamond" which indicates hardness but is probably not accurate since Israel did have access to diamonds. The modern Jewish translation has "adamant."

The analogy is not positive for Israel. God wanted soft hearts that would respond in obedience and love, but that is not what he got.[302] Ezekiel, Jeremiah's contemporary located in Babylon, saw the same thing (Ezek 3:9). For Israel to return to God they needed to have their hearts of stone removed (Ezek. 11:19) and receive a heart of flesh (a soft heart) so that God's law could be directly written on it (Jer 31:33). By referring to "heart," Jeremiah is addressing their will here, not their emotions. A huge change is needed in their intentions and mind-set.

The second analogy is just as devastating in implication. It gets to the very heart of their worship. On the Day of Atonement (Lev 16), the high priest sprinkled blood on the horns of the altar. This was to atone for Israel's sins.[303] In sharp contrast, now the people's sins were engraved on these horns. Their sin also infected the children (v. 2) so that they followed the same Canaanite idolatrous worship as the parents (2:30; 3:6). These were the same shrines that Moses had commanded to be torn down when they entered the land (Deut 7:5; 12:3).

The sins committed in the land resulted in the wealth and treasures and the gift of the land being taken away (vv.3-4). Further, they would experience judgment in a distant and strange land, the land of exile. God's gift would no longer be the place of blessing and refuge. Their sins had defiled it and they could no longer live there.

The gift of the land was the central focus of the Pentateuch and the book of Joshua – so strong a theme that one might think the gift was irrevocable, but after centuries of patience God did revoke his gift and his anger burned against them. Burning is a fitting image for God's judgment for it denotes complete destruction (*cf.* 4:4, 7:20, 15:14, 17:27, etc.). Even early in Israel's history they had experienced God's outbursts of anger against sin (Gen 19:14; Lev 10:1-2;

---

[302] Wright, *Jeremiah*, p. 197 – their hearts were set in concrete.

[303] The horn was an upward protrusion from each corner of the altar that resembled a horn. Several such altars have been dug up in Palestine and surrounding countries from the time of ancient Israel.

Num. 16:35), but the image was also a reality when Babylon destroyed Jerusalem by fire (2 Kgs 25; Jer 21:10).

The analogy is grim but must be taken seriously. The New Testament also affirms that God's judgment can be expressed in the form of fire (Matt 2:22; 18:8; Heb 10:27; 12:29; Rev 20:14). It is a terrible thing to fall into the hands of the living God (Heb 10:31).

17:5-8

Verses 5-6 stand in contrast to verses 7-8 but are bound together by the key word "trust" (vv.5, 7). The contrast is in the object of the trust. The cursed heart (v.5) trusts in men ("mere mortals"). The "curse" reminded Israel of the long list of curses in Deuteronomy 28, the consequence of disobedience. The contrast between trust in oneself or God is stark. If one does not trust in God, what are the alternatives? Very few. One might list fate, idols, myths, the self, but they all come from the same source, the human heart/mind. Jeremiah points out the ephemeral nature of the cursed heart (v. 6). It is like a shrub in a hostile environment that may exist for a while but will soon perish. One may admire their hardiness, but their fate is certain.[304]

On the other hand, those who trust in God can expect a far different outcome (vv. 7-8). The blessed heart is like a Psalm 1 person, the one who continually meditates on God's word and experiences a full, long life like a well-watered tree (Ps 1:3). Jeremiah follows many other Psalms of trust which declare their reliance on God (Ps 22:4; 26:1; 40:4). Psalm 40:4 affirms that the trusting heart does not turn from the Lord (using the same verb as in verse 5 of our text). The image of a tall tree was very effective in an area like ancient Israel where rain was scarce, and most trees were stunted from lack of water and the hot sun. A

---

[304] The language reminds us of the Dead Sea valley which was extremely hot, with high salinity in the soil, and hostile to plant and human life. See Isaiah's comments on human life (Isa 40:6-8 – like grass) and Deut 29:22-23. The latter may be the inspiration for Jeremiah's words.

tree by a spring would have been healthy, green, and fruitful.[305]

Jeremiah's contrast between the two hearts still defines the human condition. One is tempted to think that in our day people are more self-centered than ever but that may be because we do not know the past well. The trust in "mere mortals" disguised as great achievements in science or the arts or politics, is still human centered, and does not meet the deepest needs of the human heart.

17:9-11

Jeremiah now brings into his discussion of the human heart some observations from Israel's wisdom tradition, especially on the negative side. The heart has a great ability to deceive itself and others (v. 9, *cf.* Gen 6:5). Perhaps no one is more pitiful than the self-deceived, but the heart is fully capable of such delusion, of such perverseness.

Proverbs is full of warnings against the deceitful heart, the perverse heart, the proud heart, the violent heart, the heart that trusts in itself, the heart that makes its only plans.[306] This heart is self-evident, and history is full of the carnage wrought by such hearts. Who can understand these hearts? God can (v. 10; see also Ps 17:3; 139:1-6). Therefore, God apportions out justly the fruit they bear (see also Jer 11:20; 12:3; 20:12; Rom 2:6; Gal. 6:7). Often wealth becomes the goal of the perverse heart, but those who trust in it turn out to be fools (v. 11). One should not envy them but wait for their end. The obscure metaphor of verse 11 seems to imply that a bird that steals eggs to hatch will in the end, or even at mid-life, lose everything just as one will lose their

---

[305] Ps. 1 uses the image of chaff blown in the wind to contrast the wicked with the righteous which is similar to the contrast in Jeremiah but even more striking.

[306] For just a few examples see Prov 5:12; 6:14, 18; 11:20; 12:8; 16:5, 9; 19:21; 21:4; 28:26. But Proverbs also has much to say about the wise, happy, guarded, discerning, happy heart – 4:23; 10:8; 14:30; 15:13, 14; 16:21. Perhaps the best parallel is Prov 3:5-10.

wealth.³⁰⁷ Perhaps Jeremiah had in mind his contemporary, King Jehoiakim, who died at age 36 (2 Kgs 23:36).³⁰⁸ We can add that even if one dies wealthy, it is of no eternal good to them.³⁰⁹

17:12-18

Jeremiah's affirmation of praise (vv. 12-13) and his prayer (vv. 14-18) now allow us to see into his heart. It is a relief to read his doxology of praise in the midst of so much negative, even if it is brief. In the midst of doom, he affirms where he stands (*cf.* 16:19-20). He reminds us of Isaiah who was in the temple and saw God high and lofty (Isa 6:1; *cf.* Ps 2:4; 11:4). God is not only on his throne, he is the throne – he is the royal ruler of the universe, reigning in heaven and on earth (Isa 66:1). There is probably a double meaning here for God was also enthroned in the tabernacle and temple above the cherubim on the ark of the covenant in the most holy place (Exod 25:22; 30:29; Lev 16:2; I Kgs 8:29).³¹⁰ Psalm 11:4 affirms that God is both in his holy temple and on his heavenly throne.

It was fitting that God on his throne is referenced here for it was the seat of divine justice, majesty, and power (Ezek 1:26; Ps 9:7; 45:6; Isa 6:1; 66:1). The God whom Jeremiah praises is worthy, and he is the one holding his covenant people responsible.

---

³⁰⁷ Verse 10 refers in the NRSV to the mind and heart (also 11:20; 12:2; 20:12). In the Hebrew the word order is heart and kidneys. This helps us see that throughout this text the heart is referring to the will and mind, the source of our planning and intentions. The seat of emotions for ancient Israel was the kidneys or bowels, while we place emotions in the heart. Jeremiah uses kidneys here but bowels in 4:19.

³⁰⁸ We will meet Jehoiakim in chapter 36 where his blatant and arrogant opposition to God's word is on display.

³⁰⁹ See Jesus and the rich fool in Luke 12:13-21.

³¹⁰ In the future Jerusalem will be his throne – Jer 3:17. Israel did understand that God's presence on earth was an accommodation for them, for Solomon asserts that even the heavens could not hold him (1 Kgs 8:27).

The second half of verse 12 confirms that Jeremiah is thinking of God in the temple for he refers to the "place of our sanctuary" which can only be the temple (see Exod 25:22; 1 Kgs 8:6).[311] The One enthroned among them is their place of refuge, a sanctuary (*cf.* Ezek 11:16).

This enthroned One is the hope of Israel (v. 13; *cf.* 14:8). He is hope for the righteous but not for those who have forsaken God,[312] the fount of living water (2:13).[313] The motif of water and life, drought and death is strong here and elsewhere. In Amos 4:7-8 God used rain and drought as a tool to convince Israel to return to him. It did not work then, and it did not work in Jeremiah's day either. God pled for his people to seek life (Deut 30:15; Amos 5:4) but to no avail.[314] What they subsequently will experience is shame and death, not life and peace. These people are the ones whose sins are inscribed on their stony hearts (v. 1) but whose names will be written in the dust and thus easily blown away. That is, they have no future.[315]

Jeremiah follows his doxology with a prayer for vindication (vv. 14-18). The background is 15:18 in any earlier complaint when he lamented that his wounds from his enemies were incurable (*cf.* v. 18 here). God is the focus of Jeremiah's life, so he expresses confidence in his healing, but it won't come to everyone. Jeremiah has preached the word of God faithfully (v. 16) but those who have not heeded his word (v. 15) cannot expect healing. They are marked by

---

[311] The NRSV is misleading here by translating place as "shrine" for the word does not convey what Jeremiah intended to say. Most other translations do better.

[312] The verb "to turn away" occurs in verses 5 and 13 and provide a commentary on each other.

[313] The Christian thinks of Jesus's discourse on the living water in John 4:1-15.

[314] The whole of Deut 30 provides the theological grounding for Jeremiah's brief comments.

[315] The NRSV "netherworld" seems misleading. It implies *sheol* as the place of the dead, but the literal Hebrew makes sense in the context as the KJV and NIV translate. See Fretheim, *Jeremiah*, p. 260.

deep skepticism that seems to be fueled by their experience. They have not seen any results from Jeremiah's preaching so far so why should they expect that it is God's word.[316] Jeremiah could have countered that the other prophet's sermons of peace had not come true either.[317] The truth of the word of God was not important to them, only what they experienced counted as truth.[318]

Jeremiah ends his prayer with a plea for refuge (v. 17) and a wish for his persecutors (v. 18). For them he wishes shame, dismay (see 20:11), and suitable punishment which is destruction.[319] As we know from numerous sermons in the book already, Jeremiah's wish is God's plan. Still Jeremiah is intense in his plea with the emphatic "you" in verses 14b, 16b, and 17b. His appeal will be heard but he still has much to suffer, so at the present there is no answer.

1.c.ix. Unholy Sabbath – 17:19-27

Jeremiah takes up the theme of covenant breaking which he addressed specifically in chapters 7 and 11. Covenant is always in the background of Jeremiah, and he has concentrated mostly on idolatry as the major sin. In chapter 7, he listed several of the ten commandments. Now he concentrates on one specific commandment, the fourth – Sabbath breaking. His indictment has two parts: admonition and warning – verses 19-23; and blessings for obedience and warning – verses 24-27.

---

[316] Deut 18:21-22 gives the test for the true prophet. His word must come true.

[317] The exilic readers of Jeremiah would know who spoke the truth.

[318] In a certain sense it is easier to be a skeptic than to make a commitment to a cause. Israel had plenty of evidence from the covenant and their history to know that God was faithful, but they refused to believe it. Verse 19ff. in the next section gives an example of how they ignored the law. Their skepticism was not fueled by honest doubt, but disobedience.

[319] NRSV "double destruction" is a literal translation but the Hebrew idiom means punishment suitable for the offense as in 16:18.

Jeremiah addresses the nation at the "peoples' gate" (v. 19) where the royalty and people are coming and going. This is the only reference to the peoples' gate in the Old Testament and its location is unknown. In Jeremiah's day there were six gates in the outer city walls and numerous gates inside in the temple complex and palace area. City gates were the location of much community activity, especially of an official nature (see Ruth 4), so they were a natural place for proclamation. In chapter 7 he stood at the temple gate.[320]

The heart of the sermon is the warning about violating the Sabbath commandment (Exod 20:8-10; Deut 5:12-18). The Sabbath was a day of rest for man and beast, designed also to bring to memory the creation (Exod 20:11) and the exodus (Deut 5:15). It was also a holy day, sanctified by the people as they dedicated it to God. Therefore, the people were to do no work on that day. It was not specifically a day of worship but a day of rest.

Nowhere does the Law define what work might be, though a few activities are specifically forbidden such as gathering manna (early on), plowing and harvesting, kindling a fire, buying and selling, and personal pleasure.[321] Jeremiah targets doing normal business here ("burden", vv. 21-22) which seems to mean anything that was loaded on a donkey to be carried to a place of transaction. This was work. If Israelite society was involved in economic exploitation (Amos 8:5) then ignoring the Sabbath was one more example of their lack of concern for God's will for them. He willed justice and special concern for the poor, usually identified as the orphan, widow and alien (Deut 10:18, etc.). Pursuing wealth with abandon deserved the censure Jeremiah gives it. Isaiah also celebrated the joy of keeping the Sabbath as a sign of covenant faithfulness and an avenue to blessing, even for foreigners (Isa 56:1-7).

---

[320] Jeremiah also mentions other gates: the Potsherd Gate (19:2), the Benjamin Gate (20:2), the palace gates (22:2, 4), and the New Gate of the Lord's house (26:10).

[321] Exod 16:23-26; 34:21; 35:3; Amos 8:5; Isa 58:13.

What Jeremiah is attacking is a lax attitude toward the commandment which in turn indicated a lax attitude toward the law, the Covenant, and God. This indictment fits well with the other charges Jeremiah has brought against the people. The issue was not the violation of one commandment but the deeper issue of Israel's relationship with God.[322]

The Sabbath was to be sanctified, given over to God. The prohibition of work was for human benefit but essentially the day belonged to God. He had consecrated it at creation (Gen 2:2-3) and Israel was to follow suit. It was also a weekly reminder of their redemption. On the positive side permitted activities on the Sabbath included offering sacrifices, visiting sanctuaries, and singing with joy.[323]

The Christian is reminded of Jesus's many conflicts with the Jews of his day over healing and eating on the Sabbath (Matt 12:1ff.; Mark 3:2ff.; Luke 6:6ff.; 13:14ff. etc.). He was confronting a long history of legalization of the law, encumbering it with minute rule and regulations to protect it. By Jesus's day the Rabbis had defined 38 acts of work forbidden on the Sabbath. The Pharisees were particularly sensitive about the Sabbath since their ancestors had suffered death rather than break the Sabbath during the Maccabean revolt of the middle second century before Christ.

Jesus clarified his position by pointing out that the Sabbath was made for man, not man for the Sabbath (Mark 2:27) and that, ultimately, he was lord of the Sabbath (Matt 12:8). For Christians to treat Sunday like a Christian Sabbath (legalistic version), is a violation of Jesus's teaching. It also removes the joy from worshipping the resurrected Lord on resurrection day.

---

[322] The prophet Nehemiah found himself dealing with the very same issue in the post-exilic community and used almost the identical language as Jeremiah. He reminds them it was this very profaning of the Sabbath that brought God's wrath on them (Neh 13:15-18). He also refers to the loads the people were bringing into Jerusalem and these were clearly agricultural products for sale.

[323] Num 28:9-10; Isa 1:13; Ps 92; Isa 58:13.

Jeremiah 17:22

And do not carry a burden out of your houses on the sabbath or do any work, but keep the sabbath day holy, as I commanded your ancestors.

One of the tasks given to Jeremiah was to park himself at city gate and preach against the commonplace violations of the fourth commandment in Jerusalem. The people were not keeping the Sabbath.

Cities are places that never sleep. Buses run all night. Big stores never close. Restaurants are open 24/7. Clubbers do their crawls into the early morning hours. No one ever turns off the lights. While living in Los Angeles, I was amazed at how heavy the freeway traffic could be at 3 am.

Where I lived, it was common to see families dressed in orthodox Jewish garb walking together on Saturday morning, on their way to synagogue. They walk because observant Jews believe driving is a Sabbath violation. These families avoid other activities on *Shabbat*, too, things like turning on lights (considered the work of lighting a fire). Sabbath preparation on Friday afternoon includes disconnecting the light bulb in a refrigerator. Otherwise, the light would turn on when the door was opened, violating the Sabbath. Friday nights after sundown and Saturdays until sundown are periods of family and rest.

The diverse cultures of the city make it impossible to slow down and observe a city-wide day of rest together. On a personal level, this is more feasible. Without being legalistic, we should be able to take time to rest weekly, to withdraw from the endless hubbub of the city. We don't need to fill our days off with chores from dawn to dusk. We can slow down, turn off the television, put down our phones, avoid other screens, and rest without guilt.

Jewish people see two aspects to Sabbath, to "remember" and to "keep." "Remember the sabbath day and keep it holy" (Exo 20:8). They keep (observe) the Sabbath by resting and refraining from work. They remember the Sabbath by reminding themselves of their deliverance from Egypt. Christian communities that encourage personal sabbaths

> may enjoy some of the things promised by Jeremiah in this text. We can still rest and remember.
>
> *Mark S. Krause*

1.c.x. Pots, plots and Jeremiah's laments – 18:1-19:15

Chapters 18 to 20 are an editorial unit as is shown by the parallel structure in the three chapters. Pot symbolism is in 18:1-11 and 19:1-15; opposition to Jeremiah is in 18:18 and 20:1-6; Jeremiah's complaints are in 18:19-23 and 20:7-18. These parallels are supported by the repetition of key words throughout the passage. A brief example includes the word evil or disaster in 18:11 and 19:3, 15; the verb to change his mind in 18:8 and 20:16; sword in 18:21 and 19:7; 20:4; Jeremiah opposed in 18:15 and 20:1-2.[324] We see that 18:12-17 is a disputation from Judah that functions as a response to the first message from the potter.

18:1-11

The first message of pottery symbolism has two parts: the action of the potter in verses 1-4 and the application in verses 5-11. Several key words dominate the sermon: "return/repent" in verses 4, 8, and 11; "plan" in verses 8 and 11; "evil/disaster" in verses 8, 10, 11; "to make" in verses 3, 4, 6, 8, 10; and "to form" in verses 2, 3, 4, 6, 11. Many of the words appear in verse 11 which tells us the verse is a summary of the main point of the passage:

> Now, therefore, say to the people of Judah and the inhabitants of Jerusalem: Thus says the LORD: Look, I am a potter shaping evil against you and devising a plan against you. Turn now, all of you from your evil way, and amend your ways and your doings.

The sight of the potter at his wheel provides a powerful image for Jeremiah's sermon. The potter would have been a common sight in ancient Israel for pottery was one of the most useful products in use and probably every village

---

[324] See Allen, *Jeremiah*, p. 212, for more details.

would have had a potter. The potter needed a good source of water, clay and a large flat area for drying or a kiln. Pots were easily broken so the potter had a consistent market for his wares.[325] What Jeremiah saw was a potter working on his wheel with a lump of clay (vv. 3-4).[326] The potter had complete control of the clay and if the first try at making a pot did not work out for some reason, he could mash it down and start again. Perhaps Jeremiah spent some time watching a potter.[327]

The Hebrew noun for potter comes from the root verb "to form/make" (יצר, *ysr*), which is an apt verb for God, the one who formed human and animal life (Gen 2:7, 19), and who formed Jeremiah in the womb (Jer 1:5).

This image is easily transferred to divine action (vv. 5-6). God, like the potter, has complete control over his people. The image is expanded into two directions in verses 7-10, one negative and one positive. In each case God had developed a plan for nations and kingdoms, and his sovereign will would carry it out. It could be judgment, or it could be blessing based on his charge to Jeremiah in 1:10. It is noteworthy that he refers to nations and kingdoms here, not just Israel. God's sovereignty extends beyond his people to all the peoples of the world and just as they were the objects of his evangelistic concern earlier, they are consequently objects of his blessings and curses.

The application is unexpected, for the potter image suggests the potter is in full control of the clay and has no choice. In the application, it becomes clear that the nations (the clay) can influence how the potter treats them. If God

---

[325] Broken pottery is so prevalent in ancient sites that pottery sherds have become the mainstay of dating ancient ruins. Pottery changed in shape and style over the years and in different locales, so the specialist can usually estimate the date of a layer of debris in a city mound within a few years' span.

[326] The Hebrew word for the wheel has a dual ending so there were probably two wheels in action, a larger lower wheel turned by the foot which was connected to a small upper, flat wheel which held the clay.

[327] See also the potter imagery in Isa 29:19 and 41:25.

plans disaster (evil) and the nation turns or repents, then God will change his mind and not bring the disaster (vv. 7-8). In the same way if God plans to bless and the nation does evil, then God will change his mind and not bring blessing (vv. 9-10). These two scenarios set up the application in verse 11 – God has planned evil/disaster against his people which they can avert if the repent and turn to him ("amend" comes from the root "to do good," יטב, *yṭb*; see 7:3, 5).

This text prompts reflection in several directions. It shows that God is responsive to human actions. He does "change his mind" when confronted by obedience or disobedience.[328] We first encounter this aspect in Genesis 6:6 where he expresses he regret that he had made mankind because they were so sinful. He also regretted making Saul king (1 Sam 15:11). It was this aspect of his character that Moses appealed to when he asked God not to destroy Israel after the golden calf event (Exod 32:12). This demonstrates his relational side. He is a personal God, intimately involved with his creation and his people, and responds to obedience and sin. Because of this, two crucial teachings of the Bible, repentance and prayer, are possible. This is not about God's character, which does not change, but about his work in the world and how he proceeds in carrying out his will. He is not the inflexible, immutable God of the philosopher, but the loving Father of his people.

In the long term, God's will for the world will be carried out (Rev 21-22), but in the short term, his people have some say in the future. The decision for or against God "determines" what will happen to his people and to nations and kingdoms – blessing or curse, building and planting or breaking down and destroying. The readers of Jeremiah in exile would understand how their disobedience had brought them into exile, but they could also see that obedience in exile could reverse God's judgment and perhaps

---

[328] The Hebrew verb is *nḥm* (נחם) and is translated in a variety of ways – relent, be sorry, change one's mind.

lead to restoration. Jeremiah will give them more hope in chapters 29 and 31-34.

We must be careful how we interpret the plans of God here. His plans focused on the big picture and were specifically related to Deuteronomy 28 and the covenant blessings and curses. His plan for Israel always was that he would bless them in wonderful ways if they obeyed, but punish them if they disobeyed. Within these parameters, there were many ways open for Israel and the nations to be within the will of God. Micah defined this as "to do justice, to love kindness, and walk humbly with your God" (6:8). Deuteronomy defined it as to "love God with all your heart, with all your soul, and with all your might" (Deut 6:5). Moses appealed to the people to choose life (Deut 30:19). This meant obedience to the covenant, which he assured them was not hard. Consequently, this is not a text about what kind of plan God might have for an individual Israelite, or an individual Christian. There is nothing in the text to even hint at such a conclusion.[329] Individuals are not in view but Israel and the nations and the modern audience is the church, not individual Christians.

18:12-17

Israel also has a plan (v. 12). Jeremiah's warning is of "no use." All they desire is to continue to walk in "the stubbornness of their evil will."[330] This is a cry of despair.[331] Why they would respond to God's grace this way is unclear. Had sin as a way of life become so ingrained that they saw no way out? Or where they so guilt ridden that they had no

---

[329] Yet an Old Testament scholar says this: "Just as the potter works with clay until he has shaped the pot the way he wants it, so God has a plan for each believer's life (see 29:11). He does not reject us when we fail but continues his patient work until he makes us what he wants us to be (Phil 1:6)." (F. B. Huey, *Jeremiah, Lamentations* (Nashville: Broadman Press, 1993) p. 181. Here is a case of how a certain theological perspective seems to trump exegesis and the plain meaning of the text. See further my comments on chapter 29 below.

[330] See also 7:24; 9:12-13; 11:8; 13:10; 16:12.

[331] Isa 57:10 reflects a different mindset.

hope (so 2:25)? Or where they just impervious to God's word?

Whatever the reason, there was no parallel among the nations (v. 13; *cf.* 2:10-11) or in nature (v. 14).[332] Israel's stubbornness was unique. They had strayed off the path (v. 15) and brought horror to the land (v. 16; see Lam. 2:15-16). Therefore, just like the destroying, burning east wind that roared in during the summer, God would destroy them. This was a sure sign that he had turned his back on them (v. 17).[333] Jeremiah had been preaching this for years. The exilic readers would look back on this despair and perhaps wonder how they could have been so stubborn, especially as they discover in exile that God still holds out a future for them (ch. 29).

18:18-23

Just as the people had their own plans opposing God (v. 12), they have their own plans[334] (or plots) opposing Jeremiah (v. 18). They appeal to the three main classes of leadership within the nation – the priest, the wise man, and the prophet (a fourth, the king is not mentioned). The priest was entrusted with teaching the law and overseeing all the sacrifices and rituals at the temple. The wise were consulted for instruction in how to live an ordered life (*cf.* the book of Proverbs) and had great respect.[335] The prophet was called by God to be his representative to the people. Ironically, Jeremiah was also a prophet but obviously not they kind they wanted. They had apparently heard Jeremiah's sermons when he condemned all three classes (2:8; 5:13; 6:13-15; 8:8-13; 14:13-16) and especially the prophets who preached peace. Hence, arrayed against Jeremiah

---

[332] V. 14 is difficult to translate as there seems to be some textual confusion. The NRSV translation represents a widely accepted resolution. See its footnotes and compare other translations.

[333] Num 6:24-26 is a beautiful prayer asking for God's face to shine on them.

[334] The same Hebrew root is used in vv.11, 12, and 18.

[335] The wise were among the elders who are represented in 19:1.

were all the power groups in the society as well as the people.

It was a nasty coalition for they were plotting to attack him with the tongue (NRSV, "bring charges"; see the footnote), that is to lie. This was the tongue of 9:3 that shot arrows of lies. The strongest attack against truth is the lie, because people will hear what they want to hear.[336] They did not want to hear Jeremiah, but the real lie was the message of the other prophets that peace was coming or that the exile would be short (Jer 28:1-3; 29:21-23). Despite Jeremiah's message of truth, they preferred a lie and to lie. Their ultimate plan was to kill Jeremiah (v. 23).

As in the other cases Jeremiah laments to God (vv. 19-23; see 11:18-20; 12:1-6; 15:15-18). His complaint is marked at the beginning and end by references to the pit (vv. 20, 22). This was a common metaphor to describe the machinations of the opponents of the faithful (*cf.* Ps 35:7; 119:85). For Jeremiah, this took on reality when later he was actually thrown into a pit by his enemies (Jer 38:6).

Jeremiah had difficulty understanding how the good he had done in God's name could rebound back upon him as plots and suffering, that is, evil (v. 20). This was not just Jeremiah's question but also that of many other sufferers (Ps 35:12; 38:19-20; 109:1-5). Psalm 109 could have been Jeremiah's words:

> [T]hey reward me evil for good,
> and hatred for my love. (Ps 109:5)

Is there a moral order of recompense in the world or is the idea of God's justice an illusion? The question remains with us, but we must remember that in the long run God can redeem this kind of evil and turn it into good. Joseph expressed this truth to his brothers (Gen 50:20).[337]

---

[336] As we are reminded every election cycle, politicians are very good at this. They get away with it because people want to believe them.

[337] Paul put his definitive stamp on how God works in Rom 8:28.

At one time, Jeremiah had pled with God to turn away his judgment (v. 20; cf. 7:16; 11:14; 14:11) but now he wants justice. He wants God to carry out the sentence of death that he, in his anger, had promised in 7:20; 11:12, 15-16, and elsewhere. He envisions the battle siege against the land and Jerusalem, and the subsequent slaughter and famine (vv. 21-22). Jeremiah's words had already been spoken by God (6:11-12; 9:20-21; 14:12; 15:2, 7-9), so he thought his plea for justice was grounded firmly in God's will.

Wright raises an important question for the Christian: can we pray the prayer of Jeremiah?[338] The answer is no. First, we are not in Jeremiah's position as a called prophet of God who has faithfully delivered his message and been rejected and severely persecuted. Nor have we prayed continually for this apostate people. Jeremiah's condition is unique to him, his situation, and his relationship to God. Further, the teaching from the New Testament is clear: love our enemies (Matt 5:43-44; Rom 112:14, 19-21). Also, Jesus's example on the cross is our paradigm as well. Furthermore, Stephen's words instruct us to forgive our enemies (Acts 7:20). Our mission is to live out the love of Christ. We trust God to mete out justice (Rom 12:17-21). Our task is to overcome evil with good!

19:1-15

God instructs Jeremiah to undertake another symbolic action involving a pot and potter. The accompanying message is given in three parts at two locations. The first message (vv. 3-9) is delivered before the main action of pot breaking at the Potsherd gate. The second message (vv. 11-13) comes after the pot breaking. The third message (v. 15) is delivered back in the temple area.

In the first part of the drama Jeremiah buys a pot (v. 1), taking with him some elders and priests. This time the pot is a finished one, not the raw clay of chapter 18. It is a pot with a long neck which was common in ancient Israel for

---

[338] Wright, *Jeremiah*, p. 219.

storing liquids. Its Hebrew name was *baqbuq* (בקבק), an onomatopoetic word coming from the sound made as the liquid poured out of the spout. The name provides a connection to verse seven where the main verb "make void" comes from the Hebrew sound-alike root *bqq*.

Jeremiah's companions were from the well-known priestly class and the elders, an important group with civic responsibilities but not normally among the class of leaders attacked by Jeremiah. Elders had a long history of important roles in Israel's history. They were with Moses at Sinai (Exod 24:4), were a part of Joshua's covenant renewal (Josh 24:31), and they were granted important legal functions in the law (Deut 18:12; 21:2ff., 22:16ff.). Some came to Jeremiah's defense after the riot at his temple sermon (Jer 26:17). They were also leaders in the exile (Jer 29:1).

Apparently, these men were witnesses to Jeremiah's message so they could report back to the people. The Potsherd Gate's location is unknown, but its name suggests it was near the place where broken pottery was discarded.[339] The Valley of Hinnom was known as the place of refuse on the south side of the city (*cf.* 7:30-34) and as a place of sacrifice to Molech which Josiah had destroyed (2 Kgs 23:10). Therefore, their destination was an unpleasant one, the city dump – an unsavory place for a word from the Lord – but it provided a proper backdrop for Jeremiah's grim messages.

Jeremiah's initial message did not have new content though the horrors of Israel's apostasy are starkly described. They could not get much further away from the will of God than to practice child sacrifice (vv. 4-5). Such a thing is almost beyond imagination, even God's (v. 5; *cf.* 7:31) and forbidden in the law (Lev 18:21; Deut 12:30; 18:10; *cf.* Ps 106:37-38).[340]

---

[339] Perhaps it was the Dung Gate of Neh 2:13.

[340] See comments on chapter 7:30ff. above. Did they perhaps repeat the trite assertion – all religions are the same and worship the same God? Not only was it false but the contradiction between Israel's worship practices and other religions could not have starker.

The result will be destruction by an army (v. 7) and death by famine and sword. The siege will result in cannibalism (v. 9), a fact recorded about the fall of Samaria in 722 BCE to the Assyrians (2 Kgs 6:28-29) and Jerusalem to the Babylonians in 587 BCE (Lam 4:10). This was one of the covenant curses of Deuteronomy 28 (vv. 53, 55, 57). The exilic readers would have recalled the horrors of the latter event. The destruction would be so great that the world would be astonished (v. 8; *cf.* 1 Sam 3:1; 2 Kgs 21:12).

After Jeremiah broke the pot at God's instruction, he delivered the second message (vv. 10-13). The action here contrasts to the action of chapter 18. In chapter 18 when the clay did not respond well to the potter's hand, he would rework it. The implication as spelled out in the following sermon was that Israel had a chance to change their ways (repent) and return to God. The implication in chapter 19 is that the broken pot (Israel) cannot be put back together (v. 11). All hope was gone. There was no turning back. They had bought into the culture of death and death was the only possible outcome (v. 6; *cf.* 7:31-32). There would be so much death there would be no room for bodies (as in 7:30-34) as the holy city became a cemetery.

Jeremiah gave the third message back in the temple court so that all the people could hear (v. 14). It was brief because it was not new. God was going to keep his promise of bringing disaster on them because they were stubborn and refused to obey him (v. 15).

1.c.xi. Pashur persecutes Jeremiah – 20:1-18
20:1-6

The response to Jeremiah's sermon in chapter 20 parallels the response in 18:18, but it is even more severe and is initiated by a high temple official, Pashur.[341] He was perhaps second in power to the High Priest (*cf.* 2 Kgs 25:18; Jer 29:26-27). His official business was to keep order in the temple and Jeremiah was preaching a coming disorder. Although Jeremiah was God's prophet, Pashur's devotion

---

[341] The Pashurs of 20:1 and 38:1 are not the same person.

to stability and the law blinded him to the truth. In fact, he was one of those who spoke lies in God's name (v. 6). He probably was not just a priest, but one of the false prophets who preached peace, a dangerous and self-serving misreading of the times (*cf.* 6:13-14; 8:10-11; 23:26-29). Once a lie is spread it is impossible to retrieve it and makes it harder for the truth to get heard.

Pashur's way to silence the truth was through beating and torture (v. 2). He did more than strike Jeremiah (NRSV), he had him beaten or flogged (most other translations). Then he put him in some sort of confinement usually translated as "stocks." This is usually thought to be an apparatus that bound both the hands and feet which resulted in a painful twisting of the body.[342]

Pashur discovered that although he could shut up Jeremiah in stocks, he could not shut him up (vv. 4-6).[343] Consequently, Pashur received a direct word from Jeremiah that rebounded to the whole nation. He underwent a name change that involved a new status and destiny.[344] His new name was *maggor-misabib* (מגור מסביב), "terror on every side." His destiny would become that of his friends and the whole nation. Babylon would invade the land and bring the terror of war and devastation (see ch. 21). Jeremiah had been saying this for some time but here he personalizes it to Pashur and names Babylon as the destroying "foe from the north" for the first time (*cf.* 4:6 and chap. 6). Terror was coming to Pashur and Israel from every direction (6:25). As much as Pashur and Jeremiah's foes might try to intimidate Jeremiah by terror (v. 10), they would be destroyed by it.[345]

---

[342] The Hebrew word is used only here and in Jer 29:28 and 2 Chr 16:10.

[343] Wright, *Jeremiah*, p. 223.

[344] Compare for example Jacob's name change to Israel in Gen 32:22-28.

[345] Jeremiah also uses the phrase for Egypt and Kedar/Hazor in 46:5 and 49:29.

The one later reference to the priestly leadership in Jerusalem lists a different priest – Zephaniah in Jeremiah 29:25. We can surmise that Pashur did die in the exportation of the leaders (2 Kgs 24:12-16) or shortly afterwards. This is only one of several examples of authorities who had opposed God's prophet and lost. The prophets Elijah (1 Kgs 18), Micaiah (1 Kgs 22), and Amos (Amos 7) all faced the opposition of kings or priests and prevailed. Jeremiah also prevailed, but his immediate response was not that of a winner but of a man in deep despair.

20:7-18

Jeremiah's response to Pashur's persecution is immediate and visceral. He questions his relationship with God and curses the day he was born. His despair comes from his long years of faithful service and a message that has brought isolation and death threats. This was not at all what he anticipated at his call in chapter one, although God warned him at the time. The gist of his lament is that he wanted to recall his calling.

We have already examined six of Jeremiah's complaints and laments (*cf.* 11:18-20; 12:1-4; 15:10, 15-18; 17:14-18; 18:18-23). This section contains two more complaints (vv. 7-13 and 14-18) and these are the last and most bitter of them all. They are the most difficult texts in the whole book to understand and key words and ideas are hard to interpret. The first complaint takes the familiar form of the lament that we find in the Psalms: complaint (vv. 7-10), petition (v. 11), statement of trust (v. 12), and praise (v. 13).[346]

Jeremiah's complaint is shocking – God has enticed and overpowered him (v. 7). Just how God enticed him has caused much discussion. The Hebrew verb (פתה, *pth*) is used in a variety of contexts in the Old Testament. It is used of seduction of a virgin in the law (Exod 22:16), enticement into idolatry (Deut 11:16), a lying spirit enticing Ahab (1 Kgs 22:20-22) and of the Lord deceiving a prophet (Ezek 14:9). Hosea 2:14 uses it in a positive sense of God

---

[346] See Pss 3, 7, 13, and 26 as examples.

alluring Israel back into the wilderness to reconnect with him.

How has God enticed or deceived Jeremiah? He gave him fair warning at his call that he would face opposition (1:17-19). Verse 8 suggests that perhaps the content of the message was unexpected. Every time Jeremiah preached it was to announce, "violence and destruction." For a prophet, or anyone, to continually have a negative message would be depressing. His sermons in chapters 18 and 19 are a good example. Certainly, the reception of the message engendered despair as well. We have seen that his life was threatened, he was ridiculed, and he was finally put in the stocks. Also, there is more to come. Who could bear up under years (20 years, perhaps) of such a life?

God not only enticed Jeremiah, he overpowered him and naturally prevailed (v. 7). Of course, Jeremiah did not have a chance in a contest of power with God. The verb "prevail" is the key word in this lament. It may not seem like it to Jeremiah but the fact that he could not prevail against God was to his benefit. His enemies tried to entice and prevail over him (v. 10), but since God was on his side they could not (v. 11). Their destiny was shame, failure and dishonor, so Jeremiah was vindicated, and he bursts out in praise (v. 13).

There is one more key use of the verb "prevail." Part of Jeremiah's anguish was the power of the word of God within him. He did not like the message he was continually preaching because it brought him derision (v. 8). Perhaps this was partly because nothing of what he said had happened yet, however, he could not contain this word. It burned in him like a fire and he had to let it out or be consumed.[347] The power of the word was too much. It burst out against his wishes. He could not prevail against it.[348]

---

[347] Compare this thought with 15:16 where God's words were a joy and delight to Jeremiah and he ate them.

[348] The NRSV translates the verb as "I cannot" at the end of v. 9 and thus masks the verbal connection vv. 7, 10 and 11.

Jeremiah's despair was fed not only by the stocks of Pashur but the threats of his close friends (v. 10). They apply to him the words Jeremiah spoke against Pashur. There will be "terror on every side" for him.[349] The irony is that these people in the Hebrew text are called "men of peace" but they are anything but that. They were no better than his worst enemies but since they were close to him they can better find ways to trip him up.[350]

Despite Jeremiah's despair, his trust in God pushes to the foreground. He ends this complaint with a petition and a praise (vv. 12-13). His petition is the same he made in 11:20 (see comments there). Since God is the just judge and Jeremiah's cause is just, he can trust God to do the right thing, so he leaves it in God's hands. The despair of the moment eventually gives way to hope, and as he looks ahead in hope, he sees the divine deliverance that is sure to come (*cf.* Ps 13:5-6). Verse 13 is the high point of all of Jeremiah's complaints. Many of the lament Psalms were probably recited in the temple. Perhaps that is where Jeremiah is saying these words (*cf.* 19:14). The experience of just being there would overpower the lamenter and ultimately the lament has to turn to praise.

Therefore, the next words out of Jeremiah's mouth are shocking (vv. 14-18). How can he go from praise to curse? These mood swings, however, are common in laments. The emotion and pathos are not suppressed for fear of offending God. God knows the heart, so one might as well be honest.

This lament is marked by two key words: curse and womb. Jeremiah focuses on his birth and wishes he had never been born (*cf.* 15:10 for a milder wish). He cursed the day of his birth, a conviction he shared with Job (Job 3:1-2). He also cursed the man who carried the news of the birth of a baby boy, an event that usually occasioned great joy and rejoicing (vv. 15-16; *cf.* Ruth 4:10, 13-17). A son ensured the family name would continue and the father could pass on

---

[349] Compare Ps 31:13 which has a similar complaint.

[350] The parallels between Jeremiah and Jesus again seem obvious.

the inheritance. Jeremiah pronounced a curse on that day, which was equal to aligning the day with all those things God had cursed – such as the ground (Gen 3:17), those who refused Abraham's blessing (Gen 12:3), or the disobedient Israelites (Deut 28:16-19). Jeremiah did not curse his parents, though, which was a capital offense (Exod 21:17) or God which would have been blasphemy (Exod 22:28). Job resisted that temptation too although enticed by his wife (Job 2:9-10).

Jeremiah ends this complaint with three references to the womb (vv. 17-19) which recalls chapter 1:5 where God informed Jeremiah that he formed him in the womb. Jeremiah wanted to cancel out that divine act! He would have rather died in the womb than to been born to the life of toil and strife that he experienced. Job felt the same way (Job 3:11-12). Jeremiah calls into question God's action and selection of him to his calling. He wants to undo his life and thereby God's mission. Fortunately, that did not happen, and God's word prevailed (Isa 40:8). Ultimately, so did Jeremiah.

From the larger editorial perspective of the book of Jeremiah these verses form an *inclusio* with chapter one with the use of the key word womb. This is a common Hebrew rhetorical style to call attention to major units in the text. Therefore, many scholars think that chapters 1-20 form a unit and reflect the earliest preaching of Jeremiah.

Despite Jeremiah's anguish his lament provides a foundation for reflecting on the power of the word of God. It consumed Jeremiah and he could not hold it in. A Christian reflection on this word is informed by many NT texts. The Hebrews author asserts that it is living and active and a two-edged sword (4:12). Paul points out that it is the sword of the spirit (Eph 6:17). He admonishes Timothy to preach it (2 Tim 4:2). Peter, quoting Isaiah, affirms that it stands forever (1 Pet 1:23-25). Most important for the Christian, however, is that Jesus is the Word, the full and final revelation of God. He reveals God not in words but in his person and is the focal point of all the words of Scripture. The history of the church witnesses to the power of this Word.

1.d. Prophecies Against King and Prophet (21:1-25:14)

This next major section in the book of Jeremiah is addressed to the kings and prophets in Judah. These were the power groups in Judah that consistently opposed Jeremiah. The section begins and ends with an affirmation that Nebuchadrezzar[351] of Babylon is coming to destroy Jerusalem and it cannot be avoided (21:1-10 and 25:1-14). Several of Judah's kings are addressed by name. The last four kings of Judah after Josiah's death were Jehoahaz, Jehoiakim, Jehoiachin,[352] and Zedekiah (2 Kgs 23:31-24:12). In chapter 22 Jehoahaz is called Shallum (22:11) and Jehoiachin is called Coniah (22:24). The dates of these four kings were from 609 to 587 BCE. Jehoahaz and Jehoiachin each reigned only three months. This large section is not in chronological order for chapter 21 is addressed to Zedekiah and chapter 25 to Jehoiakim. Another king is also addressed, the coming righteous Branch of David (23:5-8).

1.d.i. Word to Zedekiah – Surrender – 21:1-14

If chapters 1-20 contain the early sermons of Jeremiah as many suggest, then some time has passed from the sermon in chapter 20 to this word to Zedekiah, probably about 15 years.[353] Nebuchadrezzar placed Zedekiah on the throne in 597 BCE after the first Babylonian invasion of Judah when

---

[351] There are two spellings of the king's name – with an ending of -rezzar or -nezzar. The former is closer to the Babylonian name which occurs 31 times. The name with the ending of -nezzar occurs six times in Jer. and 17 times elsewhere. Most English translations use the -nezzar ending (see the NIV, NAS, ESV) but the KJV and NRSV use the -rezzar ending. Nebuchadrezzar was king in Babylon from 605 to 562 BC. His early years are recorded in the Babylonian Chronicles which gives us extra-biblical attestation of his exploits. He was a religious man and rebuilt and built many temples throughout his country. He also built he famous hanging gardens of Babylon for his wife.

[352] Jehoiachin is referenced in the Babylonian records.

[353] Jer 36:1 refers to the fourth year of Jehoiakim as the time when Jeremiah dictated his early sermons to Baruch, which would be 605 BC

he took Jehoiachin and many leading citizens into captivity. Zedekiah was Jehoiachin's uncle and the third son of Josiah. Nebuchadrezzar expected him to be a loyal subject, which he was for several years. Eventually he rebelled and turned to Egypt (Jer 52:3; Ezek 17:12-15) which brought the wrath of Nebuchadrezzar on Jerusalem resulting in its final destruction in 587 BCE. Zedekiah was a weak king and was not blessed with wise counsel. All the experienced palace leaders were gone, and he received conflicting advice – resist Babylon, give in, ask the Egyptians for help. He was interested in Jeremiah and questioned him four different times (here and 37:3-10, 17-21; 38:14-18). But he was unable to protect him from others in his palace (38:1-6).

21:1-10

Jerusalem was under Babylonian siege and Zedekiah hoped for a miracle, so he sent two emissaries, Pashur and Zephaniah, to Jeremiah in hopes of getting a good word from the Lord (vv. 1-2). This Pashur is not the one in chapter 20 but he was not friendly toward Jeremiah either (see 38:1-6). Zephaniah was the chief of security for the temple (29:25-26). After the fall of Jerusalem, he was executed by the Babylonians (Jer. 52:26-27). Zedekiah sought a "wonderful deed" to deliver Jerusalem. Maybe he was looking for a miracle like what God used to rescue Israel from Egypt (Exod 3:20 – same Hebrew word; celebrated in Ps 77:10-20), or one of the miracles of the conquest. More likely he was thinking of God's intervention against the Assyrians in Isaiah's day when God destroyed the whole army outside of Jerusalem (Isa 37:33-38; see the promise in Isa 29:14).

The answer was a great shock to Zedekiah. God was not only not going to perform a miracle; he was going to orchestrate the Babylonian victory. He would first make the defenders outside the walls retreat into the city (v. 4) and then he would vent his anger and wrath against the people and city.[354] This was not the time for rescue but for destruction. Nebuchadrezzar was God's servant carrying out his will (Jer 25:9; 27:6). God had persistently warned the people to turn back to him, but they refused (Jer. 7:13, 25; 11:7) and continued to rebel and disobey.

God at one time fought for Israel, but now he would fight against them (v. 5). His mighty power he used to deliver them from Egypt (his outstretched arm and mighty hand – Exod 3:20; 6:1, 6; Deut 4:34) would be turned against them. As he struck down the Egyptians he would now strike down Israel (v. 6). As he struck Egypt with pestilence he would now strike them (v. 7). The Holy Warrior celebrated in song in Exodus 15 for winning victory on Israel's behalf was now on the other side. This was a devastating message.

The people would first suffer the consequences of a siege which included disease from famine and bad water (v. 6, see 52:6). Then they would experience death as the conquering army entered the city: the terrible triad of pestilence, sword, and famine (vv. 7, 9). Those who survived that horror could only anticipate execution.

Zedekiah tried to avoid this fate by escaping from the city and fleeing east toward the Jordan, hoping to gain safety and asylum in one of the trans-Jordan countries (Jer 39:4-7; 52:8; 2 Kgs 25:4-7). But he was caught, his sons executed, his eyes put out, and he was taken to Babylon where he disappears from the historical record.

Jeremiah told his audience that the only way to survive was to surrender to the Babylonians. God again held out life and death for them as he did in Deuteronomy 30 (v. 8). Here the choice is an immediate and real matter of life and death, not a call to covenant obedience. For this advice and later actions, Jeremiah was considered a traitor (Jer 38:4-5; 37:11-14). But he was right. The only way to life and escaping the coming onslaught was surrender. History bore him out. Those who did surrender were taken to Babylon

---

[354] See Jer 52:7. Near the end of the siege the army fled the city during the night.

and there permitted to settle in their own community (Jer 29; Ezek 1:1). God was still concerned about his people's future, but not in the way they hoped. That was important for the exiles to know because it was easy for them to think otherwise.[355]

Several times Jeremiah had spoken of God's wrath burning against Israel like a fire (4:4; 11:16; 15:14) as a symbol of judgment. But the Babylonian's destruction of Jerusalem made that symbol became a reality. They burned the city and temple with fire (v. 10; 39:8). This terrible picture is revisited in Jeremiah 39 and 52.

Jeremiah had already advanced the idea that God would use the Babylonians as his instrument to carry out his judgment on his people (chs. 4 and 6). This presented a theological problem to the people. Psalm 89 represents a lengthy meditation on God's loving kindness toward Israel, the consternation caused by his judgment, and the puzzlement of the length of this judgment (Ps 89:56, "How long …?").

Jeremiah 21:10

For I have set my face against this city for evil and not for good, says the Lord: it shall be given into the hands of the king of Babylon, and he shall burn it with fire.

History tells us that cities rise and fall. Why?

An example from my lifetime is the city of Detroit. World War II and its need for wartime manufacturing boosted Detroit to become the fourth largest city in the United States with a population approaching 2,000,000 residents in 1950. Since then, Detroit's population has dipped under 700,000 with vast tracts of blighted housing, abandoned factory buildings, and empty spaces. The loss of jobs and population forced the city into insolvency, declaring bankruptcy in 2013. One observer attributed Detroit's fall to a

---

[355] Fretheim, *Jeremiah*, p. 309.

combination of high taxes, poor services, oppressive regulations, and outright corruption.[356]

During the city's bankruptcy woes, some creditors sought relief through the sales of art treasures from the city's world-renown Detroit Institute of Arts. This was averted through a "grand bargain" through which various sources agreed to contribute approximately $800,000,000 to facilitate the transfer of ownership to the museum's private foundation.[357]

Through Jeremiah, God promised to deliver Jerusalem into the hands of the king of Babylon. When the Babylonians broke into the city, its population was decimated, and its treasures were looted and carried to a foreign land. The Bible understands this great tragedy to be orchestrated by the Lord, both before and after it happened.

It would be simplistic and careless to equate the fall of Detroit with the fall of Jerusalem, but it is also naïve to assume that God does not have a hand in the rise and fall of modern cities. Cities need a prophetic voice to issue an ongoing warning against injustice and corruption, a voice those called to ministry in urban centers should be providing.

Mark S. Krause

21:11-14

These verses provide a bridge between 21:1-8 and 22:1-30. Both sections address the last kings of Israel and their shortcomings. Verses 11-14 offers us the short version of

---

[356] Scott Beyer, "Why Had Detroit Continued to Decline," *Forbes*, July 31, 2018, accessed at https://www.forbes.com/sites/scottbeyer/2018/07/31/why-has-detroit-continued-to-decline/#7f8bf96b3fbe

[357] Randy Kennedy, "'Grand Bargain' Saves the Detroit Institute of Arts," *New York Times,* November 7, 2014, accessed at https://www.nytimes.com/2014/11/08/arts/design/grand-bargain-saves-the-detroit-institute-of-arts.html

the message with repetition of themes familiar from elsewhere. The addressees are the royal house (house of David) in verses 11-12, Jerusalem in verse 13,[358] and the royal palace in verse 14. However, Jerusalem and the palace are metonyms for the king.[359] Hence, the king is condemned for lack of justice, a false sense of security in the city, and knowing the right thing to do but not doing it.

The imperatives of verse 12 offer hope for the king. There is still time to turn aside the wrath of Babylon (and God) by attending to justice.

Justice was the primary duty of the king and is attested throughout the Old Testament. Deuteronomy's instructions for kingship focused on the importance of the king obeying the law (Deut 17:14-20).[360] An important part of the law was promoting justice (Exod 23:1-9; Deut 16:18-20). The theme of justice also permeates the Psalms (12, 58, 72, 101) and many proverbs (Prov 14:31; 16:12-13; 17:5, etc.). David was noted for reigning with justice (2 Sam 8:15). It characterized Solomon early on (1 Kgs 3 – see the conclusion in v. 28; 10:9), but he eventually failed and passed his failure on to his son (1 Kgs 12:1-15). After that, only the kings Asa, Jehoshaphat and Josiah achieved this ideal (2 Chr 15, 19; Jer 22:15-16). This call to social responsibility ran counter to the temptation for governments to become self-serving and self-seeking.[361] Unfortunately the latter kings of Israel failed (5:28) and all they could anticipate was God's fiery wrath (vv. 12, 14). Zedekiah was looking for a wonderful deed (v. 2), a demonstration of God's power. Jeremiah suggests the wonderful deed was within the power of the king – doing justice.[362]

---

[358] The NIV puts Jerusalem in the text although it is not in the Hebrew

[359] Just as the White House is a metonym for the President.

[360] See Hall, *Deuteronomy*, pp.278-284.

[361] Brueggemann, *To Pluck Up*, p. 185. The subject of kingship and justice recurs in 22:3 where justice is clearly defined.

[362] *Ibid.*

The observations of verses 13 and 14 conclude there is no hope for Israel. Jerusalem the city may think she is safe and secure (v. 13) high above valleys on a rocky plateau but she is not. She may think no one can swoop down from the Mt. of Olives to the east and conquer her, but Nebuchadrezzar will do that very thing. She may take great pride in her magnificent buildings, especially the one called the Forest of Lebanon (1 Kgs 7:2; 10:17, 21) but God will burn it with the fire of his judgment (v. 14).

1.d.ii. *Against the Kings – 22:1-30*

Chapter 22 features the word of the Lord addressed to the last three kings in Judah before Zedekiah. It begins with a word to the king(s) in general (vv. 1-9), then a word to Shallum (vv. 10-12), Jehoiakim (vv. 13-19), and Coniah (vv. 24-30). A brief word to Jerusalem, the seat of the kings, is inserted in verses 20-23 and a brief reference to Josiah is embedded in the address to Jehoiakim (vv. 15b-16). The chapter is characterized by a description of the Old Testament concept of justice (vv. 3 and 16; *cf.* v. 13) and a lengthy list of the sins of the kings (vv. 13-17).

A brief historical review will be helpful (see the Introduction). Josiah was killed by the Egyptians in 609 BCE and his son, Jehoahaz, succeeded him. He reigned only three months and then was taken to Egypt by Pharaoh Neco where he died (2 Kgs 23:31-34). Neco put his brother Eliakim on the throne and changed his name to Jehoiakim. Jehoiakim reigned from 609-598 BCE. Nebuchadrezzar defeated Egypt in in 605 BCE and took control of Judah as well. In 601-600 BCE, Nebuchadrezzar tried in invade Egypt and suffered a loss. This perhaps encouraged Jehoiakim to ally himself with Egypt. Nebuchadrezzar regrouped and attack Jerusalem in 597 BCE. Jehoiakim died and Jehoiachin succeeded him but reigned only three months before Jerusalem was conquered and he was taken into exile. He lived there in prison for 37 years and then was released and put on a stipend (2 Kgs 25:27-30).[363] Nebuchadrezzar

---

[363] He is referred to in Babylonian records as the King of Judah.

put Jehoiachin's uncle, Mattaniah on the throne and renamed him Zedekiah. Therefore, the material in this chapter moves backward about twenty years to address the three kings preceding Zedekiah of chapter 21.

22:1-9

This section addresses the "King of Judah" (v. 1) but the singular king represents all the kings, especially the three named ones in the following verses. The kings have one major responsibility, to do justice and righteousness. This is defined immediately as protecting the lower classes of people who are easily oppressed because of their lack of financial resources (v. 3). The specific classes named are the robbed, the alien, the orphan, and the widow.[364] The failure to do justice was a failure of leadership. The kings were obligated to obey the law (*cf.* Deut 17:14-20), and at the heart of the law, especially as expressed in Deuteronomy, was taking care of the oppressed. The orphan, widow, and alien were the defenseless ones in the society, the marginalized. They had no one to defend them or protect them. The orphan had no father and the widow had no husband. Naomi and Ruth in the book of Ruth demonstrate the plight of the widow.

The alien was an individual who had chosen for a variety of reasons to seek refuge in the Israelite society and thus had no larger family structure for support. Aliens were different from the foreigner for they had settled in the land. Foreigners were just passing through or were only in the land for trade or commerce. God loved these aliens (Deut 10:19) and Israel was to love them also. As foreigners, they had lost their rights they would have had in their homeland. Abraham was an alien in the land (Gen 15:13) and the people of Israel were aliens in Egypt, so they were to have regard for aliens among them. The law made provision for al-

---

[364] See the same list in Jer 7:3-7. See comments there and especially the other OT texts listed.

iens to participate in the religious life and they were obligated to the law's demand (*cf.* Lev 19:10; Deut 14:19; Lev 25:6; Lev 17:8-16; Exod 12:48; Lev 24:22).[365]

Both the kings and judges were expected to administer the law justly. If they did not, then the classes mentioned had little hope for justice or that they would be treated well. If justice did not prevail at the top, the likely hood that it would permeate society was slim. How the kings could get caught up in their own selfish pursuits of wealth is described in the following verses 13-17.[366] It is a sad story of the kingship from day of Solomon with few exceptions.

Two conditions are contrasted. If they obeyed, then they could live with a stable and long dynasty of kingship under God's blessing (v. 4). If they disobeyed it would bring destruction to the land (vv. 5-7), and disdain from the nations, who even as pagans, would recognize that a broken covenant caused the demise of Israel (vv. 8-9). The monarchy was subservient to the Torah and not vice versa. Kings ruled under God, not under their own authority. There were two foundations on which the monarchy could exist, the ethical and the theological (vv. 3 and 9). These were not in conflict but complementary.[367] Even the most powerful in society must pay attention to the ethical demands of the moral order or they will bring their own destruction. God will not be mocked.

One of the glories of the monarchy was the great temple and palace complex that David and especially Solomon had built in Jerusalem. Solomon contracted with Hiram of Tyre to provide the material and artisans. The best material was

---

[365] The alien concept easily became a metaphor for the life of the people of God on this earth in both the OT and the NT – Ps 39:12; 119:19; 1 Pet 1:17; 2:11.

[366] The Hebrew word for violence in v. 3 is חָמָס (*ḥāmas*). The Arabic word is the same which gives its name to the modern Palestinian terrorist group.

[367] Brueggemann, *To Pluck Up*, p. 190.

the wood from the huge cedars in Lebanon. It took Solomon longer to build his palace complex than to build the temple. One building was even called the House of the Forest of Lebanon.[368] Thus, the judgment statement in verses 6-7 speaks to a great reversal. From the heights of the magnificent mountains of the Lebanon cedars (a metaphor for power and fame), the kings will collapse like felled trees.[369] The metaphor had a reality to it also as the Babylonians burned both the temple and palace in 587 BCE. How the mighty have fallen.

22:10-12

The first of the three kings is addressed – Shallum (Jehoahaz, Josiah's son; *cf.* 1 Chr 3:15). He reigned only three months then was deposed by the Egyptians and taken to Egypt where he died. The nation mourned deeply at the death of the good king Josiah (1 Kgs 23:28-30; 2 Chr 35:24-25), but Jeremiah suggests they should mourn more for Shallum.[370] At least Josiah was buried at home. Shallum would die in a foreign land and never return to the Promised Land. He will "return no more" (v. 10), "will return here no more" (v. 11), and "he shall never see this land again" (v. 12).

22:13-19

The second king addressed is Jehoiakim,[371] who will appear several more times in the book of Jeremiah. His reign is defined by his acts of injustice, brought on by his intense greed and desire for an elaborate palace (*cf.* v. 7). He is noted in Jeremiah for his contempt for the prophet and the word of God and his attempt to get rid of Jeremiah (ch.

---

368 For the details see I Kgs 5-7.

369 Cedars appear in vv. 7, 14, 15, and 23 and Lebanon in vv. 7, 20 and 23.

370 Mourning is a main theme of vv. 10-30.

371 The Shallum of vv. 10-12 and the Coniah of vv. 24-30 each reigned only three months which suggests the focus of vv. 10-30 is Jehoiakim.

36), and for killing Uriah the prophet (ch. 26). Jehoiakim is classified in 2 Kings with his evil fathers (2 Kgs 23:37). His rebellion against the Babylonians was the direct cause of the first exile in 598 BCE even though he apparently died before it happened. His son Jehoiachin suffered the consequences of the rebellion and was taken with his family and ten thousand leading citizens into captivity.[372]

Jehoiakim's sinful actions are enumerated in verses 13-17 and his fate exposed in verses 18-19. His eleven-year reign was marked by self-seeking and self-promotion with no regard for his people. It was a dangerous decade for the nation, but the king was absorbed only with his life style. He was obsessed with a common malady of the rich and powerful – building personal mansions.[373] He built a large palace (or refurbished the one that was there) by conscripting labor in direct violation of covenant law (vv. 13-14; *cf.* Deut 24:14-15). This was in addition to taxing the people to pay tribute to Babylon (2 Kgs 23:35). The palace had upper rooms, cedar paneled walls, and red paint, all signs of luxury and power in the ancient world.[374] He got his way through corruption, fraud, murder, oppression and violence (v. 17).[375] It is hard to think of a more depraved ruler. The main charge in verse 13 covers all his sins – he ruled with unrighteousness and injustice, the very opposite of God's expressed desires in verse 3.

Jehoiakim's conduct was the direct opposite of his father Josiah as Jeremiah points out in verses 15b-16a. Josiah was the good king who did what God desired and tried to rule by taking care of the poor and needy, which God honored ("it was well with him", twice). Josiah also tried to

---

[372] 2 Kgs 24. The captives included the young Ezekiel (Ezek 1:1-2).

[373] Numerous modern examples easily come to mind, not only among tyrants but among millionaires of every kind.

[374] Compare David's palace (2 Sam 11) and Ahab's palace (1 Kgs 21:1; 2 Kgs 9:30-33 – with two floors).

[375] See a similar list of the sins of Judah's kings in Ezek 22:6-12.

eliminate idolatry from the country and return true worship to the temple. Unfortunately, Jehoiakim reversed that reform also.[376]

Jeremiah's question to Jehoiakim in verse 15 is devastating – do you think a nice palace qualifies you as king? What makes a king or any leader, superficial accomplishments or something deep like character and commitment to morality? Jeremiah leaves no doubt what the answer is by providing a radical observation in verse 16b. Taking care of the needy is the same as knowing God. Josiah knew the Lord and the proof was practical and ethical.[377] "... here we find a biblical, prophetic, inspired, luminous, *definition* of what knowing God is. Its simplicity and clarity [defy] all obfuscation. Doing righteousness and justice; defending the poor and needy- *that* is to know God"[378] In the New Testament, 1 John 2:3-4 and 3:16-18 affirm the same.

Jehoiakim's fate was clear (vv. 18-19). He would suffer an ignoble death, and no one would mourn him. There was nothing worse for a person than to have their body unburied and unmourned (*cf.* Jer 36:30). That would be the final humiliation and dash his efforts to make a name for himself. God will keep his word of verse 5.[379]

22:20-23

We know by the feminine singular verbs used that these verses are addressed to the city of Jerusalem, the city of the kings. The message is the same as to the kings. Because of

---

[376] The author of 2 Kings devotes almost two chapters to Josiah's reign (22-23) and only 3 verses to Jehoiakim (23:37-24:2 plus his death notice in 24:5-6).

[377] Wright, *Jeremiah*, p. 241.

[378] *Ibid.*, p. 140. Italics are in the original.

[379] The Biblical texts give different perspectives on Jehoiakim's death. In addition to the Jeremiah references, 2 Kgs 24:6 says he "slept with his ancestors," which is the book of Kings's normal way of referring to the death of a king. 2 Chr 36:6 says Nebuchadrezzar took him to Babylon in chains. Some suggest he may have died on the way and his body disposed of by the road.

her disobedience and arrogance, Jerusalem shall suffer shame and captivity. Like Jehoiakim she sought security through wealth (*cf.* the references to Lebanon) and foreign alliances ("lovers") but her wickedness determined her fate. Her leadership failed ("shepherds"; *cf.* 23:1-4) and will be scattered before the wind.[380]

22:24-30

Coniah (Jehoiachin)[381] is the last of the three kings to learn of his fate. He will go into exile and no descendants will follow him on the throne, ending the long-lived Davidic dynasty in Judah (v. 30). The king was supposed to be God's representative and rule for God over the nation, but God denounced him as the rightful authority and hurled him away (vv. 26, 28) as one would throw away his discarded signet ring (v. 24). This ring was like a modern day notarized signature that carried legal authority on documents and letters. The ring would have a special engraved symbol or image (seal) which was impressed on a lump of clay attached to the document. It was the most important instrument of authority in the ancient world.[382] God totally rejected Coniah as king.[383] Though God had hurled him out, the people still considered Coniah/Jehoiachin the proper Judean king thirty-seven years later in Babylon (2 Kgs. 25:27)!

The word "land" dominates the passage, occurring five times (vv. 26 [NRSV, "country"], 27, 29). This suggests a reversal of the taking of the Promised Land under Joshua.

---

[380] See Jer 4:11-12; 13:24; 18:17 for wind as an instrument of God's judgment. There is probably a deliberate word play here for the Hebrew terms for "shepherd" and "wickedness" look and sound alike, and the word for "wind" partly sounds like the word for "shepherd."

[381] Jeconiah in Jer 24:1; 27:20; 28:4; 29:2; 1 Chr 3:16, 17; Esth 2:6.

[382] These bits of clay were durable and lasted long after the documents vanished. Hundred have been found in Palestine, several with the names of Biblical kings and people, including Baruch, Jeremiah's scribe.

[383] Coniah's grandson, Zerubbabel, after the exile is made God's signet ring (Hag 2:23)!

Israel entered the land with great fanfare (literally), triumph, and hope, and settled in under God's blessing. Now after centuries of rebellion and sin Israel is being cast out in the person of her king. The triple "land" of verse 29 expresses great distress.[384]

Verse 30 raises the issue of the nature of God's promise to David in 2 Samuel 7:12-16 which seems to be unconditional and permanent. Here Coniah is the last of the line, so what about God's promise? Psalm 132:11-12 addressed this issue in covenant terms and recognized the conditional nature of the promise. Covenant obedience was required of David's descendants. This is a point that Jeremiah has made throughout his sermons. The kings were not obedient and violated the covenant. Therefore, the promise had come to an end. But can God's long-range plans be frustrated by human action? Jeremiah returns to this theme in chapter 23:5-6.

While it is true that no other descendant of David sat on the throne, Coniah did have children and grandchildren (1 Chr 3:17). One grandson, Zerubbabel, became governor in the small Judean community after the return from exile (Hag 1:1; 2:2). The end of the David line meant that Coniah's status was the same as being without children.

1.d.iii. God the King and His Branch – 23:1-8

Jeremiah wraps up his section on the kings with a surprisingly hopeful note. This comes in two parts: verses 1-4 which promises divine intervention to return the people from exile; and verses 5-8 which promises a continuation of the Davidic line through the "righteous branch."

23:1-4

Jeremiah begins with another "Woe" announcing further judgment on the kings, addressed here as shepherds. The task of the shepherd was to care for and gather the flock together to protect them, but Israel's kings had scattered

---

[384] *Cf* the three-fold "temple" in Jer 7:4.

them. They had failed in their duty and the people went into exile. Since they had not "attended" to the flock God would "attend to them" (vv. 1-2).[385] Jeremiah described in chapter 22 how God attended to these kings.

Throughout the book so far Jeremiah has relentlessly condemned the people for the rebellion and sin. Here he seems to suggest that the results may have been different with better leadership. This theme is easy to trace throughout the Old Testament and into the New Testament. Godly leadership is crucial to the spiritual health of God's people.

Since the human shepherds had failed, God himself, the true and good shepherd,[386] will come to their aid and gather[387] them from exile (v. 3) so that they may once again live under his blessing and fulfill the creation mandate to be fruitful and multiply (Deut 28:1-14; Gen 1:28; *cf.* also Jer 31:35-37 and 33:20-26). There is a slight negative note for it is just a remnant that will come back, not all the exiles (*cf.* 31:7).[388] There is also a different perspective on who caused the exile. God says here he had "driven them" into other lands. In verse two it was the shepherds and in chapter 21 it was the Babylonians. Here again we encounter how God's agency in human history works. God is the ultimate cause, but he works out his will through human agents.

New shepherds are promised who this time will carry out the will of the divine shepherd and guard the flock (v. 4). Ezekiel 34 offers an extended meditation on this shepherd metaphor. Ultimately God would set over his people a

---

[385] The verb *pqd* (פקד) is used here. It can mean visit judgment upon someone and Jeremiah has used it with this nuance before. But it can have a positive side as well as here in the first usage in verse 2. The NRSV reflects the double-sidedness in its translation. The punishment fits the crime. See the discussion of this verb above on 1:10. It occurs 49 times in Jeremiah with a wide range of meaning.

[386] Ps 23; 80:1.

[387] See Deut 30:3; Jer 29:14; 31:8, 10; 32:37.

[388] in chs. 40-42 the remnant is those left in Judah after 587 BC.

shepherd of his choice of the house of David who will rule his people (Ezek 34:23-24). This provides the crucial Old Testament background to Jesus's teaching that he is the good shepherd (John 10).

God had ended the line of David with Coniah. But if he can end it he can also restore it again in a new way. His plan for his nation and the nations will not be thwarted by his disobedient people and their history.[389] Because he is the sovereign God there is still a future.

23:5-8[390]

This future will be centered on the Davidic line.[391] The unconditional promise of 2 Samuel 7:16 will be kept, just not through the failed line that ended with Coniah (22:30).[392] "Branch" (v. 5) suggests a new growth from an old stock which is a fitting metaphor for the situation. The Hebrew word could also be translated as "shoot or bud" with the same meaning. Isaiah 4:2 uses the same word for the survivors of the exile. Isaiah 11:1-6 speaks of a "shoot" (different Hebrew word) from the root of Jesse who will rule in wisdom and justice under the direction of God's spirit. This new Davidic figure will do what the kings should have done, execute justice and righteousness in the land (*cf.* 22:3 and 16 contrasted with 22:13 and 17). He will bring salvation and security to the land. He will even take on the name of his character as God's representative, "The Lord is our righteousness" (v. 6). This is a deliberate word play on king Zedekiah's name which means "my righteousness is

---

[389] Brueggemann, *To Pluck Up*, p. 198.

[390] Vv. 5 and 6 are printed as poetic in the NIV but as prose in the NRSV. The NIV seems more accurate.

[391] "The days are coming" is a formula pointing to the future and occurs 14 times in Jeremiah.

[392] Vv. 5-6 reappear in 33:15-16 with a few minor changes.

the Lord."[393] Zedekiah may have had the name, but this new Davidic king will embody the reality.[394]

Jeremiah ends his reflections on the kings with a repetition of a vision of the future he already espoused in 16:14-15.[395] This new future will be so spectacular that the ancient confession centered on the Exodus will fade from view to be replaced by one focused on the return from exile. The future also includes the uniting of the two nations, north and south, into one again (v. 8).

This text is one of many that develop a Messianic concept in the Old Testament. The Jews in Jesus' day had developed the expectation of a Messiah who would come to deliver them from Rome. Jesus's claims to be the Messiah did not fit their interpretation and they rejected him, but the New Testament writers, taught by Jesus, proved to many that Jesus fulfilled this text and the others. Paul, the converted Jew, became the most powerful advocate of this truth.[396]

1.d.iv. The prophets denounced – 23:9-40

Jeremiah now attacks another major leadership group in Israel, the prophets, the religious leaders. We will meet some by name in chapters 28 and 29. Chapter 22 denounced the political leadership for lack of justice. This section attacks the religious leadership for their immoral life and false words. In a nation where there was no separation between politics and religion the consequences were enormous. Nationalism trumped faith and patriotism became confused with religion. A major charge against the prophets here is that they lie (vv. 14, 25, 26, 32). They were expected to speak God's truth to the nation but became

---

[393] Ironically this was not his given name, which was Mattaniah, but the name Nebuchadrezzar gave him (2 Kgs 24:17).

[394] Brueggemann, *To Pluck Up*, p. 200.

[395] See comments there.

[396] See for example Isa 9:6, 7; 11:1; Matt 1:1; 9:27; 12:23; 15:22; 20:30, 31; Rom 1:3-4.

consumed with lies, telling the people what they wanted to hear. The death of truth is the first step to the destruction of culture and of nations.

> ### Jeremiah 23:11
>
> *Both prophet and priest are ungodly;*
>   *even in my house I have found their wickedness,*
> *says the Lord.*

The twenty-first century has been rocked by revelations in major cities across the world that clergy have been involved in sexual crimes that have been covered up for decades. The greatest headlines have been from the Roman Catholic Church, where many priests who have been exposed as pedophiles and child molesters now face prosecution. The non-Catholic wings of the church have not been free from this scandal, either. Even though there are many examples (too many), it is still national news when a megachurch pastor is accused of illicit and immoral behavior. America's great mega-congregations, often located in affluent suburbs near the city center, have had an outsized impact on evangelical Christianity for the past two generations. When they blow up due to sexual sins of the lead pastor or some other prominent church leader, the fallout is ruinous.

The dark underbelly of the city hosts many versions of sexual sin and deviancy. The anonymity of the city gives opportunity for pastors to participate with little fear of being discovered. One study claimed that half of all pastors view pornography online.[397] There is certainly wickedness in God's house.

Jeremiah prophesies "disaster" for the ungodly prophets and priests of his day. Surely there is disaster awaiting today, too. The moral fall of urban church leaders does not just hurt themselves and their churches. It damages the

---

[397] Luke Gibbons, "15 Statistics About the Church and Pornography That Will Blow Your Mind," *CharismaNews*, September 18, 2018, accessed at https://www.charismanews.com/us/73208-15-statistics-about-the-church-and-pornography-that-will-blow-your-mind

> fabric of the city itself, drawing it deeper into sexual decline and chaos. Urban pastors must not go this alone. They need support and accountability to resist the city's temptations. The ungodly, anti-church forces of the city both seek to compromise them through sin and to destroy their churches when they fall.
>
> Mark S. Krause

Identifying a prophet from God, or a true prophet, was an almost impossible task in ancient Israel. The modern Christian, with the Old Testament canon in hand, has little trouble knowing who the true prophets were. Their messages have been preserved for us in the Bible. But for the ancient Israelite the task was not simple. There were many prophets, at times hundreds, vying for the attention of the people, all claiming to speak for God. For example, 1 Kings 18 and 22 shows that the king had hundreds of prophets on retainer and consulted them about major decisions.[398] At the same time, individual prophets like Elijah (1 Kgs 18) and Micaiah (1 Kgs 22) claimed to speak for God. Deuteronomy 13 and 18 offered two different methods for testing the authenticity of prophets – the content of the message (13) and the truthfulness of predictions (18). The latter test was limited because the people would have to wait an undetermined amount of time before they would know if the prophet was authentic.

Jeremiah here offers the most extensive reflection on prophets in all the Old Testament prophetic books.[399] He critiques the prophets in several areas (see below) which offers a grid by which to evaluate whether a prophet was sent by God.[400] But even this grid had its limitations and in

---

[398] Groups of prophets appear as early as 1 Sam 10:9 and throughout Samuel and Kings.

[399] See also Jer 6:13-15; Isa 28:7; Ezek 13; Mic 2:6-11; 3:5-12.

[400] Jeremiah never calls these people "false" prophets, though they clearly were. However, the LXX consistently calls them "false" prophets.

Jeremiah's conflict with Hananiah, he at first seemed reluctant to label him a liar (see ch. 28). Only after Jeremiah received a direct word from God did he condemn the prophet.

Verses 9-40 are composed of six sections, five that describe the prophets, and one that reflects on the nature of God. The exegesis will follow this six-fold division.

23:9-12

Jeremiah begins with a simple introduction, "Concerning the prophets..." (v. 9) which applies to the whole section, but his first words reflect his own reaction to the mistreatment of the holy word of God. He was mentally, emotionally and physically undone. His "heart" is a reference to his mind. John Bright suggests "My reason is staggered."[401] He is weak and seems like he is drunk. It is incomprehensible that the "holy" word of God could be treated so lightly by the other prophets when it had completely taken over Jeremiah's life (20:9). How does he know that they treat it lightly? He attacks both their moral life (vv. 10-11, 14) and the source of their words (vv. 18, 22, 25).

First, the Jerusalem prophets are adulterers (v. 10),[402] ungodly or profane men who defile everything they touch and who have perverted even the temple. Worse, the priests have joined in (v. 11; *cf.* 14:18b). The result is that the land suffers drought because of their evil (*cf.* 12:4). The consequence is set. "Therefore" (v. 12), they will suffer disaster ("evil" in the Hebrew[403]), like traveling in the darkness on a slippery road. The "therefore" marks this as a judgment speech against the prophets and matches the other "therefores" in verses 15, 30, and 39.

---

[401] Bright, *Jeremiah*, p. 151.

[402] Compare Jeremiah's treatment of spiritual and real adultery elsewhere: 3:8-9; 5:7; 9:2; 29:23.

[403] "Wickedness" in v. 11 and "disaster" in v. 12 are the same Hebrew word. Human conduct such as adultery is wicked or evil and the resulting punishment is also an evil. Disaster is an appropriate translation.

23:13-15

The second accusation is the same, against the moral life of the prophets. It shares several verbal parallels with verses 9-12. The northern kingdom prophets (Samaria) had spoken the words of Baal (v. 13; see Hos 1-2) as God's word and led the people astray. They had also adopted the Baal fertility cult with its sexual perversions. The result was well known. The Assyrians destroyed Samaria and Israel long ago.

Jerusalem's prophets were worse. They were sexually immoral (v. 14; *cf.* 7:9), liars, and encouragers of evil. The ones expected to lead in obedience to the law instead led in violating it. Jeremiah makes it clear that the moral life of an authentic prophet is just as important as his words. Leaders have an even greater responsibility for they can easily lead others astray, which is exactly what happened in Jerusalem and Judah (v. 15). Therefore, God would treat them like the people of Sodom and Gomorrah, and like the northern kingdom. They would be destroyed also. The prophets influence on the moral landscape of the nation turned it into a "ungodly" place (*cf.* v.11). As leaders, their actions did have consequences for which they were held accountable. They did not speak the word of God, so they would have to eat and drink bitterness. Often nations do not hold leaders morally accountable, but it is not so in the Kingdom of God.[404]

23:16-22

This accusation and the next (vv. 25-32) condemn the source of the prophets' words (vv. 23-24 have a different focus, see below). Verses 16-17 vilify both the source and the content of the message. The prophets do not speak for God but from their own visions.[405] They were deluded, not being able to discern between a word from God and their imagination. It is easy to say, "this is the word of the Lord,"

---

[404] The New Testament also attests this truth: 1 Tim.3:1-12; 2 Pet 2:1-3.

[405] *Cf.* 14:14 which adds divination and the deceit of their own minds.

but the real test is in the content. Their content was false because it was not the right message for the time. To preach "peace" when disaster is coming is only telling the people what they want to hear. To ignore the deep-seated rebellious spirit of the people and contradict the message of Jeremiah of coming judgment was lying to the people, but it was what the people wanted to hear. They did not want to hear Jeremiah. Peace and prosperity prevail over repent or perish every time.[406] In a sense, the people got the prophets they desired and deserved. But it still did not change God's plans for them.[407] The wrong message at the wrong time is worse than saying nothing.

There was good reason these prophets had the wrong message – they did not have a close relationship to God. They had not participated in the heavenly council, so they could not convey God's truth to the people (vv. 18, 22). Verse 22 answers the question of verse 18. The one who had participated in God's heavenly council would have had a completely different message. It would have been a message of warning and a call to repentance, not a message of peace and safety (cf. 6:14; 8:11; 14:13). In other words, it would have agreed with Jeremiah's message.

Since the prophets did not represent God by speaking his truth, they would experience the anger and wrath of God (vv. 19-20), just as the people were going to experience his anger. In chapter 28, Hananiah, one of these prophets, received a death sentence for speaking falsely.

Though Jeremiah does not explain the nature of this heavenly council, the narrative in 2 Kings 22 provides background.[408] There the prophet Micaiah relates his vision of God sitting on his throne with the hosts of heaven around

---

[406] In the modern church, peace and prosperity preaching draws huge crowds, even in poverty stricken countries in Africa. Unfortunately, the only people getting rich are the preachers.

[407] The people in exile would have read these words with a shock of recognition. They believed the prophets and not Jeremiah and ended up in Babylon.

[408] See also Job 1:6-12; 2:1-6; Ps 82:1; 89:7 Isa 6:1-6; Gen 1:26.

him. After some deliberation, a messenger was sent to carry out God's death sentence on Ahab (vv. 19-23). This scenario provides the background for understanding what Jeremiah is talking about. The true prophet would have been attuned to this heavenly council and would have faithfully delivered God's message. The "false" prophets had no such status, therefore, they could not know what God's message was. They had to make it up and of course they had only a feel-good message for the people. They wanted to be popular, not persecuted. Jeremiah stood alone to counter this prophetic populism and he suffered for it.

23:23-24

These two verses interrupt the flow of the attack on the prophets, but they provide an important affirmation of the nature of God.[409] Lest anyone think that the God of Israel was like foreign gods, either confined to local idols or identified with distant suns and stars, God attests to both his imminence (earthly presence) and transcendence (above the world). The pagan gods were one or the other, not both. God was also omnipresent (everywhere) so that no one could escape his watchful eye (*cf.* Ps 139:1-12). Thus, he filled the earth.[410] This is comforting for the faithful like Jeremiah and threatening for the disobedient such as the false prophets. For the Christian, the ultimate manifestation of God's presence is the incarnation of Jesus Christ.

23:25-32

This is the fourth accusation against the prophets, and addresses the source of their words. They are accused of proclaiming their dreams as a word from the Lord. These dreams were no better source for they were lies and deceit also (vv. 26, 32). The dream was not the same as the word of the Lord (v. 31). Jeremiah charges these prophets with

---

[409] Their place at the center of vv. 9-40 highlights their importance.

[410] Elsewhere Scripture speaks of the earth being "full of the steadfast love of God" (Ps 33:5; 119:64; 36:5; 57:10) or the glory of God (Num 14:21; Isa 6:3; Ps 72:19; Hab 3:3).

making the people forget God (v. 28), stealing words from each other and proclaiming it as God's word (v. 30), and using their own words as authentic words of God (v. 31).

Verses 30-32 are heavily ironic. The prophets were so deceived they could not tell the difference between human words and God's word and promoted the former as the latter. This was like passing off straw as wheat (v. 28), the refuse for the valuable grain. Furthermore, God's word is like a fire and a hammer to burn and shatter (v. 29). The prophets' words are false by their very nature for they had no power of their own. There was no profit in them (v. 32).

Dreams elsewhere in the Old Testament did function occasionally as conveying a word from the Lord. God warned Abimelech about Sarah in a dream (Gen 20:3, 6-7). He instructed Jacob about breeding goats in a dream (Gen 31:10-13). He established the authority of Joseph and Daniel through dream interpretation (Gen 40-41; Dan 2 and 4).[411] But dreams did not have a prominent role as revealing the word of God. Deuteronomy 13 established the rubric for authentic dreams. Even if the dreamer announces a sign ahead of time and it comes to pass, he was not sent by God if his message was about other gods. Miraculous signs were not the test, but the content of the message. That is why the prophets' dreams in Jeremiah's time did not pass the test.

New Testament Christians faced similar issues as Jeremiah – false prophets and their message. Jesus warned that false prophets would come and do all sorts of things in his name, but they would not be from him (Matt 7:15-23). The writers of the New Testament warned against false prophets, false teachers, and false apostles (2 Cor 11:13; 2 Pet 2:1-3; I John 4:1; Jude). The people of God always must be vigilant for false leaders. The modern church seems to be especially vulnerable to preachers who promise great things,

---

[411] Joseph and Daniel lived in foreign countries where dreams were an important part of discerning the will of the gods. Dream books were compiled in Babylon to guide the interpretation. Dreams of kings were especially important. Sometimes the king would sleep in the temple to try and induce dreams.

make powerful claims, and amass fortunes from gullible Christians. As for ancient Israel, so for the modern church, it is the content of the message that determines authenticity. For the Christian, the message must be focused on the gospel, the good news of salvation through our resurrected Lord (1 Cor 15). If the death, burial, and resurrection of Jesus and the good news of saving grace is not the focal point of the message then the preacher or teacher is speaking falsehood.

23:33-40

This last accusation of the prophets assesses them as a burden to the Lord. This involves a word play in Hebrew, for the word translated by the NRSV as "burden" has a homonym that means "oracle, pronouncement," which some translations use here (NIV, NAS).[412] The KJV, ESV, and TNK (the Jewish translation) use "burden" which seems to make better sense from the context.[413] The people ask, "What is the burden(some) message of the Lord" that Jeremiah is going to speak (v. 33; just as his other messages had been a burden).[414] God answers that they are the real burden and will be cast off (repeated in v. 39).

The dialogue continues with this theme throughout the passage. The people repeatedly raise questions about this burden, but they are the burden. Therefore, Jeremiah is no longer to speak to them (v. 36) for they are interested only in their own words and constantly pervert God's word. The dialogue seems somewhat convoluted, but the meaning is clear. The people, prophets and priests have continually misinterpreted Jeremiah's message and offered their own.

---

[412] The word is used often to introduce prophecies of doom against the nations in Isa 13-23 and occurs in Nah 1:1; Hab 1:1; Zech 9:1, 12:1; and Mal 1:1.

[413] Understood in the metaphorical sense of Num 11:11, 17; Deut 1:12 – the people were a burden to Moses.

[414] There is perhaps a subtle reference here to Jer 17:19-27 where Jeremiah admonishes the people to keep the Sabbath law by not bringing burdens into the city, that is, trade goods. This law and others were evidently a burden to the people.

Consequently, they will go into exile in shame and disgrace (vv. 39-40).

1.d.v. Two Baskets of Figs – 24:1-10

Chapter 24 is a vision report and its application. There are parallels with chapter one – a vision, a question, the application, and a reference to building and planting. Chapter 24 is also the first of the series of chapters through 29 that begin with a date. In these chapters three kings are mentioned: Jeconiah (24, 29), Jehoiakim (25, 26), and Zedekiah (27, 28, 29). They are not in chronological order, for Jehoiakim preceded Jeconiah. Chapters 24 and 29 address the "good" that God is going to do for the exiles.

Chapter 24 is dated just after 597 BCE when Nebuchadrezzar took the first captives away to Babylon (2 Kgs 24:8-17). These captives would have been deeply discouraged and despondent, with little hope. They went from freedom in their own land to virtual slavery in another where the religion, culture, history, and geography was foreign, opposed to their own core values. They would have thought that God had abandoned them, and they lacked all their cherished religious traditions. The only bright spot would have been that they still had with them Jeconiah, the Davidic king.

Meanwhile, the people left in Judea and Jerusalem, though poor, would have considered themselves the blessed ones. They still had their land, their holy city, their holy temple, priests, prophets, and a king. Though in a reduced state, life as they knew it could go on. They would have regarded the captives with pity and perhaps compassion, but they would have thanked God for their good fortune. The future still lay with them.

24:1-10

Then Jeremiah saw a vision of two baskets of figs. Or they could have been a real experience since the text does not say he saw a vision.[415] One basket had excellent figs, figs good enough to be offered as first fruits at the temple (v. 2; *cf.* Isa 28:4). The other basket had very bad, rotten figs not fit to eat (v. 3). This was a sharp contrast. What could it mean? We might expect a contrast between the righteous and unrighteous, or between the faithful and the kings or prophets of chapters 22 and 23.

But the exiles were the good figs (vv.4-5), the ones living under God's care, the ones who would receive God's direct attention. He had not abandoned them but was at work on their behalf. He was going to do them good and not evil (a reverse of 21:10 – addressed to Jerusalem). They would come back from exile.[416] It was not the end, but the beginning of something new. They had a future and would not be lost to God or to history.[417] They would experience the positive side of Jeremiah's commission in 1:10 – they would be built up and planted. This was a gift of God's grace. No reason is given why they had his favor.

Furthermore, God would give them a heart (v. 7) so that they could return to him. This was the circumcised heart of 4:4. The persistent stubborn heart we have heard about up to now or the hard heart would be replaced. It was Ezekiel who clarified for the exiles that this was a new heart to be accompanied by a new spirit (Ezek 36:26-28; *cf.* Ezek 11:19-20). God would initiate a total make over so that now they would once and for all know that God was the Lord. Once again, they could be faithful covenant partners with God and be his people (*cf.* Exod 6:7; Lev 26:12; Deut 26:17-19; Jer 30:22; 31:33; 32:38). This promise will be fully fleshed out in chapters 30-34.

In contrast, the Judeans left behind, who were certainly relieved to have the Babylonians depart without them, were the bad figs (vv. 8-14). They would again experience the

---

[415] Compare similar experiences in chapter 1:11-13; Amos 7:7-8; 8:2; Zech 4:2.

[416] It is interesting that this is agreement with the false prophets who predicted a return after two years – Jer 28:3.

[417] See further comments on chapter 29 below.

ravages of warfare and bear the brunt of God's judgment. We know from 2 Kings 24:19 that Zedekiah continued in the sins of Jehoiakim and his predecessors and did not lead the people back God. There was one more rebellion and one more Babylonian invasion in 587 BCE that destroyed the temple, Jerusalem, and the country. The poor remnant left would experience chaos, assassination and ultimately flight to Egypt where they would perish (Jer 39-44). The future of God's people did not lie with them.

One can imagine the astonishment when the exiles heard or read these words. They overturned the exiles' assumptions and opened the future. God still had plans for them.

1.d.vi. Judah Will Go into Exile – 25:1-14

This sermon is also given a date, the fourth year of Jehoiakim which was 605 BCE (vv.1-2; the same date as chapter 36). The Egyptian Pharaoh Neco placed Jehoiakim on the throne after Neco defeated Josiah at Megiddo in 609.[418] Therefore, Jehoiakim was his puppet, and Judah was a vassal to Egypt and paid tribute to her (2 Kgs 23:28-35). 605 BCE was also the year Nebuchadrezzar defeated Neco at Carchemish in northern Syria. Babylon then became the ruling empire in the Middle East (Jer 46:2). This was a crisis year for little Judah and the entire area as the power shifted and Judah was plunged into uncertainty. How would Babylon treat her?

Jeremiah's words were not good news. Nebuchadrezzar took some captives to Babylon in 605 BCE and Judah's security rested on Jehoiakim's loyalty to Babylon.[419] This

---

[418] Josiah was killed and his son Jehoahaz succeeded him but for only three months before Neco deposed him (2 Kgs 23:31-35).

[419] See Dan 1:1-2. The third year in Daniel is the same as the fourth year in Jeremiah. It was based on a different way of counting the beginning of the king's reign.

lasted only a few years and Nebuchadrezzar was back in Judah in 597 (2 Kgs 24:1-12).[420]

Jeremiah begins by pointing out his long ministry of calling the people to repentance. For twenty-three years, he had persisted (v. 3), that is, from 627 BCE during the reign of Josiah. But no one had listened to his preaching. They had resisted at every turn. Moreover, not only was Jeremiah persistent, but all the prophets, God's true servants were also faithful in their preaching (v. 4).[421] But their messages fell on deaf ears that would not hear and obey (*cf.* Isa 6:9-10 – because of the condition of their heart the preaching made them deaf). The message was also always the same – turn from idols and repent so they could live in the land (vv. 5-6; *cf.* 7:6-7; 23:22b). However, rather than earn the pleasure of God they provoked him to anger (v. 7: *cf.* 32:30-33). Everything they did, not just making idols, was rebelling against God, whether politics, economics, the justice system, educating the young, or priests leading in worship. It was all self-centered and self-destructive.[422]

Therefore, the consequence was disaster (vv. 8-14). We can enumerate the outcomes. First, God will bring other tribes and Nebuchadrezzar to destroy Judah and Jerusalem (v. 9). In fact, the foreign king will be God's "servant" to carry out his plans. The people had ignored God's earlier servants (v. 4) so he raised up another that they could not ignore.

This illustrates an important factor of how God works in his world. He will use human agents as he sees fit, whether good or evil, whether Israelite or pagan, to carry out his will. Already Assyria had been God's "rod" against the northern kingdom (Isa 10:5-6) and Cyrus will be God's

---

[420] The modern reader of Jeremiah knows the Babylonian's role in the destruction of Jerusalem from chapter 21. But that comes from Zedekiah's reign a few years later, so this sermon is new information for Jerusalem.

[421] These of course were not the prophets of ch. 23 but prophets like Isaiah, Hosea, and Amos.

[422] Just like secularly oriented cultures today.

shepherd and anointed to return the exiles home (Isa 44:28; 45:1). But even if Nebuchadrezzar was a servant at this moment he, too, would be held accountable. Jeremiah 50-51 detail God's later judgment on Babylon.

Secondly, God would banish all semblance of normal life from the land (v. 10): the joy of weddings, the daily routine of preparing food, the daily evening routine of lighting a lamp. Normal life was over. Thirdly, the exile would last seventy years (v. 11; 29:10). This was both a negative and a positive word. It would be long but not permanent. There would be an end to it. This was a contentious issue with the other prophets who preached peace. After 597 BCE, they could not deny an exilic experience, but they predicted it would short, just two years according to Hananiah (28:3; *cf.* 29:24-28).

The prediction of a seventy-year exile has created considerable discussion among Bible scholars. Are they a literal seventy years or a symbol of a long time? Counting from 597 BCE and the first deportation until 539 BCE and the edict of Cyrus that the exiles could return (Ezra 1:2-4) yields only 58 years. Counting from 605 BCE, the first attack of Nebuchadnezzar, to 539 BCE yields 66 years. Some suggest counting from 587 BCE and the destruction of the temple to 515 BCE when its rebuilding was completed, which yields 72 years. This is the way Zechariah understood it (Zech 1:12). This puts the focus on the temple and not the actual exile of the people. On the other hand, Daniel sees the 70 years approaching in his day, in 539 BCE (Dan 9:2).

The symbolic idea is supported by several symbolic uses of the number 70 in the Old Testament. Seventy is the number seven (the number of completion or fullness) multiplied by the number ten (which some think is the number of perfection). Seventy is the length of a good life (Ps 90:10), the number of elders who represented the people (Exod 24:9), and the ideal family size of successful patriarchs and kings (Israel, Gen 46:27; Gideon, Judg 8:30;

Abdon, Judg 12:15; and Ahab, 2 Kgs 10:1).[423] So perhaps we are not to search for precise dates.

The fourth point is that the Babylonians would not escape responsibility for their actions and would be punished for their iniquity also (vv. 12-13).[424] In verse 13, Jeremiah refers to his words "written in this book." What was that book (or scroll)? Chapter 36 relates that God commanded Jeremiah to write down all his sermons up to the year 605 BCE in a scroll. Jeremiah then dictated them to Baruch. Perhaps the two books in 25:13 and 36:2 are the same. If so, then probably all the sermons in chapters 1 through 25:12 are this book.[425] Thus, the word of God through the words of Jeremiah (1:1 and 4) became a written word. This change from orality to written form had enormous implications for the preservation of the spoken word and the subsequent history of the written word. It fixed the spoken word in a specific time and setting which became the word that was passed down to Israel and the church.

In the Greek translation of the Old Testament,[426] the oracles against the nations of Jeremiah 46-51 are placed here after the reference to the book in 25:13. There does seem to be a natural break, for in verse 15 Jeremiah is sent to the nations. Also, the other major prophetic books, Isaiah and Ezekiel, have their oracles against the nations in the middle

---

[423] See Leland Ryken, James C. Wilhoit, and Tremper Longman III (eds.), *Dictionary of Biblical Imagery* (Downers Grove: IVP, 1998, "Seventy," pp. 775-776. In Luke 10:1 Jesus sent out 70 disciples.

[424] Chaldean is an older term for Babylon and appears first in the OT in Gen 11:28. The Chaldeans were originally a tribe in southern Mesopotamia who then gave their name to the larger region. The name occurs last in the OT in Dan 9:1.

[425] The book was of course a scroll. Ch. 36 uses the Hebrew word for scroll.

[426] Called the Septuagint and designated as LXX.

(Isa 13-23 and Ezek 25-32). Our English translations follow the Hebrew Bible order.[427]

---

[427] There are many other differences between the LXX version and the Hebrew Bible in Jeremiah which has generated a great deal of discussion. For a summary see Lalleman, *Jeremiah*, pp. 27-28.

2. Introduction to Prophecies against the Nations (25:15-38)

These verses serve as an introduction to the oracles against the nations in chapters 46-51 and should be interpreted in that light. There are two parts, verses 15-29 that describe how all nations will suffer under Babylon, and verses 30-38 which show that all nations are guilty before God.

25:15-29

These verses introduce a new image, through a vision, for the application of God's judgment – a cup of wine forced on the nations, to make them drink and stagger and fall like drunk men. It is called the "cup of wine of wrath" (v. 15). God's anger and wrath against Israel's sins was portrayed earlier and associated with a fire that burns and destroys (4:4; 7:20; 21:5, 12). The image of a cup of wine also relays the idea of destruction – the drinkers who cannot refuse (v. 28) become falling-down drunk, and, unable to withstand the sword, perish. This is a powerful image of the high and mighty nations crumbling into oblivion.

It becomes clear as the text continues that the cup is the nation Babylon (51:7), a "golden cup" to make the nations go mad. Babylon under Nebuchadrezzar had just become the dominant power in the ancient Middle East and God was going to use his sword (vv. 16, 27, 29) to carry out his judgment. This accords with historical fact. When Nebuchadrezzar became king he swiftly swept through Mesopotamia, Syria and Palestine, subjecting nations and tribes as he went. He was unable to conquer Egypt but was able to pacify her and destroy her influence in Palestine. God not only used Babylon to render judgment on Israel but on all the nations.[428]

The scope of this announced judgment went beyond Israel and Judah of previous sermons and addressed all the nations (vv. 17-29). This was a part of Jeremiah's call: he

---

[428] Drinking from the cup of God's wrath is mentioned in other OT texts – Isa 51:17, 21; Hab 2:15-16; Obad 15-16; Ezek 23:32-34; Ps 75:8.

would be sent to the nations not just Israel (1:10). They were accountable to God as well (*cf.* chs. 45-51).

The list begins in verse 18 with Jerusalem and Judah. They are treated in this case like all others. There seems to be a geographical arrangement to the list, moving out in various directions from the tiny province of Judah. The list begins with Egypt to the south (v. 19), other mixed people south of Judah (v. 20a),[429] the Philistines west of Judah (v. 20b), the small kingdoms east of the Jordan River (v. 21), the Mediterranean coastland northwest of Judah and the islands in the sea (v. 22), the tribes of the Arabian Peninsula to the East (v. 23), the kings there (v. 24), and the lands east of the Euphrates valley in modern Iran (v. 25). A catchall phrase includes everyone else (v. 26a). The last word is saved for Babylon herself. Though she is God's agent she is also held responsible for her actions (v. 26b). "Sheshach" is a cryptogram for Babylon, a code word.[430] Why Jeremiah would use a code word here is unclear since he references Babylon often elsewhere.

The section continues with a repetition from verse 15 (v. 27) and a declaration that the nations cannot refuse or escape God's judgment (vv. 28-29). If God will punish his own covenant people for the evil of their deeds and idolatry, how can the nations of the world think they could escape?

Did the nations ever hear these words of judgment? Not likely. But the exiles and later generations did and found

---

[429] Uz is the land of Job but its location is unknown. Uz is also mentioned in Gen 36:38 and Lam 4:21 which suggests its location was in the area of Edom.

[430] This is called an "atbash." The Hebrew alphabet is divided into half, the first half in normal order and the second in reversed order. Then the letters from one line are substituted for the corresponding letters on the other line. Thus, Babylon, which is *bbl* in Hebrew becomes *ššk* (the second letter matches the second to last letter and so on). See also 51:1 and 41.

consolation in them as well as grounds for serious theological reflection on the nature of their God and his sovereignty.

The cup symbol appears three times in the New Testament. Jesus prays in Gethsemane that the cup be removed from him (Matt 26:39-42; Mark 14:36). In the light of Isaiah 51 and Jeremiah 25 this must to be the cup of God's wrath against the sin of the world that Jesus was to bear on the cross. Only that could have caused him such agony. But prior to that prayer was another cup, the cup of his blood at the Last Supper which became the cup of salvation for all peoples, the cup to be drunk together with our Lord in the new Jerusalem (Matt 26:26-29). John also applies the cup of wrath imagery to those who have worshipped the beast (Rev 14:9-10; *cf.* 16;19; 18:6; 19:15), a fitting application of the Jeremiah symbol. Contrary to some opinions, God's wrath is referenced in the New Testament as well as the Old, and for the same reason, to express God's judgment on sin (Rom 1:18; 2:5; 3:5 5:9; Col 3:6; Eph 2:3; 5:6, etc.).

25:30-38

A new metaphor for God is introduced in verses 30 and 38 – the roaring lion who strikes fear into the human heart comes to destroy. This image is not new in Jeremiah. In Isaiah 31:4 God as lion defended his people and Jerusalem.[431] Real lions were a threat to the Israelites during the monarchy. They resided in the Jordan River valley (Jer. 50:44) and central hill country woods, and David was famous for defending his flock against them (1 Sam 17:34-36). Foreign kings hunted them and even captured them to keep at the palace (Dan 6).[432] Their strength and prowess made them a good metaphor for both protection and destruction. Babylon as God's agent is the lion in Jeremiah 4:7; 5:6; and 51:38. The image is associated in verse 30 with the unlikely image of treading of grapes, which was a

---

[431] See also Hos 11:10 and Amos 1:2; 3:8. But in Hos 5:14 and 13:8 he came as a lion against his people.

[432] Walton, *Bible Background*, p. 739; *NBD*, "Animals of the Bible," pp. 42-43.

time of rejoicing and shouting (Jer 48:33). God is shouting in victory over his enemies.

Another surprise of the text is that God has an "indictment" or lawsuit against the nations (v. 31). That he had a case against Israel (2:9) is understandable for they were his covenant people and had broken the covenant. The lawsuit here is based on God's sovereignty and a universal concept of justice. Amos 1 calls the nations to account for they violated even their own standards of conduct and international treaties. The same is true here. The nations are accountable, and they cannot escape responsibility. The coming judgment will devastate them (vv. 32-33).

The lion was a special enemy of the shepherd as the docile, defenseless sheep were an easy target. Thus, the lion image easily leads to a warning to the shepherds, the nations' leaders (vv. 34-37; cf. 24:1-4). They do not stand a chance. They will be slaughtered like sheep. There are no Davids among them. Nothing can stand before God's wrath (v. 37).

This is the "terrible and terrifying reality of the Lord's fierce anger."[433] This is a theme that resonates through the whole Bible, into the New Testament, through Jesus, into Revelation. But this judgment is not capricious. In both the Old and New Testament God repeatedly pleads for repentance and offers a path to restoration. The ultimate path turns out to be through Jesus Christ.

---

[433] Wright, *Jeremiah*, p. 270.

3. Destruction and Restoration (26-33)

3.a. The temple sermon aftermath (26:1-24)

Commentary for chapter 26 is given above after the commentary on chapter 7.

3.b. Yoke Sermon, Hananiah's opposition, letters to exiles (27:1-29:32)[434]

3.b.i. Acted sermon of the yoke – 27:1-22

Chapters 27-29 form a unit, joined by the theme of prophetic conflict over the length of the exile. This was intensely debated during the reign of Zedekiah as following chapters will show.

The date of chapter 27 is the fourth year of King Zedekiah's reign which would be 593 BCE.[435] Zedekiah became king in 597 BCE (2 Kgs 24:18-20) after the death of Jehoiakim. Nebuchadnezzar placed him on the throne after conquering Jerusalem and taking Jehoiachin, Jehoiakim's son, into exile. Zedekiah (Hebrew, Mattaniah) was Jehoiachin's uncle and a puppet of Nebuchadnezzar. Jeremiah 51:59 tells us that Zedekiah was called to Babylon in his fourth year, but the reason is unknown. Thus, the fourth year was an eventful one for Zedekiah for envoys had come from several nations around to Jerusalem (27:3), perhaps to plot rebellion against Nebuchadnezzar.

---

[434] In the Hebrew text of Jer 27-29 the names of Jeremiah and Nebuchadnezzar are spelled differently. The end of Jeremiah is shortened by one letter and Nebuchadnezzar is spelled with an "n" in place of the "r". The NRSV reflects this change.

[435] The Hebrew text reads in verse 1 the fourth year of Jehoiakim, but this doesn't seem accurate. Some Hebrew manuscripts, the Syriac, and the Arabic have Zedekiah which is certainly correct. He is referenced in vv. 3, 12, and 21. Also ch. 28 follows closely on ch. 27 and 28:1 has the fourth year of Zedekiah. The LXX does not have 27:1.

Chapter 27 has three parts: God's word to the envoys in Jerusalem (vv. 1-11), the same message to Zedekiah (vv. 12-16), and a message to the priests and people (vv. 17-22). The message to all three is almost identical so there is much repetition in the chapter.

27:1-11

The message is grounded in a vivid symbolic act. Jeremiah is instructed to make a yoke, like those used on oxen, and wear it. This is another of the many symbolic acts God required of Jeremiah.[436] The vividness of the symbol gives power to the message beyond what just words would have done.

The yoke was a useful tool in Israel's culture, allowing them to harness the power of an ox team for hard labor such as plowing or pulling loads on a wagon or sledge. Thus, it was a ready symbol for submission, servitude, and control. Jeremiah had already used the symbol for spiritual servitude in 2:20 and 5:5. Deuteronomy 28:48 used it for political servitude and 1 Kings 12 :4, 9, 10 for taxation and forced labor. Here it refers to political servitude to Babylon.

The nations gathered in Jerusalem were the small ones to the east and north west of Judah. They were sometimes enemies and sometimes allies.[437] A common enemy now brought them together (v. 3).

God's message is certainly unwanted. These nations were seeking ways to achieve freedom from oppression. God says the only way to survive is to submit. He was the creator of the universe (v. 5) and had made Nebuchadnezzar his servant (v. 6). The nations were not in control of their own destinies, for God was not a meager Israelite deity but

---

[436] Ch. 13, the linen cloth; ch. 18, the potter's wheel and pot; ch. 19, the broken pot.

[437] God had given Edom, Moab, and Ammon their land through which Israel had to pass to enter the Promised Land (Deut 2).

the sovereign lord of the universe over nature and kingdoms (*cf.* Jer 21; 25:9; Amos 1; Ps 33:6-11). At that time, Babylon was the world power and God's servant, but its power was not absolute. In God's big picture Babylon appeared for a moment, but it, too, would come to an end (v. 7), though not for three generations. From history, we know that the Babylonians fell to the Persians in 539 BCE (see the books of Daniel and Ezra).[438]

We have two other contemporary views of God at work through his servant Nebuchadnezzar: Daniel 2 and Habakkuk 1. Daniel 2 is dated 601 BCE, eight years before Jeremiah's sermon, and relates Nebuchadnezzar's dream that Daniel interpreted for him. God calls Nebuchadnezzar's kingdom the head of gold which gives it pride of place among the nations and would have pleased the king. However, he also portrays the end of his kingdom. The result was that Nebuchadnezzar praised God (Dan 2:47), but this praise was short lived. Nebuchadnezzar's next act, according to Daniel 3, was building the golden statue and requiring everyone to worship it. Even so, the exiles living with Daniel would have heard that God was still in control of the nations.

The prophet Habakkuk was a prophet in Judah. His conversation with God probably occurred sometime immediately before 605 BCE when Nebuchadnezzar came to power.[439] Habakkuk was outraged at the sin he saw in Judah (Hab 1:2-4) and pled to God to do something. God responded that he was raising up the Babylonians to bring his judgment (Hab 1:5-11). Unlike Jeremiah, Habakkuk expressed his shock that God could use the wicked for his purpose. This theological problem has no easy answer and has been debated since Habakkuk's day. God's answer to the prophet was simple: trust me (Hab 2:4b, "...the right-

---

[438] Nebuchadrezzar reigned from 604 to 562 BC. He was succeeded by his son Evil-Merodach, 562-560 BC, and then his son-in-law Niriglissar (Nergal-sharezer the Rabmag in Jer 39:3), 560-556 BC.

[439] Gary Hall, "Habakkuk," in Mangano, *et al.*, *An Introduction to the Old Testament*, pp. 586-591.

eous shall live by faith."). Ultimately that is the hardest answer to accept but also the only one. Therefore, the witness of the Old Testament is uniform: God is sovereign over Nebuchadnezzar and his kingdom. The time calls for judgment on God's people and the Babylonians are his instrument. Jeremiah will deal with their fate at the end of his book (chs. 50-51).

Jeremiah 27 is a reminder of the place of the nations in the hands of a sovereign God. Nebuchadnezzar was confident that his political prowess and military might had achieved his goals of world dominance. The little nations shared the same view and calculated that at the right moment they could parry this power with their own combined efforts. None reckoned that Israel's God would have any role, but they were badly mistaken. God (Israel's own Yahweh) controlled history and used nations for his purpose. Israel would have been surprised as well. They understood the sovereign power of God but believed it was always used on their behalf.[440] But God was bigger than that. God as creator and sovereign of the universe provides the background for the strong missional aspect of the Old Testament which appears throughout the whole canon.[441]

There is an "if" in Jeremiah's message (v. 8). Survival of the nations depended on their submission to the Babylonian yoke. If the nations did not submit, destruction at the hands of the war machine of Babylon would follow.[442] Anyone who said the opposite was speaking lies (vv. 9-10).

Verse 9 is a laundry list of the ways ancient kings tried to divine the future and thus control it. For example, numerous clay tablets from Mesopotamia provide detailed instructions on how to read sheep livers to predict the future.

---

[440] God still works in world affairs but without a prophet like Jeremiah or Isaiah it is difficult to interpret just how he is ordering affairs (despite the confidence of some commentators).

[441] Wright, *Jeremiah*, pp. 282-283; idem., *The Mission of God*.

[442] Note the "big three" consequences: sword, famine, plague. See on ch. 14 above.

Other methods are also documented. Anxiety about the future was endemic in those cultures. These methods were condemned in the law and elsewhere in the Old Testament (Deut 18:10-14; Lev 19:31: Exod 22:18; 1 Sam 28:8; 2 Kgs 17:17; 21:6; Ezek 21:21). Only dreams were sometimes considered in a favorable light (Joseph and Daniel).

Jeremiah had condemned the false prophets in Israel (ch. 23) but the pagan nations had their false prophets as well, especially if they contradicted Jeremiah. Survival was through submission not revolt. According to God's plan there were only two choices – submission or death. The prophets and diviners thought they had a third choice, resistance, but it was no option.[443]

27:12-15

Jeremiah addresses Zedekiah with the same message – submit to the yoke of Nebuchadnezzar or die. Israel's position is no longer unique among the nations. They had forfeited it by disobedience. They were now a "nation" and the prophets were lying if they said otherwise. In the canonical order of the book of Jeremiah this message is not new. Chapter 21 addressed the place of Nebuchadnezzar in God's plan to punish his people and carry out the destruction of Jerusalem, but, chronologically, chapter 27 is earlier. The later chapters in Jeremiah that lead up to the fall of Jerusalem provide further detail on Zedekiah's inability to provide leadership that would possibly avert disaster.

27:16-22

Jeremiah next turns to speak to the priests and people to warn them about the lying prophets. These are the very groups that opposed Jeremiah and his sermon in chapter 26 and wanted to execute him. He addresses a specific false message – that the vessels taken from the temple in 597 BCE will soon be returned (2 Kgs 24:13-14). The lying message is that the exile will be short. This message is repeated by Hananiah in chapter 28.

---

[443] Brueggemann, *To Build, To Plant: Jeremiah 26-52* (Grand Rapids: Eerdmans, 1991), p. 19.

These vessels included gold and silver cups, bowls, pans and other similar articles used in the worship ceremonies of the temple. The temple represented the presence of God and taking the vessels not only provided booty but insulted God and suggested he was just a local deity. Jeremiah establishes that is not the case. God is in control of events and not limited by space or by prophetic words. There were still vessels and large items left in the temple (v. 19). The pillars and the sea were especially impressive (1 Kgs 7:15-26). Jeremiah challenges the prophets – if they are really concerned about the fate of the temple then they should pray to God that he would not continue to carry out his judgment plan and devastate the temple even more. The place of the prophet in this event was not to predict but to pray that the will of God be done. The true prophets understood this, and the center of their message was repentance. We know that prayer was at the center of the life of Old Testament prophets and the challenge to the lying prophets was clear.[444]

God assumes nothing will change and the chapter ends with the divine prediction that even the vessels left in the temple will be taken away (v. 22). We learn from Jeremiah 52:17-19 (cf. 2 Kgs 25:9) that not only were the vessels taken but the temple itself was burned.[445]

The symbol of the yoke appears in the New Testament in the teaching of Jesus, but with a positive implication. Jesus encourages his disciples to take up his yoke which is not a burden but is light and easy (Matt 11:28-30). In his context, the burdensome yoke was the demands of the Pharisaic interpretation of the law. Submitting to his teaching and will released them from this yoke. The deadliest yoke of all is sin. The core of the Gospel is freedom from sin through faith in the crucified Messiah.

---

[444] There are many current "prophecy experts" whose ministry might have a new dimension if they turned to prayer rather than prediction.

[445] We learn from Ezra 1:9-11 that 5,400 articles of gold and silver were brought back to Jerusalem at the end of the exile.

Paul argued with Jewish Christians that faith in Christ brought freedom from the law. It was a yoke of slavery (Gal 5:1). Paul also emphasized that to be a Christian was to be a servant. Submission to Christ was the beginning of the Christian life.

3.b.ii. Hananiah's Opposition – 28:1-17

Chapter 28's events occur immediately after Jeremiah's sermon in chapter 27. Jeremiah is still wearing the yoke (v. 10) and the audience is the same as 27:16, the priests and the people. Here the prophets of 27:16 are represented by Hananiah who speaks out against Jeremiah. He undoubtedly reflected their animosity and common perspective on the future. Hananiah was from Gibeon, a few miles north of Jerusalem and not far from Jeremiah's home town of Anathoth. Perhaps he was deliberately chosen to counter another rural before the Jerusalem crowds. Hananiah's name means "Yahweh is gracious" which seems to reflect his message – there is not room for harsh judgment, just grace after grace.

Hananiah used the same introductory formula for his words as Jeremiah, "Thus says the Lord of hosts, the God of Israel" (27:21), and so claimed the same source and authority as Jeremiah. He cannot deny the visible symbol of the yoke nor the reality of the 597 BCE exile, but he can contradict the interpretation of the symbol. He said the way to life was not submission to Babylon's yoke but trust in God that he is going to soon reverse the exile. He envisions the vessels, the people, and the king all returning within two years and everyone living happily ever after. Since symbols are ambiguous he could be right in the eyes of the people.[446]

---

[446] This ambiguity casts a shadow over their importance. Without an authorized interpreter, their significance is open-ended. Gideon asked for a sign but did not accept the first one offered (Judg 6:36-40). Early in my teaching career at a Christian college some students, who had formed a quartet evangelistic team, envisioned a full-time ministry. So, they put out a soda bottle and asked God to fill it with water that

Was Hananiah merely playing to the desires of his audience or did he have a theological base for his message? It is possible that his message was grounded in the long-standing Zion theology of Isaiah and God's promise to rescue all who trusted in Zion (Isa 37:35; 31:5). The current circumstances resembled those of Isaiah and Jerusalem in 701 BCE. However, theology can become ideology, put God in a box, and not allow him to act in new ways in new situations. At any rate, the audience would have warmly received his message. Besides Jeremiah's message sounded like treason.[447]

Jeremiah's immediate response was surprisingly positive (v. 6). His "Amen" was a yes, may it be true. He could imagine a short exile and return. He had left the return open (27:22) so two years might work. However, he had already called such a message a lie (27:16) so perhaps his "Amen" was sarcastic or ironic.[448]

Jeremiah had wrestled for thirty years with God's message of judgment at a personal cost, so he issues a warning (vv. 7-9). Hananiah and the audience must consider two points. First, for centuries the prophetic message had been judgment in the form of "war, famine, and pestilence." Therefore, a different message should arouse suspicion. The prophets were covenant lawyers[449] and their mission was to announce the covenant curses of Deuteronomy 28 for covenant disobedience. Their message had come true for the northern kingdom (2 Kgs 17) and was coming true for the southern. Yet, Hananiah did not agree with them.

Secondly, Hananiah's word had to pass the test of time (Deut 18:21-22). The burden of proof was on him and his fellow prophets. Prophecy had a built-in reality check, but

---

night which would be a positive sign. In the morning the bottle was empty. I asked the leader what they did. With a sheepish grin he replied that they went ahead anyway. I should add that they had an extended effective ministry to the youth in a several-state area.

[447] Hallemann, *Jeremiah*, p. 217.

[448] We cannot always tell the tone from a written text.

[449] Longman, *Jeremiah*, p. 119; *cf.* 2:9, 29; 11:1-8; 12:1-6.

his response was not to acknowledge this truth. It was to humiliate Jeremiah (vv. 10-11). He took the yoke off Jeremiah and broke it and repeated his message.

Jeremiah responded by walking away. One would expect anger and outrage and denunciation. Jeremiah had suffered much for the message, but for the moment he was willing to let events work themselves out. Still, this was a crisis point for Jeremiah for his integrity and his words as God's words were at stake. Was he the authentic prophet or was Hananiah? The crisis of truth and falsehood was not theoretical. It deeply impacted the power of Babylon, the will of God, and the future of Jerusalem.[450]

The issue was soon resolved, for Jeremiah received another word of judgment from the Lord for Hananiah (vv. 12-14). Hananiah had broken the wooden yoke but the action would not result in freedom for the nation, but an even heavier burden, a yoke of iron.[451] They will serve Babylon to whom God had given the kingdom and power (Dan 2).

God also has a direct message for Hananiah. He will die (v. 15-16). God had not "sent" him to the people, therefore, God would "send" him out from the earth (NRSV, "remove"). Hananiah was not a covenant-lawsuit prophet so God brought a covenant lawsuit against him (the form is accusation and announcement of judgment). He would not live to see if his two-year prediction was true. He was dead in three months (v. 17). Thus, Jeremiah was authenticated and God's prophet for the exiles and for future generations. The events of 587 BCE further confirmed his message of judgment as the right one, yet his authority was still contested as we shall see in chapter 29.

Scripture consistently shows that one cannot treat the word of God with contempt. Hananiah learned it, Nadab and Abihu, Aaron's sons learned it (Lev 10), Ananias and

---

[450] Brueggemann, *To Build*, p. 29.

[451] The Hebrew has "yoke" so the NRSV "bar" ruins the continued symbol.

Sapphira learned it (Acts 5).[452] Jesus warned his disciples that one could even prophesy and do miracles in his name and not be from him (Matt 7:21-23). Paul complained about "super apostles" who created hardship for him, people who claimed authority equal to his. He also warned of false preaching that denied the resurrection (1 Cor 15:12-17) and a different (false) gospel (Gal 1:6-9).

The issue of true or false prophets, true or false gospel assails the church today. Defense of the core doctrines as expressed in the Apostles Creed, for example, can bring ridicule and censure, even from "Christians." Even among evangelical Christianity self-styled "prophecy experts" predict the future with abandon, with little regard for their history of failure.

In our culture, truth has suffered. The new word for 2016 accepted by the Oxford English Dictionary was "post-truth." What exactly can that mean? If there is no truth then where does one begin to establish meaning, identity, communication, or community? In fact, if there is no truth then the statement itself is false. This may be widely believed but it is self-contradictory and incoherent. Unfortunately, it appeals to a gullible public which is committed to making decisions based on emotion and feeling, not reason or logic. Such a society is ripe for demagoguery and tyranny.[453]

3.b.iii. Letters to the Exiles – 29:1-32

Jeremiah 29 comes from the same setting as chapters 27-28 and chapter 24, sometime after the exile of 597 BCE (v. 2 – the groups mentioned are those of 2 Kgs 24:8-17). It is also tied thematically to chapters 27-28 by the controversy over the length of the exile and Jeremiah's conflict with other prophets.

---

[452] Is it irony that Ananias is the Greek form of Hananiah?

[453] See Timothy Keller, *Making Sense of God* (New York: Viking, 2016), especially chapters 5 and 6.

29:1-3

The chapter consists of three letters from Jeremiah to the exiles in Babylon (vv. 4-28 and 29-32). The first letter is to all the exiles (vv. 4-23) and the second to a certain Shemaiah (vv. 24-28) in which he quotes from a letter Shemaiah sent to Jerusalem (vv. 26-28). His third letter is also to all the exiles concerning the fate of Shemaiah.

These letters were probably written over a period of several months. The journey from Jerusalem to Babylon was a hard, three-month trek and the letters were in response to each other. Letters from person to person, city to city, and from capitals to outlying provinces were common at the time (e.g. see the books of Ezra and Nehemiah). They would have been written on small parchment or leather scrolls and sealed with a small lump of clay stamped with some one's personal seal or ring to ensure authenticity and privacy.[454]

The occasion of the first letter was a delegation Zedekiah sent to Babylon (v. 3) that included Elasah and Gemariah. Both were men of distinction in Jerusalem. Elasah was the son of Shaphan who was the secretary to King Josiah (2 Kgs 22).[455] Gemariah was the son of Hilkiah, who was probably Hilkiah the high priest who found the scroll of the law in the temple (2 Kgs 22).

---

[454] Many of these clay, stamped seals have survived the millennia in the ancient world, even in Jerusalem. One such seal bears the name of Baruch the son of Neriah, who was Jeremiah's scribe (36:4).

[455] This family had political clout and were protectors of Jeremiah. In ch. 26 Ahikam, Elasah's brother, intervened to save Jeremiah from the mob. In chapter 36 another brother, Gemariah, was among several officials who shielded Jeremiah from King Jehoiakim. After the fall of Jerusalem in 587 BC the Babylonians appointed Ahikam's son, Gedaliah, governor of Judah (40:5).

29:4-23

The first part of Jeremiah's letter was addressed to the exiles and has five paragraphs in a modified chiastic arrangement, each beginning with the phrase "this is what the Lord says."[456]

> A - Vv. 4-7 – settle in Babylon for a long stay;
>
> B - Vv. 8-9 – do not listen to the prophets I have not sent;
>
> A' - Vv. 10-15 – after 70 years, Yahweh will return and carry out his plans for the exiles;
>
> C - Vv. 16-20 – an aside to Jerusalem: God will bring judgment on the false prophets;
>
> B' - Vv. 21-23 – the false prophets Ahab and Zedekiah will die.

Two paragraphs (A and A') address the length of the exile and two address the prophets (B and B').

The first paragraph, section A, verses 4-7, is the heart of the message. For the exiles, it is a rather grim message. They no doubt were inclined to and wanted to believe Hananiah and the other prophets who promised that the exile would be short. After all Jerusalem still stood and was inhabited, and prophetic tradition going back to Isaiah had proclaimed that the Lord would protect Zion. Jeremiah's instructions were a total shock – build houses, settle down, plant gardens, start families, find spouses for your children. In other words, the exile was going to be a long one and the current generation would not see the end of it. The implications would have driven the exiles into deep depression.

---

[456] In Hebrew, *koh 'āmar Yahweh* (כֹּה אָמַר יְהוָה). There are also five occurrences of *'āmar Yahweh* within the letter and one more *koh 'āmar Yahweh* in v. 17 that does not mark a new paragraph. My outline follows the paragraph divisions in the Hebrew text, not the paragraphs of many English translations. See also Gary Hall, "Jeremiah 29: A Theological Foundation for Urban Mission? A Case Study in Old Testament Hermeneutics," *Stone-Campbell Journal*, Vol. 20, No. 1, Spring 2017

The verbs "build" and "plant" have significant pre-history in the book of Jeremiah. Jeremiah's call to ministry in chapter 1 was defined by six verbs – four of a destructive nature, and two positive. Build and plant were the positive verbs. The six were repeated throughout the book – 12:17; 18:7-10; 24:6-7; 31:4,28. It is only as the book approaches the end of Jeremiah's career that the positive verbs become prominent. But how could they be applied to living in Babylon? How could a foreign country be a place where God would build and plant his people?

Build and plant had a pre-history in Deuteronomy also. There, the verbs were applied to inheriting the Promised Land. God gave Israel the land of Canaan and would bless them in it. They would in fact live in houses they did not build and eat the produce of vineyards they did not plant (Deut 6). This was one of the many blessings of the covenant with God.

Now, they are to live in Babylon as they were to live in the Promised Land? That would seem to violate all of God's promises first made in Genesis 12, yet the admonition to multiply (v. 6) recalled the creation blessing of Genesis 1:28 and the rapid growth of Jacob's descendants in Egypt (Exod 1). This was a promise that they could flourish in a foreign land. They were after all the good figs of chapter 24.

Verse 7 was even more shocking. They were to pray for the welfare (or peace)[457] of Babylon. Jeremiah condemned the other prophets for preaching peace in the land when it was the wrong message (6:14; 8:11: 23:17), but now they could find it in Babylon! They knew about praying for the peace of Jerusalem (Ps 122:6), but a foreign city? They probably had a hard-enough time praying in Babylon.[458] In some

---

[457] The Hebrew is šālōm (שלום) which occurs three times in 29:7. Other suggested translations are wholeness, prosperity, well-being.

[458] Wright, *Jeremiah*, p. 293.

ways, it was a selfish prayer for if everything went well for Babylon and its king, it would go well for the exiles.[459]

This was not their first desire. What they wanted was revenge (Ps 137:8-9), but God would have none of that. His grace enveloped all nations and his will was for his people to pray for them. Even in exile his people had a mission. Daniel is one who understood that although in Babylon he could still carry on the work of God. Not only did he rise to a position of influence, he prayed three times a day. Did this include prayer for Babylon? Nehemiah is another who flourished in exile, rising to be the personal cupbearer of the king (Neh 1:11).

Verse 7 has become a focal point for a theology of urban mission for some people. Roger Greenway called it a "formula for city saints."[460] Robert Linthicum called it one of the most "profound ecclesiastical statements in Scripture."[461] Jeremiah 29:7 is the "'John 3:16' of urban Christians,"[462] a message "to all the urban people of God." But can this one verse taken out of its context bear such theological weight? It is indeed a revolutionary admonition for the Old Testament but there are several hermeneutical issues that must be addressed before one can invest it with such authority.

Verse 7 is better seen in its Old Testament context and understood as one of many nudges toward a missional thrust that finds its fullest expression in Jesus Christ and the New Testament.[463] Conn and Ortiz understand that the New

---

[459] Paul gives the same instructions in Rom 13.

[460] Roger Greenway, *Apostles to The City* (Grand Rapids: Baker, 1978), 31.

[461] Robert C. Linthicum, *City of God, City of Satan* (Grand Rapids: Zondervan, 1991), 145.

[462] *Ibid.*, 147.

[463] Hall, "Jeremiah 29," pp. 61-62.

Testament is the key to the text. They conclude their two-chapter study of the city in the Old Testament:

> Six hundred years after God's call through Jeremiah to seek the peace of the city (Jer 29:7), the fuller significance of the words of Jeremiah would begin to unfold in history. His prophecies to the exiles were filled with many themes – the raising up of David and the Davidic line, future blessing for Israel in God's shalom peace, Gentiles sharing in those blessings, cities tasting the fruits of Israel's good works.[464]

Romans 13 and 1 Timothy 2:1-2 provides a firmer foundation for the Christian theology of urban mission.

Jeremiah 29:7

But seek the welfare of the city where I have sent you into exile, and pray to the Lord on its behalf, for in its welfare you will find your welfare.

As Gary Hall notes, this verse has been hailed by Robert Linthicum and others as the key verse for urban Christians in the Old Testament.[465] Linthicum reminds us that the text instructs to "pray for the *shalom* of the city where I have sent you." The Hebrew *shalom* is broader and richer than English words such as "welfare" or "peace." It has the sense of well-being and prosperity.

Linthicum taught that Jeremiah 29:7 expressed a theological principle that should guide urban Christians. We should pray for the prosperity of the city we find ourselves in, no matter how foreign it might be. Only by such a commitment will we truly invest ourselves fully in our community and lead churches that do likewise. For Linthicum, this

---

[464] Harvie Conn and Manuel Ortiz, *The Kingdom, the City and the People of God: Urban Ministry* (IVP, 2001), p. 114.

[465] Editor's note: The forthcoming volume on Deuteronomy in this series, the *Polis Bible Commentary*, was written by Robert Linthicum. He mentions this verse in many of his books including *Transforming Power* (2003), *Building a People of Power* (2005), and *City of God, City of Satan* (2011).

> was the "shalom" principle that could transform urban venues into prosperous and peaceful communities.
>
> This was not easy for the people of Jerusalem in the exile. When they reached Babylon, they cried out, "How [can] we sing the Lord's song in a foreign land?" (Ps 137:4). Relocation from one city to another often brings upon "good old days" syndrome, the longing for our past city and its charms. I have lived in three of America's great cities: Seattle, Chicago, and Los Angeles, and now I live in Omaha. I still love things about Seattle; the ferries, the mountains, the sports teams, and the beauty. I still love things about Chicago; the zoos, the museums, the shopping, and the educational institutions. And I still love things about Los Angeles; the weather, the celebrities, the beach, and the famous locations. But now my love is for Omaha, a city that needs God's grace and blessing as much as any. I pray for the city in which I live, and now that is a growing city on the banks of the Missouri River that has many people who need to know God.
>
> *Mark S. Krause*

The second paragraph, section B of the letter, verses 8-9, repeats the warning about the false prophets that Jeremiah had made elsewhere. They tell lies, encourage false hope for the future, and were not speaking from God's authority.

The third paragraph, section A', verses 10-15, returns to the length of the exile, which was a focus of the conflict in chapter 28. The exile will last seventy years, not the two or less promised by Hananiah and his ilk. The seventy-year figure appeared first in Jeremiah 25:11 (see comments there). It was probably a round number to indicate a set period that would encompass the three generations of verse 5.

This was bad news and good news. The exile would be long, but it would come to an end.[466] Babylon would serve God's purposes, but it also had to account to God for its actions

---

[466] See Dan 9 for his interpretation of the seventy years and God's answer.

and would suffer his judgment (*cf.* chs. 50-51). This was a part of God's big plan for them (v. 11) which allowed them to look forward to the distant future with hope. They would experience God's blessing now in the land if they prayed for Babylon and in the future when he returned them to their land.[467]

These plans[468] were difficult for the Jeremiah's generation to appreciate for they would not experience the return. By the time the third generation appeared who knew nothing of life in Jerusalem they might not appreciate the plans either. In fact, that is what happened for many Judeans stayed in Babylon when Ezra led the first group back.[469]

God's plans included a promise of availability (vv. 12-13). He was present in Babylon, not just Jerusalem, and open to answering their prayers. Therefore, they must apply themselves to a life of prayer and seeking God. This theology comes straight from Deuteronomy 4:29–31, a text that anticipates an exile because of disobedience. It offers hope, but it also anticipates a return to covenant obedience as part of the heartfelt seeking of God. It would not be difficult to believe repentance in Jeremiah 29 is assumed.[470] Two common verbs for seeking are used together here,

---

[467] Many people's superficial and self-centered approach to Scripture is seen in the misuse of verse 11 in pop Christianity. It appears on plaques, in devotional self-help books, and as a life verse. It is intended to give us a positive, feel-good expectation of a rosy future. The context shows us that this usage is far from the meaning. Further, such an interpretation contradicts New Testament teaching on self-denial (Matt 8:24), cross carrying (Luke 14:27), and the expectation of suffering (Rom 8:17-18; Phil 3:10; I Pet 4:13, 16).

[468] In Jer 18:11, God expressed another plan, to bring disaster on them for their disobedience. He also had plans for Edom (49:11) and Babylon (50:45; 51:29).

[469] A major center of Judaism during the intertestamental period was Babylon. The version of the rabbis' teaching on the law gathered in the Talmud that is used up today is the Babylonian version, not the Palestinian.

[470] See also Deut 30:1–5; Jer 24:6–7; Hos 3:5

bāqaš (בקשׁ) and *dāraš* (דרשׁ). In such contexts *bāqaš* presupposes repentance.[471]

In condemning Israel's apostasy, Hosea said that when Israel sought God, he would not be found (Hos 5:6)—a terrible prospect. Therefore, the emphasis here is on God's willingness to be found, not on his people's search.[472] The revelation to the exiles was that he could be found in Babylon. Not only did God admonish the people to seek him, he promised that he would be found, a profound expression of his grace in the Old Testament. The people may trust in the false prophets (v. 15), they should rather trust in God.

"Restore the fortunes" (v. 14) is a key part of Jeremiah's message of hope and return. The phrase represents a radical reversal of the message of destruction and exile that has dominated the book and forms the basis for the "Book of Consolation" of chapters 30-33 (see below).[473] The phrase used two forms of the root *šūb* (שׁוב), a verb and noun. Jeremiah previously used the root to describe Israel's apostasy (turn away; 8:4-5) and God's call to repentance (turn back; 3:6-4:4). The NIV translates the phrase as "bring back from captivity"[474] but it carries more weight than just a return from exile. It for sees the restoration of Israel's covenant relationship with God with all the blessings that entails as God's chosen people once again.

The fourth paragraph, section C, verses 16-20, is addressed to the people of Jerusalem, who are the bad figs of chapter 24 (v. 17). Rather than being the blessed ones who have been allowed to remain in the land they will further suffer from the ravages of war and conquest (sword, famine, plague; see on 14:11). They had been warned often (v. 19) but had not listened. They did not learn anything from the

---

[471] C. Chhetri, בקשׁ, *NIDOTTE*, I:725. Daniel after reading this text put on sackcloth and ashes, fasted, and prayed, repenting of the wickedness of the people (Dan 9).

[472] Amos 5:4–5, 14 twice conveys God's plea, "seek me and live."

[473] The phrase occurs seven times in chapters 30-33 and forms an *inclusio* for them in 30:3 and 33:26.

[474] Usually with a footnote "or restore fortunes."

first invasion and defeat. The future was bright only for the exiles. This was verified when the Babylonians came again to Jerusalem in the winter of 588-587 BCE and destroyed the city, this time burning the temple and taking more captives (Jer 39).

The fifth paragraph of the letter, section B', verses 21-23, returns to false prophets and the status of two specific men in Babylon, Ahab and Zedekiah. They also told lies and lived immoral lives. They too would die just as Hananiah did. They would die by the direct hand of Nebuchadrezzar, suffering execution by fire (v. 22). We know from Daniel 3 that fire was one of the methods the king used to execute those who opposed him.[475] Not only would they die they would become the basis of a curse.

29:24-32

The second half of the chapter relates a conflict between a person named Shemaiah (located in Babylon) and Jeremiah. The account consists of several letters in reversed order. Jeremiah writes a letter to Shemaiah in response to his letter to Zedekiah in Jerusalem (vv. 24-28). We know the content of Shemaiah's letter only from Jeremiah's reference to a shortened form of it (vv. 25c-28). Jeremiah's account of hearing about the letter comes in verse 29. The last letter is to the exiles about Shemaiah (vv. 30-32).

Shemaiah was another prophet in Babylon, but he was proactive. He not only disagreed with Jeremiah he acted to stop him. He wrote a letter to Zephaniah demanding to know why Jeremiah, a mad-man and false prophet, was not in the stocks. He was another Pashur (20:1-3) with no respect for Jeremiah or his message. Shemaiah could not handle opposition. He would not apply Deuteronomy 18:21-22 as Jeremiah was willing to do with Hananiah (28:11). He needed to silence all opposing views.

Zephaniah the priest (v. 29) was an important official in Jerusalem, next in rank to Seriah the high priest (2 Kgs

---

[475] The Hammurabi Code, a thousand years earlier, allowed for execution by fire.

25:18; Jer 52:24). He was a confidant of King Zedekiah who twice sent him to Jeremiah with questions (21:1; 37:3). Instead of letting Shemaiah intimidate him, Zephaniah read the letter to Jeremiah (v. 29). This prompted another word from the Lord which Jeremiah sent back to the exiles in a letter (vv. 31-32). Shemaiah was denounced as a false prophet and preacher of rebellion. He was doomed to suffer the same fate as the prophets Hananiah, Zedekiah, and Ahab.

In summary, chapters 27-29 focus on prophetic opposition to Jeremiah's message. The opposing prophets meet the identical fate – death. Jeremiah is vindicated as the true prophet sent from God, but this is not the end of Jeremiah's difficulties. He meets political opposition in the last days of Jerusalem's existence that endangers his life (chs. 36-38).

3.c. The Book of Consolation (30:1-33:26)

3.c.i Book of Consolation, part 1 – 30:1-31:40

A major shift occurs in the book of Jeremiah in chapters 30-31. Through chapter 29 the major focus has been on the coming judgment and destruction, with only an occasional expression of hope (3:14-15; 16:14-15; 23:3-8; 24:4-7; 29:10-14). Now Jeremiah preaches extensively about the hopeful future in chapters 30-31. Consequently, these chapters are called "The Book of Consolation" or "The Book of Comfort." They are a pastoral counterpart to the sense of abandonment the exiles felt.[476] Often chapters 32-33 are included in the "Book" for they too focus on hope for the future. However, they differ from chapters 30-31 in format (prose verses poetry) and in time (they are precisely dated) so are considered separately below. Chapters 30 and 31 differ some from each other also, chapter 30 mixing judgment and hope, and chapter 31 expressing only hope and restoration.

---

[476] Brueggemann, *To Build*, p. 40.

30:1-3

Jeremiah has been preaching almost exclusively plucking up and pulling down, destroying and overthrowing (1:10). Now he begins preaching building and planting, which he first introduced in 29:10-14 and which chapters 30-31 fill out with extended promises. The power of the spoken word is evident in all his sermons, whether positive or negative. They shape the future and are for posterity. Therefore, Jeremiah is instructed to write them down in a book (scroll; v. 2). This seems a commonplace to us but was in Jeremiah's time an innovation. When the spoken word became the written word its character and its future were changed.[477]

The addressees of this word are both halves of the divided nation – Israel and Judah (v. 3). Although the northern kingdom, Israel, was taken into captivity in 722 BCE (100 years before Jeremiah's time) and Jeremiah primarily preached to the southern kingdom, Judah, God's message of hope was to both nations and his plan was to reunite them by returning them to Jerusalem and to the Promised Land (*cf.* Ezek 37:15-28).

God's intention was to "restore the fortunes of" of his people (*cf.* on 29:14 above), to once more endow them with all the covenant blessings of his original covenant and give them (re)possession of the land as if under a new Joshua led conquest. In light of their rebellion and sins so carefully articulated by Jeremiah, this was none other than a gift of God's grace.

The Hebrew root *šūb* (שוב, "turn, return, repent") dominates chapters 30-31 (occurring 14 times), some spoken by

---

[477] See comments on 25:13. See also chapter 36 where Jeremiah is commanded to dictate his sermons to Baruch to write down in a scroll. The ancient world was primarily an oral culture and the prophetic word was kept alive through the faithful repetition of the prophet's disciples. Writing it down gave it more stability though not necessarily more authority. See John H. Walton and D. Brent Sandy, *The Lost World of Scripture: Ancient Literary Culture and Biblical Authority* (Downers Grove: IVP, 2013), Part 1. In contrast in our culture the written word has more authority than the spoken word.

God, some by the people.[478] The phrase in verse 3, "restore fortunes" is literally "return a returning" and equals to bring about a complete restoration of the former greatness of his people.[479] God had taken them into captivity through the action of his servant, Nebuchadrezzar (ch. 21), but would restore them through his intervention also. This indicates the radical reversal of these chapters, God bringing life out of death (Deut 30:1-10).[480] This is a foretaste of the gospel in the New Testament.[481]

30:4-11

Before the message of hope, Jeremiah reminds his audience of the profound distress that accompanied the Babylonian invasion and resulting exile. It was marked by terror (v. 5), pain and fear (v. 6).[482] A woman in labor is a common Old Testament metaphor for panic and fear (*cf.* Isa 21:2-3; 26:16-23; Jer 4:31; 6:24; 13:21; 22:23; 49:24; 50:43). It is associated with men here, men who were perhaps warriors (Hebrew *geber*, גבר, is not the normal term for a man) for the army would have fled in panic from the invading armies. But there is a glimpse of hope in verse 7b which will be expanded in the following verses.

30:8-11

These verse shift to the proclamation of hope that characterize chapters 30-31. They repeat several key ideas from Jeremiah's previous sermons. First, the yoke of chapter 27 will be broken (v. 8) and their enslavement will end. In chapter 28 Hananiah broke the yoke but he learned that his action was premature, and he died. God himself would

---

[478] See comments on this root at 3:1-5 above.

[479] See Job 42:10. God restored Job's fortunes and gave his twice as much as he had before.

[480] Wright, *Jeremiah*, p. 300.

[481] *Ibid.*, p. 304.

[482] Chs. 4 and 6 described the coming terror because of the coming foe from the north.

break the yoke but in his time. His hand could not be forced by a prophet.

Second, God would raise up a Davidic king for them (v. 9; already promised in 23:5). Third, they were admonished not to fear (v. 10; *cf.* 1:8, 19) for God was with them and would deliver them. This was an ancient divine assurance formula, first expressed in Genesis 15:1 and repeated throughout Israel's history in times of distress and doubt. The exiles should not fear for they could expect a future of security and peace (*cf.* Lev 26:6; Ezek 34:28; 39:26; Mic 4:4; Zeph 3:13).

Fourth, God's presence would assure their security (v. 11; in contrast to God being against them, 21:4-5, 13) for all the nations that were oppressing the people would be destroyed (*cf.* chs. 46-51).[483] But the promise comes with a proviso – they will still suffer destruction for it is a part of God's discipline and justice (*cf.* Deut 8:5; Lev 26:18; Hos 7:12; 10:12; Jer 10:24). The discipline had a redemptive end, for it was the pathway to salvation. God's justice could not let his people go unpunished, but his grace insured a new future for them.

This text reminds the Christian of New Testament connections. The Christian is to expect discipline also (1 Cor 11:32; 2 Cor 6:9; Heb 12:4-11; Rev 3:19). More importantly, the development in Judaism of the coming Davidic king provided important background to the claim that Jesus is the one who fulfills that promise.

30:12-17

This section is arranged in a chiasm that emphasizes both the beginning and end and the middle statement.

    A - 12-14a: Israel's incurable wound.

    B - 14b: God treats Israel like an enemy.

---

[483] This contradicted the reality of the politics of the time for might made right and Israel was a pawn of the nations. But with God in control things are not as they seem. *Cf.* Brueggemann, *To Build*, p. 50.

C - 14c: Why? Because of Israel's guilt and sin.

D - 15a: Why do you cry out?

C' - 15b: Explanation: Israel's guilt and sin.

B' - 16: God will destroy Israel's enemies.

A' - 17: Israel's wounds healed.[484]

These verses have the same rhetorical move as verses 8-11, from judgment and pain to hope. The structure calls attention to the contradiction between the beginning and end, from a grievous wound that cannot be healed to the divine healing of that wound. Divine causation is behind the scenes. Ultimately God caused the wounds through the agency of the Babylonians, but he is also the only one who can heal the wound. Only with God can the impossible happen. This is grace that comes only from the Biblical God.

Depicting their suffering as an incurable wound was a powerful metaphor in that culture.[485] An injury was many times fatal. Before the time of the understanding of the importance of cleaning and covering a wound and the nature of infection, a minor cut or scratch could cause death.[486]

The structure of the passage also emphasizes the cry in verse 15a. In light of verses 12-14 it seems useless, yet the outcome in verse 17 demonstrates that it was not useless. The reason for the cry is unclear. Are they crying out because of the wounds, or crying out to God? Perhaps both. God responded to their cries for help in earlier times (Exod 2:23; 3:7; Judg 3:9, 15; Ps 107:13; 144:2; Isa 30:9; *cf.* Jer 11:11 – God will not listen to their cry); perhaps he would again. Jeremiah's contemporary, Habakkuk, struggled with

---

[484] From Wright, *Jeremiah*, pp. 307-308.

[485] See also 10:19; 14:17; 15:18.

[486] The same is true in many contemporary, remote cultures. Medical teams who visit these places often find the most horrific cases that could have been alleviated by the simplest of sanitary practices. See Dwain Ilman, *Are You Still a Doctor: A Lifetime of Medical Missions Around the Globe* (Elon Elite, 2016).

God's actions toward Judah and cried out to him (Hab 1:2). The foundation of prayer is the faith that God will respond.

Israel also learns something about God's justice. Although he allowed the nations to oppress his people it was a limited permission and in his time, he would exact retribution on them (v. 16). The retribution would be equal to the oppression; whatever the nations inflicted they would suffer.

The Christian is reminded of the blessing of healing that permeates the ministry of Jesus and the early church. Jesus heals many of diseases of all kinds and of demonic possession. The disciples in the book of Acts also carry on a ministry of healing. The most important healing begins with Isaiah's vision of the suffering servant who brings healing of transgressions through his wounds (Isa 53:5). Jesus was that servant who bore our sins and healed us by his wounds (1 Pet 2:24-25).

30:18-31:1

The climax of chapter 30 concentrates on the results of God's rescue of Israel and prepares for the extended message of hope in chapter 31. The restoration of Israel's fortunes (v. 18) will include the rebuilding of home ("tents"), the city (Jerusalem), the palace, and the reestablishment of the anointed king (David) devoted to God (v. 21). This king will be a Deuteronomy 17 king, one of their own who will rule in justice.

The result will be a continuous outpouring of singing and rejoicing because these wonderful things God did for them (see 31:4, 7, 12). This was a reversal of 16:18-19 and the only possible response to God's great mercy.[487] Psalm 126 celebrated the return with these words:

> When the Lord restored the fortunes of Zion,
>   we were like those who dream.
> Then our mouth was filled with laughter,
>   and our tongue with shouts of joy;
> then it was said among the nations,

---

[487] The description here reminds the Christian of the scenes in heaven in Rev 4, 5, 6.

> "The Lord has done great things for them."
> The Lord has done great things for us,
> 	and we rejoiced.
>
> Restore our fortunes, O Lord,
> 	like the watercourses in the Negeb.
> May those who sow in tears
> 	reap with shouts of joy.
> Those who go out weeping,
> 	bearing the seed for sowing,
> shall come home with shouts of joy,
> 	carrying their sheaves.

This was a return to the "good old days" (v. 20) when the creation blessings of Genesis 1 and 12 of numerous descendants would again prevail. The nation ("community") would once again be God's people (v. 22; 3:1; cf. Exod 6:7; Lev 26:12; Jer 24:7) and enjoy all the blessings of the covenant (Deut 28:1-14). This meant peace in the land for all their enemies will have suffered God's wrath and have no more power over them. Never again would their joy be overcome by grief.

This passage recalls all the past promise to Abraham, Moses, and David.[488] But there was more to come as we shall see in chapter 31.

31:2

Chapter 31 is a key text in Jeremiah. The tone continues the positive view of the future of chapter 30 but is even more comprehensive and emphatic. Jeremiah complained earlier that every time he opened his mouth out came violence and destruction (20:8), but here the opposite is true. It was a message he was delighted to give. The chapter contains a series of short promises of a blessed future for the nation,[489] each one introduced by a formulaic statement, either "Thus says the Lord..." (6 times) or "The days are

---

[488] Wright, *Jeremiah*, p. 312.

[489] Some scholars call these "Announcements of Salvation."

coming..." (3 times).[490] The first emphasizes the words are indeed the word of the Lord. The latter indicates the events will be sometime in the undetermined future.

These promises are characterized by three features. First, there is a strong emphasis on the coming unity of the nation by numerous references to the northern kingdom (Ephraim [10 times], Jacob [2 times], and Samaria [once]) and to Judah (4 times) and both together (twice). The restoration from exile will include both, even though the northern kingdom had been in exile for over 130 years.

Second, the past is the key to the future. There are several references to key elements in Israel's early redemptive history that will be replicated in the future in a new way. The Exodus, the wilderness wanderings, the taking of the Promised Land, the establishment of the Jerusalem and the temple all play a part in the future. Third, the basis for the bright future is the covenant relationship between God and Israel and several metaphors are used that come out of this intimate relationship: God as father, husband, shepherd, and even mother. Further, significant theological terms like redeemer, ransom and savior appear.

The Christian will find the chapter provocative because of the theological connections to the New Testament, quotes from the chapter in the New Testament, and the emphasis on the new thing God is doing. The exegesis will address these factors as we come to them in the text.

Verse 2 is a brief introduction to the chapter and invokes two ideas from the past: the wilderness and the idea of rest. The wilderness recalls Israel's wandering after receiving the law at Sinai. For Jeremiah, this was time of devotion to the Lord (Jer 2:2). But the wilderness can also refer to the place of exile. Both Israel and Judah went into and through the desert to exile. The profound idea here is that it is

---

[490] The exception is v. 3 which is marked differently and does not have a reference to the Lord saying.

where, contrary to all expectations, they will once again experience the grace of God.[491] It is this unexpected gift that makes it possible for them to return home.[492]

This redemptive aspect of the wilderness was first stated in Hosea 2:14-23, which perhaps informed Jeremiah. Also, God had earlier promised Israel rest, a special blessing and safety from all their enemies in the land (Exod 33:14; Deut 3:20; 12:9), but they forfeited this rest through rebellion (Ps 95:11, Deut 28:65). However, it is again available through God's grace. The rest of the chapter gives the details of how God's grace works in Israel's restoration.

31:3-6

The manifestation of God's grace is his eternal love and covenant faithfulness (loving kindness – NRSV). These are covenant terms and are bedrock aspects of God's character (*cf.* Exod 34:5-7). They are manifestations of his grace and will not allow God to completely abandon his people (*cf.* Hos 11:8-9).[493] The result will include a rebuilding in the land accompanied with joy like a wedding celebration (v. 4). This will reverse the joy that was taken away by the exile (7:34; 25:10). There will also be restored fertility to the land (v. 5), a common theme in promises of restoration in Hosea 14:5-8 and Amos 9:13-15 (*cf.* Deut 6:11). Equally important, the sin of Jeroboam of setting up idols in the northern kingdom (1 Kgs 12) will be reversed and the people will once again worship at Zion (v. 6).[494]

---

[491] Some may be surprised to learn that the Hebrew noun (חן) and verb (חנן) for "grace, be gracious" occur nearly 150 times in the Old Testament

[492] Earlier in Jeremiah the wilderness was the place where Israel sinned (3:2) and experienced punishment (17:6).

[493] These same words describe Israel's early devotion on Jer 2:2.

[494] Everything restored in these verses was destroyed by God's judgment (Wright, *Jeremiah*, p. 316).

31:7-9

God the father will bring the northern kingdom back from the exile. All will return, including the disabled and weak. They will return with praise, prayer, and weeping.

The promise begins with imperatives: sing, shout, proclaim, give praise, say, save (v. 7). God commands his people to respond to his saving work. God's work in this event is equal to his saving his people in the past, for example, in the time of the judges or from Egypt or the Philistines.[495] Saving the people from exile is a new exodus event as promised in 3:14-18. But there is a sad note also for just a remnant will be rescued.[496]

It will still be a glorious event (v. 8) for God is the one bringing them back. The restoration will include even the disabled (blind and lame) and the expectant mothers, normally those not expected to make the long trip. The return is inclusive. Verse 8 recalls Isaiah's song of the redeemed (Isa 35:4-6) and Jesus' reference to it in Matthew 11:4.

The journey back will be marked by tears of contrition (v. 9) as well as singing. Perhaps these are tears of joy (v. 7) but more likely they are tears of repentance for their sin. Their prayers (NRSV, "consolations") are the same.[497]

God will make the return easy, providing water and a level path (*cf.* Ps 23). The controlling metaphor of these verses is God as father (v. 9c and v. 20). He is the one who led them out from Egypt (Exod 4:22; 32:6) with kindness and compassion (Hos 11). This is intimate covenant language which shows God's great love for his wayward people. In the New Testament, the father went out to meet the prodigal son

---

[495] A prominent theme is the Psalms is many pleas to save the psalmist from his enemies – Ps 3:7; 22:21, etc. The Hebrew *yš'* (יש׳) is the root for noun "savior" which in Hebrew is *yeshua*, or Joshua, and in Greek, Jesus.

[496] See references to remnant in 6:9; 8:3; 11:23; 24:8 and in chs. 39-44. According to Isa 10:20-23, only a remnant will survive.

[497] The Hebrew is "supplications" which most translations render "prayers" which probably is correct. *Cf.* 3:21 and v. 15 below.

(Luke 15:20). In the Old Testament, the father seeks out the prodigal in the distant land to bring him out and gather him home (v. 8a).

31:10-14

God, the good shepherd, will ransom his flock from their oppressors. They will return with singing and enjoy the bounty of land as at the first. Normal life will resume. The One who scattered Israel is the one who will gather them (v. 10). The audience for this promise is the nations.

Jeremiah introduces two crucial theological terms to describe Israel's restoration: ransom and redeem (v. 11). Ransom (*pdh*, פדה) comes from the legal sphere and refers to paying the redemption price to secure freedom for a person or thing (Num 3:45, 51; Exod 13:13, 15). Thus, it became a term used of Israel's deliverance from Egyptian bondage (Deut 5:15; Mic 6:4).

Redeem (*g'l*, גאל) belongs to the sphere of family responsibility. It refers to securing the release of a family member or family property from debt (Lev 25:25-34 – part of the Jubilee year). This word was also used to describe the Exodus (Exod 6:2; 15:13). This concept created the position of kinsman-redeemer familiar from the book of Ruth. Isaiah described God's people as "the redeemed" (Isa 35:9; 51:10; 52:12). The air will resound with the joy of the redeemed for they will experience the bounty of the land as at the first (v. 12; *cf.* Deut 8:7-9). The language even suggests a new Eden with an abundant supply of water (Gen 2:25; Isa 58:11).

The "then" of the promise (v. 13) contrasts with the "now" of the exile. Now the joy of normal life was suspended (7:34; 16:9; 25:10). But then there will be no greater sign of normal life than the sound of the wedding celebration (*cf.* Isa 62:5; 51:3, 11). Furthermore, fatness[498] and good will return (v. 14; NRSV, "abundance and bounty"). The priests,

---

[498] "Fat" is a metaphor for the rich yield of the land (Isa 30:23), the life of the righteous man (Ps 92:14), or the life of the man who trusts the Lord (Prov 11:25; 13:4).

who had been the object of God's wrath will also experience God's abundant blessing.

Three words in this chapter, save, ransom, and redeem, are important theological words that provide a foundation for the salvific work of Jesus Christ. Christ redeemed his people with his blood (2 Pet 1:18; Rev 5:9; 14:3, 4; Heb 9:12). He also redeemed his people from the curse of the law (Gal 3:13; 4:5) and from iniquity (Titus 2:14). Jesus is also called the redeemer of Israel (Luke 24:21).

31:15-22

Verse 15 is a surprise. The previous words were about the sounds of joy, but we are suddenly back to weeping – bitter weeping. We are back to the now of the exile. The weeping is for those taken to Babylon. "Ramah" was the place the Babylonians gathered the captives before the long journey east (Jer 40:1).[499] This led easily to thinking about Rachel for Ramah was near her traditional burial place, five miles north of Jerusalem. She was the grandmother of Ephraim who in this passage becomes another way of referring to the northern kingdom (vv. 6, 9, 18, 20). Her bitter weeping also recalls Jacob's mourning for Joseph when told he was dead. He could not be comforted (Gen 37:35). These rich associations made a powerful impact on the reader.[500]

But her weeping cannot stand. God's response is another word,[501] an admonition to cease weeping. God has heard this as a weeping of repentance and assures her that the exiles will return.[502] Rachel does not weep as one who has no

---

[499] Ramah was in the tribal area of Benjamin (Josh 18:25) and well known as the place where Deborah held court (Judg 4:5) and the hometown of Samuel (1 Sam 1:19; 7:17). Benjamin was Rachel's son along with Joseph. She was barren and struggled to have children (see Gen 30 and 35). She died giving birth to Benjamin.

[500] The Christian is reminded of Jesus weeping over the city, Jerusalem in Luke 19:41-44.

[501] The "thus says the Lord" here does not mark a new section but responds to the previous word.

[502] "Work" probably refers to her tears of repentance.

hope (v. 17) for restoration is assured.[503] The Hebrew word for hope carries the idea of an eager expectation for the future. It is often translated as "wait," a waiting in faith on God (*cf.* Isa 8:17; 40:31; Ps 25:21; 37:7; Lam 3:21). It is accompanied by joy as in Isaiah 25:9:

> It will be said on that day, Lo, this is our God; we have waited for him, so that he might save us. This is the LORD for whom we have waited; let us be glad and rejoice in his salvation.

In the New Testament, Mathew quotes verse 15 to describe the mourning of the mothers of Bethlehem over the children killed by Herod. On the surface this quote is perplexing because it seems to take the verse out of context. However, New Testament quotes assume the readers know the Old Testament (as the Jews did) and thus also know the context. Thus, Matthew's quote provides hope for the mothers of Bethlehem for Jesus is the coming Messiah who will wipe away all tears and give them hope for the future.[504]

Ephraim responds with confession and repentance (vv. 18-19). He accepted God's discipline (*cf.* Deut 8:8; 11:2), admitted that he acted like an untrained calf (wild and uncontrollable), and repented. This confession makes explicit what has been assumed already, and clarifies that God's restoring his people is not cheap grace. It requires repentance and the shame and humiliation that accompanies true sorrow for sin (*cf.* Hos 14:2-3; Ps 51). This was a reversal of the attitude of the people in Jeremiah 8:4-6. Israel had refused to acknowledge any shame (6:15; 8:12; 12:13; 17:13) but now recognizes what abandoning God really

---

[503] "Return" in verses 16, 17 ("come back" in NRSV) and 21 is the Hebrew root *šûb* (שוב) which plays an important role in Jeremiah's theology (see on chapters 2 and 3 above).

[504] *Cf.* Wright, *Jeremiah*, p. 320.

meant.[505] This text is prophetic in a sense for we have no record of this kind of confession from Israel.[506]

God responded to the confession with love and compassion (v. 20) for Ephraim is his beloved son (*cf.* v. 9; Hos 11; Ps 103:11-14). God's voice trembles with powerful emotion.[507] Because of God's love and grace Israel will return will the same way they went into exile (v. 21). They earlier refused to acknowledge God's way (6:16-17). These sign posts could be the Torah. "Virgin Israel" recalls verse four and provides an inclusion around verses 3-21 that focus on God's compassion.

The "new thing" of verse 22 is uncertain and seems an odd expression. Perhaps it is proverbial. It is almost certainly referring to something unique and totally new. In this chapter the new thing coming is the new covenant (vv. 31-34). In the larger context of the Old Testament we hear of a new heavens and earth (Isa 65:17), a new heart and new spirit (Ezek 36:26), a new name (Isa 62:2), and a new song (Ps 98:1). The Christian understands these as pointing to the Messianic era of the New Testament and the church, and to the eschatological future of the book of Revelation.[508]

---

[505] Something they refused to acknowledge in ch. 2.

[506] In the exile and beyond the Jews, recognizing that they had gone into exile because of disobeying the law, began to develop teachings and rules designed to safeguard them from such future errors. Over the centuries this became a fence around the law and the legalistic mindset that Jesus condemned. These teachings and traditions eventually resulted in the Mishnah and Talmud, a collection of centuries of Rabbinic discussions and teachings. One often cited example is that since the law forbade work on the Sabbath, the Rabbis defined 39 kinds of work that were forbidden. One example in modern Israel, which is governed by Orthodox religious laws, is that elevators in hotels are set on automatic on the Sabbath so that they stop at every floor, thus eliminating the work of pushing a button.

[507] Wright, *Jeremiah*, p. 320.

[508] *Ibid.*, p. 321.

31:23-26

Previous promises addressed Israel (or Ephraim). This one addresses Judah and their restoration. Life in Judah will become again at it was (*cf.* v. 12) – the temple rebuilt (v. 23), towns re-inhabited, farmers and shepherds once more prosperous (v. 24), the weary and faint refreshed (v. 25). The curses for covenant breaking (Deut 28:38-42, 65-67) will be reversed.

Verse 26 is puzzling. There is no record of Jeremiah receiving any of his prophecies by a dream or vision.[509] He condemned the false prophets for making such a claim (23:16, 25-29). Interpreters have offered a variety of explanations, but they are only guesses.[510] That Jeremiah found this experience pleasant stands in contrast to the anguish he had experienced about previous prophecies and was perhaps intended to be encouragement as the following promises are.

31:27-30

"The days are surely coming" (v. 27) is one of three such statements at the end of chapter 31 (*cf.* vv. 31 and 38; "in those days", v. 29). This and other phrases[511] point to some indefinite time in the future when God will act on behalf of his people. This phrase occurs eleven times in Jeremiah, three negative and eight positive.[512]

For the first time, Jeremiah clarifies that Judah and Israel, whom he has addressed separately so far, will be re-united back in the land (v. 27). The language of sowing is indebted

---

[509] The visions in chapter one are different.

[510] It was a dream (Hallemann, *Jeremiah*, p. 233); it was a dream like hope not yet in hand (Brueggemann, *To Plant*, p. 67); the people were waking to new realities (Fretheim, *Jeremiah*, p. 439); it was a dream and thus ironic (Wright, *Jeremiah*, p. 322).

[511] "At that time" in 3:17; 31:1 and five other places; "In that day" in 30:8; "In those days" in 3:16 and eight times; and the combination "in those days and at that time" in 33:15 and 50:20.

[512] The first time is in 7:32 and is negative. The first positive is in 16:14.

to Hosea's vision of the future in Hosea 1-2 where a word play centers on his son, Jezreel ("God sows"; *cf.* Hos. 1:4-5 with 2:22-23a). The sowing fits the promise of a prosperous future in the land when once again grain, new wine and oil will be abundant. The building and planting of Jeremiah's commission (1:10) will finally be applied (v. 28). The judgments are over, and the blessed future has come. God assured Jeremiah in chapter 1 that he was watching over his word to fulfill it (1:11-12) and he now confirms it ("watch" is the same word). The long decades of preaching judgment and destruction had discouraged Jeremiah (6:11; 20:8) but this word of hope showed him that God was faithful but had his own timetable.

The promise ends with the quoting of an old proverb that the people in exile found useful for it absolved them of personal responsibility for their situation (v. 29).

> The parents have eaten sour grapes,
>   and the children's teeth are set on edge.

If one suffers because of parental sin or indiscretion, then one can elicit pity and pretend innocence. The law seemed to support this claim when it asserted that God visited the iniquity of the fathers down to the third and fourth generations (Exod 20:5; 34:7; Num 14:18; *cf.* Jer 32:18). The people in exile, at least the second generation, could claim its truth (*cf.* Lam 5:7), but Jeremiah affirms that if it was once true that day is coming to an end. Each one will be held accountable for their own sin.[513] Jeremiah had already pointed out in 16:10-12 that the children were more wicked than the fathers. The proverb shows that newness is possible and conventional wisdom is dismissed.[514]

Every generation and culture develop their own means and folk wisdom to avoid individual responsibility and pass blame onto someone or something else. Since the rise of the social sciences in the twentieth century, the economy or the environment are two favorite excuses. Many escape

---

[513] Ezek 18:1-32 treats this issue in detail and affirms Jeremiah.

[514] Brueggemann, *To Plant*, p. 69.

into fatalism and so one hears statements like "it was meant to be" or "it is what it is." Even Christians get caught in this trap. We might ask, how much Christian "conventional wisdom" is non-biblical?

The Christian can be grateful that there is one person in history who did not die for his own sins, but for the sins of others.[515]

> ### Jeremiah 31:29-30
>
> *In those days they shall no longer say:*
>
> *"The parents have eaten sour grapes,*
>   *and the children's teeth are set on edge."*
>
> *But all shall die for their own sins; the teeth of everyone who eats sour grapes shall be set on edge.*
>
> As Gary Hall says, the proverb here conveys the idea that the catastrophe of Jerusalem's destruction and the resulting exile were the fault of previous generations. The parents ate the sour grapes, but the mouths of the children pucker. It would almost be like saying the father was out in the sun far too much, but the son received skin cancer. Jeremiah corrects this to say that the parents may have sinned, but the children (his generation) are suffering because they sinned, too.
>
> In urban situations we may inherit long-standing problems that seem to be without solutions. We blame these things on previous generations. "Our city suffers from racism because our parents were racist." "We have a housing shortage because previous governments created regulations that discouraged the building of affordable housing." "Our traffic is terrible because of poor planning in the past." "Our church is in decline because of the ridiculous, non-functional building we inherited." These complaints may be true, but no one from the past is going to come back to fix these things. We alone can do this.

---

[515] Wright, *Jeremiah*, p. 322.

> I visited the Emmanuel Gospel Center recently with a group of college students. This remarkable organization is dedicated to making a difference in the south end of Boston regarding many seemingly intractable social problems. Among the things being addressed is the gun violence in nearby neighborhoods. A grassroots group of young people, ages 14-19, has been formed and taken the name "Making Youth Voices Heard." These brave young people recognize the debilitating threat of violence in their community and "... are determined to do something about it."[516] Similar groups, many of them church-based, have organized in cities all over the nation. Yes, the problem has been created in the past, and yes, there are powerful gun-rights organizations who disapprove of their efforts. But the violence and terror that bedevil people of our cities' poor neighborhoods will never be solved unless some good people stand up to end them. When we take responsibility for our own community, maybe the days of sour grapes on urban gun violence can come to an end.
>
> *Mark S. Krause*

31:31-40

Jeremiah 31:31-34 are the heart of the Book of Consolation (chapters 30-33) if not the whole book of Jeremiah. The focus is on a new covenant that God will make with Israel and Judah in the future (v. 31). Verses 32-34 describe its new features. Two affirmations of Israel's permanence follow (vv. 35-36) which are supplemented by a promise of the rebuilding of Jerusalem (vv. 38-40).

The concept of covenant is central to the book of Jeremiah. All his preaching is grounded in the assumption or conviction the Mosaic covenant was in force and that Israel had broken it. If the law found in the temple in Josiah's time was some form of the book of Deuteronomy, the pre-eminent law book of Israel, then the covenant law and theology would have been fresh in Jeremiah's mind (see 2 Kgs 22).

---

[516] See https://www.egc.org/blog-2/2018/3/28/making-youth-voices-heard-teen-anti-gun-violence-work-in-lower-roxbury

All of Jeremiah's charges against Israel are stated in the language of the covenant and the judgments are those of the curses of Deuteronomy 28.[517]

The promise of a new covenant is the next step in renewal of the old traditions that have formed a frame work chapters 30-31 (32:40 calls it an "everlasting covenant"). Jeremiah has spoken of a new Exodus, a new wilderness experience, a new entry into the land, and now a new covenant. This new covenant is designed to overcome the short comings of the old one (*cf.* Exod 19-24). God had done everything he could do to remain faithful to this covenant and to his people, as a husband would to his wife (v. 32; *cf.* Hos 1-3; Jer 3), but they broke the covenant not once but many times.[518]

Verses 32-34 explain the features of the new covenant. First, it would no longer be external, written on tablets of stone or a scroll, but it would be written on the heart within them.[519] In the Old Testament the heart (*lᵉb*, לב) is considered the seat of intellect and will, not the seat of emotions.[520] The written law had been broken, could be lost (2 Kgs 22:8), or forgotten (Hos 4:6), rejected (Jer 6:19), or altered (Jer 8:8). However, if it is on the heart it is internal, personal, and permanent.

The use of the heart here creates a tension in the context of Jeremiah. He had spoken of the heart often in negative terms. It was stubborn (3:17; 7:24), uncircumcised (4:4; 9:26), and wicked (4:4; 17:9). Could such a heart embrace a new covenant? Elsewhere Jeremiah offered an answer – God would give them a heart to know him (24:6-7) and he

---

[517] Jeremiah first addressed Israel's covenant breaking in 9:25-29 and ch. 11 (see comments there).

[518] Exod 32-34 was the first instance and only through Moses' impassioned plea was the covenant renewed.

[519] The text is probably not referring to two places within a person, but one since the heart was within the chest; *cf.* Ps 39:4; 55:5; Lam 1:20.

[520] The NIV translation expands the Hebrew to "...in their mind and write on their hearts." In Jer 4:14 – the inward part is the seat of thought because that is where the heart is.

would give them one heart (32:39). The ultimate solution was proposed by Ezekiel, Jeremiah's contemporary in Babylon. God would give Israel a heart of flesh instead of a stony heart, better yet, a new heart (11:18-20; 36:26; *cf.* Deut 30:6).

Second, there is one continuity, it was the same "law," it was not a new law. This is clearer if we understand that the Hebrew word *tōrāh* (תורה) means teaching or instruction in the broad sense, not in the narrow sense of a legalistic formulation. In the Hebrew Bible, the first five books are called Torah. These books contain narrative, poetry, songs, instruction, directions for worship, and legal formulations. All of them are teachings or instruction. It was God's will for his covenant people, designed to enable them to live a life pleasing to him.

Third, the need for a special class of instructors such as parents (Deut 6:7) or priests would cease. Each one would have direct knowledge of God. Knowledge of God in the Old Testament was more than just intellectual apprehension but included a committed relationship to God. To know God was to be obedient and faithful. If there was no faithfulness, there was no knowledge (Hos 4:1; 6:6). There was also a moral dimension to this relationship/knowledge (Jer 9:23-24; 22:16). Israel had had great teachers in the past such as Moses, Joshua, and Samuel, but in Jeremiah's day the priests and parents were part of the problem and failed to guide the people to obedience to the law (2:8; 5:31: 6:13). The new covenant will bypass them.

The new covenant would have certain continuities with the old but radical differences in how it would be experienced or practiced.[521] Therefore, some consider the "new" be more of a "renewed" covenant.[522] Longman suggests a fulfillment thrust, especially seeing that Jesus fulfilled the old

---

[521] Wright, *Jeremiah*, p. 327.

[522] Walter Kaiser, *Toward an Old Testament Theology* (Grand Rapids: Zondervan, 1978), pp.231-35.

covenant.[523] John Calvin suggested one covenant with two administrations.[524] Clements, however, points out the Mosaic covenant was radically broken so that the new was radically different.[525]

The Christian will be guided by the New Testament use of the text. The Hebrew writer quotes verses 31-34 in Hebrews 8:8-12[526] and verses 33-34 in 10:16-17. Jesus refers to his blood as that of the new covenant when instructing his disciples about the Lord' Supper (Luke 22:20). Paul also alludes to or quotes briefly from the text (Rom 11:27; 1 Cor 11:25; 2 Cor 3:3, 6). The Hebrew writer suggested that since the new covenant has come the old one will soon be obsolete (Heb 8:13). Paul points out that the coming of Christ canceled the written code which was a shadow of what was to come, and that the reality is found in Christ (Col 2:13-17). Paul also asserted that Christ was the end of the law (Rom 10:4). Mont Smith summarized the differences between the old and new covenant:[527]

Old Covenant	New Covenant
Tablets of stone	On the heart
In letter	In spirit
Kills	Gives life
Glory	Greater glory
Fading	Permanent
Brings condemnation	Brings righteousness
Moses veiled his face from Israel	Christians view the glory of the Lord with unveiled face

---

[523] Longman, *Jeremiah*, p. 13.

[524] John Calvin, *Institutes of the Christian Religion*, Book II: VII., which seems the least unlikely explanation to this author.

[525] Ronald Clements, *Jeremiah* (Atlanta: John Knox, 1988).

[526] The longest sustained quote from the Old Testament in the New Testament.

[527] Mont Smith, *What the Bible Says About Covenant* (Joplin, MO: College Press, 1981).

| Mind hardened | Mind transformed |

This suggests that the old covenant's purpose has been achieved and it is no longer useful or valid.[528] Paul rejoices that both Jews and Gentiles are now united through the blood of Christ (Eph. 2:11-22) which verified the new covenant. This new covenant theology is at the heart of God's macro plan for the world. Israel was chosen to be a witness in the world to God's love and faithfulness. They failed, but God had planned from the beginning that the old covenant would pave the way for the coming of the Messiah and the new covenant. Jesus came, established the new covenant and created a new covenant people of both Jews and Gentiles.[529] Their mission is to preach the gospel to the whole world. Israel's failure is a challenge to the church to remain faithful to the new covenant and to God's desire that all peoples and nations be saved.

In verses 35-37, Jeremiah gives two assurances that God is faithful and will not abandon his people. Both are grounded in creation (*cf.* Gen 1, day four) and both use the rhetoric of a conditional clause to emphasize the firmness of the promise (vv. 36 and 37). The unchangeable fixed order of the universe and its unimaginable dimensions attests to the eternality of God's promises. He is as committed to Israel as he is to keep the universe going.

Chapter 31 ends with another new thing (vv. 38-40)): a remarkable and specific promise about the rebuilding of Jerusalem. The theological dimension of the previous verses

---

[528] See N.T. Wright, *The End of the Covenant*

[529] Unfortunately, the unity of Jewish and Gentile Christians in the early church soon crumbled. In fact, it was threatened from the first (*cf.* Acts 15 and Gal. 1). The relationship of Jews and Christians for most of church history has been one of conflict and persecution. The horrific culmination was the Holocaust perpetrated on the soil of a "Christian" nation. The church needs to recover the Old Testament and an appreciation for its Jewish roots. See Marvin R. Wilson, *Our Hebraic Heritage: A Christian Theology of Roots and Renewal.* (Grand Rapids: Eerdmans, 2014). Paul warned the early Christians that they needed to remember that they were grafted onto the vine of God's people and should not think they were in anyway superior to the original people (Rom 9-11).

is balanced by a concrete, geographically specific depiction of the future rebuilding and growth of the destroyed city. Some of the place names are unknown (Gared and Goah) but the sense is clear. From east to west the city will be firmly established. The book of Nehemiah gives us further details of this rebuilding.

3.c.ii. Book of Consolation, part 2, Jeremiah buys a field – 32:1-44

Chapter 32 differs from chapters 30-31 in style but has the same theme. It is still part of the Book of Consolation (chapters 30-33) but is written in a wordy, prose style that resembles the book of Deuteronomy and Jeremiah 7 and 11. It is also given a precise date (v. 1). The chapter has five parts: introduction, verses 1-2; Zedekiah's question, verses 3-5; God's word to Jeremiah, buy land, verses 6-15; Jeremiah's prayer, verses 16-25; and God's response, verses 26-44. Much of the chapter repeats language and themes from earlier sermons, but there are some new elements. The heart of the chapter is another divinely directed symbolic act, the buying of a family plot, that is the basis of the message of the chapter.

32:1-2

The setting is in the tenth year of Zedekiah. The Babylonians had surrounded Jerusalem and her end was near (588 BCE). Chronologically this chapter follows chapter 37 but is placed here as part of the messages of hope in the book. Jeremiah was a prisoner of the king, confined to the royal courtyard. The city was in severe crisis and the leadership had fractured into parties with conflicting opinions on what to do. We learn from chapter 37 that there was a lull in the siege for the Egyptians had advanced into Palestine, hoping to take advantage of the Babylonians being preoccupied with Jerusalem (*cf.* 34:21-22). Nebuchadrezzar had left Jerusalem to deal with this threat and probably some Judeans thought the siege was over. Jeremiah took advantage of the calm to try to go home, but was arrested as a deserter and put into a dungeon. He appealed to Zedekiah who removed him to the courtyard (37:12-21). The timing is crucial here for the siege began in Zedekiah's ninth year and Jerusalem fell in his eleventh year (Jer 52:4-5). The prospects were hopeless.

32:3-5

Zedekiah confronts Jeremiah with a question – why? He had heard Jeremiah's many messages against him and Jerusalem and took offense. The "why" here is translated by the modern Jewish translation (NJPS) as "How dare you...."[530] Jeremiah in his first encounter with Zedekiah had told him to surrender as the only path to survival (21:8-10). The king chose to listen to other advisors and sealed his own doom. The irony of his speech here is that although he speaks, he can only repeat what Jeremiah had told him. He seemed to have memorized Jeremiah's own words, which were ultimately God's words. Verse one tells us that the word of the Lord came to Jeremiah, but the first words are those of Zedekiah. But his words are actually God's earlier words. If he knew these words so well, he certainly knew the answer to his question for Jeremiah had told him and the people over and over what God would do. Zedekiah knew Jeremiah's words by heart, but he did not take them to heart.[531] His question is not answered.

32:6-15

Ignoring Zedekiah, God gave instructions to Jeremiah concerning a piece of family property in his home town. His cousin, Hanamel, was going to show up to offer it for sale (v. 7). Under the circumstances this was absurd. Anathoth was just a few miles north of Jerusalem and had already been overrun by the Babylonians. The land was probably worthless and since defeat and exile was coming, it would remain worthless. However, Hanamel shows up as God predicted and Jeremiah buys the land. The land was apparently controlled by someone else and Jeremiah was the

---

[530] Zedekiah had numerous interactions with Jeremiah, at once both drawn to his message and repelled by it, and in the end incapable of heeding his warnings. See 21:1-7; 27:12-15: here; 34:1-7; 37:1-10, 17-21; 38:14-28.

[531] Wright, *Jeremiah*, p. 341.

nearest kin who had the right of redemption (Lev 25:25-34; Ruth 4). The transaction is explained in detail and is not much different from modern practices. Jeremiah signed an official deed before witnesses, made two copies, and deposited them for safe keeping in a clay jar (vv. 11-14).[532]

The point of the sale was a word for the future (v. 15). Despite the desperate circumstances of the time, at some future date the normal life of buying and selling property would again occur. The devastation of the land and city at present and the coming exile were not the end. Jeremiah's absurd act of buying a small plot of land was assurance that the whole land would regain its value. The land would be "born again" and there would be life after Babylon.[533] Though God had decreed the end of the city and nation, because of his grace and mercy it was not the _end_. In his creative power, he could do something unexpected and new.

32:16-25

The deed is given to Baruch to care for (v. 16). This is the first-time Baruch is mentioned in the book although he had been associated with Jeremiah for several years and was his loyal scribe (see ch. 36). As a son of Neriah he had status. His brother, Seraiah, was an officer in the army and carried a message to Babylon on Jeremiah's behalf (Jer 51:59-64).

Jeremiah's response to the surprising word from the Lord was prayer (vv. 17-25). This prayer is different from his earlier prayers which were prayers of frustration because of the word he had to speak (*cf.* 12:1-4; 20:7-12). Here he begins with doxology, praising God for his two greatest acts in history, creation (vv. 12-19) and deliverance of Israel from bondage in Egypt and subsequent settlement in the Promised Land (vv. 20-23a). The structure of the prayer is like Psalms that also praise God for these two greats acts

---

[532] Clay jars could last for centuries. The famous Dead Sea Scrolls were placed in clay jars in the second and first centuries BC and were still intact after 2,000 years.

[533] Brueggemann, *To Plant*, pp. 80-81.

(*e.g.*, Ps 136). "Great power and outstretched arm" (v. 17), and "strong hand and outstretched arm" (v. 21) are common idioms for God's work in the Exodus (Jer 27:5; Deut 4:34; 5:15; 26:8; Ps 136:12).

The doxology also contains an affirmation of God's character (vv. 18-19) – he is merciful and just (*cf.* Exod 34:6-7).[534] God's power and justice had direct implications for the situation in Jerusalem. His justice brought the city and nation to the brink of ruin for he was using Nebuchadrezzar as his servant (25:9) to punish them for defiling his good gift. Every generation was guilty (v. 18).

"Nothing is too hard for you" (v. 17; *cf.* v. 27) should be in bold type, for it is the crux of the prayer. God had shown through creation and the Exodus that he could do anything. He now was showing his power in the disaster at hand. Could he also restore them back to the land? Was that possibly too hard? This tension persists throughout the prayer and is behind Jeremiah's concluding statement in verse 25, "Yet you ... have said ...." The Hebrew literally is "But you said ..." with the "you" in an emphatic position grammatically. Jeremiah was having difficulty understanding why he should have bought the field under the current circumstances, circumstances that were the result of the work of God. Would God go against his own plans? We have again and again faced this dichotomy in Jeremiah, the twin themes of judgment and hope.[535]

32:26-44

The two themes of judgment and hope dominate God's answer to Jeremiah's prayer. He is the God of universe and nothing is too hard for him (v. 27).[536] Therefore, he can carry out his judgment on their sin (vv. 28-35), but he can

---

[534] *Ibid.*, p. 83, "utterly faithful and exactingly severe."

[535] Jeremiah's prayer models for us what prayer should be: a focus on God and his great work.

[536] This question here and the statement in v. 17 recall Gen 18:14 where the issue is Sarah's barrenness. It was not too hard for God to handle.

also, in due time, rescue them from the consequences of the divine judgment and restore them to the land (vv. 36-44). He is the Lord of the universe and beside him there is no other (Isa 45:5-6).

The reasons for the disaster that God is bringing on Israel, described in verses 28-29a, are a litany of accusations Jeremiah repeatedly brought against the people. This list is the most comprehensive in the book. It includes the evils of provoking God (v. 30), turning their backs and not accepting correction (v. 30), putting idols in the temple (v. 34), building high places to Baal, and offering child sacrifice to a foreign god (v. 35; *cf.* 7:30-31). God accused the people of promoting these evils from their first day in the land (vv. 30a, 31), the honeymoon time of Jeremiah 2:2 a distant memory.

The character of the people is sharply contrasted with God's character. They persisted in rebellion, God persisted in teaching them and disciplining them to turn them back to himself (v. 33). The unchecked imagination of the people devised a multitude of ways to make God angry. His imagination could not even conceive of their evil deeds (v. 35; *cf.* 7:31; 19:5). Israel took her cue for worship from their foreign neighbors, not from God and his law. It is difficult to comprehend what the human imagination, not controlled by God, can devise, but history and modern culture have given us a multitude of examples and one wonders if there is no limit to the depths of degradation. Israel's idolatry pales in comparison, but worse is the culture that celebrates the sell-out to the false gods rather than experiencing shame.

The second part of God's answer (vv. 36-44), introduced by another "thus says the Lord," is a drastic turn. God decreed Israel's destruction, but he also decrees her restoration. Nothing is too hard for him, even moving beyond the present crisis to a future hope. Here we see his greatest example of grace and mercy prior to the cross. The aspects of restoration here match those of chapter 31. God will "gather," "bring back," and "settle them in safety" (v. 37).[537] This is restoration language Jeremiah has used before and indicates a complete reversal of the exile. He will also restore them as his covenant people (v. 38; *cf.* 24:7; 31:1, 33). He will deal with their heart again, giving them one heart, or singleness of heart and purpose to serve and fear him (v. 39).[538] He will establish an everlasting covenant of good to them (v. 40; a feature of the new covenant of 31:31-34). Finally, he will plant them back in the land (*cf.* 1:10; 31:27). He will take great joy in doing this and will commit his whole being into the enterprise (v. 41).[539]

The answer ends with another word (v. 42) which is a direct response to Jeremiah's implied question in his prayer to his symbolic act. The time will come when normal life will return, plots of land will again have value and be bought and sold, and the whole land will be restored (vv. 43-44).

3.c.iii. Book of Consolation, part 3, Jerusalem and Judah will be restored – 33:1-26

Chapter 33 is the last section of the Book of Consolation (chapters 30-33). It is closely related to those chapters by similar words and themes. It comes from the same time and setting as chapter 32 (v. 1) when Jeremiah was imprisoned in the courtyard of the guard.[540] The chapter consists of two parts, verses 1-13 and 14-26. The first part focuses

---

[537] These promises have already appeared in 23:3; 29:14; 31:8, 10 (gather); 12:15; 16:15; 24:6; 30:3 (bring back).

[538] For comments on the heart see above on 31:33.

[539] Of course, God does not have a heart and soul, but this phrase is an idiom for the whole person (Deut. 6:5).

[540] Jeremiah's words of hope are penned from prison as were some of Paul's (Brueggemann, *To Plant*, p. 92).

on the restoration of the people and the city while the second section focuses on the re-establishment of the Davidic kingship and the Levitical priesthood.[541]

33:1-13

The first half consists of three separate words from the Lord (vv. 2-9, 10-11, 12-13). Each "word" is arranged the same, moving from a description of the present conditions to the glorious restoration of the future. This was a life-giving message of hope to the exiles whose city and land were destroyed and who languished in a foreign city under pagan rule. For them it seemed the end of everything – country, city, leadership, worship, identity, and even the presence of God (v. 5).

The present conditions are given graphic detail. The terrible siege of the city caused the inhabitants to demolish houses and palaces to fortify the wall against the Babylonian siege engines (v. 4). The city was full of dead bodies with no place to bury them (v. 5). The cities and towns in the countryside were depopulated (vv. 10, 12).[542] In other words destruction, death, and desolation marked the city and the land. God had turned his back on his people.

In the midst of this setting God offered to do for them things they could never had imagined, hidden things (v. 3).[543] He had the power and authority to do this because he was the creator and sustainer of the universe and everything in it. This affirmation pitted his power against all foreign gods. They had power only over the nations that worshipped them. It also answered the question, can God do anything for the exiles? He could and would. He would restore his people to the land, revitalize the land itself, and

---

[541] For some unknown reason vv. 14-26 are not included in the LXX.

[542] There seems to be a double perspective here – the city under siege and the city conquered.

[543] Compare Isa 55:8-9.

move them from desolation to abundance. This would be done in three acts of restoration.

First, he would bring healing and cleansing for their sin. They were thinking physically, but God was addressing the spiritual condition first.[544] They were in exile because of sin and that had to be dealt with before anything else. They had persistently and consistently rebelled against God. It was impossible for the them to begin anew without first experiencing forgiveness.

The three major Hebrew words for sin are used five times in verses 7b-8 to highlight God's grace. If they would repent (implied; *cf.* Hos 14) then would come abundance and prosperity (literally, "peace and truth"; vv. 7-9). This healing was spiritual and physical, including restoration of their earlier life, rebuilding of the city, and forgiveness of their sins. The outcome of this mercy was praise and witness to the nations of God's acts of goodness. This is one of the many missional texts in Jeremiah. This was the goal of Israel's original calling (Gen. 12:1-3) and the exile could not negate that mission.

Secondly, God would restore normal life exemplified by the return of wedding celebrations and restored worship (vv. 10b-11a). The loss of wedding mirth had been a consequence of God's judgment (7:34; 16:9; 25:10). This act would end in doxology (v. 11b) with the well-known refrain from Psalm 136 again sung in the land.

> Give thanks to the LORD of hosts,
>   for the LORD is good,
>   for his steadfast love endures forever!

Worship at the rebuilt (assumed) temple would take up the old hymns with a whole new perspective on the God they worshipped.

---

[544] See Jesus' first words to the paralytic, "your sins are forgiven." Then he heals him (Luke 5:17-26).

Thirdly, the empty, desolate land would again be filled with flocks and shepherds (vv. 12b-13) from the north to the south and everywhere in between (*cf.* 33:44).

The second half of the chapter contains four promises about the Davidic throne and the Levitical priesthood (vv. 14-16; 17-18, 19-22, and 23-26), each marked by a traditional introductory phrase. The promises here also stand in sharp contrast to the exilic situation and the portrayal of the last kings on the throne (ch. 22). These are God's "good words" or "gracious promises" (NIV)[545] grounded in his mercy (or "compassion," v. 26) and confound all expectations.

The first promise is a repeat of the promise of 23:5-6[546] with one significant change. Chapter 23:6 says Israel will live in safety, 33:16 replaces Israel with Jerusalem, focusing on the city. The new king's new name "the Lord is our righteousness" is an ironic word play on the name of the last king of Judah, Zedekiah (same meaning), which was given to him by Nebuchadrezzar! He was inept, unfaithful, and never lived up to his name.

The promise of the eternal Davidic king and Levitical priesthood were grounded in the old promises to David and Aaron (2 Sam 7:14-16; Exod 27:24; 29:9; 30:4). Both the current institutions had failed miserably, and Jeremiah had announced the termination of the monarchy in 22:30, but this promise was a part of God's hidden things and the failure of his people did not mean a failure of his word/promise. What looked like the end to the exiles was full of possibilities for God.

The surety of these promises was authenticated by God's bond with nature that went back to Noah's day (Gen 8:22) and to creation. The regularity of the day and night (vv. 20, 23) which was taken for granted but indispensable to life on earth was proof of God's faithfulness to creation and to

---

[545] The NRSV inexplicably leaves out the word "good/gracious."

[546] See comments there.

his promises.[547] Also, God's promises to Abraham concerning abundance of his descendants (vv. 22, 26; *cf.* Gen 13:16; 15:5; 22:17) were further proof of his commitment to David and the Levites. These were covenants that were made and honored. His eternal promises stand and overturn the ridicule of the nations (v. 24).

This chapter invites Christian reflection in two directions. The promise of a renewed city reminds us of the new city of the New Testament in Galatians 4:26, Hebrews 11:20 and 12:22, and in Revelation 3:12 and 21:2. This new city is from above, but it comes down to earth as a divine gift. It is here the saints will ultimately dwell with God and the limits of the old Jerusalem will be overcome.[548]

The second reflection directs us to the Davidic king and Levitical priesthood. Jeremiah's grand vision did not ever come to pass in Israel's history, either at the return from the exile or later (*cf.* Ezra, Nehemiah, Haggai, and Zechariah). The New Testament centers the fulfillment of these promises in the Messiah, Jesus Christ. He is not only the Son of David (Matt 1:1; Luke 1:32-33) but the fulfillment of the Levitical priesthood (Heb 8-10).[549] In Him both of these central Old Testament promises meet. He takes up into himself both functions to establish the new kingdom of God.[550]

---

[547] This fixed order in creation is asserted thousands of years before the rise of modern science which confirmed it through the deduction of "natural laws." Science can function only in a world that is stable and predictable. The earliest scientists were Christians who operated from this foundation. It is ironic that many scientists of our era espouse a world view that does not support this stable and ordered cosmos. Randomness and chance do not produce order. This modern scientific worldview could not have produced modern science!

[548] See Fretheim, *Jeremiah*, p. 474.

[549] See also the many quotes and allusions in the New Testament to Ps 110 which combines kingship and priesthood (Matt 22:44; Acts 2:34; Heb 1:13 for example).

[550] Wright, *Jeremiah*, p. 353.

Jeremiah 33:16

In those days Judah will be saved and Jerusalem will live in safety. And this is the name by which it will be called: "The Lord is our righteousness."

City names are sometimes casually given but endure for perpetuity. In America, many cities were named by European immigrants in honor of their former cities. Sometimes they were christened as a "new" version of the older city: New York, New London, New Orleans. Other cities were named for European royals or politicians: Annapolis, Pittsburg, Bismarck. Some have names from ancient history: Cincinnati, Memphis, Syracuse. Still others derive their names from regional tribes of Native Americans: Miami, Cheyenne, Sioux City. A few are named for figures in the history of the church: San Diego (St. James), St. Louis, St. Augustine. Some even have explicit and intentional Christian names: Sacramento, Philadelphia, Corpus Christi, Providence, even Los Angeles.

The exact origins of the city name "Jerusalem" may be obscure. Some believe it to be the same as the city of Salem, the city of *Shalom*/Peace (see Gen 14:18, *cf.* Heb 7:1-2). Jeremiah prophesies a new name for future Jerusalem, restored after its destruction and the following exile of the Judeans: The LORD is our Righteousness (יהוה צדקנו, *Yahweh Ṣidqenu*), a name also prophesied for the coming Messiah in Jeremiah 23:6. Some of our cities have acquired nicknames from bad reputations: Las Vegas (Sin City) or Chicago (the Windy City). What a joy it would be to live in a city that was characterized as the place where all residents agree, The Lord God defines our standards through his revealed righteousness. We would be *"Dikaiapolis"* the city of justice.

Mark S. Krause

4. Jeremiah and the Last Days of Jerusalem (34-45)

4.a. Jeremiah, Zedekiah, and Jehoiakim (34:1-39:18)

4.a.i. Zedekiah warned of the end and breaks a covenant – 34:1-22

This chapter begins a section that leads up to the fall of Jerusalem and details Jeremiah's interactions with the last kings of Judah. Chapters 34-36 are related thematically, enclosed by the accounts of two kings who refused to listen to God: Zedekiah (34:1-7) and Jehoiakim (ch. 36). In between are two examples of covenant keeping: a flagrant violation of a promise made (34:8-22) and a shining example of a word kept (ch. 35). Chapters 35 and 36 are also connected by place, they occur in the temple. However, these chapters are not chronological as we might expect. Chapter 34 takes place during the final siege of Jerusalem, sometime in 588 BCE. Chapter 35 occurs before the end of Jehoiakim's reign in 597 BCE. Chapter 36 takes place in the fourth year of Jehoiakim (605 BCE).

Chapter 34 has two sections. Verses 1-7 relate another prophecy of doom to Zedekiah. Verses 8-22 tell how the debt-servants were promised release but then later were re-enslaved. The two sections are enclosed by the same prophetic word – the Babylonians were going to burn Jerusalem (vv. 2 and 22).

34:1-7

Verse one portrays the Babylonian siege of Jerusalem as a "cosmic" event.[551] God had marshalled the whole world against the city – all the Babylonians, all the kingdoms of the earth, and all the peoples in Nebuchadrezzar's empire. When God was at work in the world against his rebellious

---

[551] Wright, *Jeremiah*, 356, quoting Stulman.

people all the world was involved, and its kingdoms carried out his will.

Jeremiah had already announced the fate of the city and of Zedekiah (21:10; 32:29; 32:4). The new addition here is the possibility that Zedekiah might escape torture and death, the usual fate of a rebellious king. Al-though he will meet Nebuchadrezzar face to face ("eye to eye") he could avoid the sword if he would listen to the Lord, something he was not inclined to do (vv. 4-5). These two verses are usually translated as a promise which does not fit well the context. Some have suggested that verse four introduces a conditional clause, "If you listen... then you shall die in peace." But Zedekiah had not listened before and there seems little likelihood he would at this point. His actual fate, as described in 52:7-11, suggests he did not. He tried to escape from the doomed city, was caught, brought before Nebuchadrezzar, and sentenced. After seeing his sons murdered his eyes were put out (!) and he was taken to Babylon in chains where he died in prison.

The tragedy of Zedekiah is that of lost chances. He had a complex relationship with Jeremiah. Publicly he resisted his message but privately he sent several messages to the prophet hoping for a better word (see chs. 21, 37-38). Jeremiah counseled him to surrender and save his life and that of the city (38:17) but he did not have the courage to go against the other political forces at work in Jerusalem.[552]

---

[552] V. 7 makes a historical statement that can be verified. Lachish was the strongest fortified city in Judea after Jerusalem. It was 20 miles southwest of Jerusalem and protected the country against threats from that direction. It was established by Rehoboam along with Azekah, a mountain fortress nearby (2 Chr 11:5-10). Archaeologists have found some letters at Lachish that date from 588 BC and the Babylonian attack. One states that they can no longer see the signal fires from Azekah, suggesting it had already fallen. One hundred years earlier, Lachish fell to the Assyrians in 701 BC (2 Kgs 18:17; 2 Chr 32:9) who celebrated the victory with a room full of carvings at Sennacherib's palace in Nineveh. The huge mound of Lachish can be visited today with the Assyrian siege ramp prominent on its south west corner, and the carvings can be seen in the British Museum in London.

34:8-22

This section presents a case study in fidelity and the lack of it and provides further evidence for the harsh words to Zedekiah in verses 1-7. It presents a sharp contrast between God's covenant keeping and the king's. The setting is the same as verse 1, but apparently occurred during a brief period when the Babylonians withdrew from Jerusalem (v. 21).

King Zedekiah issued a proclamation that all debt-slaves in Jerusalem should be released. No reason is given although they may have wanted more people available for the defense of the city. Debt-slavery was carefully controlled by the Mosaic law (Exod 21:2-11; Lev 25:39-55; Deut 15:12-28) and was the first law given after the Ten Commandments in Exodus. The law was associated with other laws on returning land to the original owners, cancelling debts, and fallowing the ground (Lev 25). These laws restricted the wealthy from exploiting the poor. The law on debt-slavery had a positive side. It provided an avenue for the poor farmer to work off his debt without losing the family land. It also limited the time of servitude (seven years) and provided for a generous gift when the servant was released. On the other hand, it was disruptive to the wealthy and the economy for it curbed exploitation and accumulation of land (*cf.* Isa 5:8; Mic 2:2). Unfortunately, there is little evidence that these laws were ever observed in Israel.

Zedekiah's laudable action in making the covenant to release the debt-slaves was short-lived (vv. 10-11). It was soon broken. Again, no reason is given, but one can surmise that the wealthy soon learned that the consequences cost them more then they anticipated. This brought God's full condemnation (vv. 13-21) and he compared Zedekiah's fickleness with his own steadfast, centuries-long faithfulness. Zedekiah's action was especially cruel because God had delivered the people of Israel from their own harsh slavery when he the brought them out of Egypt (Exod 20:2;

34:8; Deut 5:6).[553] This was the deep background for the debt-slavery law. All of Israel was expected to be thankful for their deliverance and demonstrate it through how they treated debt-slaves and other oppressed people.[554] Worse, Zedekiah had established the release covenant with an oath sworn in the temple, publicly invoking God as a witness. Therefore, he not only broke the law he profaned God.

God's sentence for this sin was an example of his retributive justice, the punishment fits the crime.[555] Zedekiah would not release the slaves to freedom, but God would release him and his people to the devastation of war – sword, famine, pestilence, and disdain of the nations (v. 17). The judgment of death was integral to the ritual of covenant making in the ancient world as verses 18-20 show. The word for making a covenant was to "cut" a covenant (v. 13; NRSV "made"). Genesis 15 offers an example. The parties to the covenant cut animals in half, often a heifer, then passed between the two halves, in effect saying, if I break the covenant may I become as this animal. This practice is attested in other Middle Eastern countries from that time,[556] so, in a sense, Zedekiah and the wealthy had already condemned themselves by their covenant breaking.

The cynical behavior of the wealthy and powerful described in this chapter is much too often the way of the world. It is the mark of autonomous individualism and consumerism.[557] Part of the tragedy of this episode was that the exploited poor were not some faceless, distant, lower class,

---

[553] Deut 26 on the law of the tithe gives some detail on how the Israelite should approach God – with a confession of his deliverance from slavery, with a declaration of his faithfulness, and with a commitment to take care of the poor.

[554] Christians are reminded of Jesus' parable of the unforgiving servant in Matt 18:23-35 who was forgiven a great debt but would not forgive a little one.

[555] See Hab 2:6-20 for examples against Babylon and Isa 5 for examples against Israel.

[556] Walton, *Bible Background*, pp. 48, 668.

[557] Wright, *Jeremiah*, p. 361.

but they were "neighbors and friends" (v. 17; "brothers" in the Hebrew). They were family, an intimate part of the covenant community. How could they be objectified and treated like mere property? Unfortunately, exploitation of the poor is a constant of human history no matter what the prevailing economic system is.

4.a.ii. The Rechabites Faithfulness – 35:1-19

The setting of chapter 35 is at least a decade earlier than chapter 34 and comes from the time described in 2 Kings 24:1-3. The Babylonians were making their first foray into Palestine and Jehoiakim at first submitted, then rebelled. The countryside grew dangerous and the Rechabites who are the focus of this chapter had to flee to Jerusalem for safety (v. 11).

The placement of this chapter is deliberate to contrast the faithfulness of the obedient Rechabites to the covenant breaking of Zedekiah and Israel (ch. 34). The Rechabites appear only here in the Old Testament, but their ancestor, Jonadab (or Jehonadab),[558] appears in 2 Kings 10:15-24 as an ally of King Jehu and shows his zeal by helping eradicate the family of Ahab and the Baal prophets from Samaria.

Apparently, this zeal also led Jonadab to issue stringent commands for the life style of his descendants. He gave them a "pentalogue" of five commands[559] which seemed to be a mix of codifying the "good old days" and adopting a modified Nazerite regimen (Num 6). Abraham "sojourned" in the land (Gen 12:10; 20:1; 35:27; Exod 6:4) and so must they (v. 7; NRSV "reside"). This meant living in tents, not sowing seed or owning vineyards, and not drinking wine

---

[558] It is spelled both ways in the chapter. The name means 'Yahweh is noble/liberal."

[559] Brueggemann, *To Plant*, p. 113.

(vv. 6-7). This small group had been faithful to their ancestor's words for 250 years.[560]

God instructed Jeremiah to take them into the sacred precincts of the temple, into one of the many side rooms among temple officials, and order them to violate their longstanding commitment by drinking wine (vv.1-5).[561] The pressure to comply was enormous, especially surrounded by temple officials and enticed by the great prophet of God, Jeremiah, but the group was adamant that they must keep the word of their fathers and their valued traditions (vv. 8-10).

At this point a new word of the Lord comes to Jeremiah. After seeing the Rechabites' response, God makes clear the purpose of this little tableaux. He is not concerned about the Rechabites' life style, but their obedience, their ability to "listen" to their ancestors. He finds it exemplary. It is this quality that is the focus of the whole chapter. He uses them as a foil to address the people of Judah and Jerusalem. The Rechabites had been faithful to an ancestor's word for a couple centuries, but Israel had not listened to God or obeyed his covenant for generation after generation (vv. 13-14). Jonadab had spoken to his family only once but God had spoken through his prophets to his people for hundreds of years, over and over again (vv. 15-16). Jeremiah had spoken of this persistence appeal again and again (7:13, 25; 11:7; 25:3, 4; 26:5) but it made no impact.

The key word in this chapter is $šm'$ (שמע), "to listen" which often as here means obey. It occurs nine times in the chapter (187 times total in Jeremiah) and provides the sharp

---

[560] They would have been a fringe group, living on the edges of the settled areas and probably considered strange. The word *racab* in some Ugaritic and Aramaic texts refers to chariot builders. Thus, some suggest they were itinerant metal workers, going where ever the work was (Walton, *Bible Background*, p. 669).

[561] The side rooms of the temple are where the priests and other officials lived, and where the temple implements and treasure were kept. See 1 Kgs 6:5; 1 Chr 28:12.

contrast between the two groups, the Rechabites and Israel. Seven times the Rechabites listen well to the word (are obedient to). Twice Israel did not listen (vv. 15, 17) or refused to obey. The passage invites the exilic readers to move from the lesser to the greater, from contemplating how the Rechabites were faithful in a small family matter to the enormous infidelity of Israel to God's longstanding covenant.[562] On the other hand, chapter 34 had already illustrated that Israel was incapable of keeping covenant even in "small" matters, like freeing debt-slaves.

Two "therefores" conclude God's word (vv. 17-19). "This people" (not God's people) of Judah and Jerusalem will suffer the covenant curses for disobedience (Deut 28) which God had already detailed many times. He will keep his word even if they cannot keep theirs. The second therefore addressed the Rechabites (v. 19). They would have descendants forever who served God.[563] This is the same promise given to the descendants of David and the Levites in 33:17-18. The Rechabites received the promise for lifelong obedience. In contrast, David and the Levites received their promise as a gift of God's grace.

Do the lowly and outcasts have greater capacity to listen and obey then the powerful and wealthy? The Rechabites seem to represent the poor in spirit commended by Jesus (Matt 5:3; Ps 25:16; 34:6).

The New Testament stresses listening also. Paramount is God's instruction to listen to his Son, Jesus (Matt 17:5). Jesus often commanded, listen (Matt 21:33). The sheep listen to the good shepherd (John 10:3). On the other hand, before people can hear (listen to) the gospel messengers must be sent (Rom 10:14-15). Habakkuk tells us where to start to be good listeners, *"...the Lord is in his holy temple; let all the earth keep silence before him!"* (Hab 2:20).

---

[562] The lesser to greater was a first century Jewish exegetical method that Jesus used often. See for example Matt 6:30 and the key phrase "how much more."

[563] See Neh 3:14. Some descendants helped rebuild the temple.

4.a.iii. Jehoiakim Burns the Scroll – 36:1-32

Chapter 36 has an interesting place in the book of Jeremiah and presents us with high drama. It seems to provide book-ends with chapter 26 for chapters 27-35 with certain parallels with chapter 26 (Jeremiah and the temple, Jeremiah's life threatened, he is rescued by friends at the court, some of the same people are involved, the time is in Jehoiakim's reign). The chapter also seems to provide a lead into the last days of Jerusalem recorded in 37-39. But it has parallels with chapter 35 in that they both feature kings who refused to listen to Jeremiah. There is also a connection with chapter 45 in the person of Baruch who has a crucial, but silent role in 36, but is quite vocal in 45 about it. It also has certain features that in the account that play a key role in the book of Jeremiah. We must keep all these inner-connections in mind as we study the chapter.

The structure centers on a scroll – its origin and its public life. The scroll was produced per God's instructions (vv. 1-8) and was read three times (vv. 9-10, 11-19 and 20-26). At the end, another scroll was commanded (vv. 27-32).

The setting returns to a time some fifteen years before the surrounding chapters. It was the fourth year of King Jehoiakim's reign (v. 1), that is 605 BCE. The year is crucial for it was a crisis time for Judah and Jerusalem as well as the king. Jehoiakim was placed on the throne by the Egyptians who had killed King Josiah his father in 609 BCE (2 Kgs 23:28-34). In 605 BCE the Babylonians defeated the Assyrians and Egyptians at Carchemish and become the dominant nation in the Middle East. In 604 BCE Nebuchadrezzar advanced into Palestine and destroyed the city of Ashkelon on the sea coast. This was same month that the scroll was read before the people (v. 9). Judah and Jerusalem were under serious threat. Would they be next? It must have been clear by then who Jeremiah's predicted "foe from the north" was (*cf.* 4:6; 6:1: 15:12).

This was the moment when God decided it was time for Jeremiah to have his sermons written down and read to the public (vv. 1-8). Although this is the most detailed account of prophetic sermons being put in written form there may have been precursors to the phenomenon. Isaiah's message was to be bound up and sealed for his disciples (Isa 8:16) and the peoples' quote from Micah in Jeremiah 26:18 one hundred years after Micah's time may have been from a scroll of Micah's sermons. Jeremiah's dictated sermons covered twenty-three years of his ministry which began in the thirteenth year of Josiah (Jer. 1:2; that is 627 BCE). This seems like a great feat of memory, but in oral cultures people memorized everything (and still do). Also, perhaps Jeremiah preached some of his sermons more than once and they were fresh in his mind.

The purpose of producing the scroll was centered in the great "perhaps" of verse 3 (NRSV, "It may be..."). God was still willing to give his people another chance, a perspective already declared in 18:7-8. If the people turned to him he would not carry out the disaster he had determined to do. Jeremiah repeated this hope in verse 7. The written scroll also allowed the words of Jeremiah to be read to the people and other audiences even when the prophet was absent (see below).

In the arrangement of the book of Jeremiah we have already met Baruch the scribe (ch. 32), but, chronologically, this is his first appearance. He was probably a royal scribe who had allied himself with Jeremiah.[564] He apparently had some enemies (Jer 43:3) but had easy access to the court in this event. It was an arduous task to create a scroll with all of Jeremiah's sermons. Papyrus or leather pieces had to be trimmed and sown into a scroll, then columns measured out and lined, then the text hand written.[565] This

---

[564] His brother was a part of the royal court, Jer 51:59, and he had his own seal. Archaeologists have discovered thousands of clay seals, called *bulla*, from Jerusalem from the 8th to the 6th centuries BC. These were the pieces of clay used to seal documents on which the seal ring of a scribe or royal official was stamped. Several Biblical people are named on these seals, including several kings. One seal reads, "belonging to Berechiah, son of Neriah, the scribe" which is Baruch, a shortened form of the name ("Baruch" means "blessed").

[565] The famous Dead Sea Scrolls have provided us with insight on the nature of scrolls. They were written on leather that show the stitching, lining and columns. The longest was the complete scroll of Isaiah

is part of the reason the scroll was not read until several months later (v. 9).[566]

The first reading of the scroll was to the people on a called fast day (vv. 9-10). Fast days were not a part of regular feast days and worship times but could be called for special times. Perhaps this fast was called from concern about the Babylonian sack of Ashkelon. The reading was in the temple where the people had gathered. We do not know why Jeremiah was not welcomed there but it may be related to his sermon in chapter 7 (*cf.* ch. 26; the sermon was near the time of this event, although Jeremiah has access to the temple in ch. 35). Baruch (and Jeremiah) had the support of an important official, Gemariah, whose brother had saved Jeremiah's life from the mob in chapter 26.[567] The response of the people is unknown.

The first reading of the scroll led to a second reading (vv. 11-19). A son of Gemariah, Micaiah, thought the content was important enough for royal officials to hear. At his report they agreed and invited Baruch to read it to them.[568] They were alarmed by what they heard and immediately decided the king needed to hear these words. First, they interrogated Baruch to be sure of the scroll's authenticity,

---

that was thirty feet long and ten to twelve inches high. The scrolls were rolled up on wooden spindles and unrolled as read. This was somewhat awkward and cumbersome. There were no chapter and verse divisions so finding a desired passage would have been difficult. When Jesus read from Isaiah in the synagogue at Nazareth he "unrolled the scroll and found the place..." (Luke 4:17). This implies he knew the book well and knew where to find the passage.

[566] Though Baruch is a silent partner in this chapter we learn from ch. 45 that he had strong objections to his role and did not think it would do anything for his reputation.

[567] Gemariah was the son of Shaphank the royal secretary under Josiah, the one who told Josiah about the scroll found in the temple (2 Kgs 22:3, 8, 10). A seal has been found with his name on it also.

[568] Little is known about this group but Elnathan was an emissary of the king who went to Egypt to bring back the prophet Uriah for execution (Jer 26:2-23). However, here he seems supportive of Baruch and Jeremiah (*cf.* v. 25).

then cautioned Baruch that he and Jeremiah should hide themselves. They apparently anticipated a possible negative reaction from the king.

This led to the third reading of the scroll (vv. 20-26). Since Baruch was in hiding, it became Jehudi's responsibility to read the scroll to the king. Though the king listened to the whole scroll, he responded with complete distain, cutting it up as it was read and burning it.[569] Many of the officials were shocked at this but he ignored them. Jehoiakim's contempt is emphasized twice. He was not alarmed as the other officials were and he did not tear his garments. The latter is a direct reference to his father Josiah who tore his garments in repentance when he heard the words of the scroll found in the temple (1 Kgs 22:11).[570] The great "perhaps" was in vain.

This act of defiance had two consequences (vv. 27-32). Jehoiakim received a direct word from the Lord that sealed his fate. He would die in shame and have no descendent to rule on the throne. This agrees with the judgment Jeremiah had already issued against him (22:18-19). More importantly, burning the scroll did not destroy the word of the Lord. God commanded Jeremiah and Baruch to write out another scroll with the same words, only to this one they added even more sermons. Not only could Jehoiakim not extinguish the word of God, he was a catalyst for a larger scroll.

The focus of this chapter is on the written word of God.[571] As in chapter 1 we have the tension between God's word and Jeremiah's words. God's word comes through the prophetic word so that although the words are from Jeremiah, they still are God's. There is no half and half. The oral word written down marked a significant change in how the word

---

[569] The "penknife" he used (v. 23) was the same kind that Baruch would have used to trim the sheets of the scroll for sewing together.

[570] The Hebrew text connects the cutting of the scroll and the not cutting of his garments by using the same verb.

[571] The Hebrew word for "word" (*dbr*, דבר) in noun and verb forms occurs 23 times in the chapter.

was heard and passed on. No longer was it from memory nor was it confined to the presence of the prophet. Now it could be read and heard in many places and times. Furthermore, it could not be destroyed but lived on as it was copied over and over. The prophet would die but his word (God's word) would live on. Isaiah 40:8 is proven true, "... *the word of our God will stand forever*" and it will accomplish everything that God intends (Isa 55:10-13). The written word had the same authority as Jeremiah's spoken word. Each new generation, including ourselves, can read and hear this word, and respond by accepting it or rejecting it.

This event became the model for canon making which over one thousand years has produced the Bible which is cherished by Jew and Christian alike (although in different forms). The canon was God's idea and the doctrine of inspiration assures us that not only did God initiate the canon, he was at work assuring its integrity and authority.

The Christian has the greatest gift of all, Jesus Christ is the incarnate Word and perfect revelation of God (John 1). Our salvation is found in a Person not merely in written words. But we are still dependent on the written word that bears witness to the Word. Despite Enlightenment and Post-enlightenment attacks on the Bible, it still endures, and the preached word still changes lives around the world.

4.a.iv. Jeremiah and Zedekiah – God's Word Vs. Realpolitik – 37:1-38:28

These two chapters are chronologically located nine years after chapter 36 and are connected to the story line of chapters 21, 27-29, 32, and 34. They show Jerusalem and its leaders plunging head long into disaster which unfolds in chapter 39. The events of these two chapters take place within the eighteen months that the Babylonians besieged the city before it fell (*cf.* 39:1-2; 2 Kgs 24:8-20; 25).

Though not in chronological order chapter 36 connects to chapters 37-38 by the theme of two kings, who were brothers, and who did not listen to Jeremiah. They also share the theme of endangered Jeremiah whose life was threatened by powerful parties in the royal court.

Death hovers over these chapters, either as a threat for Jeremiah or as a certainty for Jerusalem (37:21; 38:2, 4, 9, 10, 15, 24, 25, 26). Both Jeremiah and Zedekiah are faced with challenges. Will Zedekiah listen? Will Jeremiah survive? Three times Zedekiah questions Jeremiah (37:2-10, 17-20; 38:14-23). Three times Jeremiah's life is in danger (37:11-16; 38:1-6, 24-28). These dual tensions are not resolved until chapter 39.[572] Jeremiah's innocent suffering has often been compared with Jesus' suffering in his last week in the gospels.[573] In this way Jeremiah could be seen as an Old Testament prefiguring of Jesus Christ and it is fruitful to think about them in this way. Jeremiah is characterized as resolute and steadfast, remaining faithful to his divine mission at great personal danger.

Standing against Jeremiah are the court officials, some named, who see him as a threat to the security of Jerusalem and seek his death. They are not the same court officials of chapter 36, who were taken into exile with Jehoiachin, but they represent the same power politics. They are pro-Egyptian and see surrender to Babylon as treason.

Caught in between these two immovable forces is Zedekiah. He is characterized as irresolute and vacillating, eager to consult Jeremiah, but unable to stand against his court officials. He was put on the throne by Nebuchadrezzar but was disloyal and easily influenced by others.

The introduction (37:1-2) sets the stage for the timing of the events. It also tells the reader that although Zedekiah may seem open to change, he and the people would not listen to Jeremiah no matter how many times they seek a new word.

The exegesis will first consider Zedekiah's three encounters with Jeremiah and then explore the three threats to Jeremiah's life. Several scholars suggest that chapters 37 and

---

[572] Although chapter 39 chronologically belongs with chapter 37-38 it is given its own heading and will be treated separately.

[573] Wright, *Jeremiah*, 378, lists some of the parallels.

38 are two accounts of the same events, with chapter 38 providing more details. This would parallel the twin accounts of the temple sermon in chapters 7 and 26.[574] However, the exegesis will follow the text as we have it.

Zedekiah's first inquiry of Jeremiah is through a delegation he sent (37:3). He had sent a delegation earlier (21:1-2) seeking a miracle from God. Now he asks for prayer.[575] Both requests seem out of character. Jeremiah had persistently appealed to Zedekiah to turn to the Lord and obey his word, but he had refused. Now he wanted Jeremiah to pray! Pray for what? That God go back on his word? Probably, the king wanted Jeremiah to pray that God would rescue them from the Babylonians (which he had already refused to do). Jeremiah ignored the request and repeated his standard message, the Babylonians would burn Jerusalem with fire (vv. 7-10).[576]

The narrator provides a clue to the motivation for Zedekiah's request. The Egyptian Pharaoh, Apries, sent an army into Palestine to challenge the Babylonians. Nebuchadrezzar lifted the siege to meet this challenge (v. 5, 11). This provided hope that the Egyptians would prevail and the pro-Egyptian party in Jerusalem gained confidence. This included the royal officials. Jeremiah dashed these hopes (v. 8). Chapter 34 has already told us that Zedekiah used this respite to re-enslave the debt slaves they had released. The king is not only hypocritical, he is clueless.[577]

---

[574] See *Ibid.*, p. 380 for the parallels.

[575] One emissary was the same in both missions, the priest Zephaniah. The other was Jehucal, who turned out to be an enemy of Jeremiah in 38:1 (Jucal there). A clay seal with Jehucal's name has been found in the Davidic city of old Jerusalem dated from this time which confirms his important position as a government official.

[576] Jeremiah had been told twice not to pray for the people – 7:16; 11:14.

[577] Kidner, *Jeremiah*, p. 122.

Jeremiah 37:14b-15a

But Irijah would not listen to him, and arrested Jeremiah and brought him to the officials. The officials were enraged at Jeremiah, and they beat him and imprisoned him ...

Accounts of misconduct and mistreatment of poorer city residents by police and courts are sometimes so outrageous they make the national news. For people living in large cities, they are almost daily occurrences. Minor violations are accelerated into major, sometimes deadly confrontations. In depressed neighborhoods, police officers are not always seen as protectors of the order and the innocent. In areas of high crime and high levels of poverty, negative experiences with law enforcement remain in the community memory for a long time.

As Jerusalem approached its final catastrophe, Jeremiah (perhaps unwisely) sought to leave the city to deal with a family property matter. The policeman at the gate did not find his reason for leaving credible, believing he was exiting to give aid and comfort to Jerusalem's enemies. Rather than seek the truth, this man (Irijah) chose to disbelieve Jeremiah and took him to his higher-ups, where he was beaten and imprisoned.

Sorting out the stories when a crime is committed can be tedious, especially in an atmosphere of distrust. Navigating the legal system when assigned to an overworked court-appointed public defender can be frustrating. Others in the city have need of legal advice without resources to hire an attorney. Should the Christian community play a role in this?

A number of churches in urban areas have partnered with volunteer attorneys to provide legal assistance to the vulnerable in their communities, including immigrants. An example is the Park Avenue Legal Clinic, a ministry of the Park Avenue United Methodist Church in Minneapolis. This church partners with the Volunteer Lawyers Network (VLN) to provide basic legal advice at no cost. The organization also works to refer people with more serious legal

> needs to more extensive resources in the area. One advocate working for the organization said, "Justice means that an individual will not be railroaded by those with more power, money or legal know-how. It means that regardless of who you are, you have the right to equality."[578]
>
> In Jeremiah's case, King Zedekiah intervened and his received better treatment (although remained imprisoned). We cannot count on royal intervention in our cities. Churches may lack resources to resolve all the injustice in their city, but they can make a difference if they embrace the problem like Park Avenue Methodist has.
>
> Mark S. Krause

Zedekiah's second inquiry was a direct meeting with Jeremiah after he had been imprisoned by the court officials (vv. 17-21; see below for comments on vv. 11-16). Zedekiah asked if there was a word from the Lord. He apparently missed the irony. Jeremiah had for years been generous with him with the word of the Lord. Jeremiah's reply was terse, and we can imagine impatient. "There is" he replied (v. 17).[579] It was the same, bad news for Zedekiah. Most of the conversation was Jeremiah's plea to get moved to a different confinement area since he would easily die where the officials had put him. Zedekiah agreed and sent him to the "court of the guard" (v. 21; *cf.* 32:2; 38:13, 28; 39:14).

Zedekiah sent for Jeremiah a third time to meet him in the temple area (38:14-23). The third question is not stated but we can infer from Jeremiah's answer that it was the same – would God somehow save him? We also learn that Zedekiah lived in fear of some of the Judeans who had already surrendered to the Babylonians (v. 19). He presents a pathetic figure – afraid of the Babylonians, afraid of his own court officials, and afraid of his people. The one he should have feared was God! Even when Jeremiah gave him a vision of what would happen to his wives and children if he

---

[578] Jerrold Bergfalk at https://www.vlnmn.org/volunteer.

[579] "There is" is the literal translation of the Hebrew word *yeš* (שׁי) which is pronounced yesh, very close to the English "yes".

did not surrender to the Babylonians (vv. 21-23) his only concern was for his own life (vv. 24-26). Jeremiah continually counseled Zedekiah that he and Jerusalem would survive only if he surrendered to the Babylonians. Unfortunately, he was incapable of such courage and doomed the city and people.

Paralleled with Zedekiah's three questions are the three threats to Jeremiah's life. The first comes during the interlude when the Babylonians had lifted the siege (37:11-16). Jeremiah choose that moment to attempt to go home to Anathoth and see about some family property.[580] The guard at the gate interpreted his attempt to leave as wanting to go over to the Babylonians and therefore as treason. Some Judeans already had deserted Jerusalem to surrender (*cf.* 38:19) and Jeremiah had preached surrender so there were grounds for the charge. The court officials, who were pro-Egyptian and a power-block at the palace, beat him and threw him into a dungeon, or a cistern in the basement of a house (vv. 15-16).[581] Only Zedekiah's intervention saved him, an intervention that defied the officials.

The second endangerment came from the same officials when they heard Jeremiah's message that the Judeans should surrender to the Babylonians (38:1-6).[582] They charged he was not seeking the welfare of the people (v. 4) though that is exactly what he was doing. They were the ones endangering the peoples' lives by resisting Babylon. This time they threw him into an old cistern, a deep hole

---

[580] This may or may not have been the same property of ch. 32. The visit of Jeremiah's cousin there was a little later than this event.

[581] It seems it was a vaulted room and would have been dank, dark, and moist, an extreme danger to health. The same word is used for Joseph's dungeon in Gen 40:15 and 41:14. Similar cisterns can be seen in the lower reaches of old Jerusalem today.

[582] The officials are named here. A seal with Gedaliah's name has also been found in the same area as the one for Jehucal.

cut in the limestone rock and lined with lime. It had no water but only deep mud.583 This was even more dangerous than the previous dungeon for he was stuck in the stinking, filthy muck. Many Psalms bemoan being in a metaphorical pit, but for Jeremiah it was real (*cf.* Ps 28:1; 30:1-3; 69:1-2; 88). In this instance, Zedekiah did not dare defy the officials (v. 5) and did not intervene to save Jeremiah.

Jeremiah's rescue from that danger (vv. 7-13) came from a totally unexpected source – a eunuch in the king's own house from Ethiopia named Ebed-melech (literally, "servant of the king").584 His providential appearance is not explained but his appeal to the king results in orders to get Jeremiah out of the pit. The king ordered him to take thirty men (not three as in the NRSV) with him, perhaps to protect themselves from the other royal officials. Jeremiah was returned to the courtyard of the guard.585

The third danger to Jeremiah's life came from the king himself. He called Jeremiah to the temple for a private interview and warned him to say nothing of it to the court officials if they asked (vv. 24-27). Zedekiah again shows his fears and concern for self-preservation. The officials were concerned but Jeremiah deflected their threat by not revealing the nature of his conversation with the king. He remained in the court of the guard to await the fall of Jerusalem (v. 28). For the time being the royal officials had prevailed, but only for a moment.

These events demonstrate the tension that results when power politics and patriotism clash with the prophetic word of God. The court officials thought they were cleverly applying *realpolitik* when the times called for obedience to God. They sought every chance to opt for independence.

---

583 This may indicate the dire conditions of Jerusalem at the time. Water was scarce.

584 The Christian is reminded of another Ethiopian eunuch in Acts 8:26-40.

585 Ebed-melech subsequently received a message of salvation from God which is recorded in 39:15-18.

This patriotism was idolatrous for it led to resistance to God.[586] This malady has persisted through the ages and loyalty to country often trumps obedience to God. Zedekiah's hypocritical request for prayer is also still with us. One can think of societies that marginalize God, including our own, but in times of national crisis flock to churches to pray. But as in Zedekiah's case, why will God listen to those who do not listen to him?

4.b. The Fall of Jerusalem and Aftermath (39:1-45:5)

4.b.i. The Fall of Jerusalem – 39:1-18

This chapter is the climax of the book of Jeremiah. Everything he had been preaching from chapter 2 has finally come to conclusion. He is a true prophet according to Deuteronomy 18 for what he said has come to pass. Jerusalem falls to the Babylonians ("Chaldeans" in v. 5) as Jeremiah predicted back in chapter 21 and many times later, the most recent in chapters 37-38. Despite the importance of the event it is briefly told with little detail. It has neither a theological justification or an admonition of lessons to learn. The Babylonians do what powerful nations do to rebellious, little kingdoms – they destroy them and their leadership. God and Jeremiah are absent. They have said all that needs to be said. The end has come.

Chapter 39 has three sections. Verses 1-10 give the brief details of the fall of the city of Jerusalem. Verses 11-14 relate the kind treatment Jeremiah received from Nebuchadrezzar. Verses 15-18 give a message of salvation to Ebed-melech that is chronologically dislocated for it occurred before the fall of the city. It is possibly placed here to contrast the fate of Zedekiah who would not listen to God and Ebed-melech who trusted God.

---

[586] Wright, *Jeremiah*, p. 385.

39:1-10[587]

The siege of Jerusalem is precisely dated (v. 2). It began on January 15, 588 BCE and ended on July 18, 586 BCE, almost exactly eighteen months later.[588] We have already seen that several events in the book of Jeremiah took place during this time (*cf.* chs. 21, 32, 34-35, 37-38). The narrator was familiar with the leaders of the Babylonian army and lists names and positions (v. 3). The last named (Nergal-sharezer[589]) was the son-in-law of Nebuchadrezzar and took over the kingdom when the latter died.[590] They established their authority by setting up residence in the city gate.

Zedekiah, with his court, at the last moment turned tail and ran, abandoning the people to the fate he brought on them (v. 4).[591] He apparently thought he could get to one of the small kingdoms east of the Jordan River and find refuge. He almost made it, but he was captured a few miles from the river and brought before Nebuchadrezzar as Jeremiah predicted, seeing him "eye to eye" (as promised in 34:3).[592] His punishment was customary for rebellious

---

[587] A more detailed description of the fall is found in Jer 52 which equals 2 Kgs 24:18-25:30. They both have a large section on the temple and its contents.

[588] This assumes that Judah used a lunar calendar. There is some debate about this.

[589] Known from other sources as Neriglissar.

[590] The NRSV has four names; most other translations have three. NRSV is inaccurate. Shamgar is now known to be a title and Nebo-Sarsechim has been found as the name of a leading official in Babylon on a cuneiform tablet in the British Museum. See Longman, *Jeremiah*, pp. 256-57. The Rab- part of the titles means "great or chief" but the exact function of these officials is not clear.

[591] Jeremiah's contemporary, Ezekiel, described Zedekiah's fate in Ezek 12:8-13.

[592] Riblah where Nebuchadrezzar had his headquarters was north of Damascus. From there he protected his supply routes and oversaw his army's forays into Palestine. This was where the Egyptian Pharaoh Neco had taken Jehoahaz captive and put him in chains (2 Kgs 23:33).

kings.[593] The last thing he saw was the execution of his sons and court officials,[594] and he disappeared into exile.[595] According to Jeremiah 52:8 all his soldiers deserted him as he fled.

The city was burned as Jeremiah had predicted many times (*cf.* chs. 37-38 for example) and many of the people taken into exile (vv. 8-9). The numbers were not large (Jer 52:28-30), but they represented the leaders and skilled craftsmen. Those left were a few leading citizens and many poor people. The Babylonians did not want to destroy the economy, so they gave the land to the remaining poor to live on. It was ironic that the Babylonians show more care for the poor than Zedekiah and his leaders did (*cf.* ch. 35).[596]

39:11-14

In the middle of the destruction, God saves two people. Jeremiah had been accused of treason for advocating surrender to the Babylonians. Nebuchadrezzar had heard about his message and freed him. Jeremiah could decide for himself whether to stay or go (40:1-6 has more details). He apparently was treated as a captive until he got to Riblah and was released there (40:1). This experience proved his word. To surrender was to live, to resist to die. God's word was true. There is still more for Jeremiah to do as we will learn from chapters 40-44.

---

[593] Zedekiah was on the throne only because Nebuchadrezzar had put him there and loyalty was expected.

[594] From chs. 37-38 we know the names of some of these officials. Putting the eyes out was a punishment for treaty breaking. See also the example of Samson in Judg 16:20.

[595] This made two Judean kings in exile, but we only hear again about Jehoiachin who was later treated kindly by a new Babylonian king (2 Kgs 25:27-30).

[596] Though people were left in the land they did not flourish and the future of nation as an ethnic entity lay with the exiles in Babylon. See comments on ch. 29, above.

39:15-18

The word of the Lord came to Jeremiah concerning Ebed-melech (the only place God speaks in ch. 39). The message was to reward Ebed-melech for saving Jeremiah's life, and was given before the fall of Jerusalem (v. 15), but is placed here perhaps to contrast his fate with Zedekiah's. The latter would not listen to the Lord, but Ebed-melech trusted in the Lord (v. 18). This could have been Zedekiah's reward, but he lacked the ability to exhibit faithfulness during personal danger. Ebed-melech showed great courage and was saved. The foreigner did what an Israelite king was incapable of doing.[597] God would save Ebed-melech in the same way he promised to save Jeremiah (Jer 15:20-21). The victors usually received the spoils as a "prize of war" but Ebed-melech received something more valuable, his life.[598]

An early promise to Israel was choose life (Deut 30:15-20). They were encouraged to choose life and blessings in the land but there was also before them the possibility of death if they disobeyed. The sad truth is that they ultimately opted for death. All the pleading and haranguing of Jeremiah could not change their fatal choice. God was patient, willing that Israel come to repentance, but obstinateness prevailed, and time ran out. The New Testament affirms God's patience but also knows that time will run out and the final judgment will come (2 Pet 3:9-10).

4.b.ii. A Remnant Left in Judah Under Gedaliah – 40:1-16

Chapter 40 begins a long section that continues through chapter 44 and details the events in Judah after the Fall of Jerusalem. Chapter 39 suggests that many of the Judeans went into exile but there were also many left (v. 9). Though

---

[597] Wright, *Jeremiah*, p. 390.

[598] This was promised to Zedekiah, but he refused it (38:17).

most were the poor there were some with leadership ability, including Gedaliah and a few others who soon make their appearance.[599]

The narrative in these chapters is grim. Its begins with hope but soon descends into deception, betrayal, assassination, murder, chaos, fear, and the continued flaunting of God's word through Jeremiah. We also see the last remnant of the Davidic dynasty self-destruct and the people voluntarily flee to Egypt. The remnant, still in full rebellion against God, comes full circle, once again back in the land of bondage from which God had delivered them with such mighty power. We learn nothing of the exiles in Babylon, but future events recorded in Daniel, Ezra, and Nehemiah demonstrate that Israel's future lay with them, not the remnant in the land. This account would have had a significant impact on the exiles when they read it. Would it dampen any desire they had to return to the land? The account also fulfills the bad fig predictions of chapter 24.

The chapters are framed by the word of the Lord to two individuals who played an important role for Jeremiah, Ebed-melech in 39:15-18 and Baruch in chapter 45. Both receive a word of salvation which contains the phrase "I will give you your life" (39:18; 45:5). This suggests that events could have turned out differently if the people had obeyed God and listened to Jeremiah. They, too, could have experienced life.

40:1-6

The Babylonians' gracious treatment of Jeremiah is recorded a second time (*cf.* 39:11-14) with a few more details. He was originally treated like all the other inhabitants of Jerusalem and taken in chains to Ramah, the staging area

---

[599] Jer 52:28-30 gives the total exiles as only 4,600, a figure that included three deportations, in 597, 587, and 582 BC. 2 Kgs 24:14 gives the total figure for the 597 BC exile as 10,000. We are not sure who is included in these two sets of figures. The latter number may be more comprehensive, and the former figures include only the men.

for those going to Babylon. But he was freed by Nebuchadrezzar's captain of the guard, Nebuzaradan, and given the choice of going to Babylon or staying in Judah.[600] Jeremiah's position was ambiguous. Whether he went or stayed his kind treatment would have given support to those who accused him of treason (37:13-16). He chose to stay, perhaps hoping to support Gedaliah and knowing that he would be protected.

There is irony in the statement "the word that came to Jeremiah from the Lord" (v. 1) for, actually, it came through the Babylonian, Nebuzaradan (vv. 2-5).[601] The word is a reprise of Jeremiah's message to Israel for decades, something the Babylonians could have easily known. But there are also words of encouragement for Jeremiah. Whether he stays or goes he is free and safe. Nebuzaradan is possibly a foil for Zedekiah and the Jerusalem elite who refused to listen to Jeremiah.[602] He knew the word of the Lord better than they did and took it seriously. It was not unusual in the ancient world for foreigner conquerors to invoke the gods of the conquered nations. In Jeremiah 22:8-9, an imaginary dialogue in the mouths of foreigners discussed why God had dealt as he had with Jerusalem. During the Assyrian crisis of Hezekiah's time 100 years earlier the Assyrian leaders made the claim that Israel's God had sent them (Isa. 36:10). Jeremiah said earlier that Nebuchadrezzar was God's servant (25:9) and that God was fighting against Jerusalem through the Babylonians (21:5-7). The ancients were quite aware that the gods, or God, were active in the affairs of men. Nebuzaradan is unknowingly a spokesman

---

[600] The contrast between Zedekiah and Jeremiah seen in chapters 37-38 continues. Zedekiah was taken away in chains, Jeremiah was freed from his.

[601] Some have suggested that the word doesn't come until 42:7, but the context doesn't support that view.

[602] Keith Bodner, *After the Invasion: A Reading of Jeremiah 40-44* (Oxford: Oxford University Press, 2015), p, 16. Bodner's work is a narrative analysis of Jeremiah 40-44 with several insights that have been very helpful for the exegesis of these chapters.

for God.[603] A humanistic, secular world-view is a modern invention.

"[T]he land is before you" (v. 4) is a striking phrase with connections to the patriarchs. Abraham offers Lot the land (Gen 13:9), Abimelech king of Gerar makes the offer to Abraham (Gen 20:15), and Pharaoh makes the offer to Joseph and his family (Gen 47:6). This somewhat obscure allusion alerts the reader to the possibility that the refugees could have a second chance. Although the land is not theirs any longer the Babylonians are willing to allow them to settle down in peace. Events soon demonstrate their inability to take advantage of the offer.[604]

Gedaliah's appointment as governor also echoes Genesis. The same verb was used three times in the Joseph narrative. He was promoted by Potiphar (Gen 39:4-5) over his household, by the captain of the guard over the prison (Gen 40:3-4), and by Pharaoh over Egypt (Gen 41:10-12). These appointments by a foreigner book-ends Israel's history and reflects God's care for them among the world's empires.[605] The appointment was fortuitous for Jeremiah, for Gedaliah's family was loyal to God, had supported Josiah, and defended Jeremiah (2 Kgs 22; Jer 26:24; 36). Jeremiah knew he would be safe if he stayed, and he possibly foresaw a ministry to the remnant in Judah.

40:7-16

The remnant community seems to begin well.[606] Gedaliah was a prominent Judean who was trusted by both the Babylonians and his own people. His first important decision

---

[603] Later Jewish tradition considered Nebuzaradan a righteous Gentile. Is it possible there are righteous non-Christians today?

[604] *Cf.* Bodner, *After the Invasion*, p. 28.

[605] Also, Daniel gained favored with Nebuchadnezzar and later the Persians.

[606] The emphasis on the remnant dominates chapters 40-44, the noun occurring twelve times and the verb "remain" occurring three times. Earlier Jeremiah had promised the remnant in all the other countries would return (Jer 23:3) and that God would save the remnant

was to establish the new seat of government at Mizpah, an old city, about eight miles north of Jerusalem and near Gibeon and Ramah. It was a good choice for the city was important in early Israel during Samuel's time. Samuel assembled the people there for prayer and then led them in victory over the Philistines (1 Sam 7:5-12). There he raised the "stone of help" ("Ebenezer") to commemorate the battle.[607] Mizpah was also a stop on Samuel's annual tour (1 Sam 7:16) and he introduced Saul as king there (1 Sam 10:17). It later was fortified by Asa (1 Kgs 15:22), who is referenced in Jeremiah 41:9

Gedaliah apparently inspired confidence in the people because refugees from various backgrounds and locations gathered to him at Mizpah (vv. 7-8, 11-12). During the last years of Judah many had sought to escape the Babylonian oppression. Some apparently formed small "militias" in the wilderness, others scattered after the fall of Jerusalem, some prominent persons fled to nearby countries to escape (several are named in v. 8), and some would have been officers who abandoned Zedekiah as he escaped Jerusalem (52:8). This would have been a mixed group, many with their own agendas, but they all saw hope in the new leader.

Gedaliah presented his agenda to the people with an oath (vv. 9-10). He would represent them to the Babylonians who would treat them well if they stayed in the land and submitted to them (implied). He took responsibility for walking the fine line of administration – satisfying both parties. His successful mediation was crucial to the survival of the new community. The people had a responsibility to trust him and apply themselves to rebuilding the economy of the land ("as for me" ... "as for you", v. 10). The Babylonians had been generous to the refugees (39:10) and it was

---

(31:7). The term implies both doom and salvation. Jeremiah makes the most use of the noun and verb of any of the prophets with a negative sense predominating.

[607] The "Ebenezer" was made famous by the old hymn, "Come Thou Fount of Every Blessing." Newer versions of the hymn substitute another word because no knows what the reference means anymore.

time to get to work. Gedaliah sounded like Jeremiah in the latter's letter to the exiles in chapter 29. This seemed sensible and politically astute, but Gedaliah was in a very difficult position, fraught with danger. One misstep and any party could cause trouble.[608] But the initial response was positive, and the people reaped a good harvest of dates and figs.

Tension soon erupted (vv. 13-16). Different groups began their power plays. One group supported Gedaliah, led by Johanan, and warned Gedaliah of the dark plots of another, led by Ishmael. Johanan seems to think the Gedaliah should have known about the plot ("Are you at all aware…?"; v. 14). Ishmael also represented the king of Ammon, Baalis,[609] who had given him refuge and who feared a Babylonian province so nearby.[610] Ishmael was of royal blood (41:1) and had his own agenda, perhaps to claim kingship. He reasoned that assassination of Gedaliah was the first step. But Gedaliah mistrusted Johanan, even after a highly charged personal plea, and dismissed the accusation.

This would seem like a good time to have sought a word from God, but both Jeremiah and God are absent from these events, nor is there any theological reflection. Gedaliah does his best to work out the will of God in the situation but without direct appeal for divine help. Unfortunately, his good intentions, generous spirit, and calculated political judgment led to disaster. His was probably in an impossible position from the beginning. Given the inherent

---

[608] Are at least five parties implied in verse 8? At least two competing forces soon emerge.

[609] Though otherwise unknown in the Bible, a seal with his name on it has been found in Ammon, Jordan.

[610] The Ammonites appear in 27:3 as co-conspirators against Babylon. Also, after the fall of Jerusalem, Zedekiah fled in that direction, perhaps to seek asylum as Ishmael had. David early in his reign had a long conflict with the Ammonites (2 Sam 10-12). Even more interesting is the fact that the mother of Rehoboam, Solomon's son who was responsible for splitting the nation, was an Ammonite (1 Kgs 14:21). In Jer 49:1-5 the Ammonites receive Jeremiah's words of judgment.

4.b.iii. Assassination, Murder, Mayhem – 41:1-18

41:1-10

Ishmael, introduced in 40:8, takes center stage and creates mayhem. A key to understanding his brutal behavior is his royal family connection. He was from the line of David, had taken refuge among the Ammonites during the Babylonian domination, and very likely thought he should have been the new leader. He was also angry that the Babylonians had killed or taken into captivity his extended family. Accommodation with the hated occupiers was unthinkable for Ishmael.

Gedaliah, despite Johanan's warning, apparently thought he could build some bridges and negotiate with all the factions to establish his leadership. Thus, he invited Ishmael and his men to a banquet. But Ishmael had only one plan, get rid of the Babylonian puppet. This shared meal may even have had some covenantal implications; at the least it required all parties to engage in a peaceful meal. This meant nothing to the thug, Ishmael, and he slaughtered Gedaliah, his men, and the Babylonian troops.[611] If he aspired to rule in place of Gedaliah, then he was following a policy of extermination of all of his supporters on the pattern of Jehu, who slaughtered all the descendants of Ahab and Jezebel (2 Kgs 9-10).

The next event shows Ishmael's blood lust. A band of worshippers came from some northern cities to worship,[612]

---

[611] The fast in the seventh month mentioned in Zech 8:19 is usually interpreted to be a fast in memory of Gedaliah.

[612] It is remarkable that after centuries of division there were still some in the north who revered Jerusalem and the temple. The importance of the three cities of origin of the pilgrims in Israelite history is interesting and worth pursuing.

probably at the destroyed temple. They were perhaps coming for the feast of tabernacles and were in mourning.[613] Why Ishmael would lure them into the city and slaughter them is inexplicable. This is the only speech of Ismael in the narrative and shows him to be a treacherous liar. This is perhaps how he gained the confidence of Gedaliah.[614] The unfortunate men were in the wrong place at the wrong time. The grisly scene included dumping all the bodies into a large cistern dug by King Asa centuries earlier (*cf.* 1 Kgs 15:12). The cistern was dug to provide water and life, but Ishmael turned it into a death pit. Ishmael kidnapped many of the refugees, and knowing he could not stay in Judah, fled toward his old refuge of Ammon. If he had thought he might save the remnant, he ended up destroying it.[615] In this he was like the last kings of Israel (such as Jehoiakim and Zedekiah) whose conduct was self-centered and destructive for themselves and the nation.

> **Jeremiah 41:2**
>
> *Ishmael son of Nethaniah and the ten men with him got up and struck down Gedaliah … with the sword and killed him, because the king of Babylon had appointed him governor in the land.*
>
> One of the worst actors in the drama of Jerusalem's downfall is Ishamel, son of Nethaniah. Coming from the royal household himself, Ishmael disagrees with the appointment of another person from the Jerusalem royal court, Gedaliah, to be the governor of Judea on behalf of the king

---

[613] The seventh month included the Day of Atonement, the Feast of Trumpets, and Tabernacles (Lev 26). Scholars disagree on the date of these events, for 41:1 says the seventh month but does not give a year. Jerusalem fell in the fourth month of the eleventh year of Zedekiah (39:2). The city was burned in the fifth month (52:12-13). The seventh month would be just two months later, a rather brief time for all the events recorded to transpire. Since 52:30 records a third deportation in 582, some suggest this was in retaliation for Ishmael's deeds and thus four or five years had elapsed. However, most scholars think the parallel passage in 2 Kgs 25:22-26 supports the shorter period.

[614] Bodner, *After the Invasion*, p. 66.

[615] Brueggemann, *To Plant*, p. 171.

of Babylon. Ishmael assembles a posse of armed men who treacherously murder Gedaliah. Without any legal authority, they terrorize the community.

It is not a direct equivalent, but this sounds something like the gangs that plague many cities. Jeremiah's account shows that Ishmael operated by intimidation and violence. He had a group of followers who carried out murder according to his orders. Jeremiah indicates the people feared him.

One of my students tells the story of his young nephew, left fatherless when my student's brother was killed in a gang dispute. Although only college-aged, the student was attempting to be a substitute father to this boy, who was angry and bitter. Once, when asked, "What are you going to be when you grow up?" the youngster answered, "I'm going to be a killer. They killed my dad and I'm going to be a killer, too." Gang culture destroys urban lives and neighborhoods.

One response to this is the Every Youth Coalition, a multi-city network that intends to connect every juvenile offender in America with a faith-based ministry, church, or individual.[616] Believing that more policing and incarceration has proven ineffective, this group teaches that the gospel can help solve this problem, one young person at a time. It provides an alternative culture of believers to the gang culture of the street.

Christianity Today profiled and interviewed one of the most prominent members of this coalition working in Chicago a woman named Amy Williams.[617] Williams articulated her philosophy of ministry like this:

> If you think about how we feel overwhelmed by the violence,
> imagine how these families feel; they have no resources,

---

[616] See https://www.everyyouth.org/about.

[617] See "Q & A: Ministering to Gang Members Is God's Work," at https://www.christianitytoday.com/women/2017/october/ministering-gang-members-is-gods-work.html.

> no connections, and no God in their lives. It's a lethal absence of hope, as Father Greg Boyle puts it. And violence
> is just a symptom. Our communities often think that more policing and incarcerating is going to fix the problem.
> But if the root issues aren't addressed, the violence will persist.
>
> As with the violent Ishmael and his followers, when our urban communities lack hope, conflicts often arise. Armed gang members may control the streets. Courageous believers like Amy Williams look to this lack of hope as the root cause of gangs and gang violence. Christians have a message of hope like no other, but not enough Amy Williames to actualize it.
>
> Mark S. Krause

41:11-18

Johanan, who had warned Gedaliah about Ishmael earlier, came to the rescue. Not in Mizpah at the time (why?), he pursued Ishmael and caught him at the "pool of Gibeon." He overwhelmed Ishmael's men and rescued the captives who gladly joined him.[618]

Gibeon was a place of symbolic significance. The narrator implies that the end of the David dynasty was ignoble and in sharp contrast with its beginning. An important battle took place at the pool of Gibeon after Saul's death as David was consolidating his power (2 Sam 2:12-17). David was noted for his honorable treatment of Saul's son and refused to seize the throne by assassination.[619] Ishmael is almost an

---

[618] No battle is recorded but we can safely assume one from vv. 12 and 15. Ishmael escaped with only eight men.

[619] Also, Gibeon was the site of one of Joshua's major mistakes in the conquest of the land, allowing the Gibeonites to deceive him without consulting the Lord (Josh 9). Solomon also worshipped there before the temple was built (1 Kgs 3:4-5). Hananiah, Jeremiah's opponent was from Gibeon (Jer 28:1). Archaeologists have uncovered an extensive wa-

anti-David and ends the dynasty in betrayal and shame. Ishmael disappears from the scene and history, demonstrating that he is not the righteous Davidic king of Jeremiah 23:1-7 and 33:14-26.[620]

Any hope of a peaceful reestablishing of a remnant in the land was gone. Ishmael had seen to that. Johanan knew that the Babylonians would retaliate for the murder of their troops.

It was ironic that he would chose to lead them to Egypt. When Egypt had the opportunity, they had subjugated Judah after killing Josiah, yet there was a faction that always hoped they would rescue them from Babylon. Egypt for Israel was place of bondage from which God had rescued them with mighty acts of power. God had demanded they never go back there (Deut 17:16) and promised if they went back it would be under his judgment (Deut 28:68). After the establishment of the monarchy under David, Egypt came to symbolize the temptation to turn to idolatrous superpowers for help rather than God in time of crisis (Isa 20; 31:1-7; Ezek 23; 2 Kgs 18:19-25; see Jer 42).[621]

4.b.iv. Jeremiah Prays for The Remnant – 42:1-43:7

Jeremiah, notable for his absence in chapters 40-41, reappears as the remnant prepares to head to Egypt under Johanan's leadership. He and all the people suddenly decide to seek a word from the Lord. Who suggested, maybe we should pray? Jeremiah missing from the narrative perhaps suggests that Gedaliah and his supporters attempted to proceed setting up the new government without consulting God. It turned into disaster. We can assume that Jeremiah and Baruch were in Mizpah and suffered through the Ish-

---

ter system in Gibeon that includes underground tunnels, a long stairway, and a huge pit with steps down the side (the "pool of Gibeon"?). See the *NBD*, p. 419.

[620] Bodner, *After the Invasion*, p. 86.

[621] *Cf. DBI*, pp. 228-229.

mael crisis along with the other refugees. Now at last Jeremiah is given an opportunity to contribute. All other options had failed so they would try God.[622]

42:1-6

All the people and the leaders requested prayer. Only two leaders are named of the five who gathered around Gedaliah in 40:18. Had all the others been killed by Ishmael?[623] They recognized that they were now reduced to even a smaller remnant ("only a few", v. 2) and their lives were in jeopardy from the Babylonians (41:18).[624] The request seems sincere. They want God to show "where we should go and what we should do" (v. 3). Is it possible for both remnants to live in obedience to God where they are? Since this remnant is already on its way to Egypt but still near Bethlehem the request raises tensions. What will they do if God says to stay in the land?

Jeremiah had been forbidden to pray for the people before the fall of Jerusalem (7:16; 11:14; 14:11) but that restriction is lifted afterward. Jeremiah promises to pray and to be transparent about the answer (v. 4). The people swear an oath to obey what God says, whether it be for good or evil. God himself is called to be a witness (v. 5). The request for prayer recalls Zedekiah's request in 37:3 though he did not heed Jeremiah's words. Will these people be different?

42:7-22

It took ten days for God's answer, certainly a long time for those fearing a Babylonian retaliation for Ishmael's deeds. The answer to the prayer leaves the future of the people in their own hands. They were given two options – if they stay in the land (vv. 10-12) or if they go to Egypt (vv. 13-17). It concludes with an extended expansion of the second option

---

[622] Brueggemann, *To Plant*, p. 173.

[623] The NRSV follows the LXX and lists Azariah (also in 43:2). The Hebrew has Jezaniah. They are probably the same person.

[624] There were now two remnants. One wonders how the exilic remnant in Babylon reacted when they read this account.

(vv. 18-22). It certainly surprised the people to learn that if they stayed in the land they would experience blessing. Jeremiah draws on God's words from chapter one and his call narrative to explain the good things that would happen – God would build and plant them in the land.[625] Three times he declares that it is in "this land" they will experience God's care, nowhere else (vv. 10, 12, 13).[626] It is still the promised land which God gave to his people. God's judgment on it had not changed that fact. Further, since King Nebuchadrezzar was still God's servant (43:10), he would do God's bidding and show mercy even as God shows mercy. Therefore, their fear of Babylon was misplaced. God's assurance "do not fear" for I am with you is a constant assertion throughout the Old Testament beginning with Abraham (Gen 15:1).[627] This assurance is repeated from 1:8, 19. God is consistent in his care for his people. This admonition is the Old Testament equivalent of Romans 8:31:

> What then are we to say about these things? If God is for us, who is against us?

The people wanted safety and restoration. The key was to remain in the land, the same promise Gedaliah made to the people in 40:9. God would provide for them (*cf.* Gen 22:8, 16).

One reason for God's gracious treatment was his sorrow for destroying Jerusalem (v. 10). This does not mean he regretted what he had done. The whole book of Jeremiah is a justification for the righteousness of his judgment on their disobedience. He would not be just if he did not carry it

---

[625] See Jer 29:4-9 for God's word to the exiles to build and plant in Babylon.

[626] V. 12 has "your land" (NRSV, "native soil")

[627] It occurs at least 75 times in the Old Testament.

out. Still, it gave God no pleasure. He grieved at the destruction they had brought on themselves,[628] however, because of his mercy, the judgment was not the end.

The second "if" clause addresses the consequences if they do go to Egypt (vv.13-17). To the people, Judah seemed a dangerous place, but Egypt was far enough away for them to feel safe from the disasters of war. In actuality, the opposite was true. Safety was in staying, disaster was in going. God was with the exiles in Babylon, but he would not be with the remnant in Egypt. They would experience there the very thing they were trying to escape. The repeated "there" in verses 14, 15, 16 (2x), and 17 emphasize that Egypt is not a secure location. The use of the verb "settle" in verses 15 and 17 reinforces the 'there". The Hebrew for "settle" is *gûr* (גוּר), to live as a foreigner or alien. No, it is "this land" that is a place of safety.

The concluding exposition of the "if" clause (vv. 18-22) seems to assume that the remnant will not listen to God, just as Zedekiah did not. Perhaps the "when" of verse 18 could be regarded as another "if" (as the NET Bible does), but the Hebrew syntax does not support that interpretation. When the remnant goes to Egypt they will suffer what the nation did when they resisted the Babylonians – death by the ravages of war.[629] The heartfelt promise of verse 6 was apparently only a surface piety.

43:1-7

The people respond with a vicious accusation – Jeremiah is a liar. Their willingness to listen to God apparently only applied if he supported their own plans. They could not believe that God would not approve their agenda. They had already decided their future, so, they turned Jeremiah's own words against him. He had consistently accused the prophets, the people, the scribes, and the priests of lying

---

[628] A loving father who disciplines his child takes no pleasure in the act.

[629] V. 18 repeats the words of 7:20; 24:9; 25:9; and 29:18.

(5:2, 31; 7:4, 8; 8:8; 23:9-31). To accuse him of lying was the apex of self-deceit.

They also turned Baruch into a scapegoat claiming he had influenced Jeremiah to lie (v. 3). This was the ultimate insult for both Jeremiah and Baruch. Both were faithful to God and his word, but it was turned into something dark and devious. "[T]he hard sayings of Scripture are still open to attack from both these angles: first from our version of God...who we are sure would never say such things; and then in the assertion that the witnesses who speak in Scripture have listened to other voices than his."[630]

Consequently, Johanan and the leaders took all the people, including Jeremiah and Baruch, to Egypt (vv. 4-7). It is ironic that they would not listen to God's word through Jeremiah, but they took him along, so they could not escape it. He has plenty more to say.

Johanan and his compatriots are described as "insolent" (*zēd*, זֵד, v. 2). This is one of the few adjectives used to describe the character of people in chapters 40-44. Mostly, the insolent are those who oppose God and/or those faithful to him (Pro 21:24; Isa 13:11; Mal 3:13; Ps 119:21).[631] It appears that Johanan shows his true character here. One wonders if Gedaliah saw such traits and that is why he did not trust him in chapter 40:13-16.

4.b.v. *The Word of the Lord in Egypt Through Jeremiah* –43:8-44:30
43:8-13
Unfortunately for the Judeans, arrival in Egypt did not put them beyond the range of God's word. They had taken Jeremiah with them, against his will, and the first recorded event is another divinely directed prophetic symbolic act. This is the last recorded such act in the book of Jeremiah

---

[630] Kidner, *Jeremiah*, p. 131. This incident recalls 1 Kgs 22. Ahab ignored Micaiah's prediction of his death in battle, went into battle in disguise, and just happened to be struck by a random arrow and died.

[631] It occurs six times in Psalm 119.

and is similar to the broken pot (ch. 18), the yoke (ch. 27) but perhaps most similar to the hidden loin cloth (ch. 13). This one also involves something hidden – large stones hidden in the entry to Pharaoh's residence in Tahpanhes. It is unclear exactly what Jeremiah did, but he marked the spot that was going to be covered by Nebuchadrezzar's throne which he would set up when he invaded Egypt. This is reminiscent of what happened after the siege of Jerusalem (39:3).

This was devastating news to the Judeans who had fled to Egypt to escape the Babylonians. They thought Egypt was a refuge but forgot they could not escape God. God told them the place of safety was to stay in Judea and submit to Babylon, but they succumbed to their fears and were determined to plan their own future apart from God. Therefore, they would suffer again the same consequences they suffered in the siege of Jerusalem (v. 11; "quoted" from 15:2).

Nebuchadrezzar was still God's servant (v. 10) and cooperating with God to carry out judgment. In fact, God and the king would work together to destroy the Egyptian temples with fire (v. 12).[632] The destruction of Egypt's temples demonstrated the superior power of the gods of Babylon over those of Egypt.[633] Heliopolis (v. 13) was noted for its monuments to the gods, especially the sun god, Amon-Re, who was the high god of Egypt. The temple to Amon-Re in Heliopolis was approached by a procession way that was lined with rows of obelisks. Its destruction swept away any claim to power that Egypt would have.[634] Even these national gods were powerless before the God of Israel who

---

[632] The Hebrew has in v. 12 "I shall kindle a fire..." which parallels "he shall burn..." The NRSV "he shall kindle..." removes this important theological assertion.

[633] We are told that Nebuchadrezzar would "ravage" the land (v. 11) which carries echoes of the Exodus plagues. See Exod 3:20; 7:25; 9:15; 12:13; Ps 136:10. This time the ravaging did not deliver Israel.

[634] Heliopolis is called On in Gen 41:45. Jeremiah called it "bethshemesh", "house of the sun." Heliopolis is the Greek name of the city.

was orchestrating the events and Egypt's suffering was collateral damage when God executed judgment on his people.

Babylonian annuals, the ancient Greek historian Herodotus, and Ezekiel 29:19-21 tells that Babylon did invade Egypt in 568 BCE. Little is known of the details, but we can assume that God's judgments were carried out.

44:1-30

These are the last words of Jeremiah to the Judeans in the book of Jeremiah. The tragedy is that even after the catastrophe of the fall of Jerusalem, the word had not changed. The people were still mired in their disobedience and rebellion.

This word apparently came several years after the words of chapter 43, for the Judeans had had time to scatter throughout Egypt. Migdol was a fortress near Tahpanhes. Memphis was south of the modern city of Cairo. Pahos referred to all lower Egypt, that is the southern regions all the way to the first cataract on the Nile at modern Aswan.[635]

Chapter 44 consists of three of Jeremiah's speeches (vv. 1-14, 20-23, and 24-30) and one response by the people (vv. 15-19). The key theme is idolatry, a topic missing from chapters 37-43 but prominent earlier in Jeremiah.

44:1-14

The first address has three sections: a historical review (vv. 1-6), the accusation framed as four questions (vv. 7-10), and the announcement of judgment (vv. 11-14). Each is introduced by the long phrase "Thus says the Lord of Hosts, the (Lord) God of Israel." This fulsome phrase leaves no doubt who is the author of the words. The historical review summarizes the disaster their wickedness brought on Jerusalem, God's gracious sending of the prophets to warn

---

[635] Archeology has confirmed there was a Jewish colony in the southern region on an island in the Nile called Elephantine in the sixth and fifth centuries B.C.

them, their persistence in disobedience, and the inevitable expressing of his wrath, turning Jerusalem into a desolated mound. This recent history would have still been a vivid memory for the audience.

This makes the four why questions of the accusation more poignant (vv. 7-10).[636] How could they have observed and experienced the fall of Jerusalem and continue to persist along the same path that would bring disaster on themselves?[637] It is inexplicable to us that they would continue in idolatry after that experience. There is pain and astonishment in these questions.

Consequently, the Judeans will experience the fall of Jerusalem all over again. The judgment language used (vv. 11-14) is familiar from several previous sermons (*cf.* 14:11-12; 29:18; 42:15-22 for just a few). The pattern of disobedience established by the Judeans under Jehoiakim and Zedekiah was not curtailed by the fulfillment of Jeremiah's words. By God's grace a remnant of the people was left in Judea, but their flight to Egypt assured their demise as well. Only an unexplained tantalizing promise ends this judgment scene – some fugitives will go back (v. 14d; *cf.* v. 28 below). What this could have been we do not know. These refugees disappeared from biblical history.

44:15-19

We last heard the voice of the people in chapter 42, pledging with an oath to obey whatever God told Jeremiah. We hear their voice again and this time they reveal their true heart. They were not dedicated to God but to their idols

---

[636] Two whys are expressed (vv. 7, 8), two are assumed (vv. 9, 10).

[637] The word *rā'āh* (רָעָה), "evil, disaster" dominates this section (five times in verse 9) and the chapter (fourteen times total). NRSV translates the word as "crimes" and renders only two of the occurrences in v. 9. It produces a smoother translation but reduces the force of the Hebrew repetition – "the evil of your ancestors, the evil of the kings of Judah, the evil of their wives, your evil, and the evil of your wives...." The evil defines their ancestors, their leaders, themselves and all the wives, that is, it pervaded the whole society.

borrowed from other nations. They were adamant that they would not abandon them.

Jeremiah's prediction of the fall of Jerusalem happened just as he said, seemingly unassailable evidence that he had spoken the word of God (*cf.* Deut 18:21-22).[638] But the people had a different perspective on the events of the past few years. According to them disaster had come because they had ceased their worship of idols, specifically the queen of heaven (vv. 17-18). This was probably a reference to the Mesopotamian goddess of love and fertility, Ishtar. She was called Anat in Canaanite literature and Ashtoreth in the Old Testament. The worship involved the whole family, including the children, and was therefore doubly pernicious for it taught the children idolatry, not the law of the Lord.

It is not clear when they would have ceased this worship. Josiah's reform may have driven it underground (2 Kgs 22-23), but Jeremiah condemned it early in Jehoiakim's reign as if it were still going on (Jer 7:17-18). When were these "good old days" of prosperity and peace? The only possibility seems to be for a few years under Josiah when Judah achieved a brief measure of independence.

Whose view of history was correct, Jeremiah's or the people's? In the moment either could have been. The cause of events is always open to different interpretations and people come to decisions based on certain prior assumptions and perspectives. Only time would tell who was right, but for the people, their perspective worked. Their gods seemed effective. There was no answer to their argument. This was at the heart a contest between God and the gods. Where does the evidence lead? Someone is at work, but who?

---

[638] But see Deut 13:1-5. If a false prophet could make a prediction and have it come true, then the test is the content of the message. It must always call the people to obedience to the covenant.

44:20-23

Jeremiah confronts the people with a two-part reply, verses 20-23 and 24-30. They are wrong in their view of history and God is fed up with them. He will not attempt to persuade them any longer or offer them grace again. The reader of Jeremiah will be familiar with the charges Jeremiah levels against the people (v. 23.) The litany of sins comes from Deuteronomy 10:12-13 which enjoins the people to walk in the ways of the Lord, to love him, to fear him, to serve him, and to obey all his statutes and decrees. This should have reminded them of Josiah's reforms. Jeremiah had continually painted a dystopian future for the people to motivate them to repentance. If they would repent, they could avoid that future, but they preferred their "good old days" utopia which never worked and would not work, even in Egypt.

44:24-30

Since they were determined to worship the queen of heaven, Jeremiah tells them to go ahead (v. 25). Their determination has determined their future, but not the one they thought. God's determination of their future has precedent. God had been watching over his word from the beginning of Jeremiah's ministry (1:11-12) to make sure it would be carried out. For the exiles in Babylon it was for their good (29:10) but not for the exiles in Egypt (v. 27). They would reap what they had sown, death by famine and sword.

More ominously, God would remove his name from their lips (v. 26). All chance of an appeal was gone. They had not listened to God, now he would not listen them. It was in Egypt that God revealed his name to his people (Exod 3:13-15) and now it is in Egypt that he takes his name away. The first occasion was for their redemption (Exod 6:1-13), the last was for their destruction. Since their hearts were not aligned with God, possession of his name was useless. Historically, it is accurate to say that Israel gave up God, but it is more accurate to say with Paul that God gave them up (Rom 1:18-32).

The people would perish in Egypt, but perhaps a few would escape. The offer of a "few in number" returning (v. 28) is another ironic echo of Israel's earlier Egyptian experience. Their ancestors had entered into the land "few in number" (Ps 105:12; Deut 26:5). Then they became a multitude (Exod 1:7; Deut 1:10). Now they would be a tiny remnant again.[639] God had shown great power in bringing them out of Egypt and establishing them in the land. He made them into a great nation, but now they are back where it all began, and God's blessings are nullified. A great tragedy is the only phrase that can describe this disaster.

God offers them another historical sign that he is at work and that they had misread history. He will hand over the Egyptian Pharaoh, Hophra, to Nebuchadrezzar, just he had Zedekiah. This was the same Pharaoh who had failed to help Zedekiah (37:5). Would two similar events convince them? It was too late.

At the beginning of Israel's history and at the end, Egypt became that place that was determined to swallow up the people of God. From Abraham on it was a place of abundance and power, and at times safety. It became a place of bondage and oppression and after the Exodus it became a symbol for oppression. It was a place of military power and often was sought for protection, which the prophets denounced.[640] This temptation to seek security in earthly powers and not God doomed the Judean refugees. Perhaps this is a cautionary story for the church who sometimes flirts with cultural subversion and syncretism rather than trusting fully in the Lord of the church.

Jeremiah's prophetic call to speak to Israel ends with these words. The prophetic task was not one he desired, but he was faithful to his calling his whole life. It cost him deep anguish and cost him his family. He ended up in Egypt

---

[639] Deut 4:27 predicted because of disobedience they would become few in number.

[640] Especially Ezek 23 in a very graphic picture of two promiscuous sisters seeking lovers.

against his will, but he persisted. He was a good and faithful servant.

4.b.vi. The Word of the Lord to Baruch – 45:1-6

Chronologically this private word to Baruch came years earlier than chapters 40-44 and the destruction of Jerusalem. The fourth year of Jehoiakim was 605 BCE, and the word is associated with the events of chapter 36.[641] Baruch was Jeremiah's scribe who wrote on a scroll Jeremiah's early sermons (perhaps chapters 1-25 of the book) and read them in the temple. The scroll was destroyed by the king and Baruch wrote it out again. This was an arduous task.

We first met Baruch in chapter 32 when he aided Jeremiah with the deed to his property. He came from an important family in Judea. His grandfather, Maaseiah, was the governor of Jerusalem during Josiah's reign (2 Chr 34:8), and his brother was a high-ranking official in Zedekiah's court (Jer 51:59). Also, his training as a scribe gave him high status in that society.

Structurally, chapter 45 connects with two previous texts in Jeremiah. In the immediate context, it has close parallels with Jeremiah's word to Ebed-melech in 39:15-18. Both emphasize that these two faithful servants will "have your life as a prize of war" (39:18; 45:5). As an *inclusio* around chapters 40-44, these two small sections show the refugees that if they had remained obedient, they could also have lived. Instead, they chose the way of disobedience and death.

Chapter 45's connection to chapter 36 also provides a bracket for the larger section of 36-44. Many scholars refer to these chapters as "the Book of Baruch." He is the most likely candidate for the collector and final editor of the whole book of Jeremiah.

Baruch's lament (v. 3) focuses on his suffering and pain, which was long and deep. Chapter 36 hints at some of it when it tells us he had to hide for his life with Jeremiah

---

[641] See comments there.

(36:19). His lament also echoes some of Jeremiah's laments (*cf.* 8:18-9:1; 15:18). It is probable that as a faithful servant of Jeremiah he had suffered through some of the same things Jeremiah did. Repeated exposure to Jeremiah's messages of doom, writing them down, repeated observation of his people's disobedience, and anxiety over whether he and his family would survive the destruction of Jerusalem took its toll.

God's response (v. 4) doesn't seem to connect to the lament. God repeats his message of destruction for the whole land, breaking down and plucking up (*cf.* 1:10). But we need to see this statement with the emphasis given it in the Hebrew. The "I" is emphatic. He is doing something he never wanted to do but now must. We need to realize that God is suffering, too.[642] He desired to build and plant and exerted great effort on their behalf for centuries. But those plans would not come to fruition. Thus, there are tears behind his words. God takes no pleasure in the destruction of the wicked (Ezek 18:23; 33:11).[643] Compared to God's sorrow, Baruch's was insignificant.

God then exposed an unexpressed part of Baruch's lament (v. 5). He had ambitions. He wanted to be somebody. With his family connections and skills, he had the potential to play an important role in Judean society, but his identifying with Jeremiah dashed those hopes. Under the circumstances it was enough that he should live. God's gift of life was like "booty from war".[644] With death all around this was a significant promise.

Some see Baruch as representing all those who supported Jeremiah and remained faithful to God's word in those dark days. They too had suffered privation and oppression,

---

[642] Wright, *Jeremiah*, 412.

[643] And neither should we.

[644] This was the same promise made to those who would surrender to the Babylonians – 21:9; 38:2.

but here they learn that insignificant people were important to the plans of God.⁶⁴⁵

Wright reminds us that God's suffering for Israel leads us directly to the cross. There he suffered for and through his son. The suffering was to rescue us from the consequences of our sinfulness, but it also demonstrated that God could identify with our suffering, something unique among all the religions of the world. This God is appealing to everyone who is seeking understanding and release from pain, and speaks to the truth of the gospel.⁶⁴⁶

---

⁶⁴⁵ Wright, *ibid.*, p. 415 – Baruch the man was important to God, but his ambitions were not.

⁶⁴⁶ *Ibid.*, p. 416.

5. Prophecies Against the Nations (46-51)

This section turns from Judah to address the nations surrounding Judah. Prophecies against nations are a common feature of other prophets as well – Amos 1-2, Isaiah 13-23, Ezekiel 25-32, Jonah, Obadiah, and Nahum. These sermons are vivid reminders that God is not only the God of Israel, but the sovereign God of all the nations and that they are accountable to him. This was an important message for the exiles, trapped in the capital city of the strongest nation in that world.

These sermons complete Jeremiah's mission detailed in chapter 1:5 and 10. He was called to be a prophet to the nations, not just Israel. Midway through the book, he first applied this calling (25:12-13) when he offered to the nations the cup of God's wrath which they must drink. In chapters 46-51, we see the details of that wrath.[647]

Chapters 46-51 are loosely arranged geographically and chronologically. They begin with Egypt in the south, move to the nations closest to Israel, first on the west then the east, then move north and end up with Babylon to the far east. Chronologically they begin in 605 BCE (46:2), move to 597 BCE (49:34) and end in 593 BCE (51:59). Thus, they were all delivered before the fall of Jerusalem in 588-87 BCE. The audience of these prophecies was Israel. The nations probably never heard them. However, in Jeremiah's case, a possible setting for some is Jeremiah 27. Envoys from several nearby nations came to Jerusalem to coordinate rebellion against Babylon (27:3-4). Perhaps part of the word to the kings of Edom, Moab, and Ammon were the sermons in this section. If so, the envoys returned home with a totally different message than they expected. Furthermore, Jeremiah's words against Babylon were carried there by Seraiah and read there (Jer 51:59-64).

---

[647] In the LXX, these chapters are placed after 25:13a. This arrangement conforms to the macro-structures of Isaiah and Ezekiel but for Jeremiah's purposes the prophecies fit well at the end of the book.

The words of 45:4-5 prepared the way for these sermons. Baruch is told that God planned to bring disaster over the land and all flesh. The first sermon is addressed to Egypt, the country with a long history with Israel and the new home of the refugees. The last sermon is addressed to Babylon, the scourge of that era. All the other nations as well as Israel had suffered under her tyranny and power. Jeremiah's message of her downfall and destruction would have been welcome news. The onetime servant of God now was held accountable for her arrogance and pride, and just as she had uprooted and pulled down many nations, so she would suffer the same from the Medes and Persians (50:9; 51:11; *cf.* Dan 5:30).

The language of these sermons is stereotypical of judgment through warfare, with language from the Holy War genre.[648] It is vivid, often short and sharp (*cf.* 46:3-4), with powerful poetic images. Egypt and Babylon especially receive divine retribution (46:10; 50:15, 28; 51:11, 36). The other nations who suffered with Israel under Babylonian rule are accountable to God also, but not for the same reasons. There is almost a sympathetic tone to some of the sermons. In fact, there is a future hope for some couched in the same language used for Judah, *i.e.*, their fortunes will be restored (Moab – 48:47; Ammon – 49:6; Elam – 49:39).[649] Many place names occur, reflecting the specificity of the sermons. Three times God is referred to as "King, whose name is the Lord of hosts" (46:18; 48:15; 51:57) establishing who the true king is as opposed to all the earthly kings.[650]

---

[648] Fretheim, *Jeremiah*, p. 579.

[649] For the phrase used of Judah's future see 29:14; 30:3, 18; 31:23; 32:44; 33:7, 11.

[650] Ps 96 provides a hymn that celebrates this king of all the nations. His kingship and righteous judgment are fused in v. 10.

5.a. Major Oracles against Nations (46:1-48:47)

5.a.i. Against Egypt – 46:1-28
46:1-26

God's word to Egypt is presented as two battle scenes: verses 2-12 and 13-21. The first is given a precise date (v. 2), Babylon's defeat of Egypt at the battle of Carchemish in 605 BCE. The second scene describes a similar defeat at some future date. The scenes develop in parallel with each other: introduction (vv. 2 and 13); preparing for battle with imperatives (vv. 3-4 and 14); descriptions of the defeat introduced by "Why?" (*medua'*, מדוע, vv. 5-6 and 15-17); Egyptian arrogance (vv. 7-9 and 20-21); and God's orchestration of the defeat (vv. 10 and 18-19). The presentation of Egypt suffering the defeat to her shame is repeated (vv. 11-12 and 22-24). Verses 25-26 form a conclusion to both battle scenes.

Both scenes are presented with sarcasm and powerful images and metaphors. The sarcasm was designed to deflate the inflated ego of Egypt (and all nations) who thought themselves powerful enough to rule the world. Egypt would discover, as would Babylon, that there was only one King of the universe, and it wasn't Pharaoh.

Carchemish (v. 2) was in northern Syria, near Aleppo, on the Euphrates. It was an independent trade center until taken over by the Assyrians in 717 BCE (Isa 10:9). After the Babylonian defeat of Nineveh in 612 BCE the Assyrians retreated to Carchemish to make a last stand. Pharaoh Neco II of Egypt marched north in 609 BCE to aid the Assyrians against the Babylonians, seeing his chance to dominate Palestine. Josiah opposed him and was killed (2 Kgs 23:29-35) and Judah became an Egyptian vassal. Four years later the Babylonians attacked Carchemish and routed the Egyptians in hand to hand fighting and pursued them south. This battle changed the power structure of the region and

Babylon became the dominant force with disastrous implications for Judah as we have seen.[651] In 604 BCE, Babylon marched into the Philistine plain and completed her control of the region.

The Egyptian defeat is described in verses 3-12 in vivid terms with two stages: the preparation for battle is presented in short, staccato bursts marked by seven imperatives, each followed by an object (two words in Hebrew, except v. 3a which has two objects); the second stage is marked by astonishment at the sudden retreat of the army marked by "why"? (vv. 5-6, with five verbs). The powerful army of Egypt was well prepared but turned and ran in an instant. Part of the reason was the lack of resolve by the mercenaries who filled the ranks (v. 9). Egyptian arrogance was no match for a superior force (v. 8).[652] The army falls (vv. 6 and 12) and shame covers the nation.

Verse 10 is the heart of the scene. It interprets Egypt's defeat theologically. In the world changing events of the battle of Carchemish, God was working out his plans and purposes. It was his day of retribution and vindication.[653] The Hebrew word is *nqm* (נקם), which occurs eighteen times in Jeremiah.[654] Jeremiah uses it for God's actions against Israel in 5:9, 29 and in 9:9, all which say, "Shall I not punish them for these things? Shall I not bring retribution on a nation such as this?" God is a just God who demands justice

---

[651] This water-shed year, the fourth year of Jehoiakim, was the occasion of several of Jeremiah's sermons – 25:1; 36:1; 45:1 (*cf.* 35:1).

[652] The annual flooding of the Nile which gave Egypt her fertility and wealth was an apt metaphor for her arrogance. Nothing could stop the flooding, or by extension the Egyptian army, or so they thought. Amos 8:8 and 9:5 make use of the imagery in the context of judgment. See Isa 8:7-8 for a similar image for Assyria and the floods of the Euphrates.

[653] NRSV. NIV has "vengeance" in both places. Other translations have "vengeance" and "avenge". The NET translates "will pay back his enemies."

[654] The verb seven times, the noun eleven times. Chs. 50-51 contain eleven occurrences

and he will do justice. Vengeance or retribution is the punishing of evil and righting of wrongs. It is not immoral or arbitrary.[655] God vindicates his name and stands up for justice. He acts to save his people. He is holy and zealous to uphold righteousness. Therefore, he can bring retribution against his people for breaking the covenant, or against the nations for their arrogance when they try to seize power and do evil. Thus, Egypt suffers defeat for God is bringing vindication over his enemies.[656]

This principle informs all the prophecies against the nations and asserts the total sovereignty of God over the universe. This principle still operates in our world. All nations, whose arrogance moves them to play power games, should be warned of the consequences. God overturns all worldly powers and political machinations. Woe to the nation who does not consider God's rule as the King of all nations! Paul refers to this principle amid admonitions for Christian treatment of others, even enemies (Rom. 12:19). Christians are to love and forgive and let God take care of retribution. This frees the church for ministry in all cultures and settings.

The second battle scene (vv. 13-26) has a less precise setting. It refers to a coming attack on Egypt (v. 13), but does not specify when that will happen. It may refer to Babylon's campaign into the Philistine plain in 604 BCE, when Egypt came to help Jerusalem (Jer. 37:5), or to the invasion in 568 BCE. The result for Egypt is the same – total defeat (vv. 14, 24), desertion of the mercenaries (v. 21), Egypt's arrogance brought low (v. 17),[657] and the shame of the defeat (v. 24). The images of Egypt in defeat are vivid and memorable (vv. 20, 22-23).

---

[655] God is the subject of *nqm* (נקם) for 85% of its occurrences in the OT.

[656] Some suggest in Egypt's case it could be because of Neco's murder of Josiah.

[657] Literal Hebrew, "a big noise."

Verses 15 and 25 give us the theological perspective. The real issue is, who is King of the universe, Egyptian gods or Israel's God? The text is clear – the Apis bull of Memphis [658] and Amon, the god of Thebes – cannot stand before the God of Israel.[659] In the immediate context of chapter 44 this would have been a strong warning to the pro-Egyptian party in Judah who opposed Jeremiah and fled to Egypt for refuge.[660]

The surprise of this scene is the concluding brief note of hope for Egypt (v. 26b). Even a pagan nation can benefit from God's grace which often follows judgment. How this would work out we are not told, but it informed the exiles in Babylon that they were not the sole focus of a divinely directed return.[661]

Jeremiah 46:17

Give Pharaoh, king of Egypt, the name
"Braggart who missed his chance."

When King Nebuchadrezzar threatened the Egyptian armies of Pharaoh Neco, Jeremiah delivered oracles warning the Egyptians of their coming defeat. He prophesied that when the battle was over, a proper name for the Egyptian ruler would be "Braggart who missed his chance."

Braggarts are part of the fabric of any city. Politicians overstate their accomplishments to get reelected. Businesses exaggerate their economic impact to gain valuable tax concessions at the expense of taxpayers. But, most of all, cities all have celebrities who live larger than life and crave the spotlight. In many cities, these are professional athletes, whose egos are sometimes startlingly outrageous. A star

---

[658] With the NRSV translation of v. 15, which seems an accurate correction of the Hebrew text.

[659] The god of Thebes, Amon, was combined with Re the sun god to become Amon-Re the state god of Egypt.

[660] Lalleman, *Jeremiah*, p. 283.

[661] See Isa 19-20 and Ezek 29-32 for other prophetic words on Egypt. Isaiah has a word of hope for her and Ezekiel laments her demise.

player, beloved by his team's fans for his braggadocious attitude, may be quick to dump these loyalists and jump to another city for more money. This makes it difficult sometimes for young people who look to them as role models and examples of success. Once idolized by boys in the toughest neighborhoods, they become the objects of criticism and scorn. Some of these guys deserve the title, Braggart Who Missed a Chance to Be a Hero to Young Fans."

While ministering in Los Angeles, I often was asked to visit the Mattel Children's Hospital, part of the UCLA Medical Center. This marvelous facility did treatment for children from all over the region with renown doctors and the best equipment. If a pastor friend in another city had a child in the Mattel hospital, often I would get a call to visit him or her.

One of these was a boy from Arizona. His parents, small-town folk, were uncomfortable in the city but managed to find lodging in the Tiverton House, a temporary housing facility offering subsidized rates for families with a person in UCLA Med. Their immediate needs were met, but the city was wearing them down. Not only that, but the boy's prognosis was not promising, and he had become depressed and withdrawn. I would visit, talk, and pray with him, but seemed unable to lift his spirits. One day, however, I entered his room to hear happy talk and see new decorations. The theme was a sports team, the Los Angeles Lakers. Earlier that day, one of the Lakers (a strong Christian man) had made an unexpected visit. This star player visited children when the team was in town, never seeking publicity. He left the boy with an autographed, full color 8 x 10 photo, which was placed right by his bed. Rather than be a braggart, this city celebrity brought some excitement and joy to a boy who needed a lift. Celebrities are part of city life. When they are humble and willing, they can do great good.

Mark S. Krause

46:27-28

Bad news for Egypt was good news for Israel. Thus, the prophecy against Egypt ends with two brief oracles of salvation for Israel. Each verse is introduced with a standard formula "do not fear," an admonition that occurs frequently in the Old Testament. These two oracles are identical in wording to 30:10-11 where they fit into the promise of hope for Israel and her future.[662]

5.a.ii. Against the Philistines – 47:1-7

This brief judgment on the Philistines uses language and images from previous oracles whose meaning by now is clear.[663] In Jeremiah's day, the Philistines were only a small group of people in the Mediterranean coastal land who had suffered several defeats by the world powers, Egypt and Babylon. However, in Israel's early history in the land, they were a serious threat to the struggling tribes getting settled in the central hill country. Samson, Samuel, and Saul (Judg 13 through 1 Sam 31) had many encounters with the Philistines over control of the land.

The Philistines had arrived in the Mediterranean coast just prior to Israel's entrance and were intent on gaining as much territory as possible.[664] They killed King Saul and his son Jonathan (1 Sam 31) and threatened to occupy some of the most important areas of central hill country. King David's first major military accomplishment was their defeat (2 Sam 5:17-25; 8:1).

---

[662] Except v. 28a adds the phrase from 27a. See comments on 30:10-11.

[663] For other prophetic words on the Philistines see Isa 14:28-32; Amos 1:6-8; Ezek 25:15-17; Zeph 2:4-7; Zech 9:5-7.

[664] They are normally associated with the "Sea People" who migrated out of the Greek isles via Crete (Caphtor, v. 4; *cf.* Amos 9:7) to the Egyptian shores. Driven off by the Egyptians in 1190 BC, they settled along the coast of what came to be called Palestine, in five major city-states: Gaza, Ashkelon, Ekron, Gath, and Ashdod (Josh 13:2-3).

The date of verse 1 is unclear for there were several occasions when the Egyptians, or Assyrians (Isa 20), or Babylonians were marching through their territory on the way to do battle with each other. In this sense, the Philistines' choice of territory was unfortunate. Egypt could have conquered Gaza in 609 BCE on her way to Carchemish but there were other occasions also. Verse 2 suggests their demise would come at the hands of a northern power ("waters rising out of the north") which could mean Babylon (*cf.* 1:14; 4:6; 6:1). From the Babylonian chronicles, we know that in December of 604 BCE, the Babylonians sacked and destroyed Ashkelon. Verse 4 fits that attack well. Archaeological excavations at Ashkelon have uncovered stark evidence of the attack – smashed pottery, charred grain, collapsed houses, skeletons with grave injuries.[665]

Whoever the agent was, it was ultimately the hand of God that carried out this judgment (v. 6, the sword of the Lord could not be sheathed; *cf.* 46:10). Jeremiah does not highlight any specific Philistine evil. Amos pointed to their treatment of conquered peoples (Amos 1:6-8). The main reason may be the long-time Philistine opposition to Israel and the murder of King Saul.

The demise of the Philistines also had implications for two of their allies, the Phoenician cities of Tyre and Sidon (v. 4). These two cities, plus Ashkelon, were trading partners on the Mediterranean coast and all suffered the same fate. Sidon fell to the Babylonians in 586 BCE (the same year as Jerusalem) and Tyre fell in 573 BCE after a thirteen-year siege.

There is no word of hope for the Philistines in Jeremiah as for some of the other nations. However, Zephaniah 9:7b-8 and Psalm 87:4 suggest a future for them. The Philistines stand among the nations who, with Israel, will ultimately experience God's grace as an expression of his concern for

---

[665] Walton, *Old Testament Background*, p. 679.

all his creation. God's sovereignty over evil and good is again made clear.

5.a.iii. Against Moab – 48:1-47

This chapter is the longest invective against a nation other than Babylon (ch. 50-51) in this section. The reason is unknown. Moab was a prominent neighbor of Israel on the east side of the Dead Sea and had a long history of interaction with her. This may be part of the reason, but Jeremiah does not tell us.

The country in the time of Israel occupied an area between the River Arnon on the north and the River Zered on the south.[666] These rivers ran into the Dead Sea from the east and created deep chasms and natural barriers for the country. But for much of Moab's history it also extended north of the Arnon to the northern edge of the Dead Sea.

Relations between Moab and Israel were mostly ones of conflict. In Moses' time, the northern area was under the control of Sihon, king of the Amorites, whom Moses and Israel defeated (Deut 2:26-39). It was the Moabite King Balak who asked Balaam to curse Israel (Num 22-24). Moab was an oppressor of Israel during the time of the judges (Judg 3:12-30).

On the positive side David sent his family there for safety when fleeing Saul (1 Sam 22:3), and his great-grandmother Ruth came from there (book of Ruth). Later David subdued Moab (2 Sam 8:2, 12) but she broke free after Solomon's death.[667] Omri of northern Israel briefly controlled Moab but again she gained her independence (2 Kgs 1; 3:4-27). We have extra-biblical evidence of this event on a stele discovered in 1868 at Dibon, the Moabite Stone. On it King Mesha records how Chemosh helped them gain freedom

---

[666] Gen 19:37 attributes the origins of Moab to an incestuous relationship between Lot and his eldest daughter.

[667] Solomon introduced the Moabite god, Chemosh, to Israel (1 Kgs 11:7).

from Ahab, Omri's son. Moab lost its freedom to Assyria in the eighth century and later to Babylon.[663]

Chapter 48 is notable for its knowledge of the geography of Moab (vv. 3, 8, 21, 28) and the numerous references to Moabite cities, some listed multiple times (vv. 1-2, 18-19, 21-24, 34, 45). It is also characterized by a wide variety of images, metaphors, and word plays.

This long chapter repeats several themes and it is best to examine these themes under a few headings.

The major theme is the absolute destruction of the nation and its cities. Jeremiah employs six different words to describe the carnage, and several powerful images. The six words, all synonyms, occur eighteen times in the passage. Moabite cities are laid waste/destroyed (*šdd*, שדד, or *šd*, שד, vv. 1, 3, 8, 15, 18, 20, 32; *šmd*, שמד, vv. 8, 42) and broken down (*ḥtt*, חתת, vv. 1, 20, 39). Moab is shattered, and her mighty scepter smashed (*šbr*, שבר, vv. 3, 4, 5, 17, 25, 38). Moab and her cities will perish (*'bd*, אבד, vv. 8, 36, 46). Consequently, she is desolate, and all she hears are cries of desolation or anguish (vv. 3, 5). Every geographical area is affected from the valleys to the plains (v. 8), from the ascents to the descents to the highlands (v. 5) and the tablelands (v. 21). None of the cities, large of small, shall survive.

The image of the swooping eagle supports this theme (v. 40) for no-one can escape such a powerful raptor which was renowned for its speed of attack. There would be no place to hide from the attack. Jeremiah reinforces this image with a word-play in verses 43-44. All Moab can expect is terror, the pit, and the trap (v. 43). In Hebrew, the three words are *pḥd* (פחד, "terror"), *pḥt* (פחת, "trap"), and *pḥ* (פח, "pit"), a powerful alliteration.

The judgment is also pictured as Moab getting drunk and vomiting (v. 26). This recalls Jeremiah's words to the nations in 25:15-16 that they must drink the cup of God's

---

[668] For other prophetic words against Moab see Isa 15-16; Ezek 25:8-11; Amos 3:1-3; and Zeph 2:8-11.

wrath which will make them drunk. This was the sword of the Lord against them.

Another metaphor for judgment is the reference to grapes and wine (vv. 12-13, 32-33). Moab had been at ease for years and was like un-decanted wine, but that was at an end and the decanting was beginning, the pouring of the wine from one vessel to another. These jars would be shattered (*cf.* 19:10-11) and the wine (Moab) lost. Therefore, the joy of the grape harvest and wine pressing would vanish and the shouts of joy at the harvest would be replaced by weeping and wailing (vv. 32-33).[669]

The major cause of Moab's destruction was her pride and arrogance (vv. 26, 29-30, 42). Her arrogance was well established by the prophets (Isa 16:6; Zeph 2:10). Again, Jeremiah's vocabulary is impressive. Moab is prideful, lofty minded, arrogant, has a haughty heart, is boastful, and magnified herself against the Lord. These words describe not only Moab but any nation that does not recognize Israel's God as King of the universe (v. 15). Pride and arrogance are also the default position for any social group that organizes itself apart from subservience to God, whether it be a state or county or city. Individuals also suffer the same affliction. This pride and arrogance leads to idolatry, for something or someone becomes enthroned as the object of worship.

For Moab it was her god, Chemosh, who is directly addressed three times (vv. 7, 13, 46). Chemosh was powerless to save Moab and would be going into exile with her.[670] Chemosh could not bring security but only shame when his powerlessness was demonstrated. False pride and false gods go together, and both are helpless before God the

---

[669] Compare the grim use of this metaphor in Isa 63:1-6.

[670] This probably literally happened since Assyria and Babylon would carry off the idols of the nations they defeated to display at home.

judge. Therefore, Moab also endured shame for the impotency of her god (vv. 1, 13, 20, 39).[671]

Jeremiah is clear that the judgment is the Lord's work (vv. 10, 12, 15c, 35). Though the description of Moab's destruction fits well that of a conquering army coming in (*cf.* chs. 4, 6, 46), God is still the ultimate cause and authority behind the foreign powers. Verse 10 curses anyone who does not carry out the work of the sword of the Lord (*cf.* 46:10, 14; 47:6). All of this is done in God's timing (v. 12) who is the King (*cf.* 46:18; 47:6) and Lord of the armies ("hosts", v. 15c). This is the same theology of judgment that permeates the book of Jeremiah.

The most surprising theme is the strong note of lament in chapter 48. Jeremiah alerts us to this with the first word to Nebo in verse 1, "Woe for Nebo" (NRSV, "Alas"). He ends the chapter with "Woe to you, O Moab" (v. 46). The chapter is more than a judgment speech; it is a lamentation over fallen Moab. The surrounding nations are admonished to mourn (v. 17), but more surprising, it is God himself who wails and weeps for the people (vv. 31 and 36). The "I" could be Jeremiah but as we have seen elsewhere the "I" reflects both Jeremiah and God's perspective (8:21; 9:1; 13:17). Verses 31 and 36 form an *inclusio* around verses 32-35 that expresses several ways of mourning – wail, cry out, weep, removal of joy, and moaning. Verses 37-39 continue the theme. Shaved heads and beards, slashed flesh, and sackcloth are signs of lament and funeral practices (*cf.* Isa 15:2-3; Lev 10:6-7; Jer 41:5).

Moab has earned God's judgment, but it gives him no pleasure, just as it gave him no pleasure to execute judgment on Israel. This punishment is carried out through tears, just as a loving father may discipline his son through

---

[671] The two words, shame and broken down are repeated in vv. 1, 20, and 39 and perhaps suggest a structure for the chapter.

tears. In the big picture, all the nations are a part of God's people and they too cause him great heartache.[672]

Therefore, the brief promise for the future in verse 47 is not a surprise (*cf.* 46:26b; 49:6, 39). Jeremiah employs the language of restoration from his promises to Israel – God will "restore their fortunes: (*cf.* 30:18; 33:11, 26; Deut 30:3; Hos 6:11; Amos 9:14). This hope is grounded in the promise of Jer 12:15:

> And after I have plucked them up, I will again have compassion on them, and I will bring them again to their heritage and to their land, every one of them.

Again, we learn that judgment is not the end, but that grace prevails.

5.b. Lesser Oracles against Nations (49:1-39)

Chapter 49 contains prophecies against five more nations and tribes. Most are brief except for the section on Edom.

5.b.i. Against Ammon – 49:1-6

The Ammonites occupied the territory east of the Jordan River between the Jabbok River on the north and the Arnon River on the south, though Moab often controlled the area. Rabbah was the capital city, which is located within Ammon, the present capital city of Jordan.

The Ammonites had a long history with Israel going back to the time of the conquest.[673] During the conquest Israel was ordered to treat them kindly (Deut 2:19). They were trouble for Israel throughout the Judges period and into David's reign,[674] but at times they were friends.[675] The most

---

[672] This image is far removed from the uninformed caricature of the OT God popular in some kinds of modern anti-Christian writings. One thinks especially of Richard Dawkins, *The God Illusion,* and numerous on-line blogs and conversations.

[673] Gen 19:38 traces them back to Lot and his daughter.

[674] Judg 3; 10; 1 Sam 11; 2 Sam 10.

[675] 2 Sam 17:27-29; 23:37.

recent conflict was after the fall of Jerusalem when the Ammonite king, Baalis, supported Ishmael, the assassin of Gedaliah (Jer 40:18; 41:1-3, 15). Other prophets also condemned the Ammonites (Ezek 2:21; 25:1-7; Amos 1:13-15; Zeph 2:8-11).

Milcom was the chief god of the Ammonites (also called Molech) and was noted for requiring child sacrifice (1 Kgs 11:7; 2 Kgs 23:10; Jer 7:31; 19:5; 32:35). Solomon built a high place for Molech in Jerusalem (1 Kgs 11:7) and married an Ammonite woman who was the mother of Rehoboam (1 Kgs 14:21).

The key word of this prophecy is "possess/dispossess" (*yrš*, ירש, – 4 times in vv. 1-2). The word is dominant in Deuteronomy (71 times) as the Israel moved in to possess the Promised Land and dispossess the Canaanites.[676] The reference to Gad reflects the long history of conflict between Israel and the Ammonites over control of the land given to Gad, which included the territory east of the Jordan (Josh 13:15-23). The Ammonites often tried to drive out the Gadites and for that they would suffer fiery destruction.

Like the words to Moab, the Ammonite god would be humiliated and go into exile (v. 3; *cf.* 38:7b). Also like Moab, the Ammonites were judged for trusting in their own strength and their wealth. They should now lament with ashes and sackcloth (*cf.* 48:17, 31-32, 37-38) for terror is coming (v. 5) because of God's judgment, a terror created by Babylon's war machine, but a terror that came from defying God.[677] Those in obedient relationship with God feared him (revered him) but God's judgment elicited the exact opposite, a dreadful fear of the divine (Exod 15:16; Deut 2:25; Isa 2:10).

A promise of grace ends this short oracle (v. 6):

---

[676] See Hall, *Deuteronomy*, p. 44.

[677] This "terror on every side" is a unique theme in Jeremiah (6:25; 20:3, 10; 46:5).

[A]fterward I will restore the fortunes of the Ammonites

5.b.ii. Against Edom – 49:7-22

The prophecy against Edom is the longest in this chapter. Perhaps the reason is the lengthy history of conflict between the Edomites and Israel which began as Israel traveled from the wilderness up the east coast of the Dead Sea to prepare to enter the Promised Land (Num 20;14-21).[678]

Edom occupied the land south of Moab and the Zered River, through the Arabah, and south to the Gulf of Aqaba. The territory included rugged mountains and deep valleys which gave them a sense of impregnability.

Other prophets had harsh words for Edom, especially Obadiah, who devoted his short book entirely to Edom's destruction.[679] He condemned Edom for its harsh treatment of Israel. There are significant parallels between Obadiah and Jeremiah (*cf.*; 49:9-10 and Obad 5; 49:14-16 and Obad 1-4). Edom like the other nations was arrogant (v. 16) trusting in her wisdom (v. 7) and mountain strongholds (v. 16).

In chapter 25, Jeremiah had given the cup of God's wrath to the nations, including Edom, which is repeated specifically for her here (vv. 12-13). Isaiah has the most vivid description of God's wrath working out against Bozrah (=Edom; Isa 63:1-6). Jeremiah's most arresting image here is that of God as a lion coming up from the Jordan to devour the sheep and lambs of the flock (vv. 19-21; *cf.* 50;44-46). He was also a swooping eagle who would pick off what remained (v.22; *cf.* 48:40). Again, we see, it is indeed a fearful thing to fall in the hands of the living God.

---

[678] The Edomites were descendants of Esau, who was called Edom – Gen 25:30; 36.

[679] See also Isa 21:11-12; 34:5-15; 63:1-6; Amos 1:11-12; Ezek 25:12-14.

In the end, there is no hope for Edom and no lamenting for her demise.

5.b.iii. Against Damascus – 49:23-27

With this prophecy, the location moves north to Syria and its capital, Damascus. These were the Arameans of the tenth to eighth century BCE who had extensive involvement in Israel's life at that time (1 Kgs 20 – 2 Kgs 16).[680] Damascus was an old and important city located at the confluence of trade routes running both east and west, and north and south. It had a series of kings named Ben-Hadad who are mentioned in the narratives in 1 and 2 Kings.[681]

Like the other nations, the fame and power of Damascus could not stand before God and the fire of judgment was sure. This fulfilled the words of Amos a century and a half earlier (Amos 1:4). Like Edom there is no promise of hope for Damascus.

> **Jeremiah 49:25**
>
> *How the famous city [Damascus] is forsaken,*
>   *the joyful town!*
>
> As I write this, the war in Syria appears to be winding down to a conclusion. Its wake has left urban devastation. The largest city in Syria, Aleppo, saw huge areas depopulated and reduced to rubble. Damascus itself, Syria's capital city, saw damage from bombing and urban warfare.
>
> Jeremiah witnessed the damage to various cities (especially Jerusalem) with his own eyes. Cities were fortresses and therefore became battlegrounds when an invading army attacked. Soldiers died, but so did civilians. War can be an indiscriminate killer.
>
> Cities throughout history have rebuilt after being ravaged. Today, missionally motivated Christians may move into a

---

[680] Elijah and Elisha also interacted with some of the leaders.

[681] Ben-Hadad means "son of Hadad." Hadad was the Aramean storm god.

> war-torn urban area as soon as it is safe. They find damaged infrastructure, lack of health care and schools, and traumatized citizens. Open Doors ministry is one of these organizations. Founded in the 1950s by a Dutch citizen who came to be known as "Brother Andrew," Open Doors ministers to persecuted Christians world-wide. In Syria, Christians returning to their cities have encouraged Open Doors to partner with them "to help (our churches) become true places of compassion, true centers of hope."[682] The physical, mental, and spiritual ruin of these cities presents opportunities for people of compassion show the love of God for all people. The "joyful towns" crushed by a war may once again become places of hope, community, and singing. This type of urban ministry will not lack for sites in the foreseeable future.
>
> Mark S. Krause

5.b.iv. Against Kedar and Hazor – 49:28-33

These two names refer to nomadic tribes (vv. 29, 32) in the far north of the Aramean territory who would have been the first victims of a Babylonian military campaign to Palestine and Egypt. Babylonian records tell us that Nebuchadrezzar conquered them in 599 BCE, a decade before Jerusalem fell to him. As nomads, they would have been easily defeated. The sparsely settled desert would become even more so (v. 33). This was Babylon's plan (v. 30), but we know that behind the scenes it was really God's plan. There is no promised hope for the tribes.[683] However, Isaiah saw them in the future responding to the shining light of the glory of God (Isa 60:7).

---

[682] See https://www.opendoorsusa.org/christian-persecution/stories/building-centers-hope-middle-east/

[683] *Cf.* also Isa 21:16-17; Ezek 27:21.

5.b.v. Against Elam – 49:34-39

This prophecy is dated to 598/97 BCE, at the beginning of Zedekiah's reign and is perhaps the latest of these messages.[684] The text now moves geographically far to the east. Elam was located east of the Tigris River, in southwest modern Iran.[685] Its capital was Susa (*cf.* Dan 8:1; Neh 1:1; the book of Esther).

God is the subject throughout and "I" appears often. Everything that happens to Elam originates with him. This was the case with all the prophecies but is more explicit here. The words against Elam match the words against Israel throughout the book. The true King will establish his throne and destroy Elamite leadership (v. 38; *cf.* 46:18; 48:15; 51:57).[686] Their arrogant kings could not stand. Disaster would come from every direction (v. 36).

Yet there is hope for Elam (v. 39; *cf.* 46:22; 48:47; 49:6). God's grace and concern for the salvation of the nations prevails. Perhaps the presence of Elamites on the Day of Pentecost reflects this promise (Acts 2:9).

These prophecies against the various nations, and the long one to come against Babylon, repeat some important themes that all generations need to think about. We find here repeatedly the folly of human arrogance, the futility of trusting in false gods, the illusion of security if one trusts in one's own resources, divine retribution against human violence, the terrible suffering from war, and the interaction between God's judgment and hope for the future.[687]

---

[684] The only other precise date is in 46:2.

[685] The Elamites were listed in Shem's family line in Gen 10:22.

[686] This perhaps forms an *inclusio* with the reference to thrones in 43:10.

[687] Wright, *Jeremiah*, p. 426.

5.c. Oracles against Babylon (50:1-51:64)

The word against Babylon is the longest of the judgment speeches in this last section of Jeremiah. These words would have been of great interest and importance to the Judean exiles in Babylon. They would have also seemed improbable, for Babylon had been the ruling world power for some years, even defeating Egypt (*cf.* chap. 46) and would have seem firmly established as the dominant kingdom in the world.[688]

The date of these words is not given until 51:59. They were delivered and written down in the fourth year of Zedekiah and taken to Babylon by Seraiah, one of Zedekiah's ministers. The date matches other events in Jeremiah – the message of the yoke and Hananiah's response (ch. 27-28) and Jeremiah's letter to the exiles (ch. 29). Therefore, even before the fall of Jerusalem to Nebuchadrezzar the exiles learned that Babylon was doomed, but the judgment was not immediate, and the exiles had to resign themselves to a lifetime in Babylon (ch. 29).[689]

There are several parallels in these chapters with Jeremiah 4-6, which details war and judgment on Judah from an enemy from the north. Babylon will also suffer defeat from enemies from the north. There is a fitting correspondence between the evil done **by** and the evil done **to** Babylon.[690] God's retribution on evil and arrogance dominate the chapters.[691] Babylon may have been the dominant power in the world, but her future was filled with judgment and death.[692] There are also several parallels with Isaiah, who a

---

[688] The list of nations who were to drink the cup of God's wrath in Jer 25:19-26 began with Egypt and ended with Babylon, as do chs. 46-51.

[689] The fourth year of Zedekiah was 594 BC. Babylon was not conquered by Cyrus the Persian until 539 BC.

[690] These parallels suggest that chs. 4-6 and 50-51 form an envelope around the book, ending as it began.

[691] Kidner, *Jeremiah*, p. 148.

[692] Wright, *Jeremiah*, p. 429.

century earlier during Assyrian dominance addressed the coming advent and decline of Babylon (Isa 13-14).

These chapters are difficult to outline, but two themes dominate: the coming destruction of Babylon though war, and the resulting rescue of Israel from her captivity. These two themes are interconnected. Bad news for Babylon is good news for God's people. Since Jeremiah had already addressed these themes, he draws language and images from earlier material.

50:1-3

The whole oracle against Babylon is summarized in these three verses and parallels 51:54-58. The Lord is bringing a nation from the north to wreak destruction on Babylon (*cf.* vv. 8, 41, and 51:48). At the beginning of the book Israel was warned about an enemy from the north bringing evil on her (4:6; 6:1, 22). The irony was deliberate. Babylon was the enemy from the north to bring judgment on Israel, so God will bring judgment on Babylon from the north. Babylon was his servant to carry out his will, but she was also responsible for her actions, and God's justice required he also deal with her evil.

Babylon trusted in her power and in her gods (Bel and Merodach,[693] v. 2) but these gods were powerless to save the nation from the one true God (see also v. 38; 51:44, 47, 52). Isaiah had already established the impotency of idols (Isa 40-44) which Jeremiah had affirmed in chapter 10:1-16. "False gods never fail to fail."[694] But idolatry was not confined to images alone. Babylon, as well as all nations, put her confidence in her wealth, her military might, and

---

[693] "Merodach" is the Hebrew form of Marduk. Marduk was the patron deity of Babylon and his supremacy was celebrated with a yearly fertility festival. Bel Marduk became one name and continued as the patron god. Cyrus even said that he was enabled to conquer Babylon through his patronage. Bel also appears in Canaan as Baal, a familiar figure in the OT. The name Mordecai in the book of Esther comes from Merodach (Esth 2:5).

[694] Wright, *Jeremiah*, p. 434.

her political and religious leaders (*cf.* vv. 35-38). They, too, would fail her.

50:4-20

This first extended statement of judgment on Babylon is sandwiched by two words of encouragement for the exiles (vv. 4-8 and 17-20). Jeremiah had commanded the exiles to settle down in Babylon for at least three generations (ch. 29) but the time would come for their release (*cf.* 2 Chr 36:22-23 and Ezra 1:1-6). Jeremiah portrays them as coming back to Jerusalem in tears (vv. 4-5) seeking God (*cf.* 29:12-14). Their covenant would be renewed (*cf.* ch. 30-33) and they would once again be at home. So, they must "flee" Babylon at the appropriate time (v. 8, *cf.* 51:6).

Israel had suffered from Assyria and Babylon (vv. 6-7, 17)[695] but God would restore her (*cf.* 31:10; 33:11, 12) as he proceeded to destroy Babylon. In a great act of mercy God would pardon Israel and her iniquity would be forgiven (*cf.* 31:34; 33:8).

Some of the nations that God would raise up from the north (v. 8; 51:1) are named in 51:27-28 but the Medes were the major enemy (51:27-28). The Medes were a collection of tribes who allied themselves into a nation in what is now northwest Iran. They were famous for finely bred horses. They helped Babylon defeat Assyria and established their own kingdom. Cyrus the Persian was able to overcome them in 550 BCE and establish the kingdom of Medes and Persians which appears in the book of Daniel (Dan 6:17). Cyrus and his armies conquered Babylon in 539 BCE.

The destruction scenes of Babylon (vv. 9-16) are typical of earlier descriptions of Israel's judgment. The arrows will fly (vv. 9, 14, 16), Babylon will experience shame (v. 12; 51:17, 47) and become a waste land (51:1-2, 43), the city walls will be shattered (v. 15). This is God's "vengeance" on the nation (*cf.* v. 28; 51:6, 11, 36). Vengeance on the wicked is a part of God's holy character. It is retribution for evil

---

[695] The devoured sheep metaphor recalls 2:15.

and for rebellion against God. He is not taking revenge. He is establishing justice and righteousness. Specifically, this vengeance is on behalf of his holy temple and Jerusalem that Babylon destroyed (v. 28; *cf.* 51:6, 11, 36; 52:13-23). In God's world, nations cannot act with impunity against other nations and peoples and think they control their own futures. It was for this reason that Jeremiah, and other prophets, were called to speak against the nations. Revelation 18 shows that this theological principle is still active in its celebration of the downfall of Babylon/Rome.[696]

50:21-32

The pride and arrogance of Babylon will be brought low. The drive toward hubris goes back to Adam and Eve. The human desire is to throw off God's "restraints," to become like God and create one's own world. This is a great temptation for nations and kingdoms who have economic and military resources to carry out their plans. This is the height of arrogance and a recipe for disaster (vv. 31-32). Earlier the pride of Moab (48:29) and Edom (49:16) was censured. Even Israel got caught up in this rebellious spirit (13:9; 19:17; Zeph 3:11). Pride was a distinct mark of the wicked (Isa 28:1, 3). Daniel's words to Belshazzar, the last king of Babylon, echo this passage (Dan 6:22-23). He, too, exalted himself against the Lord and praised the gods of silver, wood and stone. He had not honored the God who gave him his very breath. In his case the judgment was swift. He died that night.[697]

The evil of pride is emphasized by using the epithet "The Holy One of Israel" (v. 29). This divine title is common in Isaiah, but appears only twice in Jeremiah (here and 51:5). God's holiness defines all human evil, for to sin is to violate that holiness. God's holiness sets him apart from all human

---

[696] Most of the uses for the noun and verb for vengeance in the OT refer to God's vengeance. It is his task, not man's (Deut 32:35, 41; Rom 12:19; *cf.* Isa 38:8; 61:2; 63:4).

[697] Ironically the name Belshazzar means "Bel has protected the king."

and profane spheres. Purity and holiness are the marks of obedient, Godly people, but only God can make one truly holy. Pride is the opposite of humility, which is the only way one can approach God. Only God can provide the grace to make such a humble approach possible.[698]

The timing of the coming judgment was in God's hands. To many it seemed like he delayed justice. Therefore, the words "your day has come" (vv. 27, 31) have an ominous tone. Babylon's days of iniquity were filled up (*cf.* Gen 15:16). God's wrath (v. 25; *cf.* 25:15-26) was imminent.

50:33-34

A brief interlude addresses Israel, assuring her that despite the current circumstances of Babylonian oppression, God is still their champion and he will attend to their cause. Just as he redeemed Israel from Egypt (Exod 6:6) so he will redeem them from Babylon (*cf.* Isa 43:1-4; 44:22). The language here reminded Israel of her covenant with God and his faithfulness to that covenant. Beyond the exile there was hope.

50:35-46

God's war against Babylon is again described, using language from some of Jeremiah's earlier sermons. The "sword" (*i.e.*, war) dominates this section, especially verses 35-37 (*cf.* 47:6). Nothing could save Babylon, especially not her idols (v. 38b). She would be desolated just as she desolated others (vv. 39-40).[699] The arrogant king of Babylon would shrink back in terror (v. 43).

Behind this enemy was God himself. He was the lion coming to destroy and no one could withstand his might (v. 44). The same wording occurs in 49:19-21 in the prophecy against Edom, but there the lion was Babylon! The rhetorical questions of verse 44 remind us of Isaiah 40. No one is

---

[698] Thus, all the purity laws in Leviticus were to allow God's people to maintain a relationship with him. They were not a burden but a gift.

[699] The description of the enemy from the north in vv. 41-42 matches the description of Babylon in 6:22-24.

like the God of Israel and he can carry out his plan as he wills (v. 45).

51:1-14

The description of God's war against Babylon continues using a variety of images for total defeat, interspersed with positive words for Israel. Here the enemy is like a destructive wind that empties the land (vv. 1-2; *cf.* 4:11-12 of Judah; 49:36 of Elam).[700]

A brief note to Israel (vv. 5-6) assures her that she is not forgotten. But she must flee from the crumbling nation (*cf.* 50:8). The exiles themselves speak in verse 10 that they have been vindicated by the work of the Lord which they will be very happy to proclaim.

Verse 11 is the first overt reference to the Medes as the enemy from the north. Just as Babylon was God's instrument to carry out his justice against Israel, so the Medes are his instrument to carry out justice against Babylon. This insight is available only through revelation.

The importance of the temple becomes clear for the final act of Babylon's arrogance was its destruction. Therefore, God, who forbade his people to take oaths, swore by himself that he would carry out the destruction of Babylon (v. 14). Nothing could be more certain (*cf.* 22:5; 44:26; 49:13; Gen. 22:16 for a few samples of God's swearing by himself).

Many have attempted to identify where and how God is at work among the nations, but it is presumptuous to think one knows the mind of God. On the other hand, wickedness, evil, pride, idolatry, economic injustice, and war mongering are easily identified, and God's people know

---

[700] V. 1 contains one of the cryptograms for Babylon in these two chapters – *Leb-qamai* (לב קמי). This is a code word for Kasdim which equals the Chaldeans or Babylon. Sheshach (ששך) is also used in 25:26 and 51:41. These are examples of what is called an *atbash*. The last letter of the alphabet is substituted for the first, the second to last for the second letter, the third to last for the third letter and so on. Why Jeremiah would use these code words when he already has used the real name is unclear.

what his position is on these evils. We cannot forget, however, that justice is executed according to God's time-table, not our expectations.

51:15-19

These verses are an interlude, a brief hymn describing the power of God in creation which implies that he has the power to carry out his plans detailed in chapters 50-51. These words are almost verbatim from Jeremiah 10:12-16 and remind us of similar creation hymns like Psalm 104. This is another reason that the idols are powerless and stupid (v. 17). Consequently, Israel's hope that God can and will deliver them is based on a solid foundation.

51:20-33

Though God had used Babylon as his club of judgment, she would be repaid for her evil.[701] A new metaphor is used, that of the destroying mountain, apparently referring to an erupting volcano that soon burns itself out and is harmless (v. 25). Therefore, her armies will easily fall to the enemy (v. 30).

51:34-40

This is another interlude expressing Jerusalem's perspective. She has been crushed by Babylon and desires revenge (vv. 34-35). God promises he will carry out his justice and Babylon will become a heap of ruins (v. 37). The populace will die like lambs led to slaughter (v. 40; *cf.* v. 57). They will become drunk on the wine of wrath that God will make them drink (ch. 25:26).

51:41-58

For one last time, the final destruction of Babylon is described. Armies will wash over her like a flood (v. 42; *cf.* Isa 8:7-8; 17:12) which will turn her into a desert (vv. 43, 55; *cf.* 50:12). Her gods have no power to prevent it (vv. 44,

---

[701] The NRSV heading before v. 20, "Israel the Creator's Instrument", is inaccurate. Most commentators agree that Babylon is being addressed. God never used Israel to carry out his judgment as expressed here.

47). This will cause great rejoicing in the universe (v. 48). Her pride will be brought low (v. 53), her walls breached, and her end complete (v. 58).

Scattered throughout the section are further words of hope for Israel – come out of Babylon with courage (vv. 44-45, 50-51) for she is being punished for her treatment of Israel (v. 49). The defiling of her holy places will be avenged (v. 51).

Many parts of chapters 50-51 present an interpretation issue. When Cyrus and the Medes and Persians conquered the city of Babylon in 539 BCE, they did not destroy it. It survived almost intact. Apparently, the residents welcomed Cyrus as a liberator from their own king. Therefore, we must recognize that some of the language here is stereotypical hyperbole for destruction of cities that were attacked by armies. Ordinarily the walls were torn down and the city burned, so the utter defeat of Babylon is described in those terms. The major themes of the chapter were "fulfilled." Babylon fell, and the exiles were released to go home (Ezra 1). We know from Daniel 4:30-37 that Nebuchadrezzar was humiliated, repented, and praised the Lord. This may have softened the final blow.[702]

The student of the book of Revelation will recognize that John used language from Jeremiah 50-51 in chapters 17-18. Babylon became the code word for Rome, which in turn was and is a representative of all nations and kingdoms that oppose God and oppress his people.

51:59-64

Jeremiah's words against Babylon are written down and sent to the city with Seraiah and King Zedekiah. This trip is not mentioned elsewhere but perhaps Zedekiah was going to assure the Babylonians of his loyalty. Probably Baruch wrote the scroll as he did in chapter 36. Seraiah was Baruch's brother (*cf.* 32:12). The fourth year of Zedekiah was also when Hananiah opposed Jeremiah and predicted only a two-year exile (ch. 28).

---

[702] Kidner, *Jeremiah*, 149.

Here is also another symbolic act. Tossing the scroll into the Euphrates demonstrated the surety of the fulfillment of Jeremiah's words. Utter destruction was assured.

The simple statement at the end of verse 64 is intended to round off the book of Jeremiah and parallel the opening words in chapter 1:1. The words of Jeremiah, expressing the word of the Lord, are contained in chapters 1 to 51. Though chronologically chapters 50-51 are not Jeremiah's last words, in the canonical order of the book they are. The editor (Baruch?) would have added this statement to bring closure to the book. Jeremiah is not a part of the epilogue in chapter 52.

6. Historical Epilogue (52)

Chapter 52, which serves as a historical epilogue to the book, is almost identical to 2 Kgs 24:18 to 25:21, 27-30 with additional information in verses 28-30 on the number of exiles taken to Babylon during three deportations. The story of the fall of Jerusalem and Zedekiah's fate is recounted in Jer 39 but with fewer details.[703] So this story has been told before.[704]

Why then is it repeated at the end of the book? Perhaps the most popular reason given is that the events of the fall of Jerusalem validate Jeremiah as a true prophet. Jeremiah was opposed throughout his career by other prophets who loved to tell the people what they wanted to hear (ch. 23), or who assured the people that the exile of 597 BCE would be short (chs. 27-29). Jeremiah had other opponents including his family (12:6), a priest (20:1-6), his home town people (11:18-23), and his friends (20:10). One king wanted him dead (ch. 36) and other royal officials almost caused his death (chs. 37-38). Therefore, the editor of the book of Jeremiah (Baruch?) wanted to make sure everyone understood that Jeremiah was the true man of God who spoke God's word that did not fail, and that Jeremiah's predictions of Jerusalem's fall came true.[705] Also, Jeremiah's constant warnings to Zedekiah of his fate did indeed come to pass.[706]

This chapter also completes the historical sweep of the book that began with Jeremiah's call in 627 BCE and is summarized in 1:1-3. The four destructive verbs of Jeremiah's call, "to pluck up and to pull down, to destroy and to overthrow" (1:10) had come to full fruition. Nothing was left but a few poor people in the land. The city, the temple, kings, officials, priests, artisans were all gone.

---

[703] Jer 52:4, 7a, 8-11, 13-16, parallel 39:1-10.

[704] See comments on ch. 39.

[705] See Jer 7:13-15; 16:12-13; 17:1-4; 21:1-10; 25:8-10.

[706] See Jer 21:8-9; 27:1, 12-15; 38:14-28.

The extra note in verses 28-30 gives the number of people taken into exile on three different occasions: the first in 597 BCE when Nebuchadrezzar first invaded Judah, the second in 587 BCE at the destruction of Jerusalem, and a third not mentioned elsewhere in 582 BCE. The latter may have been a delayed response to the events recorded in Jeremiah 40-42. These verses present a difficulty for the numbers of exiles differ significantly from the numbers given in 2 Kgs 24:14 and 16. There the numbers are 10,000 and 8,000. One widely accepted solution is that the 2 Kings numbers are rounded numbers and include all the people, including females and children, while the Jeremiah numbers represent only adult males.[707]

Jeremiah 52:30

"... all the persons [taken into exile] were four thousand six hundred."

The deportation of Jews to Babylon took place in several waves beginning about 597 BCE. Jeremiah apparently only reports the number of men taken to exile, giving a total of 4,600. Other sources add to that number, which may have been closer to 40,000 by some estimates. The groups taken to Babylon before the destruction of Jerusalem in 586 BC seem to have included such people as Daniel and Ezekiel. These early deportees were the best of the Jewish young men, the cream of the crop, the future of the nation.

What happens to a city when its best people leave? This sort of "brain drain" in today's world does not come from warfare, but from better opportunities abroad. Ties are maintained in the country of origin, but sometimes there is a hard push to bring family and relatives to the new country, further draining the city's human resources.

A common experience of such immigrants is a loss of status. In Los Angeles, my church employed a wedding planner who had come from Argentina. There, she had been a college professor. In the U.S. she worked a rather menial

---

[707] Kidner, *Jeremiah*, p. 161.

> and unstable job. While living in Chicago, I became acquainted with a naturopath from a Sikh area of India. He had been highly respected and well-paid in his home country, but was unable to be licensed in Illinois, therefore working as a clerk in a drug store. In both cases, moving to America may have provided economic benefits, but this came at the penalty of losing a respected place in the home community.
>
> Immigration, whether voluntary or forced (like the Jerusalemites), can be wounding to the soul in ways that are difficult to explain. What a lovely place a welcoming church can be, where all are treated with dignity as children of God! Workers in urban immigrant communities need to understand and respect a person who may have been a tribal elder in his own land but is now an underemployed janitor or fast-food worker.
>
> *Mark S. Krause*

The text's interest in the temple vessels exceeds that of 2 Kgs 25. It has more vessels listed and more detail about the tops of the two pillars (vv. 18-19, 21-23). The destruction of the temple and the theft of the vessels was a desecration and direct insult to God. This was certainly part of the reason the diatribe against Babylon in chapters 50-51 was so long and intense. God's concern for his glory was vindicated when these vessels were returned under Cyrus the Persian's decree recorded in Ezra 1.

Jehoiachin's release (vv. 31-34) in 560 BCE (after 37 years in prison) reflected a special instance of grace to a king who was in the wrong place at the wrong time (he only ruled three months). This release and kind treatment of the king also provided a faint glimmer of hope to the exiles that they too might be released.[708] This accords with Jeremiah's promises in chapters 30-33 which looked beyond captivity to restoration.

---

[708] *Cf.* Wright, *Jeremiah*, pp. 441-443.

COMMENTARY ON LAMENTATIONS

Scholars point out that Lamentations is not often used in the church. The reason is not clear, but the consequence is. Lamentations gives the people of God the words to express deep grief over a profound loss. It provides a vocal avenue to acknowledge great suffering, bring it to the surface, and offer it to God. Perhaps the American church's privatization of faith and the loss of a community that shares intense loss has contributed to its unpopularity. Also, the therapeutic approach of much preaching and the "prosperity gospel" does not have much room for lament.

Deep suffering is a part of real life and we cannot ignore it. Nor should we. Passing through sorrow and suffering can, if accepted and allowed to do its work, produce strong character and deeper faith. Even the pleasure seeker, Oscar Wilde, when confined to prison for two years discovered that surface pleasure did not bring satisfaction. Sorrow and suffering were the experiences that created meaning. "Where there is sorrow, there is holy ground" he stated in his letter written while in prison, reflecting on his change of perspective.[709]

C.H. Wright sees the loss of the use of Lamentations as a loss for the church because: 1) It disrespects the voice of those whose suffering the book represents; 2) It deprives the church of the language of lament; 3) To avoid lament is to miss the challenge and reward of wrestling with the important theological issues that permeate the book.[710]

Leslie Allen suggests the book as a helpful guide not just to the church but to the preacher or hospital chaplain who often deals with suffering and grief. To heal pain and grief one needs to talk about it. Lamentations gives the church

---

[709] Quoted from his letter *De Profundia* by Ravi Zacharias in "A Slice of Infinity" on September 20, 2017. Accessible at slice@sliceoffinity.org.

[710] C.H. Wright, *The Message of Lamentations* (Downers Grove: IVP, 2015), pp. 21-22.

the words.[711] Urban ministry encounters this kind of pain and grief numerous times.

Lamentations has parallels to other lament literature in the Old Testament, especially the lament psalms. The lament psalm is the most common type of psalm in the Psalter despite its reputation as the "Hymn Book of Israel." There are two types of lament in the Psalms, individual and community.[712] Though Lamentations shares some of the elements of these laments it is closer to a funeral dirge.[713] Lament and mourning are closely related in Lamentations. Mourning rituals in the Old Testament are described but not explained. The ritual was important to give a traditional way of expressing grief. Physical discomfort such as fasting, wearing sackcloth, shaving the beard or head, and sprinkling dust or ashes on the head were practiced. Weeping and wailing accompanied the mourning. Mourning was also public. We find these components in the book of Lamentations. Well-known narrative examples of mourning are Jacob's mourning for Joseph (Gen 37:34-35) and Joseph's mourning for Jacob (Gen 50:1-10).[714]

The setting of Lamentations is the destruction of the city of Jerusalem by the Babylonians in 587 BCE (2 Kgs 25; Jer 39). The last two decades of the city were a calamitous series of misfortunes for the little state of Judah and her cap-

---

[711] Leslie Allen, *A Liturgy of Grief* (Grand Rapids: Baker, 2011). p. 3.

[712] There are 48 individual laments and 17 community laments. See Walter Zorn, "Psalms" in Mark Mangano, *et al.*, *Old Testament Introduction* (Joplin: College Press, 2005), p. 390.

[713] Allen, *Liturgy*, p. 6 and see below on genre. Missing from Lamentations is the direct appeal to God, the statement of confidence, and the assurance of deliverance that appears in most lament Psalms.

[714] Among many other examples see David's mourning for Absalom (2 Sam 18:33-19:4), Daniel's mourning over his vision of seventy weeks (Dan 10:2), and Nehemiah's mourning over Jerusalem (Neh 1:4).

ital city culminating in the destruction of the city and temple.[715] Lamentations was generated in response to this profound crisis and the conviction of the loss of God's favor.

The book is anonymous although Jewish tradition attributed authorship to Jeremiah (*Baba Bathra* 15a). In 2 Chronicles 35:25 Jeremiah is said to have composed laments over the deceased king, Josiah, and these were written in the "Laments." Jeremiah often lamented over his people and over his role in announcing Jerusalem's destruction, so it is not surprising that authorship would be attributed to him.[716]

In the Jewish canon, the book of Lamentations occurs in its third section,[717] the "Writings," (*Kethubim*) and is placed with four other books that came to have liturgical functions – Ruth, Song of Solomon, Ecclesiastes, Lamentations, and Esther.[718] These were the five books traditionally read in the synagogue at specific festivals. Lamentations was read on the ninth of Ab (July/August) which commemorated the destruction of the Jerusalem Temple in 587 BCE and the second temple in CE 70.[719] The Septuagint Greek translation (c. 250-200 BCE) attributed the book to Jeremiah and placed it after his book.[720] The Christian canon kept this arrangement.

The title of Lamentations in the Hebrew Bible is *'êkāh* (אֵיכָה) which is the first word in 1:1; 2:1; and 4:1 ("how" in the NRSV). These are not questions but statements of fact

---

[715] See the introduction to Jeremiah.

[716] *E.g.* Jer 4:28; 6:26; 9:17-19.

[717] The first two sections are the Law (*Torah*) and Prophets (*Nebi'im*).

[718] These are called the *Megilloth* or Rolls.

[719] Zech 7:1-7 seems to reflect that this custom began soon after the fall of the city.

[720] The LXX adds at v. 1, "And it came to pass after Israel had gone into captivity, and Jerusalem was laid waste, that Jeremiah sat weeping and composed this lament over Jerusalem, saying...."

about the post-destruction state of Jerusalem and Judah. The Septuagint called Lamentations *Threnoi* (θρῆνοι, "Dirges") following Jewish scholars who called it *Qinoth* ("Dirges").

Lamentations is only five chapters long. The outstanding feature of the book is the poetic acrostic in which each line in a poem (chapter) begins with succeeding letters of the alphabet, beginning with *aleph* (א), then *bet* (ב), and so on.[721] The Hebrew alphabet has twenty-two letters, so each chapter of Lamentations has twenty-two strophes, or stanzas (or verses) except chapter three which has sixty-six verses. However, the chapters have different patterns of acrostics. In chapters one and two, each verse has three lines and only the first line in each verse begins with the required letter. In chapter three, each verse has one line, but the required letter in sequence governs three verses, hence the sixty-six verses.[722] In chapter four each verse has two lines. Chapter five is not an acrostic but follows the pattern of having twenty-two lines (verses).

The reason for the use of the acrostic is not clear but it does represent a highly artistic form. It may have aided in memory, it may have conveyed that the subject had been completely covered, from "A to Z," or it may have been an aesthetic or artistic way of imposing limits and form on the expression of grief.[723] Whatever the reason, in Hebrew it added punch to the language of the poem.

---

[721] See Ps 119 which is an acrostic and has eight-line strophes for each letter and each of the eight lines begin with the appropriate letter. There are many acrostic Psalms, but none so elaborate as Ps 119, or Lamentations.

[722] An anomaly occurs in that the Hebrew letters *'ayin* (ע) and *pe* (פ) in chapters 2, 3 and 4 are in reverse order. This may reflect a different tradition of the order of the letters in the alphabet.

[723] Norman Gottwald, *The Hebrew Bible: A Socio-Literary Introduction* (Philadelphia: Fortress, 1985), 541. Gottwald prefers a combination of the latter two reasons. See also Delbert Hillars, *Lamentations* (New York: Doubleday, 1972), xxvi.

The lament form dominates the book with its own style, the so-called *qinah* (קִינָה, *cf.* Jer 9:20, Heb. 9:19). *Qinah* has a special meter in which the second half of a parallel line is shorter than the first half, a phenomenon referred to as a 3:2 meter. This gives the line what is sometimes called a "limping" rhythm. Sometimes this can be seen in the English (see e.g. 1:1b, 2a, 3a, 5a). At other times the number of English words required to translate the Hebrew make it harder to discern the pattern (e.g. 1:3c, 4a).

Lamentations also seems to fit the funeral dirge which was sung at the funeral of a person. 2 Samuel 1:17-27 provides the earliest example, David's lament over Saul and Jonathan. In Lamentations, the dirge is applied to the city rather than the individual.[724] Dirges occur in the prophetic books also in response to announcements of judgment on the nation. In those contexts, they anticipate the death of the nation (see Amos 5).

The laments in Lamentations are communal laments, representing the mourning of the whole nation. Many Psalms reflect the same perspective (see Pss 44, 60, 74, 79, and 80 which especially reflect defeat in battle). Psalm 137 is perhaps contemporary with Lamentations for it is set in the exile in Babylon. However, Lamentations also includes other themes, such as trust (3:20-24), the meaning of suffering (3:25-39), and prayer (5:1, 20-22).

Chapter 1

In chapter 1, we hear two voices, the author or poet in verses 1-11 and Jerusalem/Zion in verses 12-22. In verses 1-11 Jerusalem is referred to as the city (v. 1), Judah (v. 3), Zion (v. 4; *cf.* v. 17),[725] daughter Zion (v. 6) and Jerusalem

---

[724] The lament was not unique to Israel in the ancient world. See W. C. Gwaltney, "The Biblical Book of Lamentations in the Context of Near Eastern Lament Literature," in *Scripture in Context II*, ed. W. W. Hallo, J. C. Moyer, and L. G. Perdue (Winona Lake: Eisenbrauns: 1983), 191-211.

[725] Zion appears 15 times in the book. Its use in ch. 1 is especially powerful for it was the name applied to the temple area and worship center, which had been destroyed.

(vv. 7, 8). She is also portrayed as a widow (v. 1). In verses 12-22 the first person dominates though we have references to virgin daughter Zion (v. 15) and Zion/Jerusalem (v. 16).

1:1-11

"How" (*'êkāh,* אֵיכָה) introduces the chapter and the book and comes from the setting of a lament. However, the English "how" does not do justice to the force of the word here. The descriptions of the weeping of a widow in the following verses suggests a howl or shriek of desperation. Allen suggests "How terrible that...."[726] The normal setting for the word was a funeral lament. There is the feeling of death throughout Lamentations.[727]

The picture of the widow in verse 1 draws our sympathy, but how is it that Jerusalem/Zion is a widow? The prophet Hosea introduced the metaphor of marriage to describe the relationship between Israel and God in the eight century BCE (Hos 1-2). Israel was the wife and God was the husband. Jeremiah followed suit (Jer 2-3). Marriage was a covenant which described perfectly the relationship between God and Israel. Using this analogy, though, the fact that Jerusalem was now a widow was not true, for God was not deceased. However, Jerusalem's grief, sorrow, and helplessness equaled that of a widow who was destitute and alone, alienated from her family and community. It is no wonder she was weeping bitterly (v. 2). Moreover, her plight was even worse than that of widow for her friends had turned against her and become her enemies. These "lovers" (v. 2; *cf.* v. 19) were unstable and deceivers.[728]

---

[726] Allen, *Liturgy*, p. 6.

[727] *Ibid.*, p. 34.

[728] "Lovers" in Hosea and Jeremiah refer to foreign countries to whom Israel turned for assistance. It is unclear here if this is what is meant. In v. 19, the lovers do seem to be other nations.

Lamentations 1:1

How lonely sits the city
  that once was full of people!

Lamentations begins with a personification of the city as a woman. The following verses refer to her as a "widow," a "princess," a "weeper," and a "lover." When a city loses population and is in decline, there is a community sadness. This does not have to rise to the level of the devastation and cruelty suffered by Jerusalem to still be worthy of our notice. The queen is in mourning.

Ruins of ancient cities are found all over the world, whether it be Manchu Picchu in Peru, Chichén Itzá in Mexico, Petra in Jordan, or Nineveh on the banks of the Tigris River in northern Iraq. These empty cities have only the bustle of curious tourists and the people who service them, not the densely populated neighborhoods and markets with which they once teemed.

Jerusalem was eventually rebuilt. Today, its economy is heavily built on visitors who come to see the Church of the Holy Sepulcher, the Western (Wailing) Wall, the Dome of the Rock, and other ancient sites. Jerusalem is again full of people. Many modern cities have sparkling new buildings next to heritage locations. Some examples I have seen are the temple precinct in Kathmandu, the Shwedagon hill in Yangon, and Westminster Abbey in London. The old, carefully preserved buildings provide a stark contrast to newer construction.

One of the most striking examples I have seen is Faneuil Hall in Boston. Famous for events that took place within, the building itself is a handsome example of colonial style with its red brick walls, arched windows and white cupola. This graceful eighteenth century landmark stands in stark contrast to the Boston City Hall across the street, an extreme example of the "brutalist" style of architecture popular in the 1960s. It is surrounded by gleaming glass office towers.

Visionary city leaders long to create cityscapes that are usable and beautiful. This may require demolition of older

> buildings. Civic leaders are acutely aware that most buildings over fifty years old have acquired some sort of constituency resistant to tearing down or even modification. Churches are often embroiled in such controversies. A city church once full of congregants may be hosting Sunday services for fifty people in an auditorium that seats 1,000.
>
> First Methodist Church in downtown Seattle endured a loss of membership in the last part of the twentieth century. Rather than deciding to close and allow their property to be sold for a parking structure, the church's leaders negotiated several things to continue the church's ministry to the urban poor. This included sharing facilities with the Church of Mary Magdalene, a ministry to homeless women. Part of the prime real estate owned by the church was sold to allow for the construction of a 43-story office tower. Later, the sanctuary itself with its historic organ was converted to be a downtown concert and banquet venue. The developer who spearheaded this conversion helped the congregation relocate to a more suitable property in another location. Rather than expend enormous resources to maintain an historic but antiquated facility in a location that no longer works, this group is to be commended for taking strategic action to preserve the church, its witness, and its need ministry to the urban core of the city.
>
> *Mark S. Krause*

The lack of a "comforter" struck the widow especially hard (repeated in vv. 2, 9, 16, 17, and 21). In ancient Israel, family, friends, and neighbors gathered to support and minister to the widow or to the one in grief.[729] There was none of that for Zion and the pain was felt deeply. God was the source of comfort to his people (Ps 23) but in Lamentations he was the cause of the problem, so widow Zion could not

---

[729] *Cf.* Job's three friends who sat with him in silence for a full week – Job 2:13.

turn to him for comfort.[730] She did, however, address her pain to him.

One thing that made the present especially difficult was the glory of Zion's past. She was great among the nations (v. 4), like royalty (vv. 1, 6), God's chosen one, used to position and authority. All that was gone, and she was now in bitter servitude (vv. 1, 3, 7). The blessing of Deuteronomy 28:13 had been reversed (*i.e.*, they were no long at the top but at the bottom). This lament of reversal recurs throughout the book.

Zion was beset by enemies all around (vv. 2, 5, 7, 9, 10). Even her friends had become enemies (v. 2). They had become her masters and enjoyed prosperity (v. 5), which was usually seen as a godly blessing. In the past God had delivered her from her foes (v. 7), especially at the Exodus and Conquest, during the Judges period, and under David. But not now. She was experiencing the great reversal of her history and she had gone back into captivity. As bad as captivity was, probably the refugees in Jerusalem were under greater stress as some of the later graphic descriptions suggest.

Metaphorically, even the roads to Jerusalem joined in the mourning for they no long knew the footsteps of the faithful going to the temple to celebrate the festivals (v. 4). The gates could no longer welcome the worshipping community for they were destroyed (*cf.* Isa 3:26). The enemy, forbidden by the law to enter the temple (Deut 23:3-4), had not only entered it but demolished it. Israel's former religious life, even for the few left in Jerusalem, was impossible.[731]

---

[730] But note all the messages of comfort aimed at the exiles in Isa 40:1; 49:13; 51:3, 12; 52:9, etc. The future was bright with comfort, but the refugees of Lamentations were in the middle of the judgment.

[731] Pss 74:4-8 and 79:1-4 detail the destruction of the temple. Ps 122:1-2 describes the joy of those who go up to Jerusalem to worship. Ps 24 details the glory of going to the temple to worship and the grandeur of the presence of God. Imagine one the great cathedrals of the world (like Notre Dame in Paris or St. Peter's in Rome) lying in ruins, or one's

The poet is blunt about the cause for this destruction and mourning. It was Zion's sin. The prophets had described her sin and warned of her demise, especially Jeremiah, so, the current situation was no surprise. Even lady Zion confessed this in verse 14. The widow's weeping could have been avoided. Repentance was repeatedly offered. Yet the stubbornness of Israel's heart prevented a turning to God (Jer 5:23; 7:26; 19:15).[732] If there is a redemptive moment in this funeral dirge, perhaps this confession of sin is it, but it was too late.[733]

The horror of Zion's experience is further described in terms of her shame (vv. 8-9). In ancient honor/shame cultures, shame was one of the worst things that could happen to an individual, family, or community. People would do all sorts of things to avoid it, including lying.[734] "Of especial importance was the sexual honor of the woman... any sexual offense on a woman's part, however slight, would destroy not only her honor, but that of all the males in her paternal kin group as well." [735] That explains the turn from honor to despising in verse 8. Even if it was because of rape in war time (*cf.* 5:11), as it likely could have been, the woman was dishonored.

Another dimension is that nakedness was associated with divine judgment in the prophets and almost always with shame (Isa 47:3; Hos 2:3; Jer 20:4; *cf.* Deut 28:48).[736]

---

own home church building being destroyed. My home church built a new building and the old one was repurposed into apartments. Though I understand it is not the building and all that, I still feel a small pang of regret when I drive past the old building on visits to my hometown. There are so many wonderful memories associated with it!

[732] Israel had earned this condemnation as early as the Exodus – Exod 32:9; 33:3, 5.

[733] More confessions are coming. See on 5:7 and 16 below.

[734] See John J. Pilch, *The Cultural Life Setting of the Proverbs* (Minneapolis: Fortress Press, 2016), pp. 189-93, 206-08.

[735] *Ibid.*, p. 193.

[736] Nudity was first associated with shame in Gen 3:7, 10 in contrast to 2:25; see also Gen 9:22-23; Mic. 1:11. It is a telling commentary

Sometimes the phrase "lift up the skirts" was used (Jer 13:22, 26; Nah 3:5). "Uncover nakedness" is used thirty-two times in Leviticus as a euphemism for illicit sexual relations. This usage was certainly in the background of nakedness in contexts like here in Lamentations. Jerusalem was an unfaithful covenant partner, an unfaithful wife, and she had sought relationships with foreign idols and foreign nations. This was spiritual adultery. Exposing her nakedness to her shame was a fitting and powerful condemnation of her actions.

The poet also likens the consequence of judgment to uncleanness occasioned by the blood of the menstrual flow (v. 9). This could also allude to the uncleanness caused by idolatry and violence (Jer 2:22-23, 34). In this shocking way the poet described how far lady Zion had fallen from her position as God's treasured possession (Deut 7:6; 14:2).

Among the poet's descriptions of the widow's grief, we are surprised by the personal appeals in the first person in verses 9b and 11b. The Lord is asked to "look" at the widow and take note of her affliction and lowly estate (*cf.* v. 20; 2:20; 5:1). This is the first time that God is addressed. These are appeals for the Lord to consider her plight and come to her rescue. We see that even in the depths of despair expressed in verses 1-11, prayer is possible.

Did God pay attention? We do not know, for God is silent throughout the book except for 3:57.[737] Lamentations 5:20 and 22 seems to give the final conclusion that God wasn't paying attention (see comments there).

1:12-22

Widow Zion now speaks for herself, describing her weeping and pain. The same themes are repeated, and she endorses the poet's perspective. The grieving widow needs to tell her story.[738] She begins by acknowledging that it was

---

on our culture that nudity is no longer shameful, but even seemingly celebrated in some circles.

[737] Wright, *Lamentations*, p. 57.

[738] Allen, *Liturgy*, p. 53.

the Lord himself who had inflicted on her deep sorrow (vv. 12-13). The cause was God's anger and burning fire, the fire of judgment that Jeremiah had warned of so often (Jer 4:4; 15:14 – "...for in my anger a fire will kindle that will burn forever"; *cf.* 21:12; Isa 42:24-25; see also Lam 2). Judgmental fire is a refrain in Amos 1:3-2:5.

Though Babylon was the immediate cause of Zion's distress, she realized who the ultimate cause was. She claims she was stunned by this, but she should not have been. Not only had Jeremiah warned her, but the covenant curses section of Deuteronomy 28:16-67 detailed the consequences of covenant breaking.

It seems that finally, Zion understood that her sin and rebellion were the causes of her destruction (vv. 14-15). She had refused the prophets' warnings, but she could not ignore the reality of Jerusalem's ruins. She finally realized the weight of her sin.[739] She had now experienced what the Lord could do, extending his wrath on her just as he did on her enemies.[740] Now she weeps, but it is too late (vv. 16-17).[741]

Despite her grief and pain, she does recognize that the Lord is doing the right and just thing (v. 18). She has no excuse. This is the theological high point of Zion's lament. God is in the right in executing his anger and wrath against her. Here and in verse 14, Zion chose the two of the strongest words that could have been used to describe her sin – two synonyms for her rebelling, *peša'* (פֶּשַׁע, v. 14) and *mārā* (מָרָה, vv. 18, 20). Her sin was more than just failing to measure up, it was deliberate turning against God and his will (as in Gen 3). In her case it was intentional and sustained, marked by persistent idolatry (Jer 7:16-20; 10:1-

---

[739] There is some irony here for in Jer 27-28 the false prophet Hananiah removed the yoke Jeremiah put on himself to symbolize Israel's future submission to Babylon.

[740] *Cf.* the wine press imagery for Edom in Isa 63:1-3.

[741] V. 17 is a brief third person interruption that marks the center point of vv. 12-22.

16). The verbal form of *peša'* (*pāša'*, פָּשַׁע) was used especially of covenant breaking (*cf.* Lam 3:42). The verb *mārā* was used as early as the wilderness period of Israel rebelling against God (Num 20:10, 24; Deut 1:26, 43). Of course, God was in the right. It was the very righteousness of God that also made it possible for Zion to cry out to him for relief. Not only was God the cause of her distress, he was the only one who could help her.

Zion's distress over the fate of her youth (v. 18b) and her leaders (v. 19) was understandable, but actions have consequences. Nothing that happened to her was a surprise.[742] Zion ends her lament/dirge with the desire to see her enemies suffer the same fate she had, for they rejoiced over her fate and did not come to her aid.[743] We know from Jeremiah 46-51 that the nations will receive justice from God also, so Zion's wishes did not go wanting. But that did not lessen her guilt and punishment.

Allen summarizes the lesson of this chapter. Zion addressed her community of faith and by expressing grief and confessing guilt encouraged an openness with God that channeled feelings of anger into prayer for justice. These were the lessons to be learned from the destruction of Jerusalem in 586 BCE. These were hard lessons, but necessary and provide a model for use with those who suffer various kinds of afflictions.[744]

Chapter 2

There are two voices in chapter two: the poet in verses 1-19 and lady Zion in verses 20-22. The poet speaks from two perspectives: in the third person in verses 1-10 and from the first person in verses 11-19. The transition to the first person apparently is the poet's own personal response to the grim picture he described in verses 1-10. The chapter is set off by an *inclusio* in verses 1 and 22, the day of the

---

[742] *Cf.* Deut 28:41 for the predicted fate of her youth; *cf.* Lam 1:5c.

[743] Perhaps an echo of Jer 27:3.

[744] Allen, *Liturgy*, p. 61.

Lord's anger. The chapter describes the consequences of God's anger for Jerusalem and for the temple.

2:1-10

The subject of this section is the unrelenting and overwhelming description of the way that the Lord in his judgment on Jerusalem destroyed every physical and spiritual facet of Jerusalem's life. There are nearly 30 verbs of destruction in these verses.[745]

As in chapter 1, Zion is addressed in a variety of ways, many with the word "daughter" which describes the tender and intimate relationship the Lord had with her, thus makings her destruction even more heart-wrenching. The most common form of address is "daughter Zion" (vv. 4, 8, 10, 13, 18), then "daughter Jerusalem" (vv. 13 15), "daughter Judah" (v. 5), "the city" (vv. 11, 12), "Zion" (v. 6), "Jerusalem" (v. 10), and "Jacob" (v. 3).

The poet begins by describing the destruction of the temple, which was both the crown jewel of Israel and the dwelling place of God (v. 1). It was the conduit between Israel and God, where he was worshipped and where the priests offered sacrifices and instructed the people in the law, but it became an object of the Lord's scorn (vv. 6-7). Even the appointed days and seasons of the festival were gone. Consequently, any attempt to worship there was futile and a mere noise. In fact, the noise that was heard was that of the victorious army destroying the buildings.

God's right hand which delivered Israel from Egypt and sustained her throughout her history had been withdrawn (v. 3). In fact, God himself had become like an enemy (vv. 4-5). The one who had always fought for Israel now fought against her. This was "Holy War" reversed, a terrifying prospect.

The Lord also destroyed the city of Jerusalem, breaking down its walls and strongholds (vv. 2, 5, 8). There was nothing left of the once proud city. God had profaned his

---

[745] Joel's description of the great and terrible day of the Lord in 2:1-11 parallels these verses.

holy city. All things the people were supposed to do were intended to honor God and move toward holiness. There are multiple references throughout the Old Testament to the holy city, the holy temple, the holy priests, the holy land, a holy God, but God's judgment reversed all of this because of his anger and wrath (vv. 1-3). This was executed through the burning fire of the invading Babylonian army.

The destruction also involved the eradication of leadership. The kings and princes provided political leadership (v. 9), the prophets, elders, and priests provided the word of God, wisdom, and instruction in the law. Without these there was no leadership at all (vv. 9, 10, 14, 20). Jeremiah had often condemned the prophets for their false message (chs. 23, 27, 28, 29) which Lamentations here affirms. Without leadership anarchy and chaos follow resulting in devastating social disruption. Jeremiah 40-41 demonstrated the result of this chaos. There was only one possible response to this desperate situation – silence and mourning (v. 10 and 5c, 8b; 1:4).

The young people were especially affected for they had no future and no hope. The day that Amos had predicted with such insight centuries before had come to pass, "On that day.... I will turn your feasts into mourning, and all your songs into lamentations; I will bring sackcloth on all loins, and baldness on every head; I will make it like the mourning for an only son, and the end of it like a bitter day" (Amos 8:9-10).

This was done without mercy or compassion (vv. 2, 17, 21; 3:43), a shocking violation of the self-revelation of God in Exodus 34:6-7. In the past, God revealed himself as merciful and gracious, slow to anger, and abounding in love and faithfulness. Does the poet suggest that God had violated his character? No. Both the blessings and curses of the covenant (Lev 26; Deut 27-28) and Jeremiah's relentless calls for repentance over forty years of preaching had warned Israel there were consequences for their persistent rebellion. Jeremiah clearly taught that God would relent if they repented (Jer 18), but they refused and the time for repenting had ended. God's justice was being executed. He was not out of control.[746] His determination or plan (v. 8) was long in the making (v. 17). Also, his self-revelation in Exodus 34 concluded with the fact he would not let the guilty go unpunished (Exod 34:7b). The destruction of Jerusalem and the temple were a disaster, but it was not unjust or unanticipated.

2:11-19[747]

The awful scene in verses 1-10 caused the poet to burst out in a personal response. He could not be a disinterested observer any longer. He broke down into tears.[748] Do we perhaps also see here the tears of God?[749] The poet identifies himself with the tears of widow Zion in chapter 1:2 and 16. In fact his weeping was so intense that he vomited – his "bile" was poured out on the ground. So, too, did the widow Zion (1:20).[750] What moved him the most was the fate of the babies abandoned in the streets (v. 11c). The suffering of the adults was at least understandable, but innocent children also?[751]

The poet, like the people, was out of words (v. 13). The destruction was so deep and broad that nothing could be done. The prophets failed with false messages (v. 14), the neighbors mocked and even quoted Scripture against the city (v. 15; *cf.* Ps 48:2), and her enemies rejoiced (v. 16; *cf.* Jer 30:12-17).

The poet returns to God's purposes once again (v. 17; *cf.* v. 8). What happened to Jerusalem was not a random series

---

[746] The accusation of K. O'Connor as quoted in Wright, *Lamentations*, p. 79.

[747] This section has many parallels with Jeremiah.

[748] Jeremiah also broke out into tears – 9:1; 13:17; 14:17.

[749] Wright, *Lamentations*, p. 89; *cf.* Jer. 8:21.

[750] The poet likes the verb "pour out", *cf.* vv. 4, 12, and 19

[751] This has been part of discussions questioning the justice of God or even his existence. This argument is most memorably made by Ivan the atheist brother in Fodor Dostoyevsky's *The Brothers Karamazov* (New York: Random House, 1950), pp. 289-90.

of events wrought by Babylon but God carrying out his word of judgment against his rebellious people. The NRSV "ordains" in verse 17 is misleading. The Hebrew has "commanded" which connects these events to the covenant law and the blessing/curse section that accompanied it.[752] God was being faithful to his word that had stood since the time of Moses. He would not have been just and trustworthy if he had not kept his word. Though the poet has deep sympathy for Zion he could not fault God or his character.[753]

The poet ends his words with a direct appeal to Zion (vv. 18-19). Though the Lord is the cause of the distress, he is the only one who can help her, so, he pleads for Zion to cry out to God. The verb he uses (ṣʿq, צעק) was from the context of the Exodus. When Israel cried out for deliverance to God she did so because he was the only one who could help them (Exod 3:7, 9; 8:12; 14:10; Deut 26:7). The verb is also frequent in prayers of distress (Pss 34:17; 77:1). The assumption is that God will hear the cry and come to aid his people because he is compassionate for the oppressed. Israel had not been disappointed in the past, for when God saw and heard, he responded (Exod 3:7; Num 20:16). If God did not respond it was because of disobedience (Jer 11:11; Mic 3:4).

The poet gave Zion instructions on how to cry out – with great tears, continuously, with lifted hands on behalf of the children. Left unsaid is the "perhaps." Perhaps then the Lord would respond as Jeremiah promised (Jer 31:15-17).

Maybe there was a long pause between verses 19 and 20.[754] What more could Zion say? All she could do was ask God again to look and consider her situation (*cf.* 1:9, 11, 20).

---

[752] The NIV "decreed" is better. Other versions such as the ESV, KJV, and NAS have "commanded." In fact, the NIV is better here for 17a as well, "The Lord has done what he planned, he has fulfilled his word, which he decreed long ago." *Cf.* Jer 9:11; 19:10-13; 21:13-14.

[753] God also had other plans for Israel, stated in Jer 29 and 32-33, but they were for after the judgment.

[754] Wright, *Lamentations*, p. 95.

When she did speak she centered her appeal on the suffering of the children with several rhetorical questions (v. 20). The implied answers were that these things should not happen, even to a people under God's judgment—cannibalism,[755] priests slaughtered in the temple, young and old lying dead in the street – especially to God's people. But these were the consequences of the day of the Lord (v. 22). Zion's indictment of God ended on a desperate note, but there was no answer from God. "...this chapter and this book as a whole relate a message hard to bear, read, or accept: when the day of the Lord comes, one can only cry out to God in a way that confesses sin, asks questions about suffering, and intercedes on the behalf of the innocent."[756]

Chapter 3

Chapter 3's style differs from chapters 1 and 2. The acrostic pattern is applied to the first word in every line, not just every three lines. Further, the same letter is used three times in a succession. Therefore, the verse count should be the same but for some reason each line is counted as a verse, hence the 66 verses in chapter three.[757] To understand the development of the chapter it is helpful to consider three verses together as one stanza.[758]

---

[755] There is an immediacy to these questions that suggest an eyewitness to the events of the fall of Jerusalem. Cannibalism was not recorded at that time, but it did occur during a siege of Samaria by the Syrians centuries earlier – 2 Kgs 6:27-29.

[756] P. R. House, *Lamentations* (Nashville: Thomas Nelson, 2004), p. 398.

[757] Ch. 4 has 44 lines and ch. 5 has 22, so the total for those two chapters is 66 lines. The result is that the book, after chapter 3 seems to hasten to the end.

[758] Some modern translations leave a slight space after every three verses.

The voice speaking identifies himself as "I am the man...."[759] Is this the same person as the poet in chapter 2? Or is he a leader of Judah who speaks on behalf of the people? Some suggest the latter and that he speaks as an archetype of the people. However, it seems best to consider him the voice of the poet who now identifies himself with the people in their suffering.[760]

The structure of the chapter is unclear although a few elements stand out. Verses 1-18 are a statement by the man of his own personal suffering along with the people. The central portion, verses 19-42, are the one bright spot in the book with a strong expression of hope in God's faithfulness. In verses 43-51 the poet/man again weeps over the destruction of Jerusalem. The chapter concludes with an ambiguous plea to trust God – verses 52-66 (see below).

3:1-18

The man now does more than weep for Zion (2:11), he tells of his personal suffering under the wrath of God (*cf.* Ps 102). He suggests he went through the siege of the destruction of Jerusalem and experienced the anger of God himself.[761] The rod of God's wrath is the rod of the father's discipline in Proverbs (10:13; 22:15) and of God's discipline in Job (9:34; 21:9). It is also the Assyrian discipline of Israel in Isaiah 10:6. It is the rod of the shepherd in Psalm 23. For the man it took the form of his affliction (v. 1) which drove him into the darkness of God's judgment and hostility (vv. 2-3). God's hand (power) could be beneficent for he rescued Israel from slavery in Egypt, but it also punished

---

[759] Hebrew *geber* (גֶּבֶר) carries the idea of strength in contrast to women and children – Exod 10:10, 11; Jer 30:6; 41:16. Sometimes it refers to a man of spiritual strength rather than physical – Job 3:3, 23; 4:17; 10:5. The related verb root *gibor* (גִּבּוֹר) means to be strong, accomplished.

[760] When referring to the author of this chapter I will refer to "the man" rather than the poet.

[761] The "wrath" in 3:1 connects ch. 3 to 2:27 and the reference to anger there.

the Egyptians (Exod 9:3, 15) and the rebellious Israelites (Deut 2:15; *cf.* Ps 32:4). For the man it was the latter and the consequence was a darkness of the soul (v. 6).

The man's personal suffering was like a wasting disease (v. 4) that led to the semblance of death. In his despair the man uses two conflicting metaphors – God had besieged him like a city (v. 5), but he had also walled him in with no way to escape (vv. 7-9). The result was that God did not hear his prayers (*cf.* the lament of Zion in 2:20-22; *cf.* Ps 22:1). The silence of God in times of crisis is unbearable. His whole body was broken.[762] The experience produced deep bitterness (vv. 5, 15, 19; *cf.* Jer 14:9; 9:15).[763]

The emotion of the man is seen in the many images he applies to God – he is a bear (v. 10a) or a lion (v. 10b; *cf.* Hos 5:14) and a hunter or warrior with a bow (vv. 12-13). He had no doubt that God was the author of his affliction. He shared the guilt of Jerusalem and suffered with them as well. In a general divine judgment on a nation the guilty and innocent suffer alike. There was no separating of the weeds and wheat (Matt 13:24-30, 36-43).

In the thinking of the ancient world individuals were not as important as the community. The collective guilt involved everyone in the community, so, although the man took his experience as a divine, individual assault, the readers would understand that he was also speaking for the community. This makes it almost inexplicable that he became a laughing stock of the people and object of taunting (v. 14; *cf.* v. 63; Ps 22:6-7). Perhaps it is because he still maintained a faith in God (vv. 22-23).[764]

The conclusion of the man was that he had lost everything – peace, happiness, glory, and hope (vv. 17-18). These were specific promised blessings of God. The man was indeed in the pit of despair, hopeless with no future. This is the low

---

[762] Bone is a metaphor for the whole body. *Cf.* Ps 22:14, 17.

[763] In Jer 23:15, wormwood and poison water were punishment for the lying prophets.

[764] In 2:15 it was the neighbors of Jerusalem that taunted her.

point of the chapter. This depth of despair is well-known to those who are subject to depression. Very little can be said or done that will encourage them. The causes are many but to feel that God has abandoned the sufferer, as here, is devastating.

3:19-42

These verses introduce a surprising and important reversal of tone. The man had no hope in verse 18, but suddenly recovers it in verse 21. He was still in despair (homeless and bowed down, vv. 19-20) but then he "remembered," which gave him hope, literally "this I cause to return to my heart." The heart was the locus of the mind and will. In the midst of deep despair, he willed himself to struggle up from the depths and look once more to God. He knew what he knew but he had to focus his energies to bring himself back to equilibrium.[765]

In Psalm 73 the same reversal happened. There, the Psalmist went into the house of the Lord and discovered again what he knew (Ps 73:16-17). What is "this" that he called to mind? God's character: "The steadfast love of the Lord never ceases, his mercies never come to an end; they are new every morning; great is your faithfulness" (vv. 22-23).[766]

How did the man come to this place after the profound distress of the previous section? Perhaps he experienced what many of the writers of lament Psalms experienced – as they poured their hearts out to God in lament, they came to focus more and more on God himself and less on themselves, they came to realize their only hope was in God (*cf.* Ps 22:1-18 and 19-31; 13:1-4 and 5-6).

---

[765] Wright, *Lamentations*, p. 111.

[766] Fortunately for the church these words have been immortalized in a favorite hymn, "Great is thy faithfulness" written by Thomas Chisholm. Unfortunately, their context amid great expressions of despair are not well-known.

It appears also that the man remembered God's self-revelation in Exodus 34:6-7.[767] He repeats the main attributes from that text – God's steadfast love, his mercy, and his faithfulness. These are rich theological concepts that describe God's absolute loyalty to Israel and his covenant with her, and his absolute reliability in keeping his word. The "great" faithfulness could also be translated "abundant" faithfulness. That is, it may be greater than anything else, but even better, it is more abundant than anything else – there is plenty for all and then some.[768] It can cover all circumstances and needs.

"Portion" (v. 24) often refers to the inherited portion of the Promised Land that God gave to each tribe. Many Psalms and the man here assert that God is their inherited portion (Ps 16:5; 73:26; 119:57) which locates their privileged place as God's people. So of course, the man can hope in him.

In another abrupt turn from 3:1-18, the man now declares that the Lord is good (v. 25). He has not forgotten the pain expressed in those verses but his determination to remember the character of the Lord led him to realize again that ultimately the Lord is good (Ps. 34:8).[769] This good he had defined in verses 22-23 – he was reliable and gracious. God had demonstrated these qualities throughout Israel's history. Thus, the people could "wait" for him, patiently seeking his face/presence (v. 25).[770] Waiting in trustful patience is the basis of hope for the future. This waiting was a mark of spiritual maturity because God functions on a different time level than do his people. God's people trust that in his time God will work out his plan for them. For that reason, not only should one wait, but one should wait quietly and in silence (vv. 26, 28).

---

[767] This self-revelation echoes throughout the OT and should remind the Christian that God's grace and mercy were established long before the incarnation of these attributes in Jesus.

[768] The NET Bible and a Jewish translation have "ample."

[769] Affirmed by Jesus in Mark 10:17-18.

[770] The same Hebrew word is translated "hope" or "wait" depending on context.

> **Lamentations 3:22-23**
>
> *The steadfast love of the Lord never ceases,*
>   *his mercies never come to an end;*
> *they are new every morning;*
>   *great is your faithfulness.*
>
> Recently, I was staying at a hostel in the Chinatown district of Boston. Because I had a free morning and had experienced a late night, I thought I might sleep in a bit. It was not to be. Beginning about 5:30 a.m., the racket from delivery trucks, trash pickup, and city busses made additional sleep impossible. Going downstairs for coffee, I saw it had rained earlier that morning. In the morning light, the streets and sidewalks seemed washed clean.
>
> God is present in every city. Even during the horrific siege of Jerusalem, God was present. As in rain-washed Boston, every morning was a new day, and God's steadfast love continued. Every day is an opportunity to experience and express the love and mercy of God to others.
>
> God is faithful in every city. He does not change and his love for us never ceases. This verse, used by many in the darkest of days, has provided comfort and inspiration for over two millennia. When the stresses of urban life seem to overwhelm, may we remember that "the steadfast love of Yahweh never ceases."
>
> *Mark S. Krause*

"Good" dominates verses 25-30 (implied in vv. 28, 29, and 30). If the Lord is good, then there are several good things his people can do – wait for salvation (v. 26), bear up under burdens while young (v. 27),[771] sit in silence (v. 27) and humility (v. 28), and accept abuse (v. 29). The man had not been silent or humble until now, but he realized there was a time to calm down and let faith take over. There is a time for raging at God and a time to be silent before him.

---

[771] Did he have in mind the youth of the exile?

For the twenty-first century Christian, the incessant noise and demands of social media for our attention make it difficult to sit in silence before God. We feel like we must be doing something. The concept of beginning each day with a "quiet time" has many spiritual benefits.

What follows is another explanation for the man's about face (vv. 31-33). Because of his character, God would not reject his people forever. These verses are the theological center of the book of Lamentations.[772] Each of the verses begins with "for." The Lord may punish but not forever (v. 31). The Lord may cause grief and pain but ultimately his compassion and love will prevail (v. 32; cf v. 22). The Lord may afflict and grieve his people but that is not what is in his heart (v. 33).[773] The judgment was, of course, the outcome of Israel's rebellion and the result of God's action, but that was not where God's heart was. God did not "wholeheartedly" bring grief. In his heart was compassion and covenant faithfulness.

Hosea asserted this truth over a century earlier: "How can I give you up…my compassion grows warm and tender" (Hos 11:8). People who accuse the Old Testament God of being brutal and judgmental are ignorant of the true heart of God or willfully ignore the truth (cf. Jer 31:20).[774] We must not make the mistake of equating God's love and God's anger.[775] God is love, that is who he is. Anger is a manifestation of his justice, which is grounded in his holiness. Anger comes for only a moment, but love endures (cf. Exod 34:7;

---

[772] Wright, *Lamentations*, p. 116.

[773] *Cf.* Mic 7:18-19.

[774] Some atheists and skeptics who condemn the God of the Old Testament fit into this category. They cherry-pick texts and don't even come close to understanding the rich concept of the God they insist does not exist. One thinks of Richard Dawkins' ranting in *The God Delusion*. Ironically, if God does not exist then their self-designation as a-theists has little meaning. The definition of God is the key. Christians probably do not believe in the god that most skeptics would describe as the object of their disbelief.

[775] Wright, *Lamentations*, p. 116.

Deut 7:9-10). If God is not just, that is, if he does not ultimately exact punishment on evil, then he is not worthy of being God.

The man also has confidence in God because God is sovereign, he does see what happen to his people (v. 36). The previous calls to God to look and see (1:9, 11; 2:20) were now answered. God does see everything that is going on. Everything comes from the Lord (vv. 37-39). He is just, so when people suffer for their sins they cannot accuse God. The man implies that Israel was being justly punished, so they should not complain. Thus, he also indicts himself. This is one of the better moments for the man.

The "bad" in verse 38 is not bad in the sense of evil which comes from God but the disaster that judgment brings. The good and bad parallel the blessings and curses of the covenant (*cf.* Jer 18).

Subsequently, the man issues a call to repent (vv. 40-42). He echoes the earlier prophets here, who had preached repentance for centuries (*e.g.*, Hos 14:1-3). Going through judgment does not cancel the need for repentance. It is still important. For reconciliation to occur a complete turning around is needed. These verses are the logical end of the reflective journey begun in verse 22. God's *ḥesed* (חֶסֶד) is the foundation for everything the man suggests – the waiting on God, the affirmation of God's compassion, the call to repentance. This passage at the center of the book provides the good news among the pain and lament. but it is only a brief respite for the man returns to lament in the rest of chapter 3 and through chapters 4 and 5.

3:43-51

The book of Lamentations exhibits a circular structure: lament (1:1-3:21), embedded reflection on God's love and compassion (3:22-42), and lament (3:43-5:22). The man does not offer any new thought in verses 43-51 but reiterates earlier themes. He can find no access to God who has walled himself off from all people (v. 44; *cf.* v. 8). The enemies have destroyed them (vv. 46-47). He responds again with tears because of the fate of the young women (vv. 48-51; *cf.* 2:10, 21).

3:52-66

The man here sounds like Jeremiah who was flung into a pit (vv. 52-54; *cf.* Jer 38). Pits were everywhere and used as cisterns or for grain storage. They were also used as prisons (Gen 38:22-24). Jeremiah was fortunate that the pit he was in was empty and only muddy at the bottom (Jer 38:6). The man here envisioned it full of water (v. 54). He was sure of his demise and had no hope.

From the pit, the man ends his lament of chapter 3 with a direct appeal to the Lord for deliverance (vv. 55-63). The meaning of these verses can be construed in different ways. Is the man reflecting a past case of divine deliverance on which he bases his appeal, or is he making a supplication? The Hebrew verb forms used here normally indicate past action (so most translations), but under circumstances they could indicate an appeal or entreaty, especially if there is an imperative in the context (as in v. 59).[776] An appeal is a possibility, for the context suggests not a statement of confidence but a supplication to God to come to his aid.[777] Then we could render the verbs "hear my supplication" (v. 56) and throughout as appeals (*cf.* Ps 130:1-2). These then would be sincere appeals for help and rescue for the lamenter. The man is asking, post-destruction of Jerusalem, for an act of God equal to the Exodus which was God's great redemptive work.

Within this section we have the only reported words of God in the book, "Do not fear" (v. 57). This is a divine reassurance common in the Old Testament, coming especially in circumstances when fear seems the logical human re-

---

[776] So Provan, *Lamentations*, 106; the NET Bible. For the technical grammar details see Bruce Waltke and M. O'Connor, *An Introduction to Biblical Hebrew Syntax* (Winona Lake, IN: Eisenbrauns, 1990), p. 494-95. For similar constructions see Pss 3:8; 22:22; 31:5-6.

[777] However, many commentators opt to interpret the verb forms as past or present certainty – Lalleman, *Jeremiah and Lamentations*, p. 362; Wright, *Lamentations*, p. 125.

sponse. It is often accompanied by words of divine assurance such as "I am with you" (*cf.* Gen 26:24 addressed to Isaac).

The man ends his lament similarly to widow Zion in chapter 1, with a plea to God to use his anger to destroy the enemies (*cf.* 1:21-22). He wants payback and curses. The anger that came on him (*cf.* 3:1) he wants to descend on them. These strong feelings may come from the wish for revenge, but they are also grounded in a confidence in God's justice. Though a nation may be used as God's instrument of judgment that nation was also accountable to God (Isa 10; Jer 50-51).

Chapter 4

It is not clear who speaks in chapter 4, the poet of chapters 1 and 2 or the man of chapter 3. There are parallels with the earlier chapters, but the style is different. The acrostic pattern continues but each verse has only two lines, not three. The lament seems to be winding down and the lamenter is running out of steam. The writer poses several contrasts and uses vivid similes, some from the animal world. He turns to the consequences of the Babylonian ravages of the temple, the people, and the leaders in Jerusalem. He had witnessed firsthand the horrors of the siege of Jerusalem. The bright hope of chapters 3:21ff. is forgotten. There is a small note of hope in 4:22. Another voice, that of the people, speaks in verses 17-20, voices of total despair.

The chapter has two main parts – verses 1-10 which describes in graphic detail the results of the siege on every part of society, but especially the children, and verses 11-22 which focus on the punishment of the leaders, with a brief diatribe against Edom.

4:1-10

The writer uses vivid images and similes to further describe the results of the sack of Jerusalem in 587-86 BCE. The constant theme is the sharp contrast between Jerusalem and its inhabitants before and after (or during) the siege.

He begins with the destroyed glory of the temple (v. 1). Its lustrous gold and gems (*cf.* 1 Kgs 7:48-50) were scattered in the street like common gravel.[778] These were of no value because there was nothing to buy, especially food (vv. 4, 10). Gold has always played a large part in the culture and economy of cultures throughout time. It was treasured for its beauty, its malleability, its resistance to tarnishing, and being easily smelted.[779] But in a time of the total collapse of the country and economy it lost its value.[780]

The children of Jerusalem, who were more precious than gold, had also been debased (v. 2). Their worth had fallen to that of a common clay pot. Clay pots were ubiquitous in the ancient world. They were easy to make but also easily broken. Broken pieces of pottery still mark ancient ruins and are used for dating purposes.[781]

Parents who were blessed with children to raise in the Lord had also failed. Their conduct had been worse than animals (v. 3). The jackal was usually associated with haunted places and desolate cities (Ps 44:19) in the Old Testament but here the writer commends the jackal for how they care for their young, contra current parents. People considered ostriches as having no concern for their young (*cf.* Job 39:13-17) but even they are better than the Israelites. Behavior in the animal kingdom shamed human behavior during the siege of Jerusalem.

The most vulnerable of society, the children, were starving (v. 4; *cf.* 2:11-12). Even the wealthy who could almost always find food were destitute and scavenging on garbage dumps (v. 5; literally "cling to ash heaps").

---

[778] *Cf.* 1:1, 4 and Ezek 7:19-20 – gold had no value. In some cultures, gold did not have value because it had no utilitarian purpose.

[779] Today it plays an important role in electronic products.

[780] In the OT, only the word of God was more precious, and it never lost its value – Ps 19:10. Gold has been associated with the perfect or divine principle – the golden mean, the golden rule. The fact that the new Jerusalem in Revelation is pure gold refers to its beauty and permanence, not its physical composition.

[781] *Cf.* Jer 18 and 19.

The fall of Jerusalem was dramatic – comparable to the destruction of Sodom (v. 6), even worse. Sodom, with Gomorrah, was destroyed in an instant by God's fiery judgment (Gen 19). It became a metaphor in the Bible for the sinful city and the destructive power of God (Deut 32:32; Isa 1:10; 3:9; Jer 23:14; Ezek 16:46-56; Amos 4:11). Even in the New Testament it was a paradigm for people who reject God and his Son (Matt 10:15; 11:23; 2 Pet 2:7-11). Its destruction was sudden and swift. However, Jerusalem's destruction was drawn out over a decade with two invasions and an eighteen-month siege. Under the circumstances, a swift punishment would have been better. Why was Jerusalem's punishment greater? Because she had known God through a covenant relationship, had experienced his grace and deliverance, and had rebelled against him.

The leaders ("princes", Heb. *nāzîr* (נָזִיר) – "devoted ones"), who were a picture of health because of their wealth, became like walking skeletons (vv. 7-8), going from white to black.[782] If would have been better if they had died quickly by the sword, than to slowly starve (v. 9).

The charge of cannibalism is made again (v. 10, *cf.* 2:20 and comments there). Allen suggests this refers to eating dead babies, not live ones.[783] History is replete with examples of dire circumstances like this one. In the history of the U.S. the Donner party stranded in the mountains (1846-47) is an example. The tragedy here is that the "compassionate" mothers who do the cooking to provide for the family end up cooking the children.

4:11-22

The writer begins this section with a theological assessment of what happened. It was the expression of the wrath and anger of God burning like a fire that destroyed Zion (v. 11).[784] Verse 11 deliberately counters 3:22 by using the

---

[782] People slowing starving turn to a grey color; Allen, *A Liturgy of Grief*, p. 130-131.

[783] *Ibid.*,

[784] *Cf.* 2:1-3; 3:1, 43, 66; 1:12-13; 2:8; Jer 7:20.

same verb – his mercies "never end" (*klh*, כלה) and his wrath is "fully vented" (*klh*, כלה). We know that mercy and grace trump wrath (Exod 34:7). However, experiencing God's wrath was the cause of the writer's distress and grief. At the moment it certainly seemed like wrath prevailed.

The spiritual leaders had failed (vv. 13-16). Prophets and priests had already been referenced (2:6, 9, 14, 20) as objects of judgment or as failing. Here they are specifically singled out for their sins. Unfortunately, religious leaders in any age can commit crimes against the people. The many religious wars throughout the centuries attest to that. Such failures were especially heinous, for the prophets and priests were charged with teaching the law and giving the people a word from God.

Shedding blood (v. 13) was a main charge. It put the prophets and priests in the same category as Manasseh, the evilest of all of Judah's kings (2 Kgs 21:16). Jeremiah also talked about them shedding the blood of the innocent (2:34; 7:6; 9:4; 22:3-4). Because of their failed leadership many had died unnecessarily.[785] The shedding of blood was so extreme that it led to the complete ostracizing of the leadership (v.15). Another reversal – those who formerly led the people were outcasts like any unclean Israelite.[786] The priests who certified when people became clean were themselves unclean. They were assigned the fate of Cain, becoming fugitives and wanders (Gen 4:12b).

The soliloquy of the writer is briefly interrupted by a cry of woe from the people (vv. 17-20). They had hoped for others to come to their aid, but it did not happen. Perhaps they were thinking of Egypt's failure during the final siege (Jer 37). Instead they were relentlessly pursued by the enemies in the street during the fall of the city. When Zedekiah fled the city, the Babylonians caught him near the Jordan so even he did not escape (Jer 52; *cf.* Jer 16:10-18). Their last greatest hope, the king, under whose protection they took

---

[785] Shedding of blood often referred to murder in the OT (Gen 9:6; Hos 4:2) since the life was in the blood (Lev 17:11 14; Deut 12:22).

[786] For blood making a woman unclean see Lev 15:19-30.

refuge, could not save them (the "Lord's anointed", v. 20; *cf.* the promise in 2 Sam 7). So, everyone had failed: king, prophet, priest, elder. Every physical asset was gone – the temple and city. Indeed, the end had come (v. 18).

This bleak section ends with a glimmer of hope that seems indirect and is still in the distant future (vv. 21-22). Even under the circumstances there was a promise of release from exile. Their punishment would end (v. 22a). The promise of Jeremiah 29:14 would be kept, but not for some time.

Corresponding to this hope was the fact that Edom would finally receive its just due also (vv. 21, 22b). Edom had rejoiced over the fall of Jerusalem (Ps 137:7) and even had a hand in it, but God's wrath would reach these people (the "cup" refers to Jer 25:21) as Jeremiah 49:7-22, Obadiah 16, and Joel 3:19-21 promised.

Chapter 5

In 3:41, the poet called upon the people to lift their hearts and hands to heaven. Chapter 5 is that prayer of repentance,[787] and is in the form of a communal lament, sharing features of several Psalms of lament. The chapter is the shortest in the book and abandons the acrostic pattern. However, it has 22 verses which retains the number of letters in the Hebrew alphabet. Each verse is only two lines long which gives it a faster pace. The meter also changes from the dirge-like three beats plus two beats to the more regular three plus three beats per line, suggesting, perhaps, a slight movement toward hope.

It seems that enough has been said and the book moves rapidly to a close. The voice of the people ("us", "our", "we") and the setting is another vivid recall of the dire events of 587 BCE recounted in Jeremiah 39-43 when Jerusalem and the temple were destroyed, and the people left in chaos in the land.

---

[787] Allen, *Liturgy*, p. 145.

A refrain line that confesses sin in verses 6 and 17 provide a structure for a poem of three parts: verses 1-7, 8-16, and 17-22.[788] The first two sections describe distress and humiliation, the third is a cry for help.

5:1-7

The Lord is called upon to "remember" and "look" (v. 1). An appeal to remember is common in laments (*cf.* Ps 106:4-5), often with covenantal implications. God is asked to remember his promises to rescue the suffering and come to their aid. Exodus 2:24 provides a model of such remembrance. Are the people hoping for such an active divine memory and a new deliverance from oppression and distress (*cf.* Ps 78:18, 22; 89:50)? God had proven over and over that he was capable.

The call to "look" matches all the previous admonitions in 1:9, 11, 12; 2:20. Each one asks God to focus on some aspect of their suffering. Here it is Judah's disgrace which is specifically enumerated in the following verses.

The first disgrace was their lost inheritance (v. 2). The land was a gift from God, and each tribe, clan, and family received a portion which was to remain in the family (Lev 25:21). It was a part of their identity and security.[789] The land was proof of a unique relationship between God and Israel (Deut 26:1). God also had a special relationship with the land. Strangers and aliens were welcome to live in this land, but they could not inherit it. In the great reversal in the present crisis the people had become like strangers and aliens in their own land and suffered great privations.

Further, they had become like the most socially deprived and defenseless group of people in their society, the widows and orphans (v. 3). A concern of the law was the welfare of these two groups (Exod 22:22; Deut 20:18; 24:17-18). The first lament we have in the book is from the widow Jerusalem in 1:1-2. It is ironical that for generations the

---

[788] *Ibid.*, p. 149.

[789] Naboth lost his life for not giving up his family plot (1 Kgs 21).

people had trampled on the rights of the poor (Isa 1:23; 10:1-2; Jer 22:1-5; Amos 5:11) but now discover that when they suffer in the same way, they cannot endure it.

It is a sad fact that in times of social upheaval it is always the women (*cf.* v. 11) and children who suffer the most. One can think of numerous examples over the centuries until today. There are tens of millions of refugees today suffering as ancient Israel did, in rural and urban areas, big and small towns, rich and poor countries. Often, women and children represent an outsized majority of these refugees.

Getting access to the necessities of life had become costly (vv. 4-6). Deprivation became a way of life lived on the edge. Such desperation led to even appealing to the oppressors for help.

The confession of sin is the first step to reconciliation and recovery (v. 7), but this initial step was only the confession that their ancestors had sinned. Personal confession was still to develop (see below in v. 16). Jeremiah 31:29-30 and Ezekiel 18 also examined the problem of suffering for the sins of the fathers, but in those texts the present generation did not acknowledge their guilt. It is always easier to blame someone else for one's short comings and suffering.

God had warned the people over and over for centuries that the judgment would come if they did not repent. The amazing factor is that he was so patient. The present generation may have been suffering, but it was long overdue. It was remarkable that it did not come sooner.[790]

5:8-16

The normal social order that provided stability and security was turned upside down so that social chaos ensued.[791] The

---

[790] Wright, *Lamentations*, p. 153.

[791] Their circumstances were similar to a post-apocalyptic world because, for the Judeans, the end surely seemed to have come. The dystopian books and movies of the early twenty-first century carry this same feeling of a senseless world.

lament enumerates the many ways this had happened. Leadership was turned upside down. The prince was killed (v. 12; *cf.* 4:20) and the lowly slave, ill equipped for the position, became the ruler (v. 8).[792] Subsequently, justice died, for the elders were shamed (v. 12; *cf.* 4:16) and disappeared from the courts (v. 14, city gates). This generation experienced what many had experienced over the centuries, the lack of justice (Amos 5:10, 15; Isa 1:17). The sins of the fathers were coming down on them. Justice was absent for everyone, not just the poor. Young men were doing the work of animals (v. 13), taking the place of servants and slaves. Their world was upside down.

Jeremiah foretold that singing and joy would cease (7:34; 25:10) and this came to pass (vv. 14b-15). The only form of expression left was lament.[793]

Lamentations 5:14-15

The old men have left the city gate,
  the young men their music.
The joy of our hearts has ceased;
  our dancing has been turned to mourning.

Lamentations 5 describes the horrors of Jerusalem as the invading Babylonians take over the city. Hunger, rape, and oppression have become constant in the lives of the people of Judah. Their joy has vanished, symbolized by joyful dancing transformed to weeping and wailing.

Especially poignant are two references. "Old men have left the city gate." The gates of the city were gathering places for older men, something like our senior centers or barber shops. I once was privileged to be invited to a weekly meeting of World War II veterans, breakfast in a local downtown café. They had a fellowship I could never be a part of,

---

[792] Though of royal blood, Ishmael tried to usurp authority, and failed totally as a leader in the months following the fall of Jerusalem (Jer. 41). It was a brief period of bloodshed and chaos. It didn't take a slave in leadership to create turmoil.

[793] Wright, *Lamentations*, p. 175.

> old men with shared experiences they needed to remember together. They were the modern old men of the city gate.
>
> While the old men have lost their companions, the young men have lost their music. Urban music, whether hip hop, country, or rock, is a shared enjoyment of many young people. Imagine a city with no more music, no more dancing.
>
> In the Benson district of Omaha, a Christian group called the 402 Arts Collective has partnered to share a building with a Christian-owned coffee shop. On Monday nights, "the 402" hosts an "open mic night" at the coffee house. It allows young people to take the stage to share their music in a safe and controlled environment. Any profits from these nights are plowed back into the ministry of the 402 to subsidize music lessons for young people in the poorer neighborhoods of North Omaha. In a real way, this ministry by dedicated Christian artists has help many young men and women find their music rather than lose it.
>
> *Mark S. Krause*

The confession of sin (v. 16) was long overdue. As long as the temple stood, the people seemed to take refuge in the continual rituals of the sacrifices, but in the post-destruction period, there was no more sacrifice for sin. Did this prompt the admission? The confession is brief but powerful, only four words in Hebrew ("Woe to-us, for we-have-sinned"). There were no excuses or dissimulation. No passing of the buck. Only honest confession (*cf.* 1:18a; compare the tax collector of Luke18:13). This is the shortest, deepest moment of self-awareness in the book.[794] It is tragic that it took the destruction of Jerusalem to force this soul-searching cry.

Confession for the Christian is also an essential part of a relationship with God (1 Jo. 1:9-10). It is a great loss to spiritual growth when confession is deleted from public worship and private prayer.

---

[794] *Ibid.*

5:17-22

Chapter 5 and the book of Lamentations ends with a final series of complaints and laments to God. Hope and despair battle with each other. The people were sick at heart (*cf.* 1:22; Jer 18:8), filled with misery, blinded by tears, and unable to envision any hope (v. 17; 2:11). Verses 17-18 round off the main theme of the book and parallel 1:1-2, providing bookends to the extended lament. Israel was completely devastated because of the destruction of Zion, and everything it represented was destroyed. Destruction of the social and political order was lethal enough, but the destruction of the temple called into question God and his promises for its permanent glory and safety (*cf.* Isa 14:32; 28:16; 31:4-5; 33:20).

Yet the object of their lament was still the eternal Lord who reigned over the universe. There must still be hope (v. 19). Under the circumstances Wright calls this statement an "astounding leap of faith."[795] Zion may be gone but God was still on his throne. His reign could not be limited to the temple in Jerusalem (1 Kgs 8:27). He still reigned over the whole cosmos (Isa 66:1-2). Psalm 102 could have been written under similar circumstances, for it too moves from despair to affirmation of the Lord who is eternally enthroned over the universe.

> But you, O LORD, are enthroned forever;
> your name endures to all generations. (Ps 102:12)

The brief, shining statement of verse 19, however, provides the basis for more lament. It leads to the most serious question of the book – why? Had the God who should remember them (5:1) really forgotten them or really forsaken them?[796] These same whys and hows echo through the Psalms (Ps 13:1-2; 22:1; 89:46; 90:13; *cf.* Job) and down

---

[795] *Ibid.*, p. 176.

[796] There are two issues: the absence of God and its duration – Allen, *Liturgy*, p. 161.

through the centuries until they burst from the lips of Jesus on the cross. For the Christian, the resolution is the cross and resurrection. The Christian may still utter these cries[797] but the cross assures us that the issue has been resolved, though we yet wait for the final consummation.

The second to last thought of the book is the recognition that if Israel is to return to God after the confession in verse 16, it still had to be at his initiative. They had presented themselves as willing; now God could act. Jeremiah asserted that God would act and in a decisive way. It would not be just restoration of the old covenant but with the gift of an entirely new one (Jer 31:31-34).

The last thought of the chapter reflects the thought of the book and ends on a negative note – maybe God has rejected them (v. 22). A clear understanding of this verse hinges on the interpretation of the compound conjunction at the beginning, *kî 'im* (כִּי אִם). Holladay's lexicon suggests a range of meaning, depending on the context and whether it affirms a statement or follows a negative and expresses exception. Or it can appear before a clause and equal "unless". Many English translations prefer "unless" (*e.g.*, NIV). The KJV and Allen opt for "but"[798] which is totally negative. Wright prefers "even if."[799] So how completely has God rejected Israel: totally or is there some hope? The ambiguity is fitting for the end of this extended lament with its disturbing images and questions.

An interpretation that contemplates complete rejection, however, ignores the glimmers of hope in and statements

---

[797] In the summer 2017 while I was working on this commentary my Sunday School class was viewing the powerful video series by Nadeem Qureshi, "Seeking Allah; Finding Jesus" (for Qureshi's testimony, see https://www.youtube.com/watch?v=HVBiELaxzAs). At the same time, he was dying from stomach cancer. One could not help but ask, why did such a powerful witness to the Gospel die in the prime of his life? Nabeel A. Qureshi, *Seeking Allah, Finding Jesus* (Grand Rapids: Zondervan, 2014).

[798] Allen, *Liturgy*, p. 178.

[799] Wright, *Lamentations*, p. 161.

of faith in 3:22-24, 31 ("the Lord will not reject forever") and 5:19-20:

> [H]e looked down from his holy height,
>   from heaven the LORD looked at the earth,
> to hear the groans of the prisoners,
>   to set free those who were doomed to die;

Lamentations leads us into the depths of despair and laments, and it tells the truth about human suffering. But it still affirms central truths about the character of God that stand the test of time. God is willing and able to deliver his people from the ravages of evil and sin. The cry from the depths of Lamentations is answered in the coming of the Messiah. God will not reject forever but will himself come to set things right in the world. This is the great hope for all generations for all time.

www.ingramcontent.com/pod-product-compliance
Lightning Source LLC
Chambersburg PA
CBHW060450170426
43199CB00011B/1154